I0128581

# SOLIDARITY ACROSS THE AMERICAS

Margaret M. Power

# Solidarity

## ACROSS THE AMERICAS

THE

PUERTO RICAN

NATIONALIST PARTY

AND

ANTI-IMPERIALISM

THE UNIVERSITY OF NORTH CAROLINA PRESS

Chapel Hill

© 2023 The University of North Carolina Press

All rights reserved
Set in Quadraat, TheSans, and Geogrotesque typefaces
by Jamie McKee, MacKey Composition
Manufactured in the United States of America

Cover illustrations: Top: U.S. Capitol Police detain Lolita Lebrón, Rafael Cancel Miranda, and Andrés Figueroa Cordero on March 1, 1954, courtesy of Library of Congress, Prints and Photographs Division, LC-DIG-ds-02972. Bottom and background: West India Islands and Central America, map, by Keith Johnston, 1912, courtesy of David Rumsey Map Collection, David Rumsey Map Center, Stanford Libraries.

Library of Congress Cataloging-in-Publication Data
Names: Power, Margaret, 1953– author.
Title: Solidarity across the Americas : the Puerto Rican Nationalist Party
    and anti-imperialism / Margaret M. Power.
Description: Chapel Hill : The University of North Carolina Press, [2023] |
    Includes bibliographical references and index.
Identifiers: LCCN 2022045661 | ISBN 9781469674049 (cloth ; alk. paper) |
    ISBN 9781469674056 (paperback ; alk. paper) | ISBN 9781469674063 (ebook)
Subjects: LCSH: Partido Nacionalista (P.R.)—History. | Nationalism—Puerto Rico—
    History. | Puerto Rico—History—Autonomy and independence movements. |
    Puerto Rico—Politics and government—20th century.
Classification: LCC JL1059.A54 P68 2023 | DDC 320.54097295—dc23/eng/20221107
LC record available at https://lccn.loc.gov/2022045661

# CONTENTS

# ILLUSTRATIONS

# ABBREVIATIONS

AFL      American Federation of Labor

APRA     Allianza Popular Revolucionario Americana
(American Popular Revolutionary Alliance)

APJP     Asociación Patriótica de Jóvenes Puertorriqueños
(Patriotic Association of Young Puerto Ricans)

ARNE     Acción Revolucionaria Nationalista Ecuatoriana
(Ecuadorian Nationalist Revolutionary Action)

CGT     Confederación General de Trabajadores
(General Confederation of Workers)

CIO     Congress of Industrial Organizations

CPUSA    Communist Party USA

CTAL     Confederación de Trabajadores de América Latina
(Workers Confederation of Latin America)

ELA     Estado Libre Asociado (Free Associated State)

FALN     Fuerzas Armadas de Liberación Nacional
(Armed Forces of National Liberation)

FBI     Federal Bureau of Investigation

FECH     Federación de Estudiantes de Chile
(Federation of Chilean Students)

FLT     Federación Libre de Trabajadores
(Free Federation of Labor)

FOR     Fellowship of Reconciliation

ILD     International Labor Defense

MIR     Movimiento de Izquierda Revolucionaria
(Movement of the Revolutionary Left)

OAS     Organization of American States

PCP     Partido Comunista Puertorriqueño
(Puerto Rican Communist Party)

PIP     Partido Independentista Puertorriqueño
(Puerto Rican Independence Party)

| | |
|---|---|
| PNP | Partido Nuevo Progresista (New Progressive Party) |
| PNPR | Partido Nacionalista de Puerto Rico (Puerto Rican Nationalist Party) |
| PPD | Partido Popular Demócrata (Popular Democratic Party) |
| PRC | Partido Revolucionario Cubano (Cuban Revolutionary Party) |
| PVP | Partido Vanguardia Popular (Popular Vanguard Party) |
| RRDC | Ruth Reynolds Defense Committee |
| SECH | Sociedad de Escritores de Chile (Writers' Society of Chile) |
| TFP | Taller de Formación Política (Political Training Workshop) |
| UNIA | United Negro Improvement Association |

# SOLIDARITY ACROSS THE AMERICAS

# INTRODUCTION

Lolita Lebrón and her three Partido Nacionalista Puertorriqueño (PNPR, Puerto Rican Nationalist Party) comrades,
Rafael Cancel Miranda, Andrés Figueroa Cordero, and
Irvin Flores, took the train from New York City to Wash-
ington, D.C., on the morning of March 1, 1954. From Union Station, they walked
through the rain to the U.S. Capitol. Although the three men showed some
hesitation, Lolita urged them on and, when it appeared they were reluctant
to continue, said, "I will go alone then."[1] According to Lebrón, Pedro Albizu
Campos, the president of the Nationalist Party, had named her "the leader of
the attack" and she was determined to carry out her duty. Although the three
men were "from a time when men ruled supreme," they accepted her leadership
and entered the U.S. Capitol.[2]

Once inside, they climbed the stairs to the spectators' gallery of the U.S.
House of Representatives and entered the chamber. Lolita gave the order to
carry out the attack. She then whipped her pistol and the Puerto Rican flag out
of her purse. As she unfurled the flag she shouted, "¡Viva Puerto Rico Libre!"
and fired several shots at the rotunda. Her comrades fired at the congressmen
below, wounding five congressmen, none of whom died. Lolita, Rafael, Andres,
and Irvin were all arrested that day and subsequently tried and convicted of
"assault with intent to kill" and "assaults with a deadly weapon." They were all
found guilty. The men received sentences of twenty-five to seventy-five years.
Lolita was sentenced to "sixteen years and eight months to fifty years."[3]

At first, superficial glance, the Nationalists' attack on Congress in 1954
might spark comparisons with the January 6, 2021, assault by right-wing supporters of former president Donald Trump. Both involved armed incursions
into the Capitol, but that is all they had in common. The four Nationalists had
no intention of overthrowing the U.S. government; nor did they aim to murder
congressmen and impose a president who had recently lost an election. Because
their goal was to bring world attention to Puerto Rico's status as a U.S. colony,
their action is best described as armed propaganda. Another difference is the

FIGURE 0.1. U.S. Capitol Police detain Lolita Lebrón, Rafael Cancel Miranda, and Andrés Figueroa Cordero shortly after they fired guns and called for a free Puerto Rico inside the U.S. Capitol on March 1, 1954. Source: Library of Congress.

punishment each group received. The Nationalists' sentences received were astronomically higher than the pitifully lenient sentences given so far to the attackers on January 6. One significant distinction is that the Puerto Rican Nationalists sought to end U.S. colonialism and establish an independent homeland while the attackers of January 6 sought to enforce racist and authoritarian rule in theirs.

Years later I asked Lolita why they had attacked the U.S. Congress at that time.[4] Her response surprised me. She said they planned the attack to "coincide with the meeting of the Organization of American States in Caracas." The four wanted the people of the Americas to know that there were Puerto Ricans who wanted independence and were willing to sacrifice their lives to get it. Her words not only recast the action in a different, more hemispheric light but also helped me appreciate the Nationalist Party's consistent efforts to gain continent-wide solidarity for the independence struggle. Instead of conceiving Puerto Rico solely through the lens of its binary connection to the United States, I realized that the Nationalists viewed Puerto Rico as a Latin American nation and defined their allies as progressive, anti-imperialist, and revolutionary Americans from New York City to Buenos Aires. Far from being isolationists who advanced a narrow and parochial sense of the nation, the Nationalists were internationalists who identified with communities beyond their borders.[5] These insights guided my research and shaped the focus of this book.

The Nationalists were not alone in their expansive vision of the nation and belief in regional solidarity. They shared both qualities with many other Caribbean actors. In the 1860s, anti-imperialist Cubans, Dominicans, and Puerto Ricans supported each other's efforts to end slavery and Spanish rule. These same forces also propounded the Antillean Confederation that would unite the disparate islands into one body and thus realize their dream of "the Antilles for the Antilleans."[6] José Martí, the Cuban revolutionary hero who died fighting Spanish colonialism in 1895, battled simultaneously for national independence and Latin American unity. As a Cuban patriot and anti-imperialist, he called on Latin American nations to overcome their differences and "grip each other so tightly that their two hands become one."[7]

In the early 1900s, anarchists, communists, and migrant workers also built transnational networks across and beyond the Caribbean. Puerto Rican anarchists read the publications of Cuban and Spanish anarchists and vice versa, supported each other's struggles, and even, as in the case of Puerto Rican feminist, anarchist, and labor activist Luisa Capetillo, worked alongside each other.[8] The Bolshevik-directed Communist International (Comintern) established the Anti-imperialist League in 1925 to unite communist parties throughout the Americas. Headquartered initially in Mexico City, it operated throughout the Caribbean (and elsewhere). Led by Cuban and Venezuelan communists, among others, the league distributed a newspaper, El Libertador; promoted the "Hands Off Nicaragua" campaign in 1926–28 opposing U.S. intervention in that Central American country; and attempted to build communist parties in places they did not yet exist, unsuccessfully in the case of Puerto Rico.[9]

Caribbean workers migrated to other islands and Central America through what historian Lara Putnam terms the "circum-Caribbean migratory sphere" or to the United States, seeking jobs.[10] For example, 90,000 Jamaicans sailed to Panama between 1905 and 1915 to obtain employment building the canal.[11] The jobs they and other Black migrants from the British West Indies found were arduous, unsafe, and poorly paid. In addition, the migrants were frequent targets of racist treatment and discrimination. Their joint experiences contributed to the development of "black internationalism," the labor rebellions that shook Jamaica from 1934 to 1939, and the decolonization of the British Caribbean.[12] So did the experience of men from the various British colonies in the Caribbean who joined the British West Indies Regiment and served under

British commanders during World War I. Assigned to substandard housing, denied adequate medical care and sufficient, let alone healthy, food, and abused and insulted by their officers, these men forged a pan-Caribbean identity and rebelled against the mistreatment they experienced from their British rulers. Fueled by growing nationalist feelings, outraged by the white colonizers' racism and the concomitant low wages they received on returning home, former servicemen joined with workers in Trinidad, Belize, Jamaica, and Grenada to protest their conditions and challenge colonial rule.[13]

The United Negro Improvement Association (UNIA) was the largest transnational movement to emerge out of the Caribbean, if not "the largest and most powerful black nationalist organization the world has ever known."[14] Founded in 1914 by Jamaican Marcus Garvey, the UNIA had chapters in the United States and the Caribbean. The UNIA's goal was to "fight for the emancipation of the race and . . . the redemption of the country of our fathers." It defined race as the primary source of Black oppression, urged Black racial unity, and advocated the establishment of a "black republic of Africa" as a solution.[15]

This book builds on these varied experiences to explore the generally unknown transnational networks of solidarity with Puerto Rican independence, the Nationalist Party, and the Puerto Rican political prisoners that flourished across the Americas from the 1920s through the 1950s. Those were the years when revolutionary nationalists and anti-imperialists, sometimes independent of and other times intertwined with communists and socialists, proclaimed the unity of the Americas in defiance of and in opposition to U.S. imperialism. For them, colonized Puerto Rico was the symbol par excellence of U.S. intervention in the Americas, just as the Nationalists were examples of courageous combatants who fought against it.

The Puerto Rican Nationalist Party was founded in 1922, twenty-four years after the United States invaded and colonized the archipelago, with the goal of obtaining independence for Puerto Rico. During the 1920s, it called for an end to U.S. colonialism but maintained fundamentally friendly relations with the U.S. government.[16] That changed in 1930, when Pedro Albizu Campos was elected president of the party. Under his leadership, the party *demanded* independence immediately, not at some unspecified time in the future. In line with this more militant stance, the party adopted a policy of *retraimiento*, or withdrawal from U.S. institutions. The PNPR did not participate in elections because it considered the U.S. occupation of Puerto Rico to be illegal and refused to legitimize Washington's presence by acknowledging its right to conduct elections.[17] It developed an armed wing of the party, which carried out a few attacks on U.S. and Puerto Rican officials in the 1930s, none in the 1940s, and, in 1950, an uprising in October in Puerto Rico and an assassination attempt against

President Harry Truman in Washington, D.C., the next month. The PNPR's last major armed action took place in 1954, when a New York City–based unit of the party described above attacked Congress to bring world attention to Puerto Rico's ongoing status as a U.S. colony. Although the party still exists today, it never recovered its prominence, membership, or influence following these military assaults. The armed actions unleashed intense governmental repression against party members and sympathizers, some of whom retreated from politics, while others joined the Partido Independentista Puertorriqueño (PIP, Puerto Rican Independence Party), in part because it eschewed violent tactics and pursued an electoral path. A solid core, however, remained Nationalists for the rest of their lives.

Many people in the United States know very little about Puerto Rico, let alone that it is a U.S. colony and that some Puerto Ricans wanted and want an independent nation. And if they do know about the Puerto Rican Nationalist Party, many just know about the uprising and assassination attempt of 1950 or the attack on the U.S. Congress in 1954.[18] I discuss those three events and other aspects of the organization's history, politics, and efforts to organize Puerto Ricans to oppose U.S. colonial rule. Primarily, however, this book focuses on the transnational expressions of anti-imperialist solidarity with Puerto Rican independence and the Nationalist Party that existed throughout the Americas.

I first learned that Puerto Rico was a U.S. colony in 1975, about the same time I heard about the five Nationalist political prisoners who had been imprisoned in the United States since the 1950s.[19] I was appalled and angry that the United States occupied another people's country and outraged that it jailed people who fought for their nation's freedom. Over the next four years, I joined with hundreds of thousands of people in the United States, Puerto Rico, Latin America, and around the world to call for the prisoners' unconditional release. I corresponded with the prisoners, wrote letters, signed petitions, marched in demonstrations, and participated in acts of civil disobedience to help secure their freedom. President Jimmy Carter heeded the clamor and pardoned Cancel Miranda, Collazo, Flores, and Lebrón in September 1979. Andrés Figueroa Cordero had been released in October 1977 after he was diagnosed with terminal cancer. (He died in March 1979.)[20]

A year and a half later, I moved to Chicago to work with the Puerto Rican community. Despite my commitment to freeing both Puerto Rico and the Fuerzas Armadas de Liberación Nacional (FALN, Armed Forces of National Liberation) political prisoners, my academic work initially focused on right-wing women in Chile.[21] Through my work on Chile, I became aware that Chileans, including Nobel Laureates in Literature Gabriela Mistral and Pablo Neruda and Socialist president Salvador Allende, held the Nationalist Party in high regard and advocated for the release of its imprisoned members. Learning about them made me curious to find out who outside of Puerto Rico and the United States worked on behalf of the Nationalists and Puerto Rican independence and how and why they did so.

This book, the result of that investigation, explores the trans-American (in the hemispheric sense of the word) bonds of solidarity between and among members of the PNPR and their supporters.[22] What is remarkable about these supporters is how varied they were. They ranged from Cubans who had fought against Spanish colonialism in the 1890s to Haitians and Dominicans who opposed U.S. occupations in their countries in the early 1900s and from communists, socialists, and both left- and right-wing nationalists who rejected U.S. rule in Latin America to anticolonial North American pacifists who believed in social justice. They included workers, trade union leaders, students, intellectuals, politicians, scholars, poets, activists, women's groups, feminists, and people of faith. Among their numbers we find women and men who held divergent political ideologies; people who spoke Spanish, French, Portuguese, and English; and those who hailed from all classes and multiple religions, nationalities, and races. They shared an antipathy to U.S. domination and the belief that Puerto Rico deserved to be a free, independent nation. And they backed the Nationalist Party in its unrelenting quest to achieve that goal.

The Nationalist Party was not the only Puerto Rican organization to advocate independence during this period. The Partido Independentista Puertorriqueño, which began in 1946, did so as well.[23] However, the Nationalist Party was the first twentieth-century Puerto Rican party that both sought an end to U.S. rule and linked Puerto Rican independence to the archipelago's reincorporation with its sister republics in the Americas.[24] The Nationalist Party's identity with Latin America was so integral to its conception of independence that the party's foundational document proclaimed, "All the Ibero-American Republics are united with us based on indestructible ties of blood and language," and "we are linked to this [Ibero-American] community by history and origin, we share in its triumphs and in the grief of its defeats."[25]

From its beginnings through the 1950s, the PNPR dedicated resources, time, energy, and members to building and maintaining bonds of solidarity with supporters throughout the Americas. They understood that Latin Americans' material and political support, which ranged from financial aid to direct pressure on the U.S. government, was critically important to their struggle. Puerto Rican Nationalists worked on different levels, in a range of arenas, across diverse geographic spaces, using a variety of tactics to obtain independence for Puerto Rico. As a result, Nationalists, particularly Albizu Campos, were recognized as the voice of Puerto Rican independence throughout the Americas.

After Albizu Campos died in 1965, Chilean Socialist Salvador Allende, then a senator, later the president (1970–73), eulogized him in the Chilean senate. He recounted Albizu's life story and quoted Gabriela Mistral's description of Albizu Campos as "the greatest Latin American of our time."[26] The Nationalists' defiance of U.S. colonial rule, despite the formidable resources arrayed against them, the tremendous sacrifices they made as a consequence of their beliefs and actions, and their commitment to efforts to defend other forces similarly opposing Washington garnered the admiration of those who upheld the vision of a hemisphere made up of independent nations, free of the depredations U.S. imperialist policies inflicted on them.

## NATIONALISM AS A FORCE OF LIBERATION

For many progressive people in the United States today and elsewhere, nationalism is synonymous with xenophobia, exclusion, racism, and hatred of others: many of the Capitol rioters of January 6 espoused these views. It is frequently preceded by the words "reactionary" or "white" and/or "fascist."[27] This has not always been the case. For much of the twentieth century, anticolonial and anti-imperialist national liberation struggles across Asia, Africa, the Middle East, and Latin America led the global fight *against* European and U.S. domination and *for* the creation of independent nations and/or socialist societies.[28] These struggles represented liberation for most of the world's people, not oppression. Instead of erecting barriers and building walls, they sought alliances with other oppressed peoples, worked with international solidarity movements, and promoted left-wing or, in most cases, progressive politics. They did so for political and practical reasons. Politically, they confronted a common enemy or enemies—imperialism or colonialism—and shared similar goals for their independent nations. Many national liberation struggles were ideologically rooted in Marxism-Leninism, which called for an end to class and national oppression and, less often, women's oppression. Practically, they needed each other and understood that their mutual support strengthened both their individual and their collective ability to obtain and sustain victory.[29]

I have no wish to romanticize or glorify national liberation movements. They had their share of shortcomings, made mistakes, committed abuses. Male supremacy, oppressive sexual and patriarchal politics and organizational hierarchies, venality, and personal rivalries existed, more in some, less in others.[30] The point I am making, however, is that members and supporters of those movements believed that anti-imperialist nationalism represented liberation and the elimination of foreign control. Further, most national liberation movements embraced transnationalism and international solidarity, for the political and practical reasons I mentioned above.[31]

Partha Chatterjee traces "the West's" (referring to the former colonial powers or the developed world) more recent disparagement of postcolonial nationalism, and by extension the anticolonial movements that preceded them, to the 1970s. By then, "nationalism [in the eyes of the West] had become a matter of ethnic politics, the reason why people in the Third World killed each other."[32] Colonial dominance is predicated on the colonizers' assertion of and belief in their own superiority and the inferiority of the colonized. Thus, it is not surprising that former or current colonial powers would look down on and seek to vilify those who challenge their rule or, even more, those who defeated them and achieved independence, thereby exposing the emptiness of the colonizers' claims of superiority. In the case of Puerto Rico, the U.S. government and media repeatedly and consistently labeled members of the PNPR, particularly Albizu Campos, as crazy, lunatics, fanatics, and terrorists. It did so to undermine the party's credibility and portray those who oppose U.S. colonialism not as freedom fighters but as irrational and often dangerous individuals, fascists, or people who simply and unreasonably hated "Americans."

The PNPR's vision of nationalism was neither xenophobic nor isolationist. Instead of drawing boundaries—or building walls—between itself and other peoples and countries, the party sought independence in order to rejoin its sister nations throughout the Americas. It needed the solidarity of other Americans to free itself from U.S. rule. For these reasons, among others, the PNPR invested energy, members, and resources in building relationships with like-minded individuals and organizations throughout the hemisphere, attending regional conferences, distributing its literature, working with supporters to set up solidarity committees, presenting its case to elected officials and the general public, and promoting the causes of other oppressed peoples.

Furthermore, Puerto Rican Nationalists did not hate "Americans." Indeed, the Nationalist Party sought alliances and successfully worked closely with a number of them. Most of these relationships developed in New York City, home to the largest Puerto Rican community outside of the archipelago as well as several juntas, or chapters, of the Nationalist Party, and the capital of the North American Left. The Nationalist Party worked with key figures in New York City's mid-twentieth-century progressive political circles and intelligentsia, including authors Pearl Buck and Norman Mailer, Congressman Vito Marcantonio, labor leader A. Philip Randolph, Earl Browder (secretary general of the Communist Party USA from 1930 to 1945), and pacifist members of the Harlem Ashram. Ruth Reynolds, an Ashram member, and Thelma Mielke had particularly close relationships with the pro-independence party. Reynolds led or participated in U.S.-based solidarity movements with Puerto Rican independence from the late 1940s through the 1970s and, following the Nationalist Party's 1950 uprising, was jailed along with several Nationalist women in Puerto Rico. So far were the Nationalists from considering "Americans" the enemy that Albizu designated Mielke to represent the Nationalist Party in the United Nations.

In short, the Nationalist Party did not preach, propagate, or practice indiscriminate hatred or violence against an enemy Other. Yes, it opposed U.S. colonial rule and targeted individuals it held responsible for enforcing U.S. control of Puerto Rico. It did so because Nationalists believed that Puerto Rico had the inalienable right to be a free nation and they had the duty to employ the measures they deemed effective, which ranged from speeches, publications, and marches to building international networks of solidarity and carrying out armed actions to secure their freedom. Far from making the Nationalists into a party of hate-filled fanatics that employed indiscriminate violence against "Americans," their approach put them in the company of other national liberation movements in the Caribbean, Africa, the Middle East, and Asia that were fighting, on multiple levels and in a variety of ways, for their independence.

## FASCISM AND THE NATIONALIST PARTY

The Puerto Rican Nationalist Party has always provoked controversy, both during the years of its most intense political activity (1920–50) and later when it became the subject of scholarly literature. One of the most contested accusations against the party is that it was fascist. Gordon K. Lewis, the renowned author of several books on Puerto Rico and the Caribbean and friend and supporter of Luis Muñoz Marín, the founder and leader of the Partido Popular Demócrata (PPD, Popular Democratic Party), defined the PNPR as a "Creole Fascist-Nationalist movement led by the fanatical genius of Albizu Campos."[33] Lewis erroneously claimed that Albizu virulently hated Americans, due to an "unfortunate experience at Harvard University [where Albizu was a student] during the period of the First World War."[34] Lewis then incorrectly asserted that many Nationalists "were members of the *falangista* group set up in the island by [Spanish dictator Francisco] Franco agents, interested not so much in a genuine struggle for democratic independence as in fomenting a neo-fascist attack upon democracy."[35]

Puerto Rican historian Luis Angel Ferrao also linked the Nationalists to European fascism. In his study of the party in the 1930s, he claimed, "European fascism inspired more than a few of the Puerto Rican Nationalists' conceptions."[36] As an example of this connection, Ferrao stated that in 1921 Italian fascists published "a decree for the organization of young fascists. It is very like the document put out by Albizu."[37] He further declared that Peruvian Laura Meneses, who was married to Albizu, "was sympathetic to fascism."[38] However, he offered no proof to back up these defamatory assertions.

Ferrao's lack of evidence was precisely one important criticism that a group of young Puerto Rican scholars in the Taller de Formación Política (TFP, Political Training Workshop) raised in their critique of his book in 1991.[39] Indeed, they not only faulted Ferrao for failing to substantiate his claims but showed that he either ignored or misinterpreted material that contradicted his thesis. For example, Albizu expressed his thoughts on fascism in a letter he wrote to Laura Meneses in 1937 when he was in prison in Atlanta. The letter was subsequently published in two important Puerto Rican newspapers, El Mundo and La Democracia. In the letter, Albizu specifically condemned German, Japanese, and Italian imperialism because they sought to subject "humanity to perpetual, brutal, and materialistic enslavement."[40] He also defended the Jewish, Chinese, and Abyssinian peoples these empires attacked. Ferrao cited the letter but did not discuss its content.[41]

The TFP publication also exposed the weaknesses of Ferrao's other attempts to paint the Nationalists as fascist. For example, Ferrao claimed that José Buitrago, leader of the Asociación Patriótica de Jóvenes Puertorriqueños (APJP, Patriotic Association of Young Puerto Ricans), a pro-independence youth group affiliated with the Nationalist Party in the early 1930s, sympathized with fascism. He quoted Buitrago, who recalled, "When we designed the uniform worn by the Cadetes de la República [Cadets of the Republic, a PNPR militia group] we did so thinking of Mussolini." However, Buitrago clarified, "but at that time we had no idea what fascism was. Simply, out of ignorance, we thought [Mussolini] was one more nationalist." Instead of proving that "fascism had a considerable influence" on the Nationalists, as Ferrao stated, the TFP authors conclude that "the sympathy certain Nationalists could possibly have had with fascism were in fact sympathies with nationalism, the defense of the motherland, and other elements of Puerto Rican nationalism that those Nationalists incorrectly attributed . . . to Mussolini."[42]

Ferrao did not distinguish between the "nationalism of an imperialist country" and that of a colonized country. Thus, for example, Ferrao neglected to mention that the picture he included of the Cadetes wearing black shirts was of the organization's Sandino Battalion. In other words, the Cadetes named their formation after one of the foremost anti-imperialist figures of the earliest twentieth century, Nicaraguan Augusto César Sandino, not a European fascist.[43] Both Lewis and Ferrao failed to recognize that Nationalists opposed U.S. colonialism in Puerto Rico, even during World War II when the United States was fighting fascism, not because they supported fascism but because they wanted an independent nation.

The Nationalists were not alone in their decision to continue their campaign for freedom during World War II. Indians fighting British colonialism in India during this same time similarly refused to postpone their struggle for independence, even though they also opposed fascism. The Congress Party, the premier anticolonial party in India, passed a resolution in 1941 that "expressed solidarity 'with the peoples who are the subject of aggression and who are fighting for their freedom' against the Axis." Nevertheless, the Congress Party, like the Nationalists, refused to end its struggle for Indian independence. As the resolution further stated, "India cannot offer voluntary or willing help to an arrogant imperialism which is indistinguishable from fascist authoritarianism."[44] The next year, Mahatma Gandhi convinced the Indian National Congress to adopt the anti-British colonialism "Quit India" campaign. The British government responded to the Quit India campaign "by arresting the entire Congress leadership the next day."[45]

Rafael Ángel Simón Arce's exhaustive study of the Spanish Falange in Puerto Rico did not uncover any meaningful link between Spanish fascism and the Nationalist Party. As he wrote, "No data establishes a link between the Nationalists and the Puerto Rican Falange."[46] Further, Simón Arce did not find even a single reference on the part of the Falange leaders to the Nationalist leaders, nor did he discover "any personal statement by Albizu in favor of Franco or the Falange."[47] He did, however, determine that two members of Nationalist organizations subsequently joined the Falange and that former PNPR president Federico Acosta Velarde made public statements in favor of the Falange; however, Simón Arce clarified, "they did so on an individual and personal basis" and, it is important to note, once Acosta Velarde was no longer PNPR president.[48] Simón Arce pointed out, interestingly, that the U.S.-appointed ruler of Puerto Rico, Gen. Blanton Winship (1934–39), along with "other civil and military functionaries of the U.S. administration in Puerto Rico," had friendly, even supportive relations with Spanish conservatives and Falangists in the island.[49]

## A DIFFERENT PERSPECTIVE ON THE NATIONALIST PARTY AND NATIONALISM

Much of the literature on the PNPR centers on Pedro Albizu Campos.[50] For example, Marisa Rosado's rich biography offers a vivid portrait of Albizu at various stages of his life while placing his history in the context of Puerto Rico and the Nationalist Party. Her extensive research uncovered a wealth of previously inaccessible or unknown documents, many of which she includes in the book and which I draw on in my discussion of Albizu's travels from 1927 to 1930. Although her study and others illuminate the life and thinking of Albizu Campos and offer important insights into the party's principal leader, they also have the effect of conflating the party with him.

When I tell people familiar with Puerto Rican history that I am writing a book on the Partido Nacionalista Puertorriqueño, they inevitably exclaim, "Oh, on Pedro Albizu Campos!" I explain that no, my book is not about Pedro Albizu Campos, although he is certainly part of it. Instead, I highlight the transnational networks of solidarity with the party and Puerto Rican independence that existed across the Americas. Albizu played a critical role in forming and furthering these connections, particularly during his tour of the Caribbean, Mexico, and Peru in 1927–30. But from 1937 until 1965, when he died, Albizu spent almost twenty years in prisons. Although he continued to lead the party despite his incarceration and prison-induced illnesses, his ability to travel, deliver speeches, meet with supporters, and write was drastically curtailed. As a result, other Nationalists, such as Juan Juarbe, the Nationalists' secretary of foreign relations; Laura Meneses, the party's plenipotentiary delegate in charge of internationalizing the case of Puerto Rico; and Carlos Padilla, the Nationalist Party under secretary of foreign relations, became the party's international spokespersons and emissaries in the Americas.

Circumscribing the study of a political party to the figure of one male leader inevitably produces a skewed understanding of the complexity and richness of an organization and movement.[51] It overlooks the political, theoretical, and practical contributions of diverse members, both women and men, as well as the inner workings and life, day-to-day functioning, and public perceptions of the party. It obscures the essential role women played in building, maintaining, and representing the organization, as well as the political and theoretical contributions they made.

In addition to highlighting the importance of transnational solidarity to the party, this book challenges the idea that nationalism and nationalist movements are fundamentally masculine projects by exploring how Nationalist Party women understood the nation, participated in struggling for it, and perceived their role in the anticolonial movement and the Nationalist Party.[52] To do this, I analyze why women joined the party in the 1930s and beyond and profile such key Nationalist women as Laura Meneses, Blanca Canales, and Lolita Lebrón as well as U.S. women, such as Ruth Reynolds and Thelma Mielke, who acted in solidarity with the Puerto Rican independence movement. I highlight the activities and thoughts of female Nationalists whenever possible, although my ability to do so to a greater extent was hampered by a lack of sources.[53]

The unrelenting U.S. and Puerto Rican governments' repression directed against the party from the 1930s onward is another major focus of this book.[54] Because Albizu Campos was the key target of these attacks, he is frequently the main, but far from exclusive, subject of this literature as well. As these studies show, U.S. and Puerto Rican governments' attempts to suppress the

Nationalists by killing and imprisoning members, infiltrating the party, and gathering intelligence on them extended far beyond Albizu and members of the Nationalist Party and their supporters to other individuals who advocated for independence and were suspected of harboring anticolonial sentiments, including members of the Partido Comunista Puertorriqueño (PCP, Puerto Rican Communist Party). Federal Bureau of Investigation (FBI) surveillance of the Nationalists began in 1936 and continued throughout the 1950s and beyond. News of the extent of the FBI and Puerto Rican police's information gathering on Puerto Ricans became public knowledge in 1987, when it was reported that "no less than 75,000 persons [in Puerto Rico] had active files that ranged from a few index cards to full dossiers."[55] Government repression was so widespread that many Puerto Ricans justifiably feared that any association with the Nationalists would lead to governmental harassment or worse, the loss of work, and/or social, economic, and political ostracization. Their concerns led many to distance themselves from the party and undermined public support for independence.

Several Puerto Rican scholars have written important publications that offer a complex picture of the Nationalist Party. Miñi Seijo Bruno's study of the Nationalist insurrection of 1950 draws on the extensive interviews she conducted with dozens of participants in the uprising.[56] Her detailed site-by-site recounting of what happened where, who was involved, and how the militants understood their actions offers an engrossing portrait of this pivotal event in the party's history. Her careful profiling of who participated in the uprising debunks the myth that the party, at least in the 1950s, was a petit bourgeois movement. According to her data, most of the participants were "non-white" men between the ages of eighteen and twenty-four living in poor urban neighborhoods. Seijo Bruno further determined that of the 126 participants for whom she was able to form a complete picture, eighteen were students and 108, or 69 percent, were workers. In other words, as she concludes, "The majority of fighters in the 1950 insurrection were from the working class."[57]

Olga Jiménez de Wagenheim's book *Nationalist Heroines* explores the histories, actions, and thoughts of key Nationalist Party women; to date, it is the only book that focuses on these women. By providing biographical insights, many of them obtained from the extensive interviews she conducted with the women, she establishes the important role these women played in the party and draws a more complete picture of the PNPR than those studies focused solely on Albizu Campos. José Manuel Dávila's work also offers new perspectives on the Nationalist Party and its affiliated organizations for women and men. His well-researched studies reveal the rich associational life of the Nationalists and the multiple actors involved in the pro-independence groups.[58] And Gladys

Jiménez-Muñoz's intersectional discussion of race, class, and gender through her profiling of two Nationalist Party women sharpened my understanding of how important these three elements are and why we know about some women and ignore others.[59] I drew on these studies, among others, to tell the history of the Nationalist Party even as I break new ground by expanding that history to include the story of its transnational networks across the Americas.

I adopt a transnational approach to examine the Nationalist Party in the context of the Americas, from Santiago, Chile, to Mexico City to New York City. Most scholars of subjects related to Puerto Rico and/or Puerto Ricans focus on the archipelago, the diaspora, relations between the archipelago and the United States, or some combination of the three. Positioning the Nationalists in a hemispheric register allows me to transcend a vision of the archipelago and Puerto Ricans in isolation from the hemisphere or solely in a binary relationship with the United States, which too often has been the scale at which the independence movement, Puerto Ricans, and the archipelago have been studied.[60] This book offers a new perspective on the Nationalists and Puerto Rico, much as maps that center Africa or Asia and not the United States or Europe allow us to see our world in a whole new light.

I recount the PNPR's efforts to obtain hemispheric solidarity with its struggle and how and why forces, individuals, movements, parties, and even governments throughout the Americas responded to the pro-independence party's appeal. To do so, I briefly explore the political context of the specific nations involved, the anti-imperialist networks that developed throughout the region, and the individuals and organizations that participated in them. This discussion thus (re)inserts Puerto Rico into both Latin American and American studies.

Examining the Nationalist Party in a transnational context led me to appreciate how much support the PNPR, Puerto Rican independence, and the Nationalist political prisoners received across the Americas from the 1920s through the 1950s, and beyond. As I note above, my work on Chile, my training as a Latin Americanist, and my work on transnationalism pushed me to consider the Nationalist Party beyond the archipelago or the diaspora and in the context of the Americas. I discovered that solidarity with the Nationalists and independence was so extensive that examples of it existed in all the former colonies of Spain, except Paraguay—and perhaps future research will reveal that it occurred there, too—as well as in Haiti and Brazil. Instead of perceiving the Nationalists as isolated activists confronting the power and brutality of the U.S. empire alone, I realized they were part of multiple trans-American, anti-imperialist networks of individuals, organizations, parties, and, in the case of Cuba after 1959, a government, all committed to ending U.S. rule in Latin

America.[61] Although solidarity was particularly strong among communists, socialists, and other left-wing parties and movements, it frequently transcended political categories, as the case of Ecuador illustrates.

Carlos Padilla, one of the PNPR's international representatives, traveled throughout South America in the 1950s to generate solidarity for Puerto Rican independence. In 1957, he worked with members of the Ecuadorian parliament who presented a "Solidarity Agreement with the Peoples of Algeria and Puerto Rico" for approval. The resolution joined the two because "year after year, they have sought political emancipation."[62] The parliamentarians' pairing of the two colonies was significant, since it linked Puerto Rico to the global anticolonial struggles then sweeping Asia, the Middle East, and Africa.[63] The document's language also exemplifies the spirit of oneness and a shared, hemispheric identity that infused most Latin American statements in support of Puerto Rican independence: "The Nation of Puerto Rico has the total right to fight to constitute itself an independent Republic and to reintegrate itself into our family of sovereign Latin American peoples."[64] Here, as in other declarations, letters, or petitions regarding Puerto Rico, Latin Americans employed the trope of family to indicate that the diverse republics were one entity.[65] They shared a common genealogy and history and, as a result, were bound by their common past and current reality.

Congressman Otto Arosemena Gómez, a centrist upper-class politician and later president of Ecuador from 1966 to 1968, questioned whether the parliament should pass a bill that could possibly contradict the position of Ecuador's president, Camilo Ponce Enríquez, although it appears he did not know what Ponce Enríquez's position was. Congressman Jorge Luna Yépez, one of the bill's main proponents and a leader of the right-wing Acción Revolucionaria Nacionalista Ecuatoriana (ARNE, Ecuadorian Nationalist Revolutionary Action) party, declared that Puerto Ricans are "our brothers" since they share the same "blood, tradition, and culture." He reminded his fellow congressmen that the parliament had recently passed one resolution in support of the Bolivian Revolution and another one that backed Albizu Campos, "the last of the Liberators of Hispanoamérica," who now "lies in prison." He concluded that "[Puerto Rico] is the last of the nations that speaks our language, has the same legacy, shares our culture [and] still lacks an independent government." In the end, an overwhelming majority of the officials voted in favor of the agreement and planned to inform "the General Assembly of the United Nations . . . of the Ecuadorian people's sentiments."[66]

News of the Ecuadorian congress's endorsement of Puerto Rican independence traveled throughout Latin America. Left-wing Chilean politicians backed the Ecuadorian agreement, and El Siglo, the newspaper of the Communist Party of Chile, published an article titled "Ecuadorian Deputies Support Independence of Puerto Rico." The article noted that the agreement "joins ... the continental clamor of the most democratic voices demanding a complete amnesty for all the prisoners, persecuted, exiled of the Movement for the Liberation of Puerto Rico, among whom is Doctor Pedro Albizu Campos." El Siglo further reported that a number of prominent Chileans representing different political tendencies, including Clotario Blest, the noted labor leader who later helped found the Movimiento de Izquierda Revolucionaria (MIR, Movement of the Revolutionary Left), Christian Democrat Juan de Dios Carmona, and Socialist Salvador Allende, the future president of Chile, endorsed the agreement and wrote a letter to President Dwight D. Eisenhower calling for "a complete amnesty for all the members of the [Nationalist] movement imprisoned in the colonial prisons on the island and in the United States."[67]

The multiparty support that Ecuadorian congressmen displayed for Puerto Rican independence and the reverberations and amplification of their action in Chile were far from unique. Indeed, such demonstrations of solidarity with a free Puerto Rico occurred repeatedly across the Americas from the 1920s through the 1950s. In recounting them, I reveal what has long been unknown or ignored: for decades Puerto Rican Nationalists have been indomitable symbols of resistance to U.S. imperialism and colonialism in the Americas.

I recognize that referring to Latin Americans or the Americas as a body can be misleading, since it implies a uniformity in identity and opinion that simply did not exist. Indeed, the term "Latin Americans" or "Americans" encompasses a widely diverse population that, to my knowledge, has never expressed itself in one shared voice. Therefore, as often as possible I identify the specific people, group(s), or organization(s) to which I am referring. However, when I do refer to Latin Americans or Americans or Latin America or the Americas I do so to denote the peoples and the region as a whole while bearing in mind the differences and dissimilarities that define them and it.

Nor do I believe that any individual, politician(s), intellectual(s), or activist(s) speaks for their nation or movement as a whole. Too often we have conflated an entire nation with the figure of the country's president, generally a man. Thus, for many in the United States Fidel Castro became a synecdoche for Cuba, and vice versa, a commingling of terms that ignores the existence of millions of other Cubans. This approach flattens nations and regions into one homogenous unit, when in fact they are riddled with differences and variances and discontinuities. Just as governments and ideologies change over time, so, too, do many people's politics, which often reflect the historical context and personal or organizational interests of the moment.[68] For example, President Carlos Prío Socarrás welcomed the Nationalist exiles into Cuba in the early

1950s, but Fulgencio Batista, who overthrew him in 1952, harassed and arrested them and forced them to seek refuge elsewhere. Why? Because Batista sought to curry favor with Washington by displaying his loyalty to the United States, thereby securing his rule. The history of the relationship of the Alianza Popular Revolucionaria Americana (APRA, American Popular Revolutionary Alliance) with the Nationalist Party and independence is similar. In the 1930s, Peruvian Victor Raúl Haya de la Torre, APRA's founder and most recognized leader, assailed U.S. imperialism, lauded the Nationalists, hailed Albizu, called for an end to U.S. colonialism, and demanded the release of the prisoners. By the 1950s, however, years of repression and life in exile or in clandestine locations, combined with APRA's leaders' desire to operate publicly and legally in Peru, tempered the party's radicalism and ended its anti-imperialism. Instead of challenging U.S. colonialism in Puerto Rico, APRA leader Luis Alberto Sánchez, who visited Puerto Rico in 1951, had coffee daily with Luis Muñoz Marín and wrote favorably about the Free Associated State, which, according to him, "will be endowed with all the features of a republic." Sánchez dismissed the uprising of 1950 as an attack "conducted by a group of Nationalists against the Fortaleza [official residence of the governor in San Juan] to assassinate Muñoz Marín."[69]

## TRACING TRANSNATIONAL MOVEMENTS

I traveled to Chile, Mexico, Peru, Puerto Rico, and various cities in the United States to research the Nationalists. Three collections in particular yielded a treasure trove of documents on the Nationalist Party, its networks throughout the Americas, and the U.S.-based solidarity movement. They are the Ruth M. Reynolds Papers at the Centro de Estudios Puertorriqueños in New York, the Ralph C. Templin Collection, housed in the United Methodist Archives and History Center at Drew University in Madison, New Jersey; and the Archivo General in San Juan, Puerto Rico. Both Reynolds and Templin were members of the pacifist Harlem Ashram, supporters of the Nationalist Party, and incredible preservers of documents. I have never understood how Reynolds managed to keep copies of both her incoming and outgoing letters while she was in prison, but I am so glad she did!

In addition, I visited the Biblioteca José M. Lázaro and Centro de Estudios Caribeños at the Universidad de Puerto Rico, Río Piedras; the Biblioteca Nacional del Perú and Instituto Riva-Agüero, in Lima; the Archivo Histórico Diplomático "Genaro Estrada" de la Secretaría de Relaciones Exteriores de México, Archivo General de la Nación, and Archivo Plutarco Elías Calles, in Mexico City; the Harry S. Truman Presidential Library in Independence, Missouri; the New York Public Library and the Tamiment Library in New York City; the National Archives and Record Administration in College Park, Maryland; the

Special Collections, Richard J. Daley Library, University of Illinois at Chicago; and the University of Chicago.

The interviews I conducted with surviving members of the Nationalist Party and the North Americans who were in solidarity with them were vital to my research.[70] The first Nationalist I interviewed was Lolita Lebrón, in 2004. Over the next eleven years I was able to interview eight surviving Nationalists and three of their North American supporters, all of whom had been active in the 1940s or 1950s and remained politically involved. All the Nationalists I spoke with had been imprisoned for varying amounts of time. Lolita Lebrón and Rafael Cancel Miranda, who had participated in the Nationalist Party attack on the U.S. Congress in 1954, each spent twenty-five years in prison.

I learned a lot about each interviewee's personal history as well as that of the Nationalist Party from my talks with them. Although each person spoke about events, ideas, and relationships that had taken place more than fifty or sixty years earlier, their memories and stories of the past were razor-sharp. The drama and deep commitment, the joys and sufferings associated with their actions and identities as Nationalists defined much of who they were to themselves, their families and friends, and the public. As a result, the past and their role in it were firmly and securely etched in their minds. Their memories were also kept continually alive through their own writings, presentations, and reminiscences, in addition to the interviews they gave over the years. My interviews afforded me insight into the subjective, the personal, and the emotional, which allowed me to obtain a better understanding of who these people were and why they thought and did what they did. Although I don't quote all the individuals I interviewed, their thoughts and feelings informed my understanding of the Nationalist Party and the U.S.-based solidarity movement.

### OVERVIEW OF THE BOOK

The story of twentieth-century transnational solidarity with Puerto Rico begins in the nineteenth century, as chapter 1 discusses. Bonds between Puerto Rico and Cuba, the last two remaining Spanish colonies in the Americas, were particularly strong. Puerto Ricans Lola Rodríguez de Tió, Eugenio María de Hostos, Ramón Emeterio Betances, and Segundo Ruiz Belvis, Cuban José Martí, and Dominican Gregorio Luperón (Spain temporarily recolonized the Dominican Republic from 1861 to 1865) joined together to end Spanish rule in the Caribbean. Nationalist consciousness developed slowly in Puerto Rico but erupted in 1868 with the unsuccessful uprising in favor of independence known as the Grito de Lares (Cry of Lares). However, the end of Spanish colonialism, which finally occurred in 1898, did not signal the cessation of foreign intervention. Instead, it opened the doors to U.S. imperialism, a danger that anti-imperialist intellectuals warned of in two of the most important ideological contributions of the latter half of the nineteenth century, Arielismo and Hispanismo.[71]

Political, military, and economic incentives drove the United States to invade and colonize Puerto Rico in 1898. Chapter 2 examines these motivations and the formation of the colonial state that followed. The ensuing deliberations about the status of Puerto Rico occurred within the context of the U.S. domestic debate about how to categorize Washington's recently acquired overseas territories. Puerto Ricans responded in a variety of ways to U.S. colonialism and Washington's efforts to "Americanize" them. Some welcomed it, others accommodated themselves to it, and still others resisted it. The Nationalist Party drew its members and support from the third category.

The Partido Nacionalista formed in 1922 to defend Puerto Rican culture and call for an end to U.S. colonialism, as chapter 3 discusses. The party's foundational document affirmed Puerto Rico's identity as a Latin American nation, a position that remained constant throughout the party's history. A major rupture in party politics occurred in 1930, however, when Pedro Albizu Campos ended the largely cordial attitudes that had characterized the Nationalists' relations with the United States in the 1920s. Under Albizu's leadership, more women joined the party, which established organizations to facilitate their involvement. The party's racial identity and profile also changed, shifting away from elite men to men, and some women, of different classes and color.

From 1927 to 1930, Pedro Albizu Campos, then the party's vice president, traveled across the Caribbean and Latin America to promote solidarity with Puerto Rican independence and the Nationalist Party. In his visits to the Dominican Republic, Haiti, Cuba, Mexico, Peru, and Venezuela he met with a range of people and received a variety of responses, recounted in chapter 4. Dominican, Haitian, and Cuban nationalists welcomed him with open arms and cemented relationships of mutual support that lasted for decades. But the Mexican government of President Plutarco Elías Calles, fiercely battling opposition Catholic forces in the Cristero War, refused even to meet with him. (Albizu was a committed Catholic.) A shortage of funds—the Nationalist Party consistently lacked money—forced a penniless Albizu to shorten his trip and remain in Peru, with his wife, children, and her family for almost two years. Nonetheless, Albizu's travels broadened the Nationalist Party's political horizons, deepened its commitment to anti-imperialism, and laid or strengthened the roots for ongoing solidarity with a host of individuals and organizations throughout the region.

Two hurricanes, the Depression, and U.S. rule had a devastating economic impact on Puerto Ricans' lives in the 1930s. To understand how the Nationalist

Party responded to these multiple crises and ongoing colonialism, chapter 5 examines the organization's program and campaigns and U.S. government policies. U.S. government plans to manage its colony relied on improving economic conditions, undermining support for independence, and repressing the Nationalists. The last tactic precipitated an increase in violent confrontations between the PNPR and Puerto Rican police, which resulted in the Ponce Massacre in 1937 and the conviction and exile of Nationalist Party leaders to the Atlanta Federal Penitentiary. Their imprisonment under harsh conditions instigated continentwide demands for their release and independence for Puerto Rico.

Discussions of the Good Neighbor Policy typically overlook Puerto Rico because the archipelago was not an independent Latin American nation. Franklin Delano Roosevelt initiated the Good Neighbor Policy in 1933 to secure improved relations between Latin America and the United States and to counter fascist Italy's or Nazi Germany's efforts to build support for themselves and undermine U.S. power in the region. Yet Puerto Rico symbolized the unwelcome intrusion of the United States in the region and exposed the hypocrisy of Washington's pledges of noninterference for many Latin Americans. Hemispheric opposition to U.S. colonialism in the archipelago and Latin Americans' impassioned demands for the release of the Nationalist political prisoners represent an important critique of the Good Neighbor Policy and evidence of significant hostility to U.S. intervention in the region. Chapter 6 shifts the discussion of the Good Neighbor Policy from Washington and U.S. officials to Latin Americans who questioned both it and Washington's intentions for the region by denouncing U.S. colonialism in Puerto Rico.

Chapter 7 focuses on the Nationalist Party in New York City during the 1940s. Between 1937 and 1943 various Nationalist Party leaders, including Pedro Albizu Campos and Juan Antonio Corretjer, secretary general of the party, were imprisoned in the Atlanta Federal Penitentiary. Earl Browder, secretary general of the Communist Party USA, was also jailed there during some of those years. The three became close friends during their time together and subsequently reunited in New York City, the headquarters of both parties, following their release. Members of the Harlem Ashram, a radical pacifist organization, also took up solidarity with Puerto Rican independence. Harlem Ashram members joined with New Yorkers to form the American League for Puerto Rico's Independence, the first U.S.-based solidarity organization for Puerto Rican independence. Another important figure in this period was New York City congressman Vito Marcantonio, a vocal advocate of Puerto Rican independence and an ardent defender of the Nationalist political prisoners.

The 1940s was a pivotal decade in the history of Puerto Rico and the Nationalist Party, as chapter 8 explores. The Popular Democratic Party, led by Luis

Muñoz Marín, emerged as a major player in Puerto Rican politics. It worked closely with the U.S. government, which sought to avert global criticism of its colonial relationship with Puerto Rico as it proclaimed itself the leader of the Free World during the Cold War. Together, Muñoz Marín and the U.S. government engineered the island's transition to a commonwealth or free associated state (which Puerto Rico remains today). The Nationalist Party, weakened by the absence of its leadership, attempted to rebuild the party and advance the struggle for independence, an undertaking that met with some success.

Chapter 9 recounts the story of the three Nationalist Party armed actions in the early 1950s: the uprising in Puerto Rico of October 30, 1950; the assassination attempt on President Truman of November 1, 1950; and the attack on the U.S. Congress of March 1, 1954. It analyzes why the Nationalists carried out these assaults and how the U.S. and Puerto Rican governments, communist parties, Latin American governments and politicians, solidarity organizations, and supportive individuals responded to them. These actions facilitated U.S. government repression against the Nationalists and contributed to the party's subsequent decline. At the same time, the imprisonment, harsh treatment, and exile of the Nationalists generated widespread protests across the Americas and fervent denunciations of the U.S. government. Nationalist Party emissaries, who traveled throughout the Americas and worked with other revolutionaries, were central actors in the anti-imperialist networks that functioned during this period and generated solidarity with Puerto Rican independence and the Nationalist political prisoners.

Puerto Ricans who resisted U.S. colonialism are the principal actors of this book. Their dedication to the struggle for an independent nation sheds light on what U.S. imperialism means to those who oppose it. It also positions the Puerto Rican Nationalists as key protagonists in the fight for independence, not as victims of U.S. domination. This book further establishes that support for Puerto Rican independence and the release of the PNPR prisoners was a central, consistent, and unquenchable demand of anti-imperialist individuals, organizations, and networks across the Americas from the 1920s to the 1950s. In so doing, it brings to life the strong bonds of anti-imperialist solidarity that animated so many people's politics during these critical decades.

# 1 THE NINETEENTH-CENTURY ROOTS OF TRANSNATIONAL ANTICOLONIAL STRUGGLE AND SOLIDARITY

The poet Lola Rodríguez de Tió was a key figure in Puerto Rico's struggle for independence in the 1800s.[1] One of only a few highly educated women in Puerto Rico, she was known throughout the Caribbean and Latin America for her literary talents.[2] In addition to opposing Spanish colonialism in the region, Rodríguez de Tió advocated for women's rights, particularly the right to education. Because of her dedication to independence, the Spanish forced her into exile in 1877, whereupon she and her husband, Bonocio Tió Segarra, went to Venezuela, where they stayed until 1880. In Venezuela she met fellow Puerto Rican patriot and exile Eugenio María de Hostos.[3] Rodríguez returned to Puerto Rico but fled Spanish repression again in 1889 and lived in Cuba until 1895, when she and her husband moved to New York City. There she joined some fifty-nine other Puerto Ricans and worked with the Partido Revolucionario Cubano (PRC, Cuban Revolutionary Party), founded by Cuban José Martí in 1892.[4] From New York she sailed to Cuba in 1899, where she lived for the last twenty-five years of her life.[5]

The unsuccessful uprising of 1868 against Spanish colonialism in Puerto Rico known as the Grito de Lares inspired one of her best-known poems, "La Borinqueña," which has since become the revolutionary hymn of the independence movement.[6] The poem is a stirring call to arms, or rather to machetes, the agricultural tool that every Puerto Rican peasant possessed and could easily employ as a weapon:[7] "¡Despierta Borinqueño que han dado la señal! ¡Despierta de ese sueño, que es hora de luchar!" (Awaken Borinqueño, the signal has been given. Awake from your sleep, it's time to fight!) "A ese llamar patriótico ¿No arde tu corazón?" (Doesn't your heart burn at this patriotic call?)

The poem eloquently conveys how Rodríguez understood and projected the anticolonial struggle in 1868. First, the title: Borinqueño referred to the people of Puerto Rico. The word comes from the Taíno, the Indigenous inhabitants of Puerto Rico, who called their island Borinquen, or the Land of the Proud Lord. Rodríguez used the word "to symbolically attribute historical depth to the nation," a practice independence leaders Ramón Emeterio Betances and

FIGURE 1.1. Lola Rodríguez de Tío, Puerto Rican poet and anticolonial activist. Source: Library of Congress.

Eugenio María de Hostos also followed.[8] Second, Rodríguez included women in her appeal: "Las mujeres indómitas también sabrán luchar" (Indomitable women will also know how to fight). She considered women unbeatable; instead of limiting them to a supportive role, she defined them as combatants.[9] Third, Rodríguez identified with Cuba, because the sister island, like Puerto Rico, was one of Spain's two remaining colonies in the Americas. Rodríguez recognized the independence movement there was more advanced than in Puerto Rico; consequently, she presented Cuba as the model for Puerto Ricans to follow. "Mira, ya el cubano libre esta; le dará el machete la libertad" (Look, Cubans are already free. The machete will grant them freedom). And, in the next stanza, "Bellísima Borinquen a Cuba hay que seguir" (Beautiful Borinquen, we must follow Cuba).

Another of her poems, "A Cuba" (To Cuba), illustrates the profound interconnection she believed existed between Spain's two Caribbean colonies. "Cuba y Puerto Rico son / de un pájaro las dos alas, / Reciben flores y balas / sobre el mismo corazón" (Cuba and Puerto Rico are / two wings of one bird / They receive flowers and bullets / in the same heart).[10] From the publication of the poem in 1893 to today, this image of the two countries joined as one has appeared in the writings, posters, works of art, speeches, music, and artifacts of countless Puerto Rican *independentistas* and Cuban revolutionaries.

Lola Rodríguez de Tió's life and poetry eloquently convey the transnationalist spirit and politics that infused Puerto Rican and Caribbean revolutionary anticolonialism in the late 1800s. Rodríguez's contributions to the development of Puerto Rican nationalist consciousness challenge the precept that "nation

CUBA Y PUERTO RICO SON DE UN PAJARO LAS DOS ALAS...

TENGO UN ALA LIBRE... YA TENDRÉ LAS DOS

FIGURE 1.2. "Cuba and Puerto Rico / Two wings of one bird. I have one free, soon I will have both." By Cuban artist René de la Nuez. Source: *Claridad*, May 16, 1972.

building is not usually associated with women," as Edna Acosta-Belén accurately points out.[11] Indeed, Rodríguez, along with Betances and other Caribbean anti-imperialists, provided an example and inspiration for Puerto Rican Nationalists in the twentieth century who saw themselves as continuing the anti-imperialist thread for freedom. The Nationalist Party consciously traced its lineage back to these 1800s pro-independence figures and struggles in order to establish itself as their legitimate heirs and to portray the two distinct phases of anticolonialism as one linked and unbroken fight. The anticolonial fighters of the 1800s shared several similarities with the Nationalists in the 1900s. Both traveled through the Americas seeking support for Puerto Rican independence. Both were members of exile networks that proliferated in the circum-Caribbean region and extended to New York City. And both groups identified themselves as Puerto Ricans who simultaneously sought the independence of their homeland and considered themselves part of the broader Caribbean and Latin American struggles against imperialist domination and for independence.[12]

The goals of nineteenth-century Puerto Rican anticolonial leaders were twofold: national independence and a Caribbean free of foreign rule. To achieve their goals, they worked in solidarity with peoples throughout the Caribbean.

The roots of the Puerto Rican Nationalist Party's transnationalist understanding of nationalism lie in the vision and practices of these anticolonial fighters and of other Latin American anti-imperialist activists and intellectuals of the 1800s and early 1900s.

## PUERTO RICO'S DELAYED FIGHT FOR INDEPENDENCE

In 1815, Simón Bolívar, the Venezuelan creole known as El Libertador for his pivotal role in uniting the disparate pro-independence forces in South America to defeat Spain, wrote his Letter from Jamaica. He had taken refuge on the island following Spanish victories over the anticolonial forces in South America. In the letter, Bolívar analyzed the status of the independence struggle. After assessing the military situation in South America, he commented specifically on Puerto Rico and Cuba. They were, he pointed out, "the lands most peacefully possessed by the Spaniards, because they have no contact with the [independence forces]."[13] He lamented this reality and posed three plaintive questions that have since echoed across Latin America: "But, are those island dwellers not American? Are they not abused? Do they not seek their good?"[14]

Indeed, Puerto Ricans did not rise up and fight for independence until 1868, more than forty years after the rest of Spanish America, with the sole exception of Cuba, had achieved liberation. Why was this the case? To fight for independence, a people need to identify themselves as a unique and unified entity, distinct from and in opposition to the colonial power they believe both oppresses and exploits them. Scholars do not agree when Puerto Ricans began to identify themselves as Puerto Ricans, different from and, at some point, antagonistic to Spaniards. Francisco Scarano sees signs of a "proto nationalist consciousness" emerging among the liberal wing of the creole class at the end of the 1700s.[15] Harry Franqui-Rivera argues that the majority of Puerto Ricans did not see themselves as a "we" (Puerto Ricans) in opposition to a "they" (Spaniards) until after the uprising of 1868 in Lares.[16] What is certain is that aside from some notable exceptions, such as Puerto Rican Antonio Valero de Bernabé, who became one of Bolívar's trusted generals, most Puerto Ricans did not participate in or necessarily support the Spanish colonies' anticolonial war in the early 1800s.[17]

In her study of the Grito de Lares, Olga Jiménez de Wagenheim points out several political and economic factors "that delayed the insurrectionary spirit in Puerto Rico until the mid-nineteenth century."[18] Puerto Rico lacked the gold, silver, or other sources of wealth that Spain's other colonies possessed and that Spain both coveted and depended on. Consequently, Spain paid less attention to, devoted fewer resources to, and maintained a far smaller presence in Puerto Rico than it did in Mexico, Peru, or its other, more resource-rich and wealth-producing colonies. Spain's relative lack of interest in the archipelago meant fewer conflicts between the *peninsulares* (Spaniards born in Spain who lived in the Americas and controlled the economic, political, military, and ecclesiastical positions of power) and the small but growing creole class in the archipelago. Thus, one reason Puerto Rican creoles in the early 1800s did not rise up and demand independence was because they did not share the sense of being excluded from desired positions of power, influence, and wealth that galvanized their peers in other Spanish colonies to demand an end to royal rule.[19]

Other elements encouraged Puerto Rican creoles, the class that led the ultimately successful wars for independence throughout the region, to accept their colonial relationship with Spain in the early 1800s.[20] When white slave owners fled Haiti after slaves revolted in 1791, they sought refuge and the opportunity to rebuild what they had lost in the welcoming environment of the neighboring islands. Their lurid stories of death and destruction terrified Puerto Rican elites and made them cleave to Spain, especially its military might, more firmly.[21] Indeed, as Francisco Scarano notes, the island's "fast-increasing slave, free black, and *pardo* [someone of mixed African, European, and Indigenous descent] population," intensified Puerto Rican creoles' fear of armed rebellion and, consequentially, their reliance on Spain's martial protection.[22]

Furthermore, the slave rebellion in Haiti had positive economic consequences for elite Puerto Ricans: it created shortages in the world market in sugar and coffee. As a result, Puerto Ricans, along with Cubans, increased production of both goods and received higher prices for them. To sweeten the bonanza, Spain "liberaliz[ed] trade restrictions" on these products, reduced export duties, and allowed some imports, such as "farm tools, machinery, and slaves," to enter the country duty-free. These reforms "helped to create in Puerto Rico the economic infrastructure that would permit colonial development."[23] These policies strengthened creoles' loyalty to the motherland and encouraged them to view their relationship with Spain favorably. In addition, pro-Spanish loyalists from across South America flocked to Puerto Rico as revolutionary wars spread across the continent. Adding their voices to those of the Haitian slave-owners, they bolstered pro-Spanish attitudes in the archipelago and contributed to making Puerto Rico "Spain's anti-revolutionary bastion in the Caribbean."[24]

As Spain's "anti-revolutionary bastion," Puerto Rico functioned as a forward military base of the Spanish imperial enterprise in the Americas, as did Cuba. The islands were already heavily fortified since many Spanish troops were garrisoned in them. When the Spanish military presence increased on the islands due to the escalating warfare on the mainland in the early 1800s, so too did the importance of Cuba and Puerto Rico to the Spanish crown. To secure the islands and ensure their military efficacy, Spain pumped money into the Cuban and Puerto Rican economies, a chunk of which flowed into the pockets of the creole upper class and weakened any inclination it might have had to break free from the crown.[25] The cumulative effect of these factors initially convinced many Puerto Rican creoles that their continued association with Spain afforded them the military protection and economic benefits they needed to maintain their wealth and position.[26]

## NATIONALIST CONSCIOUSNESS AND
## PRO-INDEPENDENCE STIRRINGS IN PUERTO RICO

Yet by 1867 sentiment had shifted to such a degree that Ramón Emeterio Betances could proclaim, "Four centuries of oppression and servitude have not extinguished our right to be free." Instead of feeling part of Spain, Betances denounced the Iberian nation's rule and asserted Puerto Rico's differences with Spain. "Everything separates us from Spain. . . . Much more than the immense ocean [is Spain's] theft and murder! . . . [And] the horrors they have submerged us in . . . from the day [Spain] occupied and bled the land of Borinquen dry."[27] Betances not only rejected Spanish rule but encouraged Puerto Ricans to pluck up their courage and advance their struggle for liberty: "Do not lose heart! Wanting to be free is the first step to becoming it!"[28]

Scores of Puerto Ricans, including poor peasant men and women of the mountainous interior, shared his feelings and heeded his call. On September 23, 1868, several hundred revolted and fought to end Spanish rule. They took over the interior town of Lares (hence the name Grito de Lares) and declared the Republic of Puerto Rico. Spanish troops and local militias defeated the pro-independence forces in a matter of days.[29] What had occurred to produce this sea change in people's attitude?

After Spain lost its colonies in the Americas, it prized its possession of Puerto Rico (and Cuba) more highly. Thus, commercial exchanges between Puerto Rico and Spain increased, as did the presence of Spanish business interests, agriculturalists, officials, and bureaucracy, with Puerto Ricans footing the bill for the island's administration. In addition, the reforms Spain introduced in 1815 encouraged landowners to improve agriculture techniques and sell their sugar and coffee abroad. However, Spain discouraged the development of manufacturing, compelling Puerto Rico to import manufactured goods, which led to a growing trade deficit. The Spanish government refused to accede to creoles' request for financial aid, which heightened creole discontent with Madrid.[30] By 1860, "The colonial economy was increasingly decapitalized and its inhabitants were still poor, barefooted and ignorant."[31]

Economic factors alone do not explain Puerto Ricans' growing dissatisfaction with Spanish control. Pro-independence forces also had political demands, the foremost being an end to Spanish rule. They also called for the right to a free press, to free speech, to possess arms, and to hold meetings; for citizen inviolability and for the abolition of slavery.[32]

Puerto Rican anticolonial leaders such as Ramón Emeterio Betances, Segundo Ruiz Belvis, Lola Rodríguez de Tió, and Eugenio María de Hostos did not act alone.[33] They formed part of a radical trans-Caribbean cohort that simultaneously fought for national independence, political freedom, and individual rights. Like the Cuban revolutionary José Martí, they supported an end to slavery and racial oppression.[34] Betances and Hostos joined Rodríguez in calling for women's rights and supported social justice more generally.[35] Paul Estrade argues that they, along with their Cuban and Dominican counterparts, had the clearest, most advanced conception of nationalism in Latin America due, in part, to the lengthy persistence of slavery and when their independence movements emerged: "The most backward region in Latin America, from the point of view of obtaining political independence in the last century, produced the most open, modern, and consistent nationalism of its time."[36] In other words, because Cuba and Puerto Rico's independence movements developed so much later, they were both influenced by and the beneficiaries of other progressive movements that had emerged in the Americas and Europe, particularly France, in the late 1840s.

Many of these figures belonged to a trans-Caribbean, anticolonial political community. Forced into exile by the Spanish government, they met each other and worked together in various nations. Rodríguez and Hostos met in Venezuela. Betances and Ruiz Belvis were in contact with Dominican revolutionaries such as Gregorio Luperón. In New York City, where anti-Spanish Latin Americans had sought refuge since the early 1800s, Rodríguez, Betances, and Segundo Ruiz Belvis worked with José Martí and a host of other Cuban and Puerto Rican exiles.[37] They also worked with the Cuban Revolutionary Party, which Cuban revolutionary José Martí had founded in Miami in 1892 but whose headquarters were in New York City. Martí's commitment to Puerto Rican independence was as strong as the Puerto Rican anticolonial leaders' was to Cuban independence. The first article of the party platform reads, "The Cuban Revolutionary Party is created to achieve . . . absolute independence for the island of Cuba and to aid and encourage that of Puerto Rico." On Martí's request, Betances in turn agreed to lead the PRC in France.[38]

Betances was born in Puerto Rico of Dominican parents. A true Caribbeanist, he found inspiration in Haiti's successful revolution, which secured both independence and an end to slavery. He cherished Puerto Rico's ties to Cuba and the Dominican Republic.[39] Betances and Hostos, along with their Cuban and Dominican comrades, promoted the Antillean Confederation, whose goal was to secure "the Antilles for the Antilleans."[40] As Betances envisioned it, the

Antillean Confederation would lead to the "formation of a multinational state with twenty-five million inhabitants," including Cuba, Puerto Rico, the Dominican Republic, and Haiti. According to his plan, the confederation would unite various "small and weak nations and ensure the independence of all the nations in the region." Betances hoped to incorporate other Caribbean countries, such as Saint Thomas, which was a Danish colony at the time.[41]

The call for Antillean unity surged from 1863 to 1865 when Dominicans were fighting to restore independence following Spanish recolonization of their nation in 1861. It reemerged from 1868 to 1874 when anticolonial Dominicans opposed President Ulysses Grant's attempt to annex the Caribbean nation, a move that had the support of both Dominican president Buenaventura Báez and many Dominicans.[42] Betances worked closely with Dominican Gregorio Luperón, who like Betances was of African and Spanish descent, to popularize the concept of the union of the Antilles and to build support for an end to Spanish colonialism and slavery. The two men published newspapers together and, when in exile in New York City, joined the Republican Council of Cuba and Puerto Rico, which supported the abolition of slavery and independence for both countries.[43] While in New York, Betances issued a call to the people of Puerto Rico, "Patria, Justicia, Libertad" (Motherland, Justice, Freedom), that summarized his sense of Puerto Rican and Cuban oneness: "Cubans and Puerto Ricans! Unite our forces, work together, we are brothers, we share the same misfortune. We shall also be one in Puerto Rico's and Cuba's revolution and independence."[44] Betances's vision, like Rodríguez's image of Puerto Rico and Cuba being two wings of one bird, presaged the Puerto Rican Nationalist Party's politics on nationalism and transnationalism, which combined a militant demand for national sovereignty with the equally powerful assertion that Puerto Rico did not and could not exist or triumph alone because it was both a Caribbean nation and a Latin American one.

## CHANGES IN LATIN AMERICAN POLITICAL ATTITUDES AFTER 1898

The U.S. victory over Spain in 1898 transformed the political panorama across Latin America. Most Latin Americans had viewed Spain, their former ruler, as their primary enemy. Spain's defeat and loss of territory in the Americas made manifest its decline in power and global reach. Henceforth, many Latin Americans believed they faced a much clearer, closer, and more potent danger: the United States.[45] Certainly, Latin Americans had eyed earlier U.S. aggressions against the region, such as the Monroe Doctrine in 1823, the seizure of Mexican land in 1836 and 1848, and Texan William Walker's invasion of Nicaragua in 1856, with concern and suspicion.[46] However, the U.S. invasion of Puerto Rico and Cuba, and the subsequent direct rule of Puerto Rico and slightly less direct control of Cuba, heightened Latin Americans' fears about the imminence of U.S. domination and prompted fairly widespread criticism. This repudiation explains the enthusiastic reception that José Martí's brief essay Nuestra América received in 1891. Martí, the hero of the fight for Cuban independence, wrote Nuestra América as a passionate call for Americans to take pride in and learn from their past and to look to themselves, not Europe or the United States, for knowledge.

For Martí, being American, in the hemispheric sense of the word, had nothing to do with race. Indeed, he disputed the very idea of race in Nuestra América, writing, "There can be no racial animosity, because there are no races." Instead, he declared, "the soul emanates, equally and eternally, from bodies different in shape and color," a sharp rebuke to all those, be they Cuban, Spanish, or from the United States, who sought to justify or assert social hierarchy based on the pseudo-scientific notion that the color of one's skin determines one's mental capacity or position in society. He ended the essay with a stirring declaration of continental unity that included far-flung nations and distinct cultural imagery: "From the Río Bravo to the Straits of Magellan, the Great Cemi, riding high astride a condor, has scattered the seeds of the new América across the romantic nations of the continent and the suffering islands of the sea!"[47]

Pro-independence Puerto Ricans who worked closely with Martí in New York City, at least one of whom, Antonio Vélez Alvarado, was a founding member of the Nationalist Party in 1922, held similar ideas about race. Vélez Alvarado, along with Puerto Rican anticolonialists and abolitionists Sotero Figueroa Hernández and Francisco Gonzalo Marín (known as Pachín Marín), who were of Afro descent, defined race using concepts that Albizu and other Nationalists would propound in the 1930s.[48] They equated race not with biology but with a common "language, customs, traditions, and sentiments." They perceived a hemispheric division between those of a "Latin race" and "Anglo-Saxons." And they rejected any association between "divisions of color or hereditary."[49]

Increased opposition to U.S. incursions in the region also accounts for the growing popularity of Hispanismo, an ideology that promoted a common heritage and identity for Latin Americans, especially those of Spanish descent. Hispanismo, as Isidro Sepúlveda defines it, was "a movement whose objective was the articulation of a transnational community sustained by a cultural identity based in language, religion, history, and customs or social use; an imagined community that reunited Spain with the American Republics, granting the former metropolis . . . a position of primogeniture . . . under the extended expression of Madre Patria."[50] The initial impetus for the movement originated in Spain. Facing domestic political conflict and the loss of Puerto

Rico and Cuba, the government determined that it "sorely needed to cultivate friendly relations with its former colonies."[51] In addition, by presenting itself as a "leader and moral tutor to its former colonies," Spain could reposition itself within Europe as a power at a time when colonial conquest "demonstrated national greatness."[52]

Latin Americans' response to Spain's efforts to define itself as the madre patria was mixed. While some embraced the idea of belonging to a transnational community anchored in a shared language, religion, and history, others rejected the superior attitudes that many Spaniards continued to hold toward their former colonial subjects.[53] Many scholars' recent assessment of Hispanismo has been critical. Sebastian Faber offers a particularly trenchant critique of Hispanismo, pointing out that it overlooks, subsumes, or denies differences in the name of promoting a continental oneness that, in fact, did not exist: "The concept of Hispanism presupposes a commonality of interests and aims that is simply not there. The concerns, focuses, struggles of distinct social classes, ethnic groups, and other communities across the Iberian Peninsula and the American continent differ widely and are, many times, even opposed to each other. . . . The concept of Hispanism . . . should be rejected precisely because it assimilates a reality whose main characteristics is its heterogeneity."[54] Nonetheless, Spain's defeat and the U.S. occupation of Cuba and Puerto Rico following 1898 heightened many Latin Americans' feelings of mistrust toward the colossus to the north and encouraged them to join together against the rising threat.

Such sentiments prompted Uruguayan José Enrique Rodó to write the widely influential essay Ariel, which launched the continentwide movement of Arielismo. The work (and movement) contrasted Caliban, who represents U.S. materialism, to Ariel, who signifies Latin American spiritualism.[55] Latin American artists, intellectuals, journalists, and political figures seized on these images, which became a simulacrum for the defense of the region's Hispanic heritage against the encroachments of the Anglo-Saxon power to the north.[56] According to Nicola Miller, Ariel shaped the elaboration of Spanish American anti-imperialism, which "developed on the basis of the arielista claim that, if Spanish America could not be economically equal to the United States, it might at least be spiritually superior."[57]

Artists and intellectuals across the continent adopted Rodó's imagery. Nicaraguan poet Rubén Dario, leader of the Modernismo literary style in Latin America, referred to the United States as the land of Caliban.[58] One of his most famous poems, "A Roosevelt" (To Roosevelt), which he wrote in 1904 after the United States backed a Colombian separatist movement to obtain the Isthmus of Panama and create an independent nation, addressed then-president Theodore Roosevelt: "You are the United States, You are the future invader."[59]

Concomitant with this repudiation of U.S. domination, anti-imperialist Latin Americans formed and sustained "networks and intellectual circuits" to defend their culture, identity, history, and sovereignty in opposition to the cultural, political, and economic onslaught launched against them by the United States, as Eduardo Devés details.[60] Participants included leading intellectuals, politicians, and artists from the Caribbean, particularly Cuba, Mexico, and Central America, as well as the Southern Cone of South America. They wrote to each other; published in the same newspapers, principally *Repertorio* from Costa Rica and *Amauta*, which Peruvian revolutionary José Carlos Mariátegui founded and directed; read each other's writings; and participated in joint campaigns. Although members of these networks did not necessarily agree on all points—some were Marxists, others later supported fascism—four themes united them. They supported democracy and freedom of expression, social reforms, and cultural development, while they opposed imperialism and outside—read U.S.—intervention.[61]

Puerto Rican Nationalists had direct connections with several important members of these networks in the 1920s and beyond. José Vasconcelos, the former Mexican secretary of education, was a leading figure in the Latin American web, and his ideas were "hegemonic among Latin American intellectuals."[62] Manuel Ugarte, an Argentine, a good friend of Rodó's, and author of *El destino de un continente* (The Destiny of a Continent) was also a respected figure in Latin American anti-imperialist circles. He, like Vasconcelos, became an international spokesperson for the Puerto Rican Nationalists.[63] They both represented the party at the Congress against Colonial Oppression and Imperialism, held in Brussels in 1927, as well as in other international anti-imperialist conferences.[64] Like many other Latin American anti-imperialists, they believed that ending U.S. intervention in the Caribbean was essential to defending the sovereignty of Latin America, which is why they steadfastly defended Caribbean nationalist movements and served as the international voice of the Puerto Rican Nationalist Party.

Latin Americans, particularly those living in the Caribbean, shared ideas and ideals and jointly built solidarity networks during the mid- and late 1800s that extended into the early 1900s and beyond. These connections explain, in part, the warm reception Pedro Albizu Campos received on his trip through Latin America in the years 1927 to 1930. Certainly, not all Latin Americans identified themselves as anti-imperialists, rejected the United States, welcomed Albizu, or supported Puerto Rican independence. Some preferred the United States, which "represented modernity and progress," as opposed to Spain, which they considered "backward and authoritarian."[65] However, many Latin

Americans did uphold the ideals of national sovereignty and regional solidarity and clamored for Puerto Rican independence.

Nor did all Latin Americans embrace Hispanismo. Many—particularly those of Afro, Indigenous, or mixed-race descent—felt, and in many cases were, excluded from this Hispanic-dominated community. They also understood that the promotion of *hispanidad* as the link that tied people together effectively erased the genocidal nature of Spanish colonialism, the oppressed position they occupied in the post-Spanish colonial world, and the value and importance of their own religions, languages, and cultures.

However, much of the Puerto Rican Nationalist Party, and certainly Albizu, who was of mixed African and Basque descent, held a different definition of Hispanismo and *raza*. For Albizu and other Puerto Rican Nationalists, *raza* included people of Afro, Indigenous, European, and mixed-race descent. They used the term to signify that all those who were part of Hispanoamerica should unite in opposition to the Anglo-Saxon empire that controlled Puerto Rico and threatened Latin America. To understand why Puerto Rican Nationalists objected so strongly to U.S. rule and advocated independence, chapter 2 discusses the basic features and development of U.S. colonial rule in Puerto Rico.

# 2 SETTING UP THE U.S. COLONIAL STATE

On July 16, 1926, the Puerto Rican Nationalist Party held a public meeting in San Juan to commemorate the day patriot José de Diego died in 1918.[1] José Coll y Cuchí, one of the founders of the pro-independence party, closed his speech by saying, "American flag, I salute you because you represent freedom and the first republic of the Américas."[2] Pedro Albizu Campos, the last speaker, strode to the podium, which was festooned with small U.S. flags, and proceeded to remove the flags and stuff them in his pocket. In a voice fired with "emotion and patriotic anger,"[3] he declared, "Flag of the United States, I do not salute you. Although it is true you are the symbol of a free and sovereign country, in Puerto Rico you represent piracy and pillage. This flag was raised on the backs of North American Blacks and is maintained by these same unfortunate [souls] along with the exploited European immigrants. Today, it is a symbol of mourning for all of humanity."[4] According to his biographer Marisa Rosado, "The entire plaza burst into cries of '¡viva!' and applause for the courageous and decisive speaker." And henceforth, "U.S. flags were never again used in Nationalist events."[5]

U.S. flags arrived in Puerto Rico in July 1898, when U.S. troops invaded the archipelago during the Spanish-American War. Lieutenant General Nelson Miles, known for killing and conquering Native Americans in the so-called Indian Wars, led the U.S. invasion of Puerto Rico in 1898, twenty-eight years before the scene described above.[6] When U.S. troops marched into Puerto Rico, some inhabitants opposed them, but many more welcomed them, believing that the United States had come to help liberate them from Spain, not recolonize them.[7] Subsequent events, unfortunately, showed these hopes to be illusions and contributed to the formation of the Puerto Rican Nationalist Party in 1922.

The transnational solidarity networks with the Nationalist Party this book focuses on begin in, flow from, and bring together a range of local contexts. I discuss these contexts throughout the book. To understand why Puerto Rico and the Nationalists generated such support across the Americas, I begin by exploring U.S. colonialism in Puerto Rico.

The United States colonized Puerto Rico in pursuit of its political, economic, and military interests, at the expense of the needs of most Puerto Ricans. To accomplish its goals, the United States denied Puerto Ricans a voice in the legislative and judicial decisions that shaped their lives. Puerto Rico was key to Washington's plans to extend its military, political, and economic power in the Caribbean and Latin America and, after the completion of the construction of the Panama Canal in 1914, Asia. U.S. economic interests saw Puerto Rico as a site from which to extract profits. U.S. racial conceptions, which designated Puerto Ricans as inferior and uncivilized, justified their political exclusion from the seats of power. Labor policies consigned the majority of the population to the status of peons. Their function was to toil in the torrid sugar and tobacco fields or overheated and unsanitary mills or to painstakingly produce exquisite needlework in their homes or workshops. The goods and most of the profit from their low-paid work flowed to U.S. consumers and investors.

Puerto Ricans reacted to U.S. colonialism in a myriad of ways. The level of full-scale resistance that the Nationalist Party embodied beginning in the 1930s did not manifest itself in the first two decades of U.S. rule, although, as the opening vignette illustrates, we catch glimpses of it. Instead, many Puerto Ricans initially welcomed the United States, and many sought to adjust to the new situation, even as they attempted to understand it, survive it, and secure what benefits they could from it. Workers, for example, took advantage of the more lenient labor laws the United States introduced and unionized to secure higher wages and better conditions. Women struggled to obtain suffrage rights. Others, mainly men, formed, led, or joined political parties whose platforms variously called for statehood, workers' rights, autonomy, or independence.

For most Puerto Ricans, resistance, and perhaps that is too strong a word, operated on a low, but nonetheless meaningful, register. Despite U.S. efforts to enforce English on the education system, the majority of Puerto Ricans continued to speak Spanish, eat Puerto Rican food, listen to Puerto Rican music, and dance Puerto Rican dances. Some accepted or adapted to U.S. notions of a racial hierarchy, which defined those of European descent as superior to people of color. They did so, in part, because these concepts mirrored Spanish ideas of white supremacy with which they were accustomed, even though Spanish constructions of race were neither as binary nor as rigid as those of the United States in the early 1900s. Others realized that being white offered greater material benefits and a higher position in a society dominated by U.S. colonizers or Puerto Ricans of European descent. Still others rejected U.S. definitions of race, as well as U.S. rule. This latter response acquired an organizational expression in 1922 with the emergence of the Nationalist Party. It gathered force after 1930, when Pedro Albizu Campos, who was of Afro and Basque descent, became president of the pro-independence party and militantly called for an end to U.S. colonialism.

## STRUCTURING U.S. COLONIALISM IN PUERTO RICO

The U.S. government established the basic framework of its rule early on. Every significant decision affecting Puerto Ricans' judicial, political, economic, and military life would be made in Washington, D.C., not San Juan. The U.S. military directly ruled Puerto Rico until 1900, when the Foraker Act instituted civilian rule in the archipelago.[8] It established a thirty-five-member House of Delegates in Puerto Rico but permitted only Puerto Rican men over twenty-one who could read and write and paid taxes to vote.[9] U.S. presidents appointed Puerto Rico's governor, cabinet, and five-member supreme court.[10] From 1900 to 1946, when President Truman named José T. Piñero governor, no Puerto Rican held that position. Puerto Rico had a resident commissioner in the U.S. Congress who could voice his (and much, much later her) opinions but had no right to vote on any issue, even ones that affected the archipelago.[11] In 1948, the U.S. government authorized Puerto Ricans to vote for their governor, and Luis Muñoz Marín of the Popular Democratic Party became the archipelago's first elected head of government.[12]

The U.S. Congress determined Puerto Ricans' political status in relation to the United States. Although the Puerto Rican House of Delegates had issued a statement rejecting U.S. citizenship in 1914, the U.S. Congress passed the Jones Act in 1917, which conferred U.S. citizenship on Puerto Ricans but did not grant them the right to vote in federal elections.[13] Jim Crow attitudes dominated U.S. politics at the time, and the U.S. Congress had no desire to extend voting rights to Puerto Ricans, whom it considered nonwhite and therefore inferior. Later that year Congress did, however, pass a law that drafted Puerto Rican men into the U.S. military.[14]

Washington officials debated the nature of the relationship and the appropriate legal status of the archipelago and its inhabitants throughout the first two decades of the 1900s. The discussion was part of a broader conversation regarding how the United States should classify Puerto Rico, Cuba, the Philippines, and Guam, which it had secured following its victory in the Spanish-American War, along with Hawai'i, which President William McKinley annexed in 1898. The United States was no stranger to the conquest of other people's lands; indeed, the entire history of the country is based on conquest. However, as César Ayala and Rafael Bernabe point out, the acquisition of Native American lands and northern Mexico was "a republican form of expansion, insofar as the new territories were expected to and did successively join the Union under the same conditions as the founding states."[15] Puerto Rico and the above-mentioned territories were different, and not primarily because they were geographically separate from the United States. What distinguished them was the numerical superiority of the local, nonwhite population, the absence of a majority white population, and the likelihood that this basic ratio would not change.[16]

The issue of whether or how to classify the newly acquired territories and their inhabitants fundamentally boiled down to how voting citizens in the United States, most of whom were white Protestants, all of whom were men, conceived of race and nation. In the late 1800s and early 1900s, most white people in the United States understood race as a, perhaps the, key factor that defined where people lined up on the scale of civilization.[17] As law professor Mark Weiner notes, most white, Protestant inhabitants of the United States believed "Anglo-Saxon peoples are characterized ethno-juridically, above all, by their capacity for state-building . . . with a special genius for efficient administration."[18] However, and necessarily, "the darker races were incapable of legal order. . . . They were slavish children living in earlier stages of evolutionary development."[19]

The debate over the status of the recently acquired territories became a topic of public discussion. Did the refusal to fully incorporate these peoples into the U.S. body politic signify that the United States was becoming an empire? Did it violate the Constitution? Those who opposed overseas expansion enjoined the debate and formed the American Anti-imperialist League in 1899.[20] Although their reasons for doing so varied, most anti-imperialists believed that the acquisition of foreign territories without the granting of citizenship to the inhabitants violated the Constitution. They concluded that because so many in the United States, including a number of the anti-imperialists themselves, considered the peoples of these newly acquired islands to be inferior and savage, they would not be granted citizenship. Historian Robert Beisner's summary of the views of Carl Schurz, one of twelve anti-imperialists he profiles, conveys the fears many anti-imperialists held. Their main concern was not ensuring political justice and representation for the inhabitants of the newly conquered islands but maintaining the U.S. political system, which they admired. According to Beisner, Schurz feared that "Filipinos and Puerto Ricans would corrupt the whole American system; as second-class subject peoples with no rights, they would give the lie to America's free political traditions and be a standing reproach to the ideals of American history."[21]

A minority of anti-imperialists opposed the U.S. conquest and colonization of other peoples because they thought that it ignored, if not violated, the wishes of the inhabitants of the new territories. They also voiced their concern that the practice of governing people without granting them political rights would damage the United States. They spoke out against "any extension of the sovereignty of the United States over the Philippine Islands . . . and over any other foreign territory without the free consent of the people thereof, believing such action would be dangerous to the Republic, wasteful of its resources, in violation of Constitutional principles, and fraught with moral and physical evils to our people."[22] Some anti-imperialists even took up the cause of the invaded populations. They supported Filipino guerrilla forces' armed resistance to the U.S. military's ultimately successful campaign to defeat the rebels and take over the archipelago.[23] However, far too many anti-imperialists argued against the formation of an overseas empire because they abhorred the addition of millions of nonwhite, hence inferior and backward, peoples who would undermine what they considered the democratic integrity of the United States.[24] They, like most white people living in the country at the time, believed that the unquestionable power and future advance of the United States stemmed from and rested on the evolutionarily superior composition of its population. For that reason, they fervently sought to maintain the United States as an Anglo-Saxon, Protestant nation, proud of its heritage and confident of its ability and destiny to rule.[25]

The outcome of the elections of 1900, which "largely turned on the so-called issue of Imperialism," appeared to settle the matter. William S. McKinley, the Republican candidate, stoutly defended the recent U.S. victory in the Spanish-American War and argued that the Constitution did not follow the flag. William Jennings Bryan, the candidate of the Democratic Party, said that it did, and he contended that the permanent possession of colonies violated the spirit and the law of the U.S. Constitution.[26] McKinley received 284 electoral votes out of 447 possible ones; Bryan obtained 155, which many have interpreted as meaning, "The voters sanctioned imperialism."[27]

Although this presidential election affirmed U.S. voters' political support for overseas expansion, it defined neither Puerto Rico's status nor Puerto Ricans' rights or lack thereof. (At the time, women, Native Americans, and African Americans living in the U.S. South lacked voting rights, which did not prevent the voting population from considering the United States a shining example of democracy.) Those battles regarding status and rights were fought in the Supreme Court from 1901 to 1922 in a series of cases known as the Insular Cases. As José Fusté points out, the justices adapted "the kind of classification that US courts had used to give the US government near absolute power over Native American tribes and their lands" in earlier cases.[28] Essentially, their rulings sanctioned U.S. power over Puerto Rico and the other territories while simultaneously denying enfranchisement to the inhabitants. As the Court ruled, "We are therefore of the opinion that Porto Rico is a territory appurtenant and belonging to the United States, but not a part of the United States."[29] Thus, although the U.S. Congress made Puerto Ricans U.S. citizens in 1917, Puerto Ricans living in Puerto Rico could not—and still cannot—vote in any federal election, not for president, not for senator, not for congressperson.[30]

U.S. rulers justified their governing of Puerto Rico by infantilizing Puerto Ricans and declaring them unfit to run their own country. From 1898 to 1900, when the Foraker Act introduced civilian rule, U.S. armed forces ruled Puerto Rico. Military officers submitted extensive annual reports detailing the state of affairs in the archipelago. In his concluding remarks to the report of 1899, Maj. A. C. Sharpe, inspector general of U.S. Volunteers in Puerto Rico, recommended how the United States should best advance its rule in Puerto Rico. He first compared Puerto Ricans favorably to the "wild animals and savage tribes" that roamed New Mexico and Arizona before U.S. "acquisition" of these lands.[31] Puerto Ricans, he stated, "though bowed down by centuries of [Spanish] oppression, still retain the spirit and capacity for higher and better conditions."[32] However, he cautioned, "this capacity and these conditions can be developed only under a system which will wisely *control, guide, and support them,* until they attain sufficient vigor to support and control themselves."[33] As of 2023, the U.S. government apparently does not think that Puerto Ricans have yet attained the vigor they need to run their own country.

Other U.S. government officials shared Sharpe's paternalistic and condescending opinions. Brigadier General George W. Davis, military governor of Puerto Rico from May 1899 to May 1900, offered a virtually identical assessment of Puerto Ricans.[34] He, however, characterized Puerto Ricans as being of a "foreign race and tongue," thus betraying his failure to grasp that Puerto Ricans were hardly the foreigners in Puerto Rico. Davis said, "The inhabitants, *all of a foreign race and tongue,* largely illiterate and without experience in conducting a government in accordance with Anglo-Saxon practice, [the correct way!] or indeed to carry on any government, were not deemed to be fitted [sic] and qualified, unaided and without effective supervision, to fully appreciate the responsibilities and exercise the power of complete self-government."[35]

The image of Puerto Ricans as children who needed the wise counsel of the benevolent U.S. government to mature into adults capable of governing themselves was not confined to U.S. officials serving in Puerto Rico. It permeated U.S. society, as the cartoon shown here illustrates. In it, Puerto Rico, depicted as white, is the good boy. He's clean, neatly dressed in U.S.-style clothing, obediently holding Uncle Sam's hand, and looking askance at bad boy Cuba. Cuba is Black, dressed in tattered clothing, and armed with a pistol and a gun, having just broken into a safe box full of debt, mortgage, and more debt. The caption implies that thanks to Uncle Sam's wise decision to maintain direct

FIGURE 2.1. U.S. cartoon infantilizing and racializing Puerto Ricans and Cubans. Source: Chicago Inter Ocean, 1905.

control over Puerto Rico while granting nominal freedom to Cuba, Puerto Rico, the docile, well-behaved good boy, escaped sharing the presumably unwelcome fate of Cuba, the rebellious, dangerous bad boy. Further, as the image of Uncle Sam towering over little Puerto Rico suggests, Puerto Ricans need to heed Uncle Sam's paternal guidance and adopt the U.S. model of behavior if they wish to advance.

## PUERTO RICO: A U.S. MILITARY OUTPOST IN THE CARIBBEAN

In the early 1800s, land and the products generated from it were the prime measure and principal means of obtaining wealth in the United States. As the United States industrialized and urbanized and capitalist economic relations steadily expanded during the 1800s, the need for labor, resources, and markets intensified.[36] The seizure and occupation of other peoples' territory and the subsequent acquisition of additional markets and resources were essential to the continued success of capitalist development.

In his persuasive book *The Influence of Sea Power upon History*, navy captain Alfred T. Mahan argued that to attain and retain great power status, a country needed a powerful navy. Once the United States possessed a "Central-America" canal, which Mahan assumed it soon would, "the Caribbean will be changed from a terminus, and a place of local traffic, . . . into one of the great highways of the world."[37] However, he warned, to protect its assets, the United States "will have to obtain in the Caribbean stations fit for contingent, or secondary,

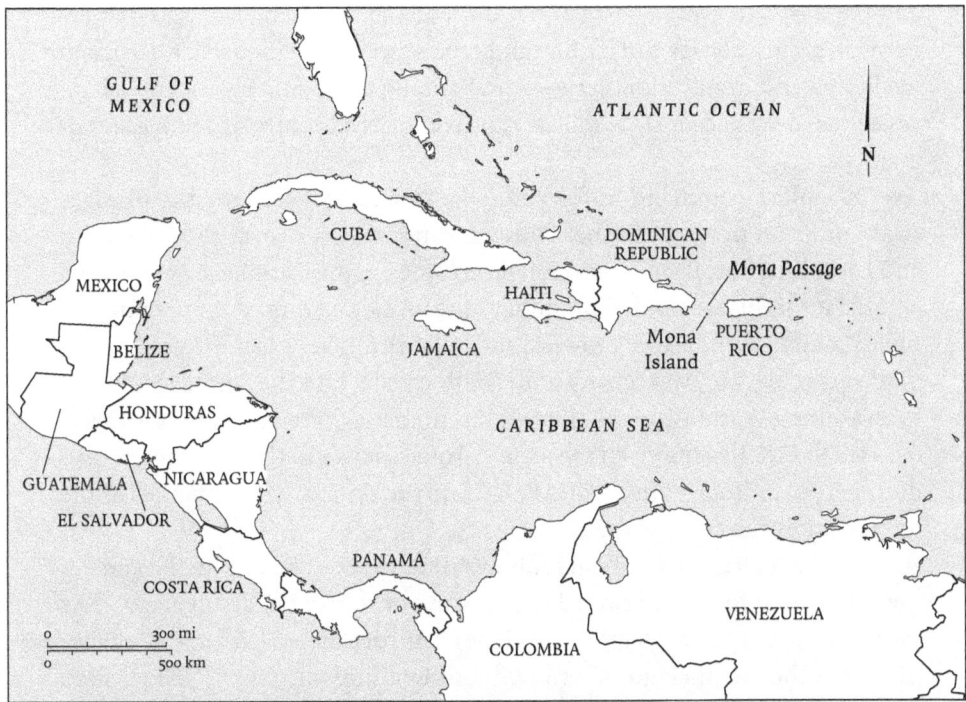

The Mona Passage. Key passage into and out of the Caribbean.
Source: Naomi Robles.

bases of operation."[38] Powerful figures in the United States embraced his
ideas. Mahan communicated frequently with Theodore Roosevelt and "was
instrumental in shaping his thinking on the necessity of a modern navy to
achieve regional hegemony."[39]

Mahan's argument on the importance of constructing a strong navy and
securing essential bases to fuel and house it fell on other receptive ears as well.
U.S. manufacturers, traders, politicians, and the armed forces coveted the
Caribbean, with its promises of rich resources, potential markets, and territory
for military bases. Puerto Rico offered the United States a key beachhead in
the Caribbean. The Mona Passage, which lies between Puerto Rico and the
Dominican Republic, connects the Atlantic Ocean to the Caribbean and is an
important point of entry and exit. Control of the Mona Passage was critical to
establishing U.S. domination of the circum-Caribbean area.[40]

Control of the Caribbean was central to U.S. geopolitical designs on the
area. Once completed, the Panama Canal became a prime shipping route
through which traffic to and from Mexico, Central and South America, Asia,

and the East and West Coasts of the United States passed. The islands were home to military bases and coaling and cable stations that housed, fueled, and facilitated communication between and among the U.S. navy and merchant vessels needed to secure U.S. military and commercial control in Latin America and Asia.

To achieve command of the zone, the United States needed to displace rival European powers that held direct or indirect sway over the Caribbean and Latin America. Britain, which held colonies in the Caribbean and exerted significant political clout throughout Latin America due to its preeminent financial system, industrial prowess, and military might, was the United States' main rival. Germany was an ascending one, especially in the period leading up to and during World War I, but its defeat terminated, if temporarily, the threat it posed to U.S. hegemony in the area.[41] British power in the hemisphere also declined precipitously after World War I, and the United States emerged as the foremost force in the region.

Although direct U.S. military rule over Puerto Rico ended with the Foraker Act, the armed forces continued to play a major role in the archipelago.[42] As early as 1923, the "[U.S.] navy . . . used the island of Culebra [one of the smaller islands of the archipelago] for amphibious landing practices."[43] The United States built the mammoth Roosevelt Roads naval base in Puerto Rico during World War II to safeguard the waters from the Germans. The base was so large that it could accommodate "the entire British navy in the event of a Nazi invasion of Britain."[44] During the Cold War, Puerto Rico's tropical location was an ideal environment in which to train U.S troops or agents that were later deployed to Korea and Vietnam or participated in the overthrow of President Jacobo Arbenz of Guatemala in 1954, the invasion of Cuba at the Bay of Pigs in 1961, the invasion of the Dominican Republic in 1965, and the invasion of Grenada in 1983.[45]

### COLONIALISM, THE ECONOMY, AND LABOR

The United States transformed the Puerto Rican economy into one that served the interests of U.S. investors, absentee landowners, industrialists, and manufacturers. U.S. capital dominated the Puerto Rican economy. By 1928 U.S. investors owned 27 percent of Puerto Rico's wealth.[46] U.S. investors successfully penetrated, pumped up, and profited from the most dynamic sectors of the Puerto Rican economy: sugar, tobacco, and needlework. Most U.S. investments, 78 percent, poured into sugar and tobacco, the areas that offered the highest rate of profit.[47] All three industries exported the lion's share of their products and profits to the United States and generated the most jobs for Puerto Ricans. Coffee production, long a mainstay of the economy, declined. Coffee workers were the lowest paid agricultural laborers. Men received fifty to sixty cents per day, women eighteen to thirty-two cents, and children fifteen to twenty-eight cents.[48]

Sugar generated the highest profits. The Foraker Act allowed Puerto Rican sugar to enter the United States duty-free, which greatly increased its competitiveness.[49] This arrangement encouraged U.S. interests to purchase Puerto Rican–owned sugar land and the *centrales* (mills) that ground the sugar, thus effectively acquiring a large share of sugar production. One year later, in 1901, the United States imported 91,000 tons of sugar from Puerto Rico.[50] By 1930, four U.S. sugar companies "owned or leased 23.7 percent of all cane land" and ground almost half of the sugarcane produced in Puerto Rico.[51] However, Puerto Ricans continued to own the largest share of the sugar industry, as César Ayala and Laird Bergad show. "Puerto Ricans owned about 60 percent of the island's sugar industry in the 1920s, and this share remained fairly constant for the next two decades."[52] Nonetheless, U.S. entrepreneurs injected capital into the production and milling of sugar, which led to a greater concentration of the mills in fewer hands.[53] It also allowed the industry to introduce technological advances and increase production. By 1930, the amount of sugar produced "was more than ten times the level of 1900." Profits expanded as well. As James Dietz notes, "From 1920 to 1935, [three of the four U.S. sugar companies] distributed $60,562,000 in dividends to their shareholders. . . . These three companies invested about one-quarter of their profits and distributed 75 percent to absentee, mostly U.S., shareholders."[54]

Puerto Rican tobacco growers maintained control of their land, as Teresita Levy shows. They could do so because U.S. capital found it more profitable to run the facilities that prepared the tobacco for market, the systems of transport that conveyed it to the United States, and the "marketing strategies for the vast U.S. mainland consumer market" than in investing in the small farms where tobacco was grown.[55] Although tobacco farmers earned much less than workers in the sugar or needlework industries, owning their land allowed them to grow crops and raise animals to supplement their otherwise meager diets.[56]

The massive infusion of U.S. capital hastened the development of the working class, particularly in the sugarcane, tobacco, and needlework industries. Conditions for workers, who received extremely low wages, did not improve under U.S. rule. The governor's report characterized labor conditions as "far from satisfactory" in 1922. Not only were wages "far below [those] in any of the States," but they were "so small as not to allow the wage earner with a family sufficient income to live in comfort and educate his children."[57] Workers labored long hours, and in many cases, the pace of work quickened. Rural workers typically worked from sunrise to sundown, ten to twelve hours.[58]

Women increasingly joined the paid labor force in the early twentieth century. They dominated the needlework industry, were important in the tobacco-processing sector, and found employment as domestics. In 1918, domestic workers were paid between twenty-five and thirty cents for a ten-to-twelve-hour workday.[59] Women needleworkers either labored in their own homes, often incorporating other members of their family into the process to obtain a barely livable income, or in small workshops alongside other women. Wherever they worked, conditions were abysmal, production demands were high, and pay was low. Many needleworkers put in nine-to-eleven-hour days, every day.[60] In 1922, they earned thirty-nine cents a day for their labor and in 1925 seventy-eight cents.[61]

Those who worked in the tobacco-processing plants also endured difficult conditions, long hours, and little pay. Women received between fifty cents and two dollars a day.[62] They did, however, learn about history, politics, and culture, along with the need to organize collectively for better conditions. They were exposed to new ideas and a "vast political culture" through the daily readings of literature, political essays, and anarchist, socialist, and union newspapers by readers whom the workers hired.[63] As a result, many women tobacco workers joined the Federación Libre de Trabajadores (FLT, Free Federation of Labor) and the Socialist Party (Partido Socialista) and struggled for workers' rights and women's suffrage.

The FLT began in 1899 and affiliated with the American Federation of Labor (AFL) in 1902. Recognizing the need to form an organization capable of representing workers in the political arena, FLT members formed the Socialist Party in 1915.[64] The Socialist Party and the FLT, which became the largest labor association, backed striking and imprisoned workers during the first two decades of their existence.[65] In 1929, the Socialist Party formed a coalition with the Partido Republicano (Republican Party). The Republicanos supported statehood for Puerto Rico, and many of its leaders were owners of the large sugar estates that dominated the island. The conflicts that such a disparate coalition inevitably engendered came to a head during the sugarcane workers' strike in 1934, when workers rejected the FLT and called on Nationalist Party president Pedro Albizu Campos to represent them.[66]

Although women did not occupy top positions in the Socialist Party, they played an important role in the union movement.[67] For example, Luisa Capetillo, an anarchist and a member of the FLT, worked in both the needle trade and tobacco factories. She fought for workers' rights and women's rights and rejected many of the gender norms that dominated Puerto Rican society. She abhorred the reigning definition of women as wives and mothers that

FIGURE 2.2. Dominga de la Cruz in Cuba, 1978. Nationalist Party activist and heroine of the Ponce Massacre of 1937. Source: Margaret Randall.

consigned them to an inferior status in relationships, the home, the workplace, and politics. Boldly donning pants at a time when women were supposed to wear dresses and skirts, she equally audaciously condemned "bourgeois exploiters" of the working class, a sexual double standard for women and men, and the idea that marriage should be based on anything other than love.[68]

Dominga de la Cruz was also an important figure in Puerto Rican labor and political struggles. A central member of the Nationalist Party in the 1930s, she was orphaned at an early age and forced to earn a living to support herself.[69] She married, not because she loved her husband, but because "women needed to find a husband in order to eat."[70] After her husband left her, she was so poor that her two children died of starvation. She first labored in workshops sewing blouses, with "oil lamps for light, until two in the morning, day after day."[71] She then worked in a tobacco factory in the late 1920s, where she read to the workers, educating them and herself in the process.[72] Through her reading she learned about the Bolshevik Revolution and that Nationalist Pedro Albizu Campos traveled to Latin America in the late 1920s to generate solidarity with Puerto Rican independence. Both news items impressed her greatly. In 1932, she heard Pedro Albizu Campos speak in Mayagüez, where she lived. She was so moved by his speech, in which "he got rid of the ghost that the Yankees were a type of God," that she joined the Nationalist Party in 1933.[73]

## U.S. EFFORTS TO "AMERICANIZE" PUERTO RICO

U.S. policymakers believed that for their colonial project to succeed they needed to "Americanize" Puerto Rico and Puerto Ricans. To that end, they reoriented the Puerto Rican economy to produce the commodities and revenues U.S. manufacturers, consumers, and investors sought and imposed U.S. political institutions and practices on the archipelago, as we have seen above. Their policies simultaneously weakened Spanish political traditions, undermined the ways of doing thing Puerto Ricans were more familiar with and adept at, and introduced new methods that reinforced U.S. control. To be employed by, let alone advance up the new colonial hierarchy, Washington officials expected Puerto Ricans to conform to U.S. ways of conducting politics. Some U.S. officials demanded that Puerto Ricans reject political positions challenging U.S colonial rule or forfeit their jobs and professional future. And, as we shall see in chapter 3, this is precisely the situation some of the founders of the Puerto Rican Nationalist Party confronted in 1922, when Governor E. Mont Reily declared that no one who supported independence could work in the colonial bureaucracy.

Not limiting themselves just to economics and politics, U.S. government representatives, educators, and missionaries also attempted to transform Puerto Rican culture and society to reflect U.S. values, ways of doing things, and interests. Puerto Ricans would continue to live in Puerto Rico, but as "Americans," not Puerto Ricans. One area in which U.S. functionaries concentrated their efforts was education. Colonial officials attempted to overhaul and refashion Puerto Rican schools, declaring that henceforth English, not Spanish, would be the language of instruction. Not only did U.S. educators and officials expect classes to be conducted in English, but they also reshaped the curriculum and the school year to replicate U.S. ideology, holidays, and practices. And they trumpeted the correlation between education, modernity, progress, and Americanization.[74]

To achieve their goals, the United States pumped money into building schools, training teachers in U.S. pedagogical methods and ideology, and rewriting the curriculum to reflect U.S. values and beliefs (Jorge Washington is the father of your country!). A U.S. Civil War veterans' organization even jumped on the Americanization of Puerto Rico bandwagon. It raised enough money to provide U.S. flags to almost every school building in the archipelago, the construction of which was central to colonial authorities' Americanization plans.[75] In 1898, there were only 529 schools in Puerto Rico; by 1910, there were

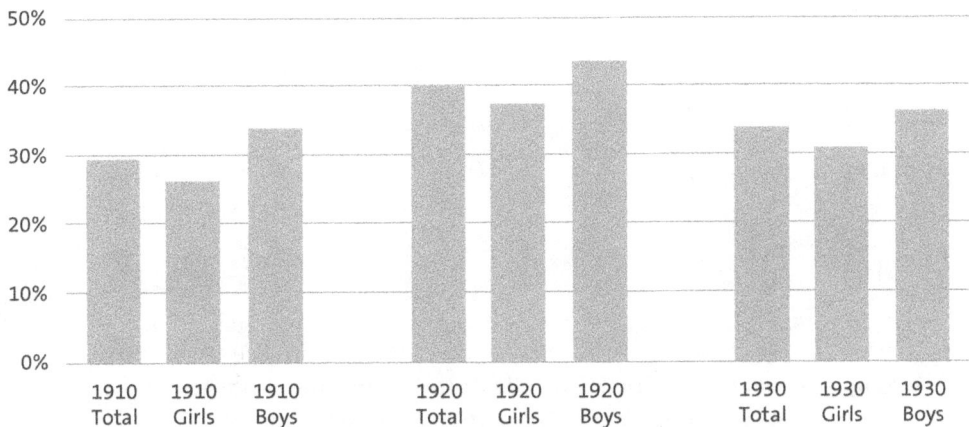

Percentage of girls and boys attending school in Puerto Rico, 1910–30.
Sources: U.S. Bureau of the Census, *Fifteenth Census*, 134, 140; Naomi Robles.

1,025 lower schools that went up to fifth grade and nineteen high schools.[76] A report from the chief of the Bureau of Insular Affairs touted these advances in 1910. It boasted, "Nearly nine and a half million dollars were expended on educational activities during the past 10 years." And "nearly 90 percent of the graded schools were taught wholly in English as compared with 66 percent the preceding year."[77]

Indeed, the U.S. government's focus on education appears to have met with success. The number of young people attending school rose in the first two decades of the 1900s. In 1910, 30 percent of Puerto Ricans between the ages of five and twenty went to school; by 1920, the number had risen to roughly 40 percent but dropped to 32 percent in 1930, probably because the economic hardships of the Depression forced parents to rely on their children's labor either at home or on a job.[78]

The percentage of boys that attended school was higher than that of girls. Only 27 percent of girls went to school in 1910; 33 percent of boys did. In 1920, 43 percent of boys attended classes; 37 percent of girls did. In 1930, the gap narrowed to 31 percent of girls and 35 percent of boys, but the overall number of children going to class dropped.[79] The gender gap reflected ideas about male and female roles and responsibilities. Men traditionally had more visible and important roles in the public sphere, as the family's principal breadwinner and the patriarch who controlled and was responsible for the movement, labor, fate, and sexuality of those under his control.[80] Education was a source, confirmation, and consequence of this power, which explains why Puerto Rican boys were more likely to attend school and be literate than girls.[81]

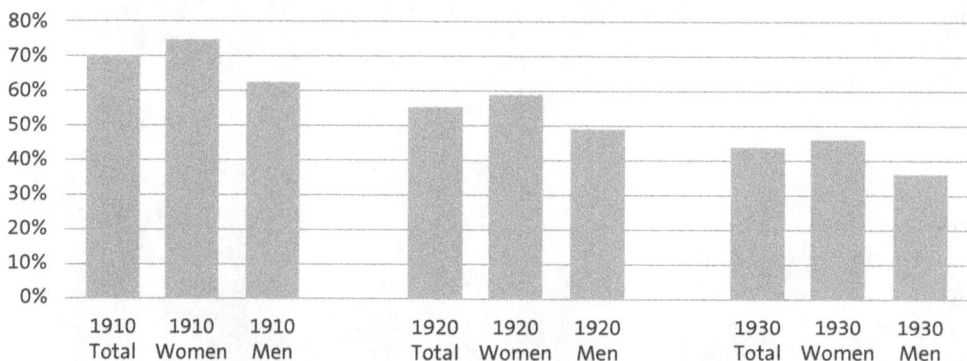

Percentage of illiteracy by total population, women, and men, 1910–30.
Sources: U.S. Bureau of the Census, *Fifteenth Census*, 141; Naomi Robles.

Declining rates of illiteracy offer further evidence that the U.S. investment in education paid off. In 1910, 69 percent of the total population over ten was illiterate. The corresponding gendered percentages were 62 percent for men and 71 percent for women. By 1920, the percentage of Puerto Ricans above age ten who could not read dropped to 55 percent, and the gap between men and women decreased, if only slightly. Close to 51 percent of men were illiterate while 59 percent of women were.[82] By 1930, the average rate of illiteracy dropped to 44 percent, 46 percent for women and 37 percent for men.[83]

Yet despite U.S. efforts to make English the primary language, Puerto Ricans continued to speak Spanish.[84] In 1910, 96 percent of the population over the age of ten was unable to speak English. Ten years later, only 10 percent of Puerto Ricans could speak it.[85] In 1930, Spanish remained the principal means of communication for four-fifths of the archipelago's inhabitants, as it did in the 1940s.[86] Alejandrina Torre's story offers some insight as to why this was the case.

Alejandrina Torres grew up in the small town of San Lorenzo in the 1940s. Her mother, a widow, raised nine children and was active in the Socialist Party because she believed in workers' rights. Alejandrina remembers that her teachers taught the students a song in Spanish about Jorge Washington, one she learned so well she could sing it in 2018, some seventy years later. Some of the words to the song were, "I never told a lie because I want to imitate George Washington."[87] She, like most of her fellow students, did not learn English, mainly because outside of English class no one spoke it and she saw no need to learn it. She does, however, recall a song from her English class: "Pollito/chicken, gallina/hen, lapiz/pencil and pluma/pen; ventana/window and puerta/door, maestro/teacher and piso/floor." But, she added, "that's about the only English I got."[88]

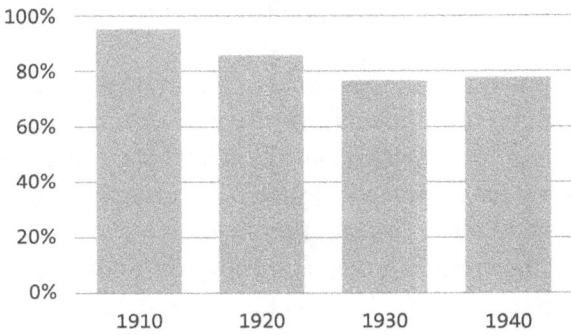

Percentage of Puerto Ricans speaking only or primarily Spanish, 1910–40. Sources: U.S. Bureau of the Census, *Fifteenth Census*, iv, 143; Naomi Robles.

Another plank of U.S. efforts to Americanize Puerto Ricans was the push to "morally reform" them, which meant encouraging Puerto Ricans to adopt U.S. ideas and practices regarding sexuality and relationships. The lower-class practice of cohabitating and reproducing outside the bonds of matrimony represented what U.S. policy makers considered immoral standards that had to be eliminated, as historian Eileen Suárez Findlay points out. The perception that lower class equaled people of color, an opinion shared by Puerto Rico's creole elite, only compounded colonial officials' certitude that moral uplift was required.[89] To remedy this, colonial officials worked to "reduce diverse popular sexual practices and morals to a unified standard of heterosexual marriage . . . thus instilling their Anglo-Saxon, bourgeois social and cultural ideals in the island's populace."[90]

Protestant missionaries also descended on the archipelago following the passage of the Foraker Act, which eliminated the "Catholic Church's privileged position" and opened the door to U.S. Protestants seeking to convert Puerto Ricans.[91] Working in tandem with U.S. colonial authorities, the missionaries established a variety of institutions, ranging from schools to orphanages to hospitals and, of course, churches, all of which would serve to Americanize the inhabitants, by "providing . . . needed services and encouraging Puerto Ricans' conversion to Protestantism."[92]

Programs to instill the colonizers' values and social mores typically enjoyed varied degrees of success. Puerto Ricans were neither passive victims of U.S. Americanization projects nor uniform in their response to U.S. plans. Their responses varied depending, in part, on whether their material assets, standing, and power improved or worsened following the economic and political changes introduced by the United States. Sugarcane workers who labored under inhumane conditions for little pay and no benefits were much less likely to be beguiled by promises of modernization, Americanization, and dreams of upward mobility than those Puerto Ricans who profited from their economic ties to U.S. sugar interests.[93]

Many Puerto Ricans adjusted as best they could to U.S. rule, seeking to adapt themselves to their changed reality in a manner that best accommodated their interests and goals. As historian Solsiree del Moral reminds us, Puerto Rican teachers were not empty vessels who blindly imbibed and implemented U.S. pedagogical methods and values. Instead, they held their own "class, gender, and race biases" and therefore "represented an obstacle for the Americanizing intentions of the US colonial state."[94] After U.S. authorities legalized divorce as part of their efforts to enhance marriage and link it to modernity by making its dissolution possible, scores of Puerto Rican women sued for divorce, thus breaking the bonds that had tied them to their husband.[95] High school students at a school established by Protestant missionaries learned to speak, read, and write in English and then used their skills to challenge the anti–Puerto Rican aspects of their education.[96]

Many Puerto Ricans clung to their cultural traditions, U.S. efforts notwithstanding. In 1907, colonial officials eliminated Three Kings Day, January 6, from school holidays, presumably because it represented a Spanish and Catholic custom, not an Anglo-Saxon and Protestant one. Many Puerto Ricans simply flouted the United States' attempt to do away with this important date.[97] Alejandrina Torres recalls that in the 1940s she, and everyone she knew, celebrated Christmas on December 24, Noche Buena (Christmas Eve), and on January 6, Tres Reyes (Three Kings Day), not on December 25.[98] People in rural areas did not sing U.S. Christmas carols. They composed *aguinaldos*, their own Christmas songs, which they performed on the *güiro* (a hollowed-out gourd with notches, played by rubbing a stick or tine across the ridges) and the *cuatro* (a ten-string guitar).[99]

Puerto Rican songs and dances—the bomba, plena, bolero, and jíbaro music—continued to fill the airwaves or were played and performed in homes and plazas.[100] Rafael Hernández, one of Puerto Rico's foremost musicians, composed "Lamento Boricano," in 1929. The haunting, initially upbeat song tells the story of a *jíbaro*, a poor farmer, who transports his products to the city, hoping to sell them and make some money. Unfortunately, all he finds is poverty, so he returns home, his goods unsold. On a broader level, the song presents a dismal picture of life in Puerto Rico after thirty years of U.S. rule. The lyrics convey the dire poverty many Puerto Ricans experienced in the late 1920s and the disappearance of the rural population's lifestyle and livelihood due to U.S. backed monopolization of the land and industrialization. The song was a hit in Puerto Rico and throughout Latin America, where it was recorded by singers as diverse as Puerto Rican Marc Anthony, Mexican Pedro Infante, and Chilean Victor Jara.[101] Its popularity seared into many Latin Americans' minds the image of impoverished Puerto Rican peasants, the unwilling victims of U.S. economic policies.

Puerto Ricans' response to U.S. rule was far from uniform. Some, particularly members of the landed creole elite, embraced it, in part because they believed it was in their economic and political interest to do so. They also believed, as sociologist Julian Go argues, that accepting U.S. "tutelage," at least nominally, was their surest path to autonomy.[102] Other Puerto Ricans simply refused or failed to adopt U.S. ways of doing things because they either preferred their own practices or found U.S. customs confusing or unappealing. Still others rejected the unwelcome imposition of a foreign power's arrogant and insulting norms. Members of the Nationalist Party chose to directly confront U.S. colonialism and dedicated their lives to ending it, as this book will recount.

## COLONIAL RACIALIZATION OF PUERTO RICANS

As U.S. attitudes and policies toward Puerto Rico made clear, U.S. officials, politicians, and much of the general public considered Puerto Ricans inferior, members of a lower race, feeble children who needed the guiding hand of the wise but stern United States to shepherd them forward to become second-class citizens. This path, the colonizers believed, offered Puerto Ricans entry to the civilized world, which the United States defined, embodied, and controlled. Since every action and almost every utterance colonial authorities made echoed and reinforced this perspective, it is inconceivable that Puerto Ricans were unaware of how their new rulers and employers considered them. Further, colonial attitudes were more than just ideas: they directly and most often negatively affected Puerto Ricans' position in the new colonial society the United States constructed and dominated. They greatly influenced the jobs Puerto Ricans held or were fired from, the low pay they received, the typically bad conditions they worked in, and the political rights and positions extended to or withheld from them. They explain why Puerto Ricans had no say in who their governor was and why they could not vote for the congressmen, senators, or presidents that ruled them. They justified the teaching of English and a U.S.-centric view of the world and Puerto Rico's place in it, which was unquestionably below that of the United States.

The United States was not the first country to introduce racial classifications to Puerto Rico. Spaniards had operated with a racial hierarchy that placed Spaniards born in Spain (peninsulares) at the top, followed by Spaniards born in Puerto Rico (criollos) directly below them, followed by people of mixed European and Indigenous ancestry (mestizos), then those of mixed European and African ancestry (mulattos), with those primarily of African descent at the bottom. However, as historian Jesse Hoffnung-Garskof's examination of baptismal records in 1800s Puerto Rico shows, although the classification system suggests a formidably rigid construction of race, colonial society allowed for some degree of fluidity. Phenotypical factors alone did not determine an individual's social classification; nonphenotypical factors also played a role. For those of Afro descent, the "degree of blackness" affected one's standing, but so did being free or enslaved, married or unwed, "legitimate" or "illegitimate."[103] Indeed, as Suárez Findlay points out, "money, 'good manners,' a 'respectable' lifestyle, and stylish dress could 'whiten' a person."[104]

The United States, however, operated with a binary notion of race that defined anyone with even a drop of African blood as Black and therefore inferior.[105] But this even more fixed racial classification system also allowed for varying amounts of flexibility, depending on time and place.[106] In any case, according to U.S. officials in Puerto Rico and the United States, most Puerto Ricans exhibited some type of "race mixture" and were, therefore, not white. How did Puerto Ricans respond to these assumptions about themselves and what they meant for their social, political, and economic standing?

Although more work needs to be done to uncover the variety of ways Puerto Ricans understood what it meant to be Puerto Rican under their new rulers, one piece of evidence is telling. Between 1910 and 1930, the number of Puerto Ricans listed as white increased from 65.5 to 74.3 percent.[107] Sociologists Mara Loveman and Jerónimo Muñiz conclude, "Puerto Rico whitened rapidly in the second decade of the twentieth century primarily through a shift in the social definition of whiteness itself."[108] In other words, this self-defined change in race reflected people's attempts to reposition themselves; there was not a significant biological transformation of the population. Loveman and Muñiz reason that the primary factor that caused this shift was the "perceived and actual costs of being seen by Americans as nonwhite."[109]

Mara Loveman adds another piece to this racial puzzle by dissecting elite attitudes toward race, Americanization, and modernization. She notes that most of the enumerators "might be likened to the local elites" who backed and saw themselves as participants in and beneficiaries of "America's campaign to bring 'progress' to the island." Because they were aware of U.S. attitudes toward race, they sought to whiten the Puerto Rican population since "they recognized the potential collective and individual disadvantages of being seen by the Americans as non-white." In short, they classified nonwhite Puerto Ricans as white in the census as a defensive measure against "the intensification of Puerto Rican's subordinated incorporation into the United States."[110]

Jorge Duany also examined censuses to discover how Puerto Ricans understood race. He developed a table listing "Major Folk Racial Terms Used in

Puerto Rico," which presents nineteen terms Puerto Ricans used to categorize themselves and another table on the census categories available to Puerto Ricans from 1899 to 2000. Duany offers two important insights into why Puerto Ricans increasingly self-identified or were identified as white. First, both the Puerto Rican enumerators and the adult population were used to thinking of themselves and others in terms of a range of possibilities, as he shows. But the census offered them only these choices: White, Mulatto or Mestizo, and Black. As a result, many mixed-race people, who would have been classified as Black in the United States, were either classified or classified themselves as white. And second, this whitening of the population is the product of racial prejudice, since "many people prefer to identify as white to avoid racial stigmatization."[111] Franz Fanon, the renowned psychiatrist from Martinique, wrote about the psychological and emotional toll that French colonialism took on Algerians. He argued that "internalized colonialism" teaches the colonized to adopt the image the colonizer has created of them and accept their inferiority to the colonizer, an attitude that justifies both their own oppression and colonialism.[112] Did the growing numbers of Puerto Ricans who identified themselves as white in the census confirm his diagnosis of the impact colonialism had on the colonized? Or was theirs a pragmatic response to the realities of U.S. colonialism? Most likely, it was some combination of both.

Using Puerto Ricans' answers to the census as a speculative synecdoche for their attitudes to colonialism, we see that the elites used the survey to advance their interests and affirm their status. They accurately comprehended the importance U.S. rulers placed on whiteness and skewed the census to make Puerto Ricans appear whiter. A whiter population, they reasoned, would enhance Puerto Rico's status vis-à-vis the United States and ensure their privileged position in the colonial structure that Washington erected. Other Puerto Ricans adapted, at least formally, to this new racial standard and reality by declaring themselves white on the census, despite their mixed-race ancestry. However, they, like so many Puerto Ricans, continued to speak Spanish and maintain many of their cultural traditions, even as they attempted to adapt to and survive, even thrive, in the new reality. Some of the founders of the Nationalist Party in 1922 likely declared themselves or were listed as white on the census. However, the PRNP embraced a very different idea of raza, one that lined up with Hispanic American anti-imperialist ideological currents. Far from accommodating themselves to U.S. colonialism or internalizing a negative image of themselves, they fought to establish an independent nation that would both affirm and assert Puerto Rican dignity and strength, regardless of skin color and one's racial or ethnic background, as we see in the next chapter.

# 3 BECOMING THE NATIONALIST PARTY

In her biography, Nationalist Blanca Canales portrays herself as a woman who supported independence since childhood.[1] She begins by telling the reader, "Since I was a little girl, pro-independence feelings coursed through my veins." She attributes these sentiments to her family. "My family . . . all belonged to the Union Party, whose fifth programmatic point called for independence. We read the newspapers and magazines papa received and the adults talked about these ideas at the dinner table."[2] She concludes the story of her childhood by foreshadowing the behavior that would mark her as a future Nationalist leader: "One of my favorite things to do from the time I was nine to eleven was to stand on a chair on the balcony behind our house and make patriotic speeches to the girls of the family and to the kids in the neighborhood. I was imitating what I had listened to in meetings."[3]

From 1926 to 1930, Canales pursued her bachelor of arts degree at the University of Puerto Rico, Río Piedras. She recalled that she repeatedly disagreed with one teacher who presented the Monroe Doctrine, Manifest Destiny, and the United States' Caribbean policy as good. She listened to the speeches of several political leaders, but it was Pedro Albizu Campos who won her over. In 1931, she joined the Nationalist Party, and in 1932, she and a few others founded a branch of the party in Jayuya, her hometown. That same year she began to work closely with the party's national leadership. "From that time on I took on missions and carried out a type of underground work. I never officially figured in the party assemblies or meetings, although I attended all of them."[4] Canales was arrested after the uprising in 1950 and convicted of various charges, including murder, burning a post office, and "conspiring to overthrow the island's government by force and violence."[5] She spent seventeen long years in prison, first in Alderson, West Virginia, and then in Vega Alta, Puerto Rico. Governor Roberto Sánchez Vilella pardoned her in 1967.[6]

Through Canales's life story we learn how one woman became–and remained—a Nationalist. But how did the Nationalist Party become the Nationalist Party? The party's identity and politics evolved during the first ten years of its existence, the period this chapter examines. I explore these differences by contrasting the thoughts and practices of the first Nationalist Party president, José Coll y Cuchí, with those of Pedro Albizu Campos, party president from 1930 until his death in 1965. The initial cohort of men who led the party were dissatisfied with the Union Party's acquiescence to U.S. policies. They sought to create an alternative to the existing Puerto Rican political parties that would challenge U.S. colonialism. Yet despite their goals, many of the middle- and upper-class men who led the party pretty much played by the established rules of the colonial politics game. They saw themselves and expected to be treated as gentlemen. They held conventional ideas about gender, which meant that they considered politics to be something men did. As educated, well-off men of European descent, they considered themselves eminently and exclusively qualified to run both the party and the future independent republic. They overlooked the privileges their position and circumstances afforded them, particularly in relation to Puerto Ricans of Afro descent and the working class, whose situation and potential contributions they ignored.

The party's politics changed after Pedro Albizu Campos was elected president in 1930. Under his leadership, the Nationalists engaged in an energetic effort to organize women, a policy that remained constant in the party from then on. Far from believing that men of European descent were the natural leaders of the party, Albizu, who was of African and Basque descent, advanced a different understanding of race, one that both critiqued U.S. policies of white supremacy and insisted that Latin Americans were all one race, la raza. The Nationalist Party employed this different interpretation of race, which is also problematic, as I discuss below, as part of its efforts to distinguish and distance Puerto Ricans from the United States and deepen their identification and sense of oneness with Latin America.

They disagreed on one other issue: how to end U.S. rule. The early leaders believed that independence would be achieved through an amicable agreement between themselves and U.S. officials. They assumed that these officials would recognize them as their peers, therefore qualified to govern free of U.S. tutelage or control. The Nationalist Party, with Albizu at the helm, was under no such illusions. It defined the relationship between Washington and Puerto Rico as antagonistic and identified the United States as an opponent and oppressor. The Nationalists' efforts to incorporate all Puerto Ricans in the anticolonial movement, regardless of race or gender, coincided with their conception that theirs was an us-versus-them struggle. Despite these significant differences, the Nationalist Party consistently agreed that Puerto Rico was part of Latin America. As a result, it unfailingly pursued connections with the archipelago's sister republics throughout the hemisphere.

## PUERTO RICAN POLITICS FOLLOWING THE U.S. INVASION

Puerto Rican political parties formed, splintered, merged, allied, and dissolved in the first decades of U.S. rule (see table 3.1). The fluidity of Puerto Rican parties can be largely explained by their reactivity and lack of real power since all weighty decisions concerning the archipelago were made in Washington, not San Juan. As a result, the parties tailored and adapted their programs and positions in response to evolving U.S. policies.[7] Educated, professional, and well-off men led most Puerto Rican parties. Women, peasants, the lower middle class, and the incipient working class—the majority of the Puerto Rican population—did not. All men had the right to vote since passage of the Jones Act in 1917; no women did. Literate Puerto Rican women obtained voting rights in 1929, and all women did in 1935.[8]

The Republican Party formed in 1899. It supported statehood for economic and ideological reasons. Access to the U.S. market benefitted the sugar-producing landowners who led the party. Party leaders also aspired to replicate the democratic ideals and practices they associated with the United States in Puerto Rico.[9] The party subsequently affiliated with the Republican Party in the United States.[10] José Celso Barbosa, a Black man and U.S.-trained doctor, led the party from its founding until 1921.[11] Political scientist Pedro Cabán characterizes the party as "loyal apologists for U.S. rule" and notes that it attracted members who "stood to gain from permanent annexation."[12] As part of its push for annexation, the party advocated that English be taught in the schools and become the official language.[13] Party membership extended beyond the elite classes. Afro Puerto Ricans joined the party, which they called the "party of the men of color" and "the party of Lincoln," because they viewed the United States as a democratic country that had defeated slavery and the Republican Party as the party of emancipation.[14]

The Socialist Party represented very different interests than the Republican Party, but it, too, advocated statehood for Puerto Rico. Founded in 1915 to organize the working class, it was a political extension of the Federación Libre de Trabajadores (Free Workers Federation, FLT).[15] The FLT originated in 1899 as a politically independent workers' organization. In 1901, it affiliated with the American Federation of Labor, then under the leadership of U.S. unionist Samuel Gompers.[16] Like the Socialist Party, it, too, rejected independence and supported annexation.[17] Santiago Iglesias Pantín, who headed the FLT, enthusiastically backed Puerto Rico's full incorporation into the United States because he believed that U.S. rule offered workers the right to organize and unionize that Spanish law had denied them.[18] He also had a personal reason for associating the United States with freedom: Washington's defeat of Spain in 1898 resulted in his release from El Morro, the Spanish citadel in San Juan

**Political parties in Puerto Rico, 1899–1920s**

| Party/year founded | Composition of leadership | Base | Position on status |
|---|---|---|---|
| Partido Republicano (Republican Party)/ 1899 | Educated, elite men of European and, in one case, Afro descent | Sugar and tobacco interests, professionals, Afro Puerto Ricans | Statehood |
| Partido Unión (Union Party)/1904[1] | Educated, elite men of European descent | Sugar and tobacco interests, professionals, Afro Puerto Ricans | Self-government: independence, autonomy, statehood |
| Partido Socialista (Socialist Party)/1915 | Skilled workers, party functionaries, mainly men, some women; multiethnic | Tobacco and sugarcane workers, the FLT | Prostatehood, prolabor[2] |
| Partido Nacionalista (Nationalist Party)/1922 | Educated, elite men of European descent | Urban professionals, laborers, small landowners, middle and lower middle class | Independence |

Notes:
1. The various coalitions that formed between parties with substantially different programs demonstrate the ideological fragility, opportunism, and general instability of Puerto Rican politics under U.S. rule. In 1925, the Partido Unión joined with a section of the Partido Republicano to form the Alianza. In 1929, part of the Alianza split off to form the Partido Liberal, while another part joined with the Partido Republicano and the Partido Socialista to form the Coalición. Ayala and Bernabe, *Puerto Rico in the American Century*, 143.
2. Ayala and Bernabe, *Puerto Rico in the American Century*, 65.

where he had been jailed for his labor organizing efforts.[19] Iglesias was so enamored of U.S.-style democracy that he named his daughters "América, Justicia, Libertad, and Igualdad." U.S. troops called him "Mr. Liberty."[20]

During the first two decades of their existence, both the Socialist Party and the FLT organized to improve workers' conditions and lives. They supported unionization, fought for higher wages, and supported equal rights for male and female workers. For example, when FLT-associated workers in the southern coastal region of Puerto Rico went on strike in 1905, they called for an equal minimum salary for both men and women and the abolition of child labor.[21] Their organizing paid off. Workers' militancy increased, and they carried out at least 335 strikes between 1915 and 1920.[22] Although neither organization sought to end U.S. colonialism despite its exploitation of Puerto Rican workers, historian Jorell Meléndez-Badillo argues that they challenged the economic and political power of the Puerto Rican bourgeoisie. They established workshops and published newspapers to educate and empower workers, promote their voices, amplify their leadership, and improve their organizational skills, reach, and effectiveness.[23]

In contrast to other political parties, women were very active in the FLT and Socialist Party in the 1910s and 1920s. They spoke at rallies, participated in strikes, and led the FLT's Women's Organization Committee.[24] Despite the large number of women in the Socialist Party, very few occupied leadership positions.[25] They did not fare much better within the FLT, even though women like Luisa Capetillo and Juana Colón were prominent working-class activists and spokespersons.[26] Not content with their subordinate position, women "used party and labor congresses to challenge Socialist leadership and demand greater participation."[27] Although the male leadership was unwilling to cede power to women within the organization, the Socialist Party was the first Puerto Rican party to call for women's suffrage. It did so in response to women's demands and because the leaders believed that enfranchised poor and working-class women would vote for the party.[28]

From its founding in 1904 until 1922, the Partido Unión (Union Party) advocated self-government, which different tendencies thought could be achieved through statehood, autonomy, or independence.[29] The Unionist leadership was a potpourri of owners of coffee haciendas and sugar estates and "the urban-elite coterie of professional-managerial personnel and literati."[30] Due to their elevated position in Puerto Rico, Unionist leaders mistakenly assumed that the United States would turn to them to run the country. Washington's failure to do so alienated a sector of the party and contributed to their dissatisfaction with U.S. rule. The base, much of which had a clientelist relationship with the leadership, consisted of "impoverished small tobacco farmers, rural squatters, and sharecroppers linked to the haciendas."[31]

In February 1922, the Partido Unión held its national assembly and eliminated independence from the party platform.[32] It did so largely in response to the colonial government's announcement in 1921 that it had created a list of government employees who held "radical ideas" and were considered "enemies of the government."[33] The heads of the departments where they worked were directed to "ask them to resign at the earliest opportunity."[34] U.S.-appointed governor E. Mont Reily's declaration that no member of the party who supported independence could hold a government position convinced some Unionists employed in the colonial bureaucracy that they would lose their jobs.[35] The leadership's decision to revise the party's platform to safeguard the employment of its members angered the pro-independence wing of the Unionists. This conflict led directly to the creation of the Nationalist Party, whose central mission was to end U.S. colonial rule and "revindicat[e] Puerto Rican dignity."[36]

## THE FOUNDATION OF THE NATIONALIST PARTY

The pro-independence wing of the Union Party had constituted itself as the Nationalist Association of Puerto Rico in 1919. Leaders of this tendency traveled throughout Puerto Rico to discuss the formation of a party committed to independence with other Unionists and potential members. Their visits bore fruit, and juntas municipales, local governing boards of the soon-to-be Nationalist Party, were set up in at least twenty-three towns and cities between late August and the end of September 1922.[37] The organizing campaign culminated in September 1922. Participants from across Puerto Rico attended a Constituent Assembly in Río Piedras, where they officially formed the Partido Nacionalista Puertorriqueño.[38]

All twenty-five men who initially comprised the Nationalist Party's Supreme Council were Catholic, of European descent, educated, and urban. Membership in the party, however, included Puerto Ricans from across the racial spectrum (fig. 3.1). Party leaders had professional or honorific titles before their names that reveal their middle- or upper-middle-class background. Three were doctors, three were professors, seven were referred to as Don, and six were Licenciados, which means they had either a B.A. or a B.S. degree.[39] Marisa Rosado characterizes the party's early leadership as one that "lacked a socio-economic program, w[as] composed of a professional elite, . . . and w[as] completely disconnected from the social and economic problems facing the country."[40] Unlike the Socialist Party, the Nationalists had no links to the peasantry or the working class in the 1920s. Nor did they represent the tobacco or sugar producers, as the Union and Republican parties respectively did. The party's initial leaders were, however, earnestly dedicated to preserving Puerto Rican culture and establishing political sovereignty, causes to which many of them devoted their life. Brief sketches of three of the founders give us a sense of these men's backgrounds and political trajectories.

One of the founders, Antonio Ayuso, a lifelong Nationalist, purchased the publication El Imparcial in 1933. Under his direction, it became the second largest newspaper in the archipelago from the 1930s through the 1950s.[41] During those years, El Imparcial published news stories favorable to the Nationalist Party and other pro-independence forces.[42] Another leader, Antonio Vélez Alvarado, designed the Puerto Rican flag in 1891 in his New York City printshop.[43] Vélez Alvarado worked closely with other Cuban and Puerto Rican opponents of Spanish rule living in New York.[44] His shop printed Patria, the weekly publication

FIGURE 3.1. A Nationalist Party assembly in the Broadway Theater in Ponce, 1922. Source: Colección Antonio Mirabal (CP2), Archivo General de Puerto Rico.

that Cuban revolutionary and pro-independence fighter José Martí edited. One day, Vélez Alvarado was sitting at his desk when he looked up and saw the Cuban flag. He decided to design the Puerto Rican flag using the Cuban one as his model. In his words, "I thought if Cubans and Puerto Ricans were going to fight together like brothers, what could be more appropriate than to have sister flags, with only a slight inversion in the colors?"[45] That explains why the Puerto Rican flag is a stylistic replica of the Cuban one. The only differences are that the Cuban triangle is red and the Puerto Rican one is blue and the Cuban stripes are blue while the Puerto Rican ones are red.

Ramón Mayoral Barnés, also a founder of the Nationalist Party, was an attorney in Ponce. Mayoral was editor of El Nacionalista de Ponce, which was little more than a printed sheet of paper mailed to interested local parties in the early 1920s but later became El Nacionalista de Puerto Rico and was distributed throughout the archipelago and the Caribbean.[46] He mentored Albizu Campos, who returned to Ponce in 1921, having obtained his law degree from Harvard University. Mayoral's pro-independence politics influenced Albizu Campos, who quit the Union Party in 1924 to join the Nationalist Party.[47]

Moderation, not radicalism, defined the PNPR in its early years, in marked contrast to the party's politics after 1930, when Albizu Campos became president. Under José Coll y Cuchí's leadership (1922–25), the party promoted cultural identity, intellectual discussions, and a cordial relationship with the United States.[48] In these early years, the party lacked organizational strength, a coherent political message or economic program, and a popular base, which could be why it did not participate in the elections of either 1924 or 1928. Many self-identified Nationalists remained in the Union Party, and it was only in Caguas, the party's stronghold, Ponce, Santurce, and Yabucoa that people even registered themselves as Nationalists.[49]

## COLL Y CUCHÍ VERSUS REILY

Like the PRNP founders profiled above, José Coll y Cuchí, the party's first president, was a member of Puerto Rico's urban, professional elite. He was a lawyer and an official of the Ateneo Puertorriqueño, a prestigious San Juan cultural institution founded in 1876 to promote "Science, Letters, and the Fine Arts."[50] Coll y Cuchí experienced Governor Reily's threat to fire any government employee who refused to renounce independence personally and directly. Coll y Cuchí had been named president of the Commission of Workers' Compensation, a lucrative and important position within the colonial hierarchy. On August 10, 1921, he received a letter from Governor Reily ordering him to resign within twenty-four hours and informing him that should he not do so, he would be forcibly removed from his office. Coll y Cuchí's public airing of his treatment made manifest how humiliated and angry Reily's dictate made him feel.[51] In one interview, Coll y Cuchí established his professional credentials as "a lawyer, journalist, and agriculturist." He then simultaneously asserted his manliness, responsibility to his family as breadwinner and provider, and patriotic dedication to Puerto Rico.[52] He defined himself as a man "who has sufficient energy to give life to my beloved home where I, along with my dear wife, am raising nine children for the Motherland."[53] When Coll y Cuchí responded to Reily the next day, August 11, 1921, he sent a copy of the letter to Puerto Rican newspapers to ensure a broader audience. In it he demanded to know why he was being fired and indignantly pointed out, once again asserting his professional acumen, that the previous governor had named him president of the commission, "which implies his recognition of my ability . . . to carry out this important responsibility."[54]

Coll y Cuchí's attempt to retain his position as a functionary of the colonial state and establish his worthiness as a colonial bureaucrat by referring to the previous governor's decision to name him to his position reflects a degree of ambivalence vis-à-vis the United States that characterized the Nationalist Party during the 1920s. The middle-class men who led the party during that decade called for independence but maintained a fundamentally friendly attitude toward Washington that, perhaps, attests to their unwillingness to anger and thereby alienate the United States. They were, after all, respectable Puerto Rican men who conducted their political affairs like gentlemen and expected to be treated as such, even by the colonial forces that occupied their homeland. They also, it appears, preserved sufficient faith in the promises of U.S. democracy to expect that U.S. officials would respond favorably to their message.

The correspondence between Reily and Coll y Cuchí hints at how personal interactions and the emotions they engender can influence political choices and the larger context in which they transpire. It suggests that Coll y Cuchí had erroneously anticipated that Reily would recognize him as the product of a civilization equivalent to his own and, therefore, his equal. Instead, the U.S. governor's patronizing treatment of Coll y Cuchí manifested his assumption of the Puerto Rican's inferiority and mirrored the U.S. colonial relationship with Puerto Ricans more generally. Equally, Coll y Cuchí's response to Reily's overt attack on his job and position and explicit undermining of his masculinity may well have contributed to the former's decision to found the Nationalist Party. Coll y Cuchí's reaction to the governor's casual insults and the asymmetrical power relationship between them raises the possibility that party founders considered independence as the necessary solution to the mistreatment and lack of respect they and their homeland suffered at the hands of U.S. officials.

However, instead of issuing anything approximating a declaration of war against the United States, at the Nationalist Assembly in September 1922, the party agreed to "officially communicate" the founding of the party to President Warren G. Harding, the U.S. Congress, and none other than the aforementioned Reily. The message to Harding informed him of the party's establishment and expressed hope he would "support our legitimate aspirations to obtain [our] full rights [as] Puerto Ricans." They asked Congress to "favorably consider the Puerto Rican people's aspirations [to] sovereignty."[55] The letter to Reily, dated September 20, was longer and included a copy of the party's Declaration of Principles and the wish that the "U.S. government and its representatives in Puerto Rico consider our respective peoples as brothers, and mutually respect the rights of each."[56] As was true with Coll y Cuchí vis-à-vis Reily, Nationalist Party leaders naively expected that their colonial rulers would consider them their peers and treat them in a manner befitting civilized gentlemen's codes of behavior.

In his reply on September 27, 1922, Reily rephrased and twisted Coll y Cuchí's remarks on brotherly relations between the territory and the United

States to reflect Reily's belief that Puerto Ricans didn't know how to govern themselves. Like previous and subsequent U.S. governors, he considered Puerto Ricans unruly children in need of U.S. guidance. Instead of wasting time bickering among themselves, Reily advised, Puerto Ricans should work together with the United States. As he wrote, "I fully agree that every citizen in each of the island's [political] parties should feel like . . . brothers."[57] He then admonished the newly elected president of the Nationalist Party that he, Reily, "will acclaim with jubilation the day that all Puerto Ricans unite across the abyss of their disagreements and forget the [interparty] struggle and [instead] defend all that promotes greater unity between Puerto Rico and America."[58]

Puerto Rican newspapers published the exchange between Reily and Coll y Cuchí. Reily's letters made all too tangible the paternalistic attitudes U.S. officials adopted toward Puerto Ricans, as did the military reports and the cartoon discussed in chapter 2. They likely concretized for Puerto Rican men in particular U.S. officials' power and superior status and attitude and their corresponding impotence and lower standing, a position they might well have found emasculating and degrading. Coll y Cuchí clearly did. In his correspondence with Reily, he stoutly defended his honor, capabilities, and virility in the workplace and the home, indications that he perceived Reily's firing and arrogant treatment of him an insult to his image, status, and manliness. It is certainly possible that Reily's belittling attitudes toward Coll y Cuchí and crude enforcement of power relations contributed to Coll y Cuchí's desire to free himself from U.S. rule, just as other U.S. officials' similar treatment of other Puerto Rican men likely stimulated theirs.[59] Indeed, as Ann Laura Stoler points out, "The demasculinization of colonized men and the hypermasculinity of European males are understood as key elements in the assertion of white supremacy."[60] Thus, if we substitute U.S. for European males, it is possible that Coll y Cuchí interpreted Reily's disparaging attitude toward him as undermining both his masculinity and his belief in his own racial superiority vis-à-vis other Puerto Ricans.

Reily was wildly unpopular across the archipelago. Puerto Rican opposition to Reily also extended to the "Porto Rican colony of Greater New York," which held a meeting to determine how to respond to his despotic rule. Reily's refusal "to appoint members of the Independence [Union] Party to office" and his advocacy of "the elimination of Spanish in favor of English in the curriculum of the public schools" antagonized them.[61] Speaking only in Spanish, members of the gathering called on President Harding to remove Reily from his position as governor of Puerto Rico.[62] Recognizing his lack of support, Reily resigned his post in February 1923.[63]

## NATIONALISM AND RACE

Just as individual experiences can influence political choices, as the exchanges between Coll y Cuchí and Reily illustrate, so, too, can ideas about race reflect an individual's broader set of political beliefs. Coll y Cuchí's notions about race influenced his definition of who was Puerto Rican and his view on relations with the United States. His attitudes diverged sharply from those of future party president Albizu Campos, as we shall see. Their differences illustrate how the Nationalist Party's thinking on race evolved from the 1920s to the 1930s.

Coll y Cuchí's conception of raza, which it is fair to assume other party leaders shared since they elected him president, reflected his understanding of what it meant to be Puerto Rican. According to him, "The people of Puerto Rico have, in their immense majority, the same origins." However, "the *raza de color* [colored race], which has a different origin, lives in perfect harmony and [enjoys] fraternal relations with whites."[64] In other words, Puerto Ricans were of European descent; those of the raza de color were Others. Coll y Cuchí circumscribed his definition of who was and who was not Puerto Rican to include those whose ancestors were European, as were his and those of his peers, while excluding those of "a different origin," read African or mixed race. By adopting a binary definition of race in Puerto Rico, Coll y Cuchí denied the diversity of the Puerto Rican population, positioned the white race as the authentic and superior race, and silenced and marginalized Puerto Ricans of African descent.[65] His perception that the raza de color "lives in perfect harmony and [enjoys] fraternal relations with whites," a statement that likely causes reactions of disbelief or anger in many modern readers, betrays his blindness to the relations of power, exploitation, and oppression that existed between many Puerto Ricans of European descent and those of Afro descent. It further ignores the very real privileges men of his class enjoyed, typically as a result of the labor of those of the raza de color. And it justifies the raza de color's exclusion from positions of political power or even participation in politics.[66] Coll y Cuchí's attitudes were neither unique nor limited to the Nationalist Party; both the colonialized elite and the colonizers shared them. As Ileana Rodríguez-Silva points out, "For the white dominant class specifically, racial impurity [i.e., nonwhite] was an impediment for the full and conscious exercise of citizenship rights and responsibilities. As a result, colonialisms and nationalist struggles reproduced the marginalization of blackness."[67]

Coll y Cuchí's class- and race-based vision of Puerto Rico aligns with his notion of why "the Island" deserved to be an independent nation. When the United States invaded Puerto Rico in 1898, Puerto Ricans were, he asserts, "a people with a language, history, culture, and customs of the highest level of any civilized people of the world."[68] Therefore, they have the right—and the capacity—to govern their nation. On one hand, his defense of Puerto Ricans' dignity and ability to rule themselves is understandable in light of U.S. colonial officials' continual assumptions, statements, and policies that infantilized Puerto Ricans and defined them as inferior and incapable of ruling themselves.[69] On the other, it mirrors his race- and class-inflected idea of who is Puerto Rican, since by civilized he meant those of European descent, not those of Afro or mixed-race descent. Further, his frequent references to Puerto Ricans' high level of civilization indicate that he adopted European and U.S. standards as to what civilization meant and who was and who was not worthy of self-government. His race- and class-based definition of civilization, and his assumption that he and the other male leaders of the Nationalist Party embodied it, also explain why he, and other early Nationalist Party leaders, believed that it was possible to achieve an aimable settlement with the "civilized" men who ran the U.S. government that would result in Puerto Rican independence.

Pedro Albizu Campos, who was vice president of the Nationalist Party in the 1920s and president in 1930, occupied a very different position in Puerto Rican society than did the elite men who founded the party. He was the mixed-race son of a father of Basque descent and a poor woman whose mother had been a slave. His father acknowledged his paternity only after his wife died and Albizu was twenty-three and studying at Harvard.[70] Albizu's experiences as a poor, lower-class mulatto distinguished not only his lived reality from that of other party leaders but his conception of race and his fixed determination to end U.S. colonial rule.

Albizu, who obtained both his BA and law degree from Harvard University, ascended to the vice presidency as a result of his dedication to the party and to independence and his brilliance as a thinker, orator, and writer. It is certainly possible that both his race and his radical politics caused a certain amount of malaise among the leadership. When José Vasconcelos, the former Mexican minister of education (1920–24), visited Puerto Rico in 1926, he met with members of the Nationalist Party. Vasconcelos found one Nationalist's contemptuous remark about Albizu so disturbing that he recorded it in his recollections of this trip. This unidentified Nationalist said, referring dismissively to Albizu, "But, look, he's a mulatto." This overtly racist comment prompted Vasconcelos to observe, "As if being a mulatto were not the most illustrious identification of citizenship in the Americas! Even Bolívar was a mulatto!"[71] Juan Antonio Corretjer, who was secretary general of the Nationalist Party in the late 1930s and early 1940s, confirmed the Nationalist Party leadership's early discomfort with Albizu. He wrote that one reason they chose Albizu to embark on a tour of Latin America in the late 1920s was it allowed them to "remove an unwanted Black element from the top leadership" by sending him abroad.[72]

In any case, Albizu simultaneously opposed white supremacy and, like José Martí in *Nuestra América* and the adherents of Hispanidad, understood the peoples of the Americas to be one. Albizu rejected the idea of race as a biological reality, while at the same time he opposed the racist ideas and practices he observed and experienced while in the United States.[73] For Albizu, raza had nothing to do with genetics or physiognomy or, as he put it, "with biology, nor with a dark complexion, kinky hair or slanted eyes."[74] Instead, it designated the peoples of the Américas who shared a common religion (Catholicism), language (Spanish, but the Nationalists were flexible on this point, since they included Brazilians and Haitians in their conception of raza), and history of European colonialism.[75] As Albizu saw it, the peoples of Iberoamérica (the former Spanish and Portuguese colonies in the Americas) "are distinguished by our culture, our courage, our nobility [*hidalguía*], our Catholic sense of civilization."[76] Albizu's exaltation of Catholicism stemmed from his own religiosity and from his rejection of Protestantism, which he equated with Washington's efforts to insinuate U.S. culture and ideology in order to undermine Catholicism and Americanize Puerto Rico. At the same time, Albizu's conflation of Latin Americans with Catholicism privileged Spanish heritage and ignored African and Indigenous spiritualities. However, Albizu's discussion of raza at a Nationalist Party event to commemorate Día de la Raza (Day of the Race) in 1933 confirms his nonracial interpretation of the word.

In 1917, Argentine president Hipólito Yrigoyen instituted October 12 as Día de la Raza (Day of the Race) to commemorate Christopher Columbus's "discovery" of the Americas, which he considered "the most transcendental event that humanity has realized" because "all the subsequent renovations derive from this astonishing event."[77] Yrigoyen apparently overlooked or denied that this "transcendental event" ushered in the enslavement and/or genocide of millions of Indigenous peoples and Africans. Nonetheless, the Nationalist Party embraced Día de la Raza and used its commemoration of it in 1933 to define race.[78] In his speech Albizu noted that "many laughed and said, 'Día de la Raza?'" They mockingly asked, "Whose day is it? Blacks? The Indigenous? Italians . . . the Portuguese, the French . . . the Spanish . . . the Yankees?" presumably in an attempt to disparage the lack of racial distinction among Latin Americans the title of the day implied.[79] By race, Albizu explained, he meant "la raza iberoamericana [the Iberoamerican race]."[80] He then clarified that this raza iberoamericana included Africans, who were part of his own heritage. "African blood. Yes . . . I also carry this [blood] in my veins, with supreme pride and human dignity."[81]

Coll y Cuchí's definition of race and what it meant to be Puerto Rican was not Albizu's. Coll y Cuchí considered Puerto Ricans to be of European descent and exemplars of civilization, thus worthy and capable of leading an independent nation. Albizu Campos's more capacious definition of Puerto Rican, which from the 1930s onward represented the party's understanding, included all those who inhabited the archipelago. However, he emphasized Spanish heritage as a force that united both Puerto Ricans and Latin Americans while failing to consider the contributions made by Indigenous and Afro-descent populations.[82] Despite their various interpretations of it, Nationalists consistently employed race to distinguish Puerto Rico from the United States and to assert why the archipelago should be an independent nation.

### NATIONALISM, WOMEN, AND GENDER

Distinct opinions on race was not the only difference between Coll y Cuchí and Albizu Campos and the Nationalist Party in the 1920s and 1930s. So, too, were ideas about women's involvement in the party. Men dominated the Nationalist Party in the 1920s. They were the public face, spokesmen, and most of the party's members (fig. 3.1). True, women attended party events and participated, albeit minimally, in public programs, as the two following examples illustrate. On July 15 and 16, 1922, the Nationalist Party sponsored a program to commemorate the death of José de Diego, whom it considered a national hero.[83] The party invited the public to attend and encouraged local chapters to send as many people as possible.[84] The elaborate program included music, poetry, and speeches on various issues, all delivered by men. One woman, Carmen María Gusti, appeared on the platform, dressed in the Puerto Rican flag, symbolically conflating the nation with women.[85] She recited the poem "Hymn to the Flag," written by a man.[86] The commemoration closed on the sixteenth with a procession to de Diego's tomb, led by "hundreds of young people of both sexes" carrying "the beautiful flag with one star."[87] In short, women had a role to play in the party, but it was a silent and decorative one, not a deliberative and intellectual one.

The second example occurred in Comerio, a town nestled in the central mountains south of San Juan. During the fall of 1923, Nationalist leaders traveled around the island to meet with members, consolidate local juntas, and attract new members. Sometime in early November, party leaders traveled to Comerio. They planned to hold a rally in the central plaza from two to six in the afternoon, but due to heavy rainfall they managed to speak only from seven to seven thirty in the evening. The male speakers criticized the Union Party for abandoning independence and heralded Ramón Emeterio Betances and José de Diego as true examples of Puerto Rican patriots. According to a reporter who covered the event, "The plaza was packed . . . circles of elegant ladies decorated the scene." The reporter's passing comment attests to women's presence at the gathering.

By focusing on their dress, the journalist simultaneously indicates that the women were from the local elite and implies they had little to do with politics and served mainly as beautiful adornments.[88] Both events convey the image of a party dominated by men with minimal, passive participation by women.

Women's participation in the party greatly expanded in the 1930s due to three interrelated factors. First, under Albizu's leadership the Nationalist Party launched an archipelago-wide drive to organize women to the anticolonial struggle. To facilitate their incorporation, the Nationalist Party set up *secciónes femeninas* (women's branches). The second reason, largely overlooked by scholars, is that women clamored to join the party. They wrote letters to the party and made public statements indicating their desire to be part of the pro-independence organization. Third, the decades-long and women-led suffrage movement politicized many women, defined them as political actors, and encouraged them to participate in politics. Through working and identifying with the transnational suffrage movement, sectors of the suffrage movement also developed their transnational consciousness.[89] Puerto Rican women exchanged newspapers with American feminists in Peru, Mexico, and the United States.[90] *Heraldo de la Mujer*, a Puerto Rican newspaper that "defended the rights of women," routinely carried global news of actions and statements in favor of women's voting rights.[91]

The Nationalist Party kicked off its campaign to attract more women to the party in Vieques, an island municipality to the east of the main island, in November 1930, when it established the first sección femenina. Another sección femenina formed almost simultaneously in Naguabo, on the east coast of the Island.[92] One more sección femenina was set up in San Lorenzo, with Trina Padilla de Sanz as the honorary president.[93] Padilla de Sanz was also active in the push for Puerto Rican women's suffrage, about which more below.[94] The next month, women in Lares, the mountainous town where anti-Spanish rebels declared the first Republic of Puerto Rico in 1868, set up a sección femenina. The ceremony in Lares that launched the sección femenina mirrored those in other towns. Nationalist men presided over the meeting, which included a large number of women. Once the sección femenina was established, the assembly elected women as president, vice president, secretary, treasurer, and *vocales* (officers), who then took charge of the organization.[95]

One of the biggest events took place in Río Piedras in December 1932—over seventy-five women attended—and women organized it. They sat on the stage alongside male party members and spoke at the event. Following the speeches, the gathering elected the officers for the newly formed sección femenina. The reporter covering the program referred to the women as both "abnegadas" (self-sacrificing) and feminists, terms not typically used together. "There can be no doubt that these enthusiastic and self-sacrificing ladies will be the militant vanguard of Nationalist feminism in Río Piedras."[96]

Albizu's speech in Vieques welcomed women into the party and defined their gendered role as mothers, instigators, fighters, and creators: "Women are the physical and moral mothers of the nation. When men forget their patriotic duty and play the game of illegitimate politics, then it is the role of women to call on them to fulfill their duty; women need to remind their husbands and brothers to carry out their debt of honor."[97] He reminded his audience that the young Joan of Arc "saved France when men lacked the courage" and that the Puerto Rican Mariana Bracetti, a nineteenth-century patriot who opposed Spanish rule in Puerto Rico, had designed Puerto Rico's first flag.[98]

Scholars Nira Yuval-Davis and Flora Anthias have analyzed the roles nationalist ideologies assign women in the construction and maintenance of the nation. They point out that women biologically and culturally reproduce members of the nation; actively transmit, reproduce, and produce national culture; embody national boundaries through their sexual and/or marital relations; carry national honor (or, conversely, dishonor); and participate in national struggles.[99] We can correlate these attributes with Albizu Campos's words: women are the physical reproducers and moral mothers of the nation; they, like Joan of Arc, save the nation or, like Mariana Bracetti, transmit national culture by making the country's flag. Of course, Albizu's description of women's roles did not adequately convey the complexity of women's relationship to, understanding of, and contributions to nationalism for the simple reason that it overlooks women's own definition of their role and the impact their thoughts and actions had on themselves, other women, and men. To understand why women joined the Nationalist Party, we now turn to them.[100]

Women across the archipelago responded favorably to the PNPR's efforts to attract new members and forthrightly stated why they thought they and other women should join the party. One woman from Aguadilla wrote to Albizu in November 1930, stating, "Women should be Nationalists not to advance themselves, but out of idealism." Another woman writing at the same time commented on "the spectacle offered by men, dividing the Puerto Rican family." She continued, "Women should not lend their support to the . . . parties that have deceived the multitudes. Nationalism organizes to constitute the Motherland, not to chase after posts in the colonial government," referring to members of the Union Party who renounced independence in order to keep their jobs. She then called on God to "illuminate the conscience of the Puerto Rican woman so she will join the Nationalist [movement], heal the corrupt colonial politics, and collaborate with the noble task of freeing Puerto Rico." She ended her letter with the words, "Sign my name to the party's official register and count on my loyalty."[101] These two representative writers argue that women should affiliate with the party not out of self-interest but in pursuit of an ideal: Puerto Rican independence. The second writer implies that women need to step forward and clean up the mess created by men who view politics as a path to enhancing their own status. Her comments simultaneously present women as moral housekeepers, tidying up the disorder men have made, and echo Nationalist Party appeals to all Puerto Ricans to join the noble cause of independence.[102]

Women repeatedly drew on gendered images of themselves to express why they should be party members. One woman from Utuado called on her female compatriots, "whose abnegation and sacrifice are traditional," to contribute to the generation of "our perpetual nationality." She wrote that now that women have the vote, "we have obtained a formidable arm that we can use to advance [against] the colonialism that oppresses us." She urged other women to join the Nationalist movement because "not only men are called on to defend the motherland." She ended her statement declaring that she was "following the example of many other women, [and] joining the Nationalist movement."[103]

One such woman was Blanca Canales, whose words opened this chapter. She not only joined the party but was a main leader of the uprising of 1950 in Jayuya (detailed in chapter 9). A few other women served as PNPR leaders in the 1930s. Dominga de la Cruz, whose story I told in chapter 2, was a national leader, as was Isolina Rondón, PNPR secretary from 1937 through 1938.[104] A number of women were elected to serve as vocales in the juntas municipales in Juncos, Barranquitas, Isabela, Guayama, Cabo Rojo, and Caguas, among others in the late 1930s.[105] However their names, contributions, and histories are largely forgotten—or overlooked—as are those of the women who wrote the letters cited above.

From the 1930s onward, women played more active roles in the PNPR. Instead of adding color to events or reading poetry written by men while draped in the Puerto Rican flag, they addressed crowds, ran the women's branch of the party, held offices in both the secciónes femeninas and the PNPR as a whole, and asserted their right and duty to participate in the fight to free their homeland. Women's heightened interest in pro-independence politics took place in the context of, and was influenced by, the intensifying struggle for women's suffrage.

## NATIONALISM AND WOMEN'S SUFFRAGE

Diverse forces, including the FLT, the Socialist Party, a smattering of politicians, and a number of women's suffrage groups had agitated for women's voting rights for decades. Pushed by women workers, the FLT first called for women's voting rights at its Congress of 1908, a demand taken up by the

Socialist Party after it began in 1915.[106] Nemesio Canales, the brother of Blanca Canales and a member of the Union Party, presented a bill "For Women's Emancipation" in 1909.[107]

Although the ratification in 1920 of the Nineteenth Amendment, which enacted voting rights for U.S. women, did not include Puerto Rican women, it did contribute to the formation of various women's suffrage organizations. These groups differed as to whether or not all women or just those who were literate should gain voting rights.[108] The Socialist Party advocated universal suffrage rights for all women, both because it recognized women's right to vote and because it knew that the majority of poor and working-class women, who were illiterate, would back its candidates. Some of the upper-class women suffragists and both the Republican and Union parties advocated limited voting rights for women because they sought to defend the class-based nature of the electorate and their own interests.[109] In 1929, the Puerto Rican legislature granted literate women the right to vote, and in 1935, all women received that right.[110]

Nationalists' position on women's suffrage was largely connected to their overall perspective on politics and elections, as articulated by Albizu. For Albizu, voting rights reflected power relations in any given nation. Thus, in a white supremacist nation like the United States, "More than sixteen million North Americans still can't vote in their country because they have African blood in their veins." He added, however, "One virtue of suffrage . . . is it [gives voters] the power to . . . modify the constitution." But this benefit did not apply to Puerto Rico because the "imperial occupying force—the United States—sets up the rules" governing the archipelago. For that reason, Puerto Rico could not hope to achieve liberation by voting to end U.S. colonialism because "neither citizenship nor [real] suffrage exists" in the archipelago.[111]

In May 1930, the year after literate Puerto Rican women obtained voting rights, Albizu wrote two short essays on women and elections that were published days apart in El Mundo. He wrote them in response to Angela Negrón Muñiz's series "Talking with the Principal Feminists" in El Mundo. For Albizu, the justification for women's suffrage revolved around their position on independence, not on their intrinsic right to elect those who governed them. Both essays addressed feminists who were struggling for the vote. In the first essay, Albizu asked if women wanted voting rights "to reinforce colonialism in their homeland?" Or, he queried, "Are feminists ready to fulfill their unavoidable duty" to end colonialism? He answered, "It appears they are."[112]

His second essay similarly contained a number of questions. "Why do women want [voting rights]? To reinforce colonialism? To annex Puerto Rico to the United States? Or to use them in favor of independence for la patria [the motherland]?"[113] Isabel Abreu de Aguilar,[114] president of the Island Associa- tion of Women Voters, apparently responded to his queries from the first essay because Albizu cited her in his second essay: "The ideal proclaimed by the Nationalist Party is so beautiful . . . that no well-founded argument, one based on high ethical principles, can oppose it. We will awaken women's awareness of their strength and their responsibility and exhort them to use them honor- ably for the good of Puerto Rico."[115] To which Albizu responded, "We salute *la mujer libertadora* [the liberating woman]. La patria wants her to immediately add her strength [to the struggle for independence]."[116] However, because Albizu believed that women's and men's "most important civic duty . . . was to immediately constitute the free, sovereign, and independent republic," the right to vote in the U.S. colony was of little consequence to him.[117]

Albizu's was certainly not the only Nationalist voice calling on women to become politically active. In 1931, Nationalist Fernando Torregrosa also called on women to align themselves with independence and the Nationalist Party. He apparently believed that women's gendered identities, "especially [those of] feminists," made them more disposed to support independence than men because "women are endowed with a more delicate sensibility than are men." As a result, "They are more capable of defending the grand ideals." As evidence of this, he connected women's and national liberation, by referencing Abigail Adams because she "defended the emancipation of women" prior to the Dec- laration of Independence.[118]

Inés María Mendoza was a Nationalist and a feminist.[119] A member of the Island Association of Women Voters, she campaigned for women's rights, includ- ing suffrage. She believed that women should obtain their full rights as women and simultaneously "see ourselves as Nationalists" and fight for an independent nation.[120] Trina Padilla de Sanz supported independence and considered herself a Nationalist but was not a feminist. In 1931, she spoke on "Puerto Rican Women on the Heroic Proclamation of the Republic" at the PNPR's commemoration at Lares.[121] She had more conservative ideas about women's role in society and politics than did Mendoza, Albizu, or Torregrosa.[122] Padilla de Sanz believed that politics was something that men did. If women got involved in "public things," they should only do so to "help men." In fact, she stated, "I detest women who are involved in politics, but I understand them defending their rights." Women should concentrate on the home, "which is their center." Their most sacred duty is "the child they must raise, the husband they must take care of, in short, the family." Yet even as she expressed her aversion to women's involvement in politics, her sense of nationalism propelled her to speak in public and approve "women doing all they can for the welfare of their motherland" because she was opposed to the United States' ongoing abuse of Puerto Rico.[123]

As this brief discussion of suffrage illustrates, ideas about race, class, and gender influenced political parties' positions on women's right to vote, as they did everywhere. Puerto Rico's status as a U.S. colony complicated the issue but did not produce uniformity of opinion among the parties. Indeed, not even members of the Nationalist Party agreed among themselves, as the examples of four Nationalists show. While Albizu considered it of no importance, Mendoza worked hard to obtain it.

## NATIONALISM AND THE AMERICAS

A discussion of the Nationalist Party that ignored its relationship with Latin America would be incomplete. Indeed, one of the major programmatic points and fundamental beliefs of the Nationalist Party was that Puerto Rico was part of Ibero-America or, as they variously called it, Hispano America (the former Spanish colonies in the Americas).[124] Puerto Ricans, like other Hispano Americanos, were the product of Spanish colonialism. They spoke Spanish, were Catholics, and shared a common past. These cultural and historical factors distinguished them from the English-speaking, Protestant North Americans who occupied their island, sent missionaries to convert them to Protestantism, insisted that education be conducted in English, and taught them that the father of their country was Jorge Washington, whose birthday they should celebrate.[125] The party established the importance of Puerto Rico's relationship to Ibero-America in one of its foundational resolutions:

> Whereas all the Ibero-American Republics are united with us based on indestructible ties of blood and language;
> Whereas since their founding these republics have cherished the ideal of a free homeland;
> Whereas we are linked to this community by history and origin, we share in its triumphs and in the grief of its defeats;
> Therefore, this Assembly resolves: we will communicate to all the Ibero-American Republics that on this date [September 17, 1922] a party named the Nacionalista Puertorriqueño was constituted in Puerto Rico whose essential goal is to work for the establishment of the Republic of Puerto Rico.[126]

The Nationalists proclaimed their cultural dissonance with the United States and their emotional, political, and historical bonds with Latin America for three reasons.[127] First, they firmly believed that Ibero-America was their home, where they belonged, where they fit. This belief was integral to their identity as Puerto Ricans and as Nationalists. Rejoining their sister republics of the Americas was one key reason they sought to establish the independent Republic of Puerto Rico. In addition, they thought that strengthening Puerto Rico's ties to the Americas and weakening their links to the United States was critical to convincing Puerto Ricans they should reject the United States, establish an independent nation, and become part of Latin America. Third, the Nationalists knew that to achieve independence they needed the political and material support of Latin America. They understood that the deck was stacked against them, given the enormous power the United States enjoyed and employed in Puerto Rico and the world. Alone, Puerto Ricans lacked the resources and numbers to successfully defeat the United States in a political, a diplomatic, and certainly a military confrontation. Therefore, the party believed it was essential to obtain the backing of other Latin American nations. At the same time, as Coll y Cuchí made clear, Puerto Ricans would be their own liberators: "We do not expect that our victory will come from outside Puerto Rico; we expect [it will be due to] the power of our rights, and support from the exterior will be a natural consequence of this."[128]

The response from Puerto Ricans living abroad to the formation of the Nationalist Party was positive, if limited. El Nacionalista de Ponce published congratulatory letters from Puerto Ricans living in Cuba and the Dominican Republic. Puerto Ricans residing in Barahona, Dominican Republic, were so enthusiastic about the formation of the pro-independence party that they published a flyer denouncing the Union Party and calling on all "good Puerto Ricans who want [to ensure] the success of the Puerto Rican Nationalist Party" to attend a meeting. The Nationalist Party also received "valuable [but unspecified] demonstrations of support" from "Mexico, Honduras, Costa Rica, Colombia, and Chile."[129]

Under the more aggressive leadership of Federico Acosta Velarde, Nationalist Party president from 1925 to 1928, the party issued direct calls for Puerto Rican independence and sought Latin American solidarity with its struggle.[130] Acosta Velarde decried the imposition of U.S. citizenship on Puerto Ricans in 1917, which, he asserted, was a matter of "national convenience [to the United States] as war with Germany approached."[131] He defined Puerto Rico as "an exploited colony," adding, "[We are] like a sugar factory for Wall Street, with all the duties and none of the rights."[132]

Acosta Velarde made it a priority to inform the world "and especially the people of our [same] blood" about the party. One month into his leadership, he had 25,000 copies of a Nationalist Party manifesto printed and distributed throughout the Spanish-speaking world. They were sent to "every major publication in Iberoamérica and Spain."[133] The Havana newspaper El Diario de la Marina reprinted it, and Dominican nationalist Américo Lugo and Venezuelan writer Rufino Blanco Frombona wrote "brilliant articles" commenting on it. Five thousand copies in English were sent abroad, mainly to the United States, including to every U.S. senator and congressman.[134]

## SUPPORTERS RESPOND

In 1926, Colombian Julio Alfredo de Guzmán sent Acosta Velarde an article Guzmán had written titled, "Puerto Rican Sovereignty." Guzmán distributed the article to newspapers in Colombia and informed Acosta Velarde that he was going to visit universities in Bogota to set up programs on Puerto Rican independence and talk with students about forming a solidarity committee that would send propaganda to students throughout the Americas asking them to support the Nationalist Party.[135] His efforts were apparently well received, because several months later he joined with others to form a "Committee in Favor of Puerto Rican Independence."[136]

In 1926, Panama hosted the Pan American Centennial Congress to commemorate the Congress of Panama, which Simón Bolívar, the liberator of South America, had organized in 1826. At the conference, Honduran delegate Alfredo Trejo Castillo delivered a passionate speech in which he sharply condemned "the Colossus of the North."[137] His speech "electrifi[ed] . . . the audience" and was reportedly received with "greater fervor than any other presentation."[138] However, the resolution he presented to the Congress calling for Puerto Rican independence failed to pass.[139] Because his was one of the first declarations of support the Nationalists had received in a Latin American congress, the party was very grateful to Trejo Castillo. They cabled him while he was still in Panama and thanked him for his "noble and generous actions" on their behalf.[140] Trejo Castillo was so stirred by the situation of Puerto Rico that he wrote to Acosta Velarde expressing his desire to "join the ranks of the Nationalist Party."[141] In a later communication with the Nationalists, Trejo Castillo added, "No cause is as moving as is yours; nothing more elevated and worthy of cooperation and help."[142]

In 1926, the University of Puerto Rico invited Mexican José Vasconcelos, the nationalist and highly respected intellectual and anti-imperialist known throughout the Americas, to present a series of lectures. After one lecture, two students delivered impassioned speeches denouncing the depredations of U.S. colonialism on the island. One then asked Vasconcelos whether Puerto Ricans could count on him to "remind the continent of the martyrdom of Puerto Rico."[143]

Vasconcelos replied, "I am a nationalist in Mexico, I could not be any less a Nationalist in Puerto Rico. Convictions are not like a thermometer; they don't change depending on the temperature. . . . After I leave the island I will be a spokesperson for nationalist goals and, frankly, for independence."[144] Vasconcelos also spent a day talking with Pedro Albizu Campos. He was so impressed with Albizu that he later wrote, "Few persons have taught me so much in only one day as has Albizu Campos."[145] Vasconcelos's visit to the island and meeting with Albizu converted him into an ardent supporter of Puerto Rican independence, for which he became an international spokesman. The next year, 1927, he represented the Nationalist Party at the Congress against Colonial Oppression and Imperialism, held in Brussels.[146]

The Brussels congress was an international gathering whose goal was "to deter imperialist governments from oppressing weak nations." Among the attendees were Jawaharlal Nehru, general secretary of the Indian National Congress; French writers Henri Barbusse and Romain Rolland; the U.S. author and radical Upton Sinclair; and Soviet writer Maxim Gorky.[147] Vasconcelos was not the only non–Puerto Rican to represent the Nationalist Party at the Brussels Congress.[148] So, too, did Argentine Manuel Ugarte, Peruvian César Falcón, and Luis Casabona of France.[149] Vasconcelos delivered a major speech at the conference in which he sought to educate participants about the importance of Latin America, an area he believed was "not well-known in Europe."[150] It should be better known, he stated, because it is at the "centre of the world conflict."[151] Vasconcelos then decried the control the U.S. empire exerted over the region and ended by proclaiming, "We claim the right to be absolutely independent."[152] He did not, oddly enough, mention Puerto Rico specifically. However, the final congress documents included a German translation of a Nationalist Party document that stated the organization's program and goals.[153] The gathering approved the Nationalist Party's message, and the congress's resolution on Latin America called for the "absolute liberation of all the colonies such as Puerto Rico and the Philippines."[154]

Angered by the Unionist Party's decision to remove independence from its platform, a number of (male) members left the organization and formed the Nationalist Party in 1922. The example of José Coll y Cuchí suggests that a combination of factors, including the contempt U.S. officials manifested for Puerto Rican culture and for them personally, as well as their realization that U.S. rulers had no intention of relinquishing control, prompted these men to act. Although they broke with the Unionist Party, they retained the gendered and racist beliefs of the Puerto Rican elite. They took as a given their own superiority and the corresponding inferiority of women and Puerto Ricans of color, whose participation and thoughts they apparently did not solicit. They also persisted in believing that they could achieve an amicable solution with the U.S. government regarding its colonial relationship to Puerto Rico.

Albizu's election to the PNPR presidency in 1930 heralded a significant change in the party's thinking and practice on all three issues. The party now sought to draw women to its folds, if not necessarily the leadership, and welcomed all Puerto Ricans into the organization. Although it valued women's contributions and established groups like the secciónes femeninas to facilitate their incorporation, the party did not critique women's oppression or address the reality of male supremacy. Nor did it explore and denounce racism in Puerto Rico or within its own ranks, instead limiting its criticisms of white supremacy to the United States. The party did, however, radically transform its approach to the United States and its strategy for ending U.S. domination. Militant condemnations replaced polite communications as the party moved to prepare itself for armed confrontations with the United States. Despite these changes, the party's interest in and need for Latin American solidarity remained constant.

The support the PNPR received from other Latin Americans encouraged it to invest more time, energy, and resources to obtain hemispheric backing for Puerto Rican independence. Although Nationalist leaders resolved that Puerto Ricans would be their own liberators, they were keenly aware of the critical need for regional solidarity with their struggle. To obtain it, they sent Albizu to inform Latin Americans about conditions in Puerto Rico under U.S. rule and convince them to support the Nationalist Party's fight for national sovereignty. Albizu's 1927–1930 trip cemented political relationships that stretched back to the nineteenth century and laid the groundwork for ones that would continue through the 1950s.

# 4 BUILDING LATIN AMERICAN SOLIDARITY WITH PUERTO RICAN INDEPENDENCE

In September 1927, just before Pedro Albizu Campos boarded the *Guantánamo*, the ship that would take him from the Dominican Republic to Cuba, he learned the next stop would be Port-au-Prince, Haiti. He immediately dashed off a telegram to Dominican nationalist Enriquillo Henríquez García asking him to "alert the Haitians" that he would like to meet them, "if convenient."[1] When the *Guantánamo* arrived in Port-au-Prince, Albizu disembarked, despite the protests of the ship's Cuban captain, who feared for Albizu's safety in U.S.-military-occupied Haiti. Albizu hailed a taxi and visited the statue of Jean-Jacques Dessalines, the first ruler of independent Haiti from 1804 to 1806. He then went to Haitian nationalist Antoine Pierre-Paul's home to pay his respects. Albizu returned to the ship, and a half hour later Pierre-Paul, accompanied by nationalist Joseph Jolibois, arrived and invited him to a reception with 200 people in his honor. During the event, speakers "raised their glasses [and] with elegant discourses toasted the independence of Puerto Rico and the restoration of the Haitian Republic."[2] Albizu then sailed to Cuba to consolidate the Nationalist Party's ties with anti-imperialist forces there.

This vignette evokes some of the principal ideas and shared experiences that united these Puerto Rican, Dominican, and Haitian nationalists. Opposition to U.S military intervention ran high across the Caribbean, from Puerto Rico to Haiti, the Dominican Republic, Cuba, Mexico, and Nicaragua during the 1920s. Anti-imperialist nationalists throughout the region opposed U.S. domination of their countries and felt solidarity with other anti-imperialists throughout the region who, they believed, were fighting for identical causes: sovereignty and regional unity. They considered themselves to be part of the same Ibero-American region, facing a common oppressor, the United States, and in need of one another to regain or retain their national sovereignty. Thus, Albizu, a Puerto Rican, wrote to Henríquez García, a Dominican, to ask him for an introduction to Haitian nationalists.

Caribbean nationalism was transnational during the 1920s. Puerto Rican nationalism, like Cuban, Dominican, and Haitian nationalism, was both rooted in the specific conditions of its respective nation and deeply enmeshed with the struggles, victories, and defeats of its sister islands in the Antilles and, albeit to a lesser extent, of Latin America. The specific political, social, economic, and, in the case of Haiti, linguistic contours of each nation were distinct. Yet nationalists in these four countries evoked the image of their common histories of oppression by European powers and the United States to link their fate to the joint community that they had been part of for many decades. Thus, for these Caribbean nationalists, transnationalism reflected their lived realities, confirmed their shared identities, and served as a source of strength and empowerment in a world dominated by nations, most especially the United States, whose power and resources dwarfed their own.

In his award-winning book *The Invaded*, Alan McPherson offers a powerful, well-researched portrait of the Haitians, Nicaraguans, and Dominicans who opposed U.S. occupation of their nations in the 1910s and 1920s. He writes, "In all three countries those who resisted invasion were motivated not primarily by nationalism, but by more concrete, local concerns that were material, power-related, self-protective, or self-promoting."[3] However, is it accurate to counterpoise nationalism and "concrete, local concerns" or to deny the idealistic or altruistic reasons people fought to throw out the invaders? I argue that Haitian, Dominican, Puerto Rican, and Nicaraguan nationalists defended the local, the material, and the national—people's ways of life and livelihoods, their state of being, and, in some cases, their very existence. Their nationalism involved, of necessity, a simultaneous struggle for power and the protection of the local and the national against the foreign and the invader. Part of the contest was deciding whose vision of the nation would prevail, that of the invaders and those who sided with them or that of the nationalists who were determined to regain national sovereignty.[4] The nationalism these anti-imperialists imagined and propounded in the 1920s often created, reflected, and inspired profound emotions. These feelings combined the material, spiritual, and political and contributed to forging the will to resist, not necessarily for personal gain, but for what nationalists perceived to be the good of what they defined as the nation and its people.

This vision of nationalism explains the depth of anti-imperialism, solidarity, and sacrifice that existed among and between the peoples in the Caribbean and Latin America during this period. Anticolonial nationalists in the Caribbean did not see themselves as disconnected, isolated, nation-bound collectivities. Instead, they perceived themselves to be unique yet united entities joined in a shared struggle against U.S. imperialism. They combined their sense of the national with their promotion of transnational unity and solidarity against a common enemy. They drew on the joint tradition of solidarity established by nineteenth-century anticolonial activists such as Ramón Emeterio Betances, Eugenio María de Hostos, and Lola Rodríguez de Tió (Puerto Rico); José Martí (Cuba); and Gregorio Luperón (Dominican Republic), whom we met in chapter 2. Many twentieth-century Caribbean nationalists employed the shared vocabulary, sentiment, and sense of community that the pro-independence leaders of the previous century had fashioned. Puerto Rican Nationalists used these figures from their shared pasts as beacons and symbols to establish the historical basis, longevity, and legitimacy of their struggle. They also employed them to encourage themselves and others to persist in their struggle against the United States, a most powerful and aggressive enemy.[5]

These attitudes and expectations inspired Pedro Albizu Campos and other Puerto Rican Nationalists who sought both sovereignty and reincorporation into Hispanoamérica, a region with which they shared a common history, religion, language, and culture. Puerto Rican Nationalists advocated not just the independence of Puerto Rico but the end of U.S. imperialist rule in the region as well. The president of the Puerto Rican Nationalist Party, Federico Acosta Velarde, expressed this sentiment well in his farewell speech to Albizu, just before Albizu departed in June 1927 for his Latin American tour. "Puerto Rico is not just fighting for Puerto Rican nationalism; we are also fighting for Mexican, Dominican, [and] Nicaraguan nationalism because we are the same people, from the Rio Grande in North America to Patagonia in South America. [We are] one homogenous people [with shared] customs, language, religion, race. What affects Santo Domingo and Nicaragua also affects Argentina and Puerto Rico; it affects our common interests as a people united by the same bonds."[6] For Puerto Rican Nationalists, national sovereignty went hand in hand with trans–Latin American solidarity and anti-imperialism.

## EARLY TWENTIETH-CENTURY LATIN AMERICAN OPPOSITION TO U.S. IMPERIALISM

Nationalists in many Caribbean countries led campaigns of resistance to the United States' increasingly aggressive and bellicose efforts to establish control over their nations. They galvanized domestic political opposition and, in Nicaragua and Haiti, formed armed movements to oppose U.S. endeavors. They appealed to progressive forces in the United States, Latin America, and Europe, especially in Paris, a center of anti-imperialist organization, for solidarity.[7] Their efforts extended the work of nineteenth century anticolonial movements and provided the PNPR with concrete examples of how and with whom to build transnational networks of solidarity.

Of course, not all Latin Americans opposed U.S. intervention in the region. Some, including many Puerto Ricans, at least initially, welcomed it, believing that it represented the gateway to modernization, democracy, and economic growth. Those who stood to gain economically from their relationship with the financial power to the north developed a mutually beneficial if asymmetric modus vivendi. But many Latin Americans opposed it. As Pablo Yankelevich writes regarding the regional response to U.S. threats against the revolutionary government in Mexico in the late 1910s, Latin Americans not only "raise[d] banners of freedom and justice," in support of the Mexican Revolution, they did so "in open defiance of a neighbor [the United States] that generated little sympathy in the rest of the continent."[8]

Opposition to U.S. intervention in Nicaragua galvanized widespread enthusiasm across the hemisphere. In 1927, U.S. Marines landed in the Central American country and occupied it until their withdrawal in 1933. Augusto César Sandino led the Nicaraguan resistance to the marines until he was assassinated in 1933.[9] Sandino located the Nicaraguan struggle in the context of Latin American unity and anti-imperialism. As Peter Smith points out, Sandino "sought to reawaken the Bolivarian dream" and called "for the abolition of the Monroe Doctrine, regional control of the Panama Canal, and other collaborative measures."[10] Newspapers across the region condemned U.S. activities in Nicaragua, while students, intellectuals, and politicians protested it; solidarity organizations sprang up to support the fighting forces led by Sandino.[11] Barry Carr characterizes solidarity with Sandino's national liberation struggle in Nicaragua as "the first modern, networked anti-imperialist campaign in Latin America."[12]

The example of transnational solidarity campaigns, such as the one with Nicaragua; the existence of hemispheric networks and contacts; and the backing of a world-recognized anti-imperialist, José Vasconcelos, among others, opened doors and smoothed paths for Albizu as he journeyed through the Caribbean. In addition, Albizu was recognized throughout the Caribbean as editor of *El Nacionalista de Ponce*. Both he and the newspaper had opposed dictatorial regimes in the region and supported the struggles of the Dominican Republic, Haiti, and Nicaragua to end U.S. occupations of their nations.[13]

### ALBIZU CAMPOS'S GRAND TOUR

Planning for Albizu's Latin American tour had begun in September 1925, following the Puerto Rican Nationalist Party's General Assembly in Ponce, Puerto Rico. The assembly chose Albizu, then the party's vice president, to represent it on the tour. It named him "Delegate on a Special Mission to Iberoamérica" to invest him with what the party considered the necessary dignity and status to successfully complete the mission. Party president Acosta Velarde, following established protocol at the time for those who hoped to be

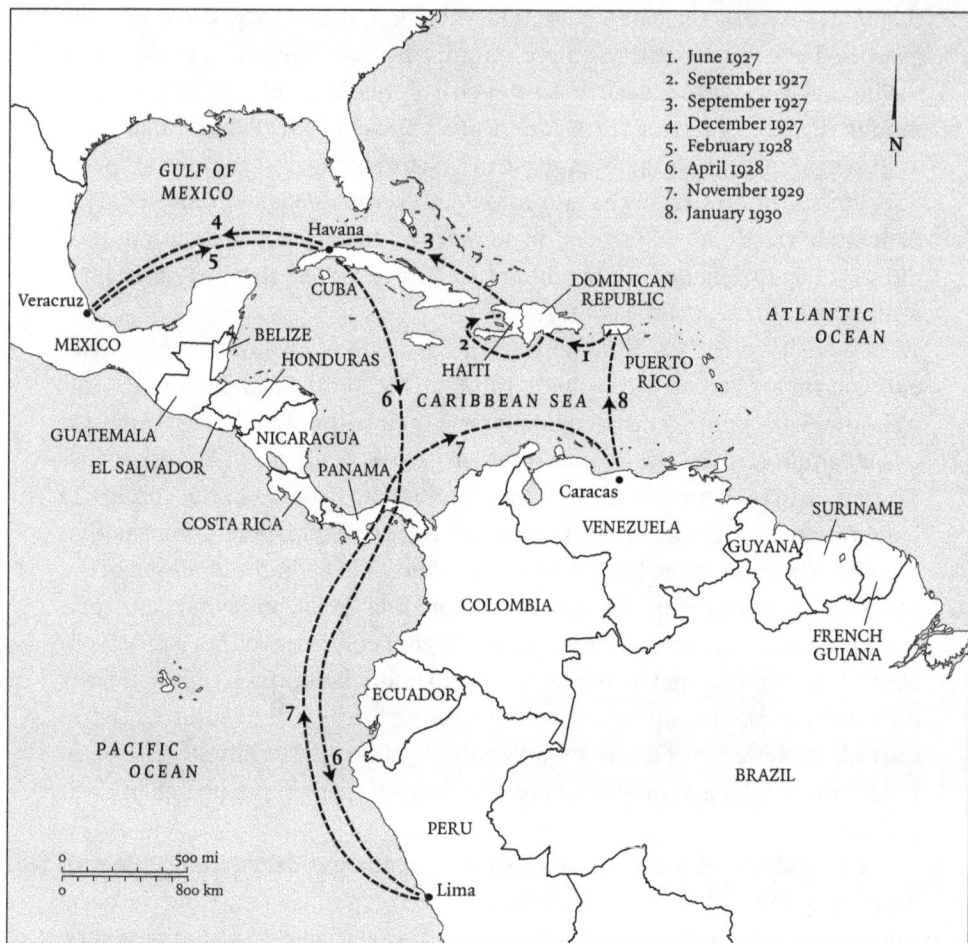

Routes and dates of Pedro Albizu Campos's tour, 1927–30. Source: Naomi Robles.

received as an official visitor, sent cablegrams and wrote letters of introduction to nationalist leaders throughout the Caribbean, informing them of Albizu's upcoming visit.[14] Because the party lacked the necessary funds, Albizu and Laura Meneses, Albizu's wife, sold most of their possessions to finance the trip. Meneses, who was Peruvian, had studied botany at Radcliffe College from 1920 to 1921 and met Albizu when they both attended a presentation by Indian writer and nationalist Rabindranath Tagore at Harvard. When they married in 1922, she automatically lost her Peruvian citizenship and then became a U.S. citizen.[15] Along with the couple's two children, Meneses returned to her parents' home in Lima; neither the couple nor the party had the resources for her to accompany her husband or support herself and the children. Had money been available to allow her to travel with Albizu, it is likely she would have done so as his wife and the mother of their children, not as an emissary of the party, given the patriarchal realities of Puerto Rican politics in the 1920s.

The party's failure to generate the money required to pay for the tour remained an ongoing problem. The wrenching devastation wrought by Hurricane San Felipe in 1928, which, until Hurricane Maria in 2017, was the worst storm in Puerto Rico's history, sharply reduced, if not eliminated, the Nationalist Party's ability to collect money and finance Albizu's trip. The lack of funds meant, ultimately, that Albizu was unable to travel to Argentina or Europe, which had been part of the original plan. It is also possible that the party's lack of financial support reflected its discomfort with Albizu's radical politics and his being of Afro-descent, as noted in chapter 3.[16]

Despite these challenges, Albizu departed on what the PNPR labeled a "patriotic tour . . . of the Américas" on June 20, 1927.[17] Albizu hoped that his presentations would demolish the myth that U.S. rule had led to prosperity and freedom in Puerto Rico. As Nationalist José Alegría proclaimed in the farewell banquet before Albizu's departure, a key goal of the mission was to "expose the painful political situation Puerto Rico is going through under Yankee hegemony and the obstacles that prevent us from attaining [independence]."[18] The party further anticipated that the trip would build or reaffirm regional solidarity with Puerto Rican independence and establish or strengthen ties with other Latin Americans, goals it considered essential to obtaining independence. Party leaders based their expectations on the experiences of nineteenth- and early twentieth-century independence leaders who had similarly traveled throughout the Americas seeking and receiving solidarity for their struggles. They were also counting on the region's long history of shared colonial or neocolonial oppression and joint efforts to end European and U.S. colonialism, invasions, and occupations.

### THE DOMINICAN REPUBLIC: SOLIDIFYING SOLIDARITY

Albizu's visit to the Dominican Republic was a success. After occupying the country for eight years, U.S. Marines had withdrawn three years earlier. Opposition to U.S. imperialism ran high there, as did sentiments of solidarity with the sister island of Puerto Rico. Thus, when Albizu stepped off the ship on June 21, 1927, he was met by a large and enthusiastic group of Dominicans from "all social classes." The welcoming committee included Dominican nationalists, "members of the press[,] and the general public."[19] During his two and a half months on the island, Albizu sought to "unify Dominican sentiment in favor of independence" by appealing to shared opposition to U.S. occupation and educating Dominicans about conditions in Puerto Rico under U.S. rule.[20] He gave press conferences, spoke to large and enthusiastic crowds in Santo Domingo, La Romana, and San Pedro de Macorís, met with Dominican nationalists and Puerto Ricans living in the Dominican Republic,[21] and "denounced North American imperialism which [has] equally tried to silence our sister nation."[22] In a speech titled "U.S. Imperialism, the Case of Puerto Rico and the Systematic Destruction of Puerto Rican Nationality," he explained that to maintain U.S. hegemony in Puerto Rico, the U.S. government had to destroy Puerto Ricans' sense of themselves as a people and nation.[23]

Both Albizu and his Dominican interlocutors correlated their previous, shared histories of fighting together for independence in the nineteenth century to Puerto Rico's struggle for sovereignty in the twentieth century. For example, Listín Diario, the principal newspaper in the Dominican Republic, editorialized, "The work [to free Puerto Rico] reflects the same vision as the continental thought of Bolívar when he sought the liberation of all the peoples of America. It is the glorious continuation of [Segundo Ruiz] Belvis, [Román] Baldorioty, [Rosendo] Matienzo, [José] De Diego, [Eugenio María de] Hostos, [Ramón Emeterio] Betances, and [Gregorio] Luperón, all brothers with the goal of resurrecting the Antillean ideal."[24]

Puerto Rican Nationalists, like their Dominican counterparts, harkened back to nineteenth-century struggles and heroes they shared to emphasize the historic basis of their current relationship. Puerto Rican Nationalists evoked this link when they described Albizu's tour as "the continuation of the great continental campaign begun by the illustrious and ill-fated José de Diego who propagated the ideal of independence in Puerto Rico and throughout Latin America."[25] The joint fight of these male heroes (the early twentieth-century list of heroes seldom, if ever, included women) against Spanish colonialism personified the ties of solidarity that linked the two countries.

More than the memory of these independence leaders united the two nations: they both shared the unwelcome and unfortunate experience of U.S. military domination. The wounds left by the U.S. Marines' occupation of the Dominican Republic from 1916 to 1924 were still fresh when Albizu arrived on the island in 1927, as were the memories of the indignities, economic losses, tortures, and murders U.S. troops had inflicted on Dominicans during their eight-year occupation, which persisted in Puerto Rico. Recognition of this common oppression linked nationalists in the two countries. The PNPR sent Dominican president Horacio Vázquez a congratulatory message in 1924, after "civilian rule was restored in Quisqueya." "We share the same bitterness Dominicans [did] seeing their nation invaded. . . . We long to [have] the honor of building the free, sovereign Republic [of Puerto Rico] just as you have."[26] The joint struggle against Spanish colonialism and the shared sufferance of U.S. rule linked the two Caribbean nations in a common battle for independence and dignity.

Dominicans manifested their support for Albizu and an end to U.S. rule in Puerto Rico. Listín Diario extravagantly praised his ideas, mental clarity, and oratorical skills; the paper extolled him as a person.[27] For example, a journalist writing about Albizu's presentation in the Colón Theater in Santo Domingo rhapsodized that "Doctor Pedro Albizu Campos . . . was gallant and enthusiastic," and the evening was "a splendid cultural event." And the attendees were "avid to hear the calm and serene words of the notable speaker, whose noble, patriotic propaganda awoke among us unanimous sympathy." The Dominican and Puerto Rican audience responded positively to Albizu's call for an end to U.S. colonialism. According to El Mundo, one large rally held in Santo Domingo ended with the crowd shouting "enthusiastic vivas in favor of Puerto Rican independence."[28]

Two of the most prominent Dominican nationalists, Federico Henríquez y Carvajal and Américo Lugo, enthusiastically backed Albizu's appeal for Puerto Rican independence and Dominican solidarity. They formed and presided over the Junta Nacional Dominicana Pro Independencia de Puerto Rico, which they launched in Santo Domingo on July 16, 1927.[29]

Officers of the junta and Albizu sent cablegrams to PNPR president Acosta Velarde to inform him of the new organization. Albizu wrote, "Dominican Junta magnificent. Composed of clergy, senators, deputies, doctors, lawyers, journalists, and university students." In reply, Acosta Velarde wrote, "The Nationalist Party sends cordial greetings. . . . We are honored by the illustrious Junta, which will tighten the bonds of affection that unite us with the noble Dominican people."[30] Dominican and Puerto Rican supporters also organized pro-independence juntas in the Dominican towns of La Romana and San Pedro de Macorís.[31] The Nationalist Party's official banner, which the San Pedro junta adopted, was hoisted outside the office to "welcome all dignified Puerto Ricans" (that is, those who supported an end to U.S. colonial rule).[32]

Although many who attended Albizu's conferences in venues such as the Colón Theater or the Casa España were intellectuals and middle- and upper-class Dominicans, it appears that support for Puerto Rican independence extended beyond these sectors. The Federación Local del Trabajo de Santo Domingo (Local Workers' Federation of Santo Domingo) publicly endorsed Puerto Rican independence. It issued a statement, signed by the president and general secretary, that "offered its ideological cooperation to the movement for absolute independence of the neighboring island." Reflecting its proworker politics, the statement described the plight of 100,000 unemployed Puerto Rican workers "whose lands have mysteriously passed from their hands to the black-gloved hands of capitalism, backed by soldiers' bayonets."[33]

Dominican Nationalists offered more than political statements in favor of Puerto Rican independence. They also shared their experiences and contacts from their earlier trip to South America seeking the removal of U.S troops, as well as direct, material support. Federico Henríquez y Carvajal's assistance was particularly valuable. Following his brother Francisco's ouster from the presidency by the United States in 1916, the two moved to Cuba, where they worked to generate international, particularly Latin American, support for the restoration of Dominican sovereignty. They and other Dominican nationalists sent reports and articles protesting the U.S. occupation to receptive news outlets throughout the Americas. Determined to generate more backing for their cause, several Dominican nationalists appealed directly to South American political leaders. In December 1920, "Federico Henríquez, Max Henríquez Ureña, and for part of it, Tulio Cestero went on a five-month tour to the capitals of Brazil, Argentina, Chile, Peru, Paraguay, and Uruguay."[34] As Alan McPherson explains, the Dominicans met with the minister of foreign relations and president in every country except one, held well-attended public meetings, and received favorable press coverage. Although officials privately expressed their support for the Dominican cause, most were unwilling to do so publicly for fear of U.S. retribution. Presidents Hipólito Yrigoyen of Argentina and Baltasar Baum of Uruguay were two defiant exceptions, while the Brazilian government was a later one.[35] Bruce Calder labels their mission a success because it "pushed the matter of North American imperialism into the forefront of daily discussion" and added "further tension to the United States' difficult relationship with Latin America."[36]

Federico Henríquez's experiences and willingness to share his insights and contacts with Puerto Rican Nationalists were both a concrete expression of Antillean solidarity and eminently helpful to Albizu during his trip. Dominican nationalists included Albizu and Puerto Rican Nationalists in their transnational networks of solidarity, provided Albizu with contacts and letters of introduction to key Caribbean nationalists, and even supplied Albizu with money when he needed it. In gratitude, Albizu wrote to Federico Henríquez thanking him for his financial support on July 8, 1928: "I have suffered greatly these last months when no economic aid reached me, except for the generous help of Dominicans. I must admit that without it I would not have been able to do anything."[37]

## HAITI: AN EMOTIONAL ENCOUNTER
## IN DANGEROUS CONDITIONS

When Albizu departed Santo Domingo in September 1927, he must have felt pleased with the results of his visit. He had accomplished his goals in the Dominican Republic. He had established lasting bonds with leaders of the Dominican nationalist movement. He had been welcomed warmly by both Dominicans and Puerto Ricans residing on the neighboring island, received accolades from the press, and witnessed the establishment of three committees in solidarity with Puerto Rican independence. And he left with valuable letters of introduction from Federico and Enrique Henríquez to Cuban nationalists, whom he planned to visit next.[38]

Although Haiti had not been part of Albizu's original itinerary, possibly due to the presence of U.S. troops, once he learned that his ship would stop there, he was eager to meet Haitian nationalists. Haiti in 1927 was a very different country from its Dominican neighbor. When Albizu visited, U. S. Marines ruled the country, as they had done since they invaded it in 1915. Mary Renda succinctly summarizes the situation: "Marines installed a puppet president, dissolved the legislature at gunpoint, denied freedom of speech, and forced a new constitution on the Caribbean nation—one more favorable to foreign investment."[39] In 1927, the puppet president Louis Borno "had bribed the Council of State to make him president in 1922," according to McPherson.[40] U.S. Senator William King bluntly described Borno as "a mere figurehead, a creature of our Government." In fact, King continued, High Commissioner Gen. John H. Russell, a former commander of the marines in Haiti, "was the real ruler of the republic."[41]

The Haitians Albizu met with were active in the movement to oppose the U.S. occupation. Joseph Jolibois was a journalist and editor of *Courrier Haïtien*.[42] Antoine Pierre-Paul was a politician and former *caco* (insurgent) leader.[43] In June 1927, just three months before Albizu arrived in Haiti, Jolibois, along with seven editors of different Haitian newspapers, and two officers of the Union Patriotique (Patriotic Union) had been jailed in Haiti.[44] They were imprisoned because they had sent a cable to *Diario de la Mañana*, a Cuban newspaper, refuting a description of conditions in Haiti published in that paper.[45] It is highly probable that Albizu knew of their arrest since he was in the Dominican Republic at the time and an article discussing an event he had spoken at was printed right next to the one describing the Haitians' arrest. Despite the risks, Albizu was determined to meet with Haitian nationalists, and they were evidently eager to meet with him. Solidarity with the Haitian people formed a critical piece of Albizu's and the Nationalist Party's anti-imperialist outlook. Albizu had made that clear in the Dominican Republic when he proclaimed, "The end of [U.S. military] occupation of Haiti is necessary for all Ibero-American people."[46]

Although Haiti had been primarily a French colony, not a Spanish one, and the people spoke French or Kreyòl, not Spanish, they were officially Catholic; had been enslaved and colonialized by Europeans, like other Caribbean territories; and were part of the Antillean world, members of the to-be-formed Antillean Confederation.[47] These factors explain why Albizu was determined to visit Haitians who, like himself, were struggling to end U.S. rule in their country. As sociologist Kelvin Santiago-Valles points out, "This broader anti-imperialist and pan-hemispheric interpretation of 'the Race,' as (trans)national-civilizational patrimony, obliged the Nationalistas to . . . publicly denounce the U.S. occupation of Haiti and collaborate with part of that country's anti-U.S. occupation forces."[48]

Pierre-Paul and Jolibois introduced Albizu to Victor Cauvin, secretary general of the Patriotic Union, writers for various Haitian newspapers, including Le Temps, Nouvelliste, and L'Haïtien, and Dantès Bellegarde, a former minister, as well as other politicians and activists. It was with this group of men that Albizu ended his visit, following speeches and a champagne toast.[49] Le Temps, a Port-au-Prince newspaper, reported, "Mr. Campos arrived this morning on the steamship 'Habana' [Guantánamo] and left around noon. We wish him a good trip and much success in his campaign."[50] Albizu's message to Haitians conveyed the Nationalists' vision of América: "The entire continent is interested in our struggle, which is that of the Hispanic-American people since we strive together against a common danger. I don't defend the cause of Haiti, nor that of the Dominican Republic, nor that of Puerto Rico; I defend the cause of the entire Hispanic-American continent. Express my sympathy to the Haitian people and give this message to each Haitian: Learn Spanish. It is through the use of a common language that Haiti will take part in the vast movement of defense that is being organized across all of Latin America."[51]

To twentieth-first-century readers schooled in the idea of respect for other peoples, cultures, and languages, such advice smacks of hispano chauvinism. And certainly, Albizu's hispanophilia framed his admonition to Haitians. Albizu believed that hispano culture and civilization were both admirable and superior to Anglo-Saxon culture, to which he frequently and positively compared them. The comment also reflects Albizu's conviction, which only intensified during his travels, that the peoples of America needed to unite to successfully confront and defeat U.S. imperialism. Although Albizu knew French, as well as German, Portuguese, Italian, Latin, and Greek, he believed that a shared language and the ability to communicate with each other would promote a common vision and purpose.[52] While this could be true, his approach ignored the critical role that French and Kreyòl played in maintaining Haitians' national identity in opposition to U.S. attempts to dominate their nation and control the population.[53] It also overlooked the social and racial distinctions among countries and ignored the different forms that U.S. occupations assumed in the various countries.[54] However, no such concerns appear to have disrupted the encounter between Haitian nationalists and Albizu, and everyone parted on very good terms.

The Haitian pro-independence forces Albizu met with were also desirous of international solidarity. Jolibois wrote to Acosta Velarde and asked the Nationalists to form a Committee in Support of Haitian Independence and whether he would serve as the Puerto Rican representative of the Haitian Patriotic Union. On October 8, 1927, the leadership of the PNPR met and agreed to form the solidarity committee, a decision it cabled to Jolibois, thus confirming the reciprocal nature of their solidarity with other oppressed peoples.[55]

## CUBA: AFFIRMING AN UNBREAKABLE BOND

From Haiti, Albizu proceeded to Cuba, where he arrived on September 16, 1927. Albizu had experienced a range of governments in the preceding two months. He departed from the U.S. colony of Puerto Rico and arrived in the Dominican Republic, where civilian rule had been restored following the withdrawal of U.S. troops in 1924. In Haiti, President Borno ostensibly ruled the country, but the U. S. military, which occupied the country, called the shots. General Gerardo Machado, a virtual dictator closely allied with the United States, was in power in Cuba.

Machado was elected on a platform that pledged to end the widespread corruption that plagued Cuba, appealed to Cuban nationalism by promising to abrogate the Platt Amendment, and pledged to institute measures to improve the economy.[56] However, by 1925, it was eminently clear that Machado had not and would not fulfill his campaign assurances. As social unrest and political opposition grew, Machado turned to intimidation, violence, and prison to quell the opposition. This repressive reality framed Albizu's visit and strengthened his connections with the opposition.

In Cuba, Albizu met with nationalists who had fought together with Puerto Ricans against Spanish colonialism, anti-imperialist intellectuals who decried U.S. domination in Cuba, the Caribbean, and the Americas, and students who opposed the Machado dictatorship. These sectors, like many Dominicans, enthusiastically embraced Albizu and the cause of Puerto Rican independence. As he had done in Haiti, Albizu visited the statue of the country's national hero, José Martí, where he delivered a speech critical of the Machado dictatorship on

October 10.[57] He met with members of the anti-Machado opposition, Rubén Martínez Villena, Juan Marinello, Francisco Ichaso, and Alejo Carpentier.[58] Ichaso and Carpentier worked on *Revista de Avance*, which published the anti-dictatorial, anti-imperialist, prodemocracy, and pro–Latin American politics of these men and the broader social circles of which they were part. *Revista de Avance* was connected to the Latin American network of newspapers that included *Amauta* of Peru and *Repertorio Americano* of Costa Rica. These publications and the political forces they represented sought "the unity of Latin Americans against the ever more aggressive policy of Yankee imperialism."[59] Reflecting these transcontinental politics, in 1927, *Revista Avance* demanded the freedom of Peruvian Communist and political prisoner José Carlos Mariátegui and the independence of Puerto Rico.[60]

In early October 1927, Cuban anti-imperialists formed the Junta Nacional Cubana Pro Independencia de Puerto Rico, an organization that persisted, albeit with different names and members, through the 1950s. A distinguished roster of Cubans led the junta: Enrique José Varona, president; Emilio Roig de Leuchsenring, vice president; Enrique Gay Galbo, secretary; and Juan Marinello Vidaorreta, treasurer.[61] Many of these Cubans were affiliated with an anti-imperialist, anticorruption group known as Los Minoristas. The group began in 1920, when young artists, intellectuals, journalists, and professionals met in the Café Martí in Havana to discuss art. As the group became more political, members identified themselves as "intellectual workers who had a social responsibility."[62] Many were or would become members of the Cuban Communist Party and remained lifelong supporters of Puerto Rican independence. Albizu did not meet with Juan Antonio Mella, the founder of the Communist Party of Cuba, because the Cuban government had exiled Mella to Mexico before Albizu arrived.[63]

The newly formed junta held a banquet to honor Albizu Campos and publicize its first manifesto. Jorge Mañach, who had been friends with Albizu, "like two brothers," since their student days at Harvard, presided over the ceremony, and Emilio Roig de Leuchsenring read the junta's manifesto.[64]

> Since 1892, when Cubans and Puerto Ricans established the Partido Revolucionario Cubano to obtain the absolute independence of Cuba and foment and aid that of Puerto Rico, both goals and ideals were always united, not only in the heart of Martí, but also in the revolutionary propaganda work and in the sympathy and support that he found in the various Latin American countries he visited. Together we will work for the Antillean cause of Cubans and Puerto Ricans Martí, Hostos, Betances.

All the peoples of the Americas who find ourselves within the radius of Yankee imperialist action should pay attention to the Puerto Rican people, not only out of brotherly sympathy or because we identify with their cause. We should also act out of self-interest, since the current military occupation of Puerto Rico is one of the many examples of North American imperialism's advances southward, with the goal of submitting our nations to permanent economic exploitation, whether by diplomatic or military means, peaceful penetration or violent interventions as they did in Santo Domingo and are doing in Nicaragua.[65]

The manifesto traced the islands' common history and shared struggle as the last two remaining Spanish colonies in the Américas, expressed outrage at the continuation of U.S. colonial rule in Puerto Rico, pledged undying solidarity with the fight for Puerto Rican independence, and echoed the theme of American unity in the face of a common enemy.

Mariblanca Sabás Alomá was a member of the Junta Nacional Cubana council, but her name was not mentioned in any of the newspaper accounts or reports about Albizu's visits that I have come across.[66] Sabás Alomá was a feminist, writer, and leader of the Club Femenino de Cuba (Cuban Women's Club), which worked on social issues to improve women's lives, including securing the right to vote.[67] She, like other Cuban women, was involved in Los Minoristas and/or in one of the vibrant women's organizations that existed on the island. These women were public speakers, writers, and activists in the suffrage, anti-Machado, and/or anti-imperialist movements. It is likely they supported Puerto Rican independence, attended meetings with Albizu, or heard him speak. However, their names, contributions, and thoughts did not appear in the documents, coverage, or testimony of Albizu's tour. What emerges, instead, is the image of a political world dominated by men, one in which women were not noticed and whose absence men did not appear to lament or comment on. This perspective defined politics as a masculine activity, not a human endeavor. Women were not leaders of political parties in Cuba, the Dominican Republic, Haiti, or Puerto Rico, but Cuban, Dominican and Puerto Rican women participated in a range of political and/or labor movements, including the struggle for the vote in the 1920s. Their activities challenged the notion that women were not critical to and deserving of full membership in the polity to which they belonged.[68] Nonetheless, the press and writings discussing Albizu's visits to these countries failed to mention their presence and contributions, thus effectively presenting a portrait of his trip as one in which women played no substantial part.

Albizu apparently did not pay much attention to women's political struggles or contributions before or during his travels, although after he returned to Puerto Rico in 1930 he most certainly did. He then encouraged women to get involved in the PNPR and pro-independence politics, as we saw in chapter 3. However, in the 1920s he focused on securing support for Puerto Rican independence, and in most cases, the people who were in positions of power and able to advance his cause were men. The letters he wrote to leaders of the PNPR about his trip did not mention women; instead, they focused on his activities, the men he met, and the men who formed the solidarity organizations he helped to create.[69]

However, a different side of Albizu emerges in a letter he wrote to Laura Meneses months later when he was leaving Mexico. Meneses was then with their three children and her parents in Peru.[70] The letter is warm and affectionate and reveals that he deeply missed her and valued her political opinions. He addressed her as "mabebé" (my baby) and ended the letter with "kisses to the little children, my love." He wrote that after attending the Congreso Mundial de la Prensa Latina (World Congress of the Latino Media) in 1928 during his second visit to Cuba, "I will travel directly to Lima. I can no longer stand being separated from my family." He obviously considered Meneses a trusted and valued compañera, writing, "I read your letter with relish. You have seen everything very clearly, as always." He also shared with her news of his political victories and defeats, his assessment of the political situation in the countries he visited, and the challenges the PNPR faced: "I just learned of [party president] Acosta Velarde's resignation. Without someone putting them to work, they [party leaders or members] don't do well."[71]

Albizu concluded his first visit to Cuba on a high note. He had established or reinforced political relationships with leading Cuban figures that persisted for decades. Anti-imperialist Cubans formed a committee in solidarity with Puerto Rican that lasted into the 1950s. With these positive achievements in mind, he boarded a ship and sailed to Mexico, where he arrived in December 1927.

### MEXICO: AN UNEXPECTED DISAPPOINTMENT

Albizu's visit to Mexico, however, bore little fruit. The Mexican government did not offer him the warm welcome he had expected, and he left the country without having established a solidarity organization, as he had done in the Dominican Republic, Haiti, and Cuba. What went wrong?

Albizu's visit occurred during a challenging time for President Plutarco Elías Calles (1924–28). Calles was convinced that Mexico needed to expurgate what he considered the backward teachings and practices of the Catholic Church in order to modernize and advance. He also sought to "create nationhood 'by forging the Nation,'" which, he believed, required centralizing power in the hands of the state.[72] His administration sought to debilitate the power, resources, and influence of the church in Mexico by implementing the anticlerical provisions of the Constitution of 1917.[73] Militant Catholic forces, encouraged by antigovernment bishops, took up arms to oppose the administration's attacks on the church, clergy, and faithful in what has come to be known as the Cristero War (1926–29). The Calles government struck back, repressing those who fought against implementation of its modernizing and secularizing project.[74] However, from the fall of 1927 through the spring of 1928, the Cristero forces were ascending. In Jalisco, the center of the uprising, the government could no longer protect the haciendas or the foreign-owned mines. By January 1928, the rebels had amassed 35,000 fighters in twelve states.[75] That was the situation in Mexico when Albizu stepped off the ship in Veracruz in December 1927.

It is not surprising the Mexican government did not welcome Albizu, a confirmed Catholic, with open arms. In fact, Albizu was not able to secure a meeting with Calles or any government official at all.[76] Albizu's friendship with José Vasconcelos, a Catholic who was out of favor with and critical of the Calles administration, could hardly have curried favor with the president.[77] Although Albizu and Vasconcelos's friendship and shared Catholicism possibly contributed to Calles's refusal to meet with him, another, probably more significant, factor was at play: the hostility that had defined relations between the United States and Mexico during and after the revolution had begun to dissipate earlier in 1927.[78]

As Albizu wrote to Meneses, "Yankees currently rule, especially in Mexico. My visit was considered damaging to the supposed good relations with the United States. This is the most hostile environment I have encountered so far."[79] Was Albizu right? Indeed, the United States had viewed the threat the Mexican Revolution and Mexican nationalism posed to U.S. economic and political interests with extreme disfavor. However, the appointment of a new U.S. ambassador, Dwight Morrow, in 1927 ushered in a rapprochement between the two countries. By early 1928, President Calles had developed such a friendly relationship with Morrow that the two conducted their meetings over breakfast.[80] Calles likely had no desire to undermine his friendship with the top U.S. diplomat to Mexico or jeopardize improved relations with the United States by meeting with Albizu or supporting Puerto Rican independence.

It appears that Albizu also failed to meet with members of the Anti-imperialist League of the Americas, then headquartered in Mexico. The Communist Party of Mexico had founded the league in 1925 in conjunction with the Communist International. The league sought to unite anti-imperialist forces across the Americas under the Comintern's leadership.[81] One possible explanation for the lack of contact between Albizu and the league was Albizu's earlier unwillingness to work with the Comintern to establish a Puerto Rican branch of the league in 1925. In that year James Sager, a U.S. citizen and Comintern agent, arrived in Puerto Rico. He proposed that the Nationalist Party, the largest anti-imperialist organization in Puerto Rico, join forces with him to set up a branch of the league in the archipelago. Although Albizu, who was then PNPR vice president, was receptive to the idea, he ultimately rejected it because he believed that the party had to maintain its independence and not fall under the control of the Comintern or any other force.[82] As a result, he most likely did not seek out the organization in Mexico. That could also be why there is no record that Albizu communicated with Julio Antonio Mella, founder of the Cuban Communist Party, who arrived in Mexico in 1926, along with other members of the Cuban exile community.[83] What is surprising about this, though, is that Albizu had built relations with Mella's comrades in Cuba. Perhaps Mella's connections with the league in Mexico meant that neither was favorably disposed to encounter the other.[84]

Although Albizu did not achieve what he had hoped, the visit did have some important outcomes. It built on or initiated relationships with individual Mexicans who subsequently facilitated future Mexican-based solidarity work with Puerto Rico. This would prove to be especially beneficial to the PNPR in the early 1950s, when Laura Meneses and the PNPR leader Juan Juarbe lived and worked in Mexico City.[85]

During his time in Mexico, Albizu was exposed to the history and presence of Indigenous peoples, a population that had been largely decimated in Puerto Rico and throughout the Caribbean in the first decades of Spanish colonization and was virtually nonexistent in the 1920s. His interpretations of the meaning and importance of Indigenous and mestizo history and culture, most of which many would find fault with today, reinforced his belief in the superiority of Hispanoamérica and fueled his antipathy to the United States.

When he returned to Puerto Rico in 1930, he gave a lecture at the University of Puerto Rico called "The Formation of Mexican Nationality on the Base of Its Indigenous Population."[86] He mistakenly observed that "Mexicans don't worry about death" because when Aztecs inaugurated their temples, they "sacrificed 20,000 young people who offered their lives with great serenity . . . an attitude toward death . . . that persists in the collective consciousness of Mexicans." Betraying his misplaced faith in the nobility of Catholics, he inaccurately asserted that Spanish conquistadores treated the Indigenous women better than the English did because "Catholicism ordered [the former] to respect women and to recognize the offspring that resulted from these unions." He ended by stating, "Mexico's integration of its ethnic elements and national consciousness is an advance and strength that guards the treasure of our culture and our race."[87] Despite the shocking misperceptions of Mexican history and reality his commentary reveals, his three-month stay in Mexico broadened and reinforced his identification with Hispanoamérica, heightened his awareness of the importance of Indigenous peoples, and offered him visceral evidence of the power and sweep of U.S. imperialism in Latin America, a reality that he confronted directly when he returned to Cuba after his visit to Mexico.[88]

### THE TOUR ENDS ON A MIXED NOTE

Albizu revisited Cuba on February 25, 1928, to attend the Congreso Mundial de la Prensa Latina. As editor of El Nacionalista de Ponce, he had the necessary press credentials to participate. Once the congress opened, Albizu submitted a series of anti-imperialist resolutions for the assembly to discuss and vote on, all of which generated energetic debate. The resolutions condemned "U.S. intervention in the affairs of Latin American nations," called on the "world press and especially the Latin press to carry out a systematic campaign against the occupation of Haiti and Nicaragua," and proposed that representatives of "the publications edited in Latin nations that are, in reality, branches of non-Latin nations not have the right to take part in the Latin Press Congresses."[89] In the ensuing dispute, many delegates protested the interjection of politics into the congress, while others responded that politics were integral to the meeting. As one delegate stated, "If the Congress does not deal with issues vital to latinidad, it would be better to simply dissolve it."[90] Of the seven resolutions Albizu proposed, only two were discussed; the other five were tabled. Neither of the two was approved; twenty-two delegates voted against them and six in favor.[91]

Frustrated again, Albizu left Cuba and sailed to Peru on April 23, 1928, where he joined his wife, three children, and in-laws.[92] I have not been able to ascertain what political work Albizu and Meneses carried out during the year and a half they were both in Peru. Albizu wanted to go to Buenos Aires but was unable to finance the trip.[93] Although one of Albizu's biographers writes that Meneses "provided him with access to APRA," what that really amounted to is unclear.[94] The American Popular Revolutionary Alliance was a populist, anti-imperialist organization founded and led by Peruvian Victor Raúl Haya de la Torre, who was also the party's principal ideologue. A supporter of Puerto Rican independence, Haya de la Torre derided the results of U.S. rule in Puerto Rico by citing examples of the economic hardships people in the archipelago experienced in his essay, "Puerto Rico, the Model Colony?"[95] However, in the late 1920s, APRA barely operated in Peru because Haya de la Torre was in exile in Europe and the core of the party was located outside the country.[96]

Unable to work with a largely inactive APRA, financially strapped and thereby prevented from continuing his solidarity tour, and eager to rejoin the work in Puerto Rico, the Albizu Meneses family left Peru in November 1929. They disembarked in Venezuela, where they spent several weeks. While there Albizu visited the tomb of Simón Bolívar and met with opponents of dictator Juan Vicente Gómez. From the port city of La Guaira, the family sailed to San Juan, arriving in January 1930.[97] Albizu arrived buoyed by the successes he had achieved. Conversations with anti-imperialist nationalists throughout the Americas had heightened his awareness of and opposition to U.S. imperialism and made him more determined than ever to end U.S. rule in Puerto Rico. He therefore resolved to transform the PNPR into a more vigorous, effective, and militant organization committed to securing Puerto Rico's independence. In the next few months, he worked hard to convince other Nationalists the party had to awaken from the stupor into which it had fallen and advance the anticolonial struggle. His efforts paid off. In May 1930, the PNPR elected him president, thus radically altering the safer, less controversial course the party had followed since its founding in 1922.[98]

Because control of Puerto Rico was key to U.S. rule in the region, the U.S. government paid close attention to Albizu's travels through the Americas, tracking the people he met, the activities he participated in, the speeches he gave, and the responses he received.[99] General Frank McIntyre, head of the Bureau of Insular Affairs, the most powerful U.S. agency in Puerto Rico from 1902 to 1934, detailed Albizu's meetings in Santo Domingo, noting that Albizu had "quite a following among Dominicans and quite a large number of Porto Ricans [sic] who are in the Macorís sugar district."[100] Another posting reported on Albizu's "tour throughout Latin America" to "propagandiz[e] the Nationalist ideal."[101] In yet another memorandum Francis White, a career diplomat, informed the U.S. secretary of war that "Dr. Albizu Campos . . . has been engaged in an anti-American campaign in the Dominican Republic."[102]

U.S. government surveillance of the Nationalists increased in the 1930s, as unrest and dissatisfaction with U.S. rule grew in the archipelago. The PNPR intensified its resistance by calling for an immediate end to U.S. colonialism, reorganizing the party, expanding its base, conducting patriotic programs, and forming new organizational structures, some of which imparted military training to members. The direct confrontations that ensued between the Nationalists and the U.S. government ultimately resulted in the imprisonment of the PNPR leadership in 1937. The solidarity networks that Albizu had fostered during his travels in the Americas responded robustly. Supporters across the Americas sprang into action in defense of the incarcerated Nationalists and in condemnation of U.S. repression and colonialism.

# 5 DEPRESSION, REPRESSION, AND MILITANT RESISTANCE IN THE 1930S

Feelings of excitement spread through the crowd of Nationalists lined up in the southern coastal town of Ponce on Palm Sunday, March 21, 1937. They had gathered to commemorate the abolition of slavery in Puerto Rico in 1873 and to call for the release of Nationalist Party leaders. The Cadetes de la República (Cadets of the Republic) were positioned at the head of the procession, followed by the Enfermeras de la República (Nurses of the Republic).[1] They didn't anticipate any problems. The mayor of Ponce had issued them a legal permit to march a few days earlier. However, Gen. Blanton Winship, the U.S.-appointed governor of Puerto Rico, had no intention of allowing the peaceful assembly to parade, so he ordered the chief of police to stop the march. To ensure that Winship's command was carried out, police, some armed with tear gas and Thompson submachine guns, were mobilized from across the island and positioned in front of and behind the unarmed protestors. As the marchers waited to step off, musicians played "La Borinqueña," the pro-independence national anthem written by Lola Rodríguez de Tió.[2]

Ignoring police orders not to advance, the leader of the cadetes addressed the crowd, "¡Atención, firmes, de frente, marchen!" (Attention, be strong, forward, march!). As the Nationalists began to march, the police opened fire, killing nineteen and wounding somewhere between 150 and 200 men, women, and children from among the Nationalists, members of the crowd that had gathered to observe or support the event, and even some of their fellow officers. Dominga de la Cruz, whom we met in chapter 2, led the contingent of enfermeras from the west coast town of Mayagüez. When she saw the flagbearer get shot and drop the flag to the ground, she sprang forward, "swept up the bloodied flag[,] and continued marching."[3]

This mass killing of peaceful civilians, which has come to be known as the Ponce Massacre, shocked and angered Puerto Ricans. Ten to fifteen thousand people joined the funeral procession that carried the bodies to the cemetery in Ponce. They listened when Julio Pinto Gandía, interim president of the Nationalist Party, "accused Governor Winship, Police Colonel Enrique de Orbeta, and the police of being responsible for the massacre."[4] Gandía asked the people "to swear this crime would not go unpunished."[5] Three thousand people attended services in East Harlem, where Congressman Vito Marcantonio and Albizu's lawyer, Gilberto Concepción de Gracia, denounced the attack.[6] Sadly, few people in the United States have even heard of one of the largest police murders of unarmed citizens in U.S. history.[7]

The Ponce Massacre of 1937 epitomizes the defiance and determination of the Nationalists and the repressive and unyielding nature of U.S. officials. It thus encapsulates key contours of the conflict between the two forces during the 1930s. Because the 1930s were decisive years for the Nationalist Party, in terms of its political evolution and relations with the U.S. government, this chapter narrows the lens to focus on conditions in Puerto Rico, the Nationalist Party's politics, programs and activities, and the U.S. government's aggressive response to the pro-independence organization.

The 1930s was a particularly challenging decade. Two hurricanes devastated the archipelago. The Depression plunged many Puerto Ricans into desperate poverty, which contributed to their increasing dissatisfaction with U.S. rule. Galvanized both by the growing misery and unrest that swept Puerto Rico and by the heightened sense of urgency to end U.S. colonialism that Albizu imparted to members, the Nationalist Party intensified efforts to mobilize Puerto Ricans to demand immediate independence. For its part, Washington attempted to improve economic conditions in its Caribbean territory, undermine support for independence, and repress the Nationalists, thereby eliminating the threat they posed to its control. One year after the Ponce Massacre, the U.S. government convicted and exiled PNPR leaders to the Atlanta Federal Penitentiary, an event that produced continentwide demands for their release and Puerto Rico's independence.

### THE DEPRESSION HITS PUERTO RICO

Victor S. Clark was a Columbia University–trained economist. Between 1928 and 1930, he worked with a team assembled by the Brookings Institution and sponsored by the Social Science Research Council to study "the Island's persistent economic difficulties."[8] The group's findings painted a grim picture of conditions in Puerto Rico. Thirty years after U.S. rule began, "the condition of the masses of the Island people remains deplorable. While distress has, of course, been intensified by the disastrous hurricane [San Felipe] of 1928, even during the most favorable periods the picture of life on the Island is drab indeed." The authors pointed out, "A daily wage of 70 cents, with employment four days out of seven, represents approximately the earnings of the larger part of the daily laboring population." They added, "The earnings of the town laborer, taking into account the higher costs of living in the city, are not greatly in excess of the country laborer."[9] In short, most Puerto Ricans lived in extreme poverty in the late 1920s.

In September 1928, Hurricane San Felipe, a Category 5 monster with winds reaching between 160 and 200 miles per hour, slammed Puerto Rico. Like Hurricanes Irma and Maria ninety years later, San Felipe left death and destruction in its wake.[10] The archipelago had not yet recovered from the damage caused by San Felipe when the Depression struck in the early 1930s. As if confirming the adage that misfortune comes in threes, another hurricane, San Ciprián, smashed Puerto Rico in 1932, "killing 225 people and causing damage estimated at $30 million."[11] The triple whammy dealt a blow to the economy, people's standard of living, and support for U.S. rule.

The tobacco industry was hit hard. San Felipe "destroyed many newly planted seedbeds and curing ranches" as well as "the future crop that was in the seedling stage."[12] This enormous loss initially resulted in higher prices for the remaining tobacco, but the crash of the U.S. stock market in 1929 lowered both the demand for and the price of tobacco. San Ciprián delivered a crippling blow. It devastated the tobacco sector, as did the growing popularity of cigarettes (high-quality Puerto Rican tobacco was principally used for cigars) and U.S. smokers' increased preference for cheaper cigars. As a result, the average price tobacco farmers received for their product dropped from twenty-five cents per pound from 1920 to 1929 to fifteen cents per pound from 1930 to 1939.[13] San Felipe and the Depression also sharply undermined coffee production, which had declined since the United States invaded in 1898. The loss had both economic and social repercussions. It eliminated jobs and "meant the decline of Puerto Rico's nineteenth-century productive elite."[14] Sugar fared substantially better than either coffee or tobacco because the storm did not inflict long-term damage on the cane and U.S. sugar interests buttressed the industry.[15] In chapter 2, I explained that U.S. and Puerto Rican sugar interests acquired or retained huge swathes of Puerto Rican land in the first two decades of the twentieth century. Some small and medium-sized Puerto Rican farmers lost their land and livelihood and became poorly paid workers on the sugar estates or in the sugar mills or migrated elsewhere.[16] This transformation meant that land previously devoted to producing crops for family and domestic consumption now harvested sugar for export. As a result, Puerto Ricans relied on food imported from the United States, since according to U.S. law all goods entering the archipelago had to arrive on U.S. ships, which drove up costs and increased dependency on the United States.[17] This maritime arrangement had dire consequences for Puerto Ricans, which the Depression exacerbated. According to the Puerto Rican Chamber of Commerce, the cost of living rose 25 percent at a time when "the depression had practically paralyzed commerce and industry, . . . employment had declined, and privation and want had reached alarming proportions."[18] For example, a bag of rice, a dietary staple, cost two dollars in 1932 and four dollars in 1933.[19] The cost of other core elements of consumption, such as *bacalao* (cod), beans, milk, and lard also increased.[20]

Agricultural laborers and needleworkers—the majority of the paid workforce—suffered the most from the triple disasters. Unemployment ran as high as 65 percent in 1933.[21] Wages and prices moved in opposite directions, with calamitous consequences. Puerto Rico's enforced dependency on the United States had much to do with this reality. To paraphrase, when the United States sneezed, Puerto Rico got the flu. Research by statistician Artemio Rodríguez starkly conveys the misery that afflicted many Puerto Ricans. His study concluded that in 1933 one person could maintain an adequate diet on $3.19 a week, or $11.17 for a family of four, a sum that does not include clothing, medical, or housing expenses. Yet the average weekly wage for laborers in most industries that year was only $3.00. While needleworkers required 1,800 calories a day to survive, farm laborers needed somewhere between 3,200 and 4,100 daily calories. Clearly, people's earnings did not cover what they needed to survive at even the most basic level.[22] For hundreds of thousands of Puerto Ricans, the situation was bleak, even desperate.

Hunger, poverty, and distress are powerful forces. While they certainly contributed to weakening many Puerto Ricans' support for U.S. rule, they alone cannot account for the heightened pro-independence sentiment and support for the Nationalist Party that occurred in the 1930s. Because data to quantify this growth do not exist, this chapter explores several qualitative manifestations of the movement, such as the sugarcane workers strike in 1934, the growth of membership in the cadetes and enfermeras, the outpouring of sympathy and anger the Ponce Massacre sparked among Puerto Ricans, the absence of sorrow the murder of U.S.-appointed police commissioner Francis E. Riggs elicited, and the refusal of the Puerto Rican jury to convict Nationalist Party leaders in 1936.[23] For their part, the Nationalists took decisive steps to expand their base and heighten pro-independence sentiment during the 1930s. They unveiled a new political program, conducted highly visible campaigns, increased their involvement in workers' struggles, and issued stirring declarations and passionate exhortations to enhance people's belief in themselves and in Puerto Rico's capacity to obtain national sovereignty and rejoin its sister republics of the Americas.

## A NEW PRESIDENT AND A NEW PROGRAM

In April 1930, four months after Albizu returned from his Latin American travels, the Nationalist Party announced that it would hold a national assembly "to completely reorganize" itself. Albizu sought to reinvigorate the membership and (re)define the party's direction. The party had floundered while he was gone, and four different presidents had run it. Federico Acosta Velarde (1925–28) had to step down due to poor health. José S. Alegria (1928–29) resigned after a few months and joined the Partido Liberal (Liberal Party).[24] The venerable Antonio Vélez Alvarado (1929), who had designed the Puerto Rican flag in New York City in the 1890s, withdrew soon after accepting the position due to poor health. Antonio Ayuso Valdivieso served as provisional president until Albizu was elected president in 1930.[25]

Albizu and his supporters wanted the party to call for an immediate and unequivocal end to U.S. rule; embark on a campaign to incorporate more members; directly confront symbols, institutions, and representatives of U.S. power; and build solidarity networks across the Americas. Signaling the importance of the upcoming assembly, the party invited "all nationalist organizations constituted by Puerto Ricans or foreigners in the Americas," as well as "preeminent men in the Americas and Europe who sympathize with the nationalist cause, such as Romain Rolland, Henri Barbusse, [José] Vasconcelos, Manuel Ugarte, the director of El Sol in Madrid, and the director of the [Spanish] magazine La Rabida" to attend.[26]

Photographs of the assembly reveal that all the delegates were men, primarily of European descent, neatly dressed in suits and ties, a few with bow-ties, seated attentively in rows in the Ateneo Puertorriqueño.[27] During the meeting, Albizu reported on his travels. He recounted the warm reception he had received in the Dominican Republic, where he was overwhelmed by "the generosity of the Dominican people, who offered him fraternal economic and moral cooperation." He spoke "succinctly" of his visit to Haiti, praising the homage Pierre-Paul and the Patriotic Union had given him. He noted that in Cuba, "the Machado government had placed many obstacles" in his path, but "the youth openly manifested they were on [our] side."[28]

The gathering elected Albizu president. When the results were announced, the assembly rose to its feet in a standing ovation.[29] The delegates approved the following resolution: "We must *immediately* end North American colonialism and commit ourselves to holding a constituent convention that will establish the government of the free, sovereign, and independent Republic of Puerto Rico, as soon as we have received the majority of the votes."[30] The resolution called on all Puerto Ricans to "fight for an independent motherland" and "join the Nationalist Party." The party announced its eight-point program. While being neither prosocialist nor anticapitalist, the PNPR offered an alternative to the economic sufferings the mass of Puerto Rican peasants and laborers experienced as a result of U.S rule. The program announced a bold critique of U.S. rule and offered a vision for the creation of a more equitable economic system that would primarily benefit the poor, those who paid the highest price of U.S. domination. Anticipating ideas that would circulate throughout Latin America decades later, the program included elements of import substitution and dependency theory.[31]

Point 1 of the program pledged to "organize the workers so they can recover their share of the profits appropriated by foreign interests." Point 2 addressed the sugar monoculture and export of profits that had occurred since U.S. interests had monopolized much of Puerto Rican land. To counter this process, the party would "destroy *latifundismo* [large estates] and absentee land ownership and divide [the land and] the buildings among the greatest number of [small] landowners." The party called for an end to the *cabotaje* system between the United States and Puerto Rico, "which only benefits the invader."[32] Points 5 through 7 spoke to the need to reorient the economy so that agricultural production, exports, shipping, and the banking system would function to satisfy the needs of Puerto Rico, not U.S. capitalists. Point 8 advocated establishing a national financial and business system that would ensure Puerto Rican money was deposited in Puerto Rican banks, and "free the country from private and public foreign companies so that agriculture, business, and industry [return to] Puerto Rican hands."[33] As the program makes clear, the Nationalists blamed the country's economic woes on U.S. economic and political rule, made no mention of domestic capitalists, and believed that if Puerto Ricans managed the economy, they would do so in the best interests of the Puerto Rican people. The meeting ended with Albizu's inauguration speech, in which he proclaimed,

> It is impossible, compañeros, for this shameful colonialism to continue. . . . We cannot tolerate our nation's desperate situation one more minute!
>
> A philosophy of optimism must inform all our actions. A doctrine of pessimism reigns in our country, one that demoralizes and makes us cowards; one that we must put an end to. We need to lift the spirits of Puerto Ricans and tell them they can be what they want to be and overcome their dependency if that is what they desire. . . . We need to boost the morale of our people so they will once again believe in their future and their possibilities.[34]

His address ended with the oath all members took upon joining the party: "We solemnly swear to defend the nationalist ideal and we will sacrifice our wealth and our life if necessary for the independence of our motherland."[35] The standing crowd burst into applause at his words.

The party worked to reenergize its followers and rally new supporters. Nationalists sought to inject hope and pride in Puerto Ricans by extolling their history, culture, and traditions. They knew that to overcome the dependency Albizu cited in his speech, they needed to assure people they had the ability, talent, and resources to break with colonial rule and govern themselves. To accomplish this, the party held well-attended public rallies at which Nationalist leaders explained the negative economic impact of U.S. domination and argued that if other countries could be independent, Puerto Rico could, too.

The party also worked to inspire patriotism and convince people that Puerto Rico should be a sovereign nation. It did so by educating Puerto Ricans about past anticolonial struggles and creating a pantheon of national heroes to admire and emulate while simultaneously emphasizing the archipelago's historical and cultural ties to Latin America. The party aimed to expand organizationally by developing nationalist associations for young people, women, and men that would mobilize and link them to the Nationalist Party. A third component of the campaign was performative. Nationalists regularly staged public manifestations of patriotism that included calls for national independence.[36] As indicated in Albizu's presidential acceptance speech, the party also paid attention to Puerto Ricans' emotional and psychological state. It strove to restore people's faith in themselves and in other Puerto Ricans and convince them they could cast off the bonds of dependency that tied them to the United States and not only survive but thrive.

One activity that combined all four elements was the annual pilgrimage to Lares, the town where anti-Spanish rebels rose up in 1868, declared the Republic of Puerto Rico, and were soundly defeated by royalist forces. Under Albizu's leadership, the Nationalist Party disinterred the history of Lares and the nineteenth-century struggle for independence from the oblivion to which they had been consigned and traced the origin of the nation to them.[37] The first of many commemorations of Lares took place on September 23, 1930.[38] Two weeks before the event, the municipal assembly in Lares discussed the upcoming commemoration. Demonstrating the high regard the town leaders had for the Nationalists, assembly members unanimously approved a resolution to welcome the "distinguished compatriots" traveling to Lares and treat them as "guests of honor." They further called on all "the business and commercial leaders and professionals" to close their offices and establishments for the day and named a special commission to welcome the visitors.[39] The event educated people about the history of the Lares uprising and the dedication and sacrifice of the nineteenth-century nationalists who fought to end Spanish colonialism, while organizing Puerto Ricans to participate in the commemoration. An emotional and evocative performance of patriotism, the activity aimed to build national pride and inculcate a sense of dignity and confidence among Puerto Ricans.

The mayor and municipal commission of Lares greeted the procession on its arrival. The group marched to the Plaza de la Revolución, singing the "Himno de Lares" (Hymn of Lares), then attended an official reception in the town hall and a mass in memory of "The Martyrs of Independence."[40] Silence was observed while participants placed a floral offering in the Plaza de la Revolución to honor those who had fallen in defense of independence. An open-air assembly followed at which Nationalist leaders, a university student, and a priest spoke, a group of girls sang the "Himno de Lares," and children and adults recited poetry. The crowd sang "La Borinqueña," and the day ended with a dance.[41]

In 1931, the Nationalist Party launched a second campaign that, like the pilgrimages to Lares, incorporated educational, organizational, performative, and emotive elements. It sold *bonos*, or bonds to be drawn on the Treasury of the Republic of Puerto Rico.[42] Each bond featured the picture, name, and a brief description of an independence figure from the nineteenth century, most of whom were largely unknown. For example, one bond displayed a photograph of Francisco Ramírez, the "president of the Republic of Lares." Another featured a drawing of Mariana Bracetti, the woman who participated in the Lares uprising and sewed the flag of Lares.[43]

The bonds both educated Puerto Ricans about their "heroes" and served several organizational purposes. They generated sorely needed funds for the party and created an emotional and political link between the party and contributors, who now had a financial as well as political interest in the party's success. The purchaser bought a stake in the future creation of an independent nation. Each bond stated that it would become due "five years after international recognition" of the Republic of Puerto Rico occurred, when the treasurer would pay the bond owner "one golden peso drawn from the Treasury of the Nationalist Party of Puerto Rico to reconstitute the Republic."[44]

On a performative level, the issuing of bonds figuratively enacted the operations of a national treasury. Those who created the bonds, as well as those who sold and bought them, demonstrated their belief in the reliability of the Nationalist Party and the future viability of the nation. Together they conducted themselves as if they were citizens of the Republic of Puerto Rico, thus acting out their faith in the party and the independence struggle.

## BUILDING MILITANT ORGANIZATIONS

To further the party's new emphasis on mass organizing and heightened militancy, the Nationalists endorsed the formation of two new bodies, the Enfermeras de la República (Nurses of the Republic) for girls and women and the Cadetes de la República (Cadets of the Republic) for boys and men. Both entities embodied and projected the militaristic, confrontational turn in the party's politics. They also reflected, reinforced, and challenged ideas about women's and men's gendered roles in society and politics.

The Enfermeras de la República evolved from Hijas de la Libertad (Daughters of Freedom), an organization founded and run by a high school student, Lamia Azize Mawad, who started the group in 1932 when she was fifteen years old. Her goal was to organize other young girls to "fight for the Independence of Puerto Rico."[45] The organization grew to include between 200 and 300 members and existed in eleven towns across the island.[46] Members believed in transnational nationalism, as preached by three men they admired: Simón Bolívar, José Martí, and Albizu. They upheld the "revolutionary Antillean Hispano American tradition" and supported "the union of Hispano America and the Antilles in an anti-imperialist bloc." They worked with nationalist women in Cuba and the Dominican Republic and established chapters of hijas in both countries.[47] The Hijas de la Libertad then transitioned to the Enfermeras de la República. Dominga de la Cruz, the future heroine of the Ponce Massacre, brought a petition from Nationalist women in Mayagüez calling for the formation of the Enfermeras de la República to the party's National Assembly in 1932. The assembly approved her proposal, and the group began. In keeping with the Nationalists' growing militancy, the women in the group wore uniforms—black or white skirts and white blouses—and, like the men, received military training. Their stated role, however, was as auxiliaries: to take care of men who got hurt in battle.[48]

Angelina Torresola was an enfermera during the 1930s. Like other members of her family, she became a Nationalist after she heard Blanca Canales, her cousin and future leader of the uprising of 1950 in Jayuya, talk about independence.[49] Torresola reminisced about her early years as an enfermera: "We conducted exercises in the plaza dressed in white. A young man from [Jayuya] trained us and we followed his orders. We dressed in white because we were supposed to be the nurses for the army. In a war there is an army and if blood is shed you need nurses for the wounded." She added, "We also received military training, but that only lasted a little while."[50] Blanca Canales was also a nurse. In addition to receiving medical and military training, the nurses "raised money for the party's work to send delegations to carry out our international work."[51] Torresola recalled that she and other Nationalist women went "from business to business asking [for money]." Many of them contributed, "maybe because in the small pueblos we all knew each other, everyone liked me and the others [Nationalists], and we were honest."[52]

In addition to training and fundraising, women participated in processions and events. In 1933, they joined with cadetes, the combined forces numbering in the hundreds, to march to the main cathedral in San Juan to commemorate the death of a Nationalist the previous year. The carefully chosen date coincided with the anniversary of the Antillean Confederation, the nineteenth-century organization that called for unity among Caribbean nations. The women's organization, like other units in the march, carried the Puerto Rican flag, not the U.S. flag.[53] Roughly 700 enfermeras and cadetes mobilized in 1937 in support of independence and the Nationalist Party. Although these numbers are small, they indicate both sustainability and growth.[54]

As we saw in chapter 3, women clamored to join the party because they wanted to be part of the movement to secure an independent homeland. Once in the organization, women carved out roles for themselves as political actors in the anticolonial struggle. The designation of female members as nurses suggests that the Nationalists saw women primarily as supportive helpmates to the men. But viewed from a different perspective, the party accepted women's petition, as presented by de la Cruz, and agreed to their request to form the organization. In so doing, it formally included women in an official and important capacity, albeit in a gender-defined position, which nonetheless represented a step forward for women. Indeed, pictures of the Nationalist Assembly in 1932 indicate more women in attendance than had been true in the 1920s. Not only were women seated in the audience, but they made up four of seven people seated at the main table.[55] Participating in public marches and events, going door to door asking for money, shaped women's view of themselves as part of the anticolonial struggle. They perceived themselves as responsible for the destiny of Puerto Rico and its inhabitants.

Isabel Rosado became a Nationalist in the 1930s. She was from a poor peasant family but managed to get a scholarship to study in the University of Puerto Rico in the 1930s. When she read about the murders in Ponce in the newspaper, she thought, "For them [the United States], we are nothing. We are second or third class. So, we need to fight until we are who we are."[56] Which is exactly what she did. Rosado spent over twelve years in prison following the Nationalists' uprising in 1950 and the attack on the U.S. Congress in 1954 and dedicated the rest of her long life—she was 107 when she died in 2015—to Puerto Rican independence.[57]

The Cadetes de la República emerged out of the Asociación Patriótica de Jóvenes Puertorriqueños, which formed in March 1931. The APJP sought and obtained direction from Albizu and named him honorary president and counsel. Under Albizu's influence, the association began military training for its members and adopted the uniform of white pants and black shirt. By 1932, the APJP had become the cadetes, which many young Nationalist men (the official age of members was eighteen to thirty-eight) joined.[58] Estanislao Lugo was one of thirteen children. His father owned a small business that sold food, and his mother "was a housewife." He became a cadete when he was seventeen years old. He joined because, he said, "I was convinced that Puerto Rico had to be free. . . . I dreamed of being a citizen of the Republic of Puerto Rico." The cadetes "met every two weeks, [and] we learned about the *patria* and what freedom meant." Lugo described Nationalist Party meetings as "extraordinary." "Many people who weren't party members went to the meetings just to hear Pedro Albizu Campos because he was such a moving speaker." Lugo recalled that the organization had three goals: "instill discipline in members, draw them more closely into the party, and project the image of men committed to fighting to free Puerto Rico from U.S. rule as an example for other Puerto Ricans."[59]

Heriberto Marín was also a cadete. He was one of eight children who grew up in Jayuya, near the home of Blanca Canales. Like many local families, his house lacked running water and electricity and his parents did not own any land. He became a cadete and a Nationalist because, he said, "I believe we have the right to be free." For him, the cadetes "were like an army, only one without weapons. We practiced, but our weapons were symbolic since they were made of wood." He rejected the idea that Albizu Campos, the PNPR, or the uniform the cadetes wore had anything to do with fascism. "Albizu was opposed to Franco, Mussolini, Hitler, the Nazis, because they were tyrants. We [the cadetes] wore the Cross of Malta, because it symbolized Christians who fought in the Crusade."[60]

A glance at the uniform worn by the cadetes could suggest links between the pro-independence organization and European fascism, since there is a certain sartorial similarity. However, this would be a mistake. European fascist groups were doctrinairely and in practice racist. The cadetes was a multiracial organization that opposed U.S. racist treatment of Puerto Ricans and called for independence.[61] As I pointed out in the introduction, the Nationalists opposed fascism. The movement that inspired the cadetes was actually Irish Republicanism, not Italian or Spanish fascism.

Albizu came in contact with Irish Republicanism when he attended Harvard University from 1916 to 1921, first as an undergraduate and then as a law student.[62] While there he mixed with students from all over the world and became president of the Cosmopolitan Club, an organization that "united Harvard's international students, entertained foreign dignitaries, and discussed world affairs."[63] Albizu learned about British colonialism in Ireland and India from his interactions with club members and guests. He was so moved by the Irish fight for independence that he formed an organization at Harvard that called for recognition of the Irish Free State.[64] Albizu met Éamon de Valera in 1919 when the Republican Irish leader traveled to the United States seeking political and financial support for the ongoing fight against the British, and he introduced de Valera when he spoke at Harvard.[65]

Albizu drew parallels between the Irish and Puerto Rican struggles: two Catholic peoples, colonized by Protestant nations, who were expected to abandon their language, identity, and culture to embrace those of the oppressor.[66] Not only did he see similarities between their situations, but he also adopted some of the Republicans' political perspectives and military tactics.[67] Albizu was particularly influenced by James Connolly, the Irish Republican and socialist, founder of the Irish Citizen Army in 1913, and commander of the Dublin Brigade during the Easter Rebellion in 1916.[68]

Many Nationalists, like their Irish counterparts, fused Catholic religious concepts and politics.[69] One central trope they adopted was the merit of sacrifice and martyrdom. The willingness to give one's life for the freedom of the motherland was baked into being a member of the PNPR, as reflected in the oath cited above. Joan of Arc was a role model for Nationalist women. When Albizu inaugurated the party's first women's section in Vieques in 1930, he reminded his audience that the young Catholic saint "saved France when men lacked the courage to do so."[70] Blanca Canales carried a medallion with a picture of Joan of Arc on one side and the words "Saint Joan of Arc, intercede for the independence of Puerto Rico" on the other.[71]

The emergence of the cadetes and the enfermeras marks an important stage in the history of the Nationalist Party, as both groups signaled the party's adoption of a more confrontational stance toward the United States. They also reveal members' resolve to go beyond belligerent statements and develop the organizational and personnel capacity to undertake aggressive action against institutions and individuals that represented and executed U.S. colonial policies in Puerto Rico. And while the gendered distinctions between the two organizations and the designated roles men and women played in each reflected societal norms of the day, if we look at how women conceived their participation in the enfermeras, a different picture emerges. The enfermeras existed because women wanted to play a more significant part in the struggle to free Puerto Rico. When they appeared uniformed in public as official members of the Nationalist Party, they understood themselves as, and indeed were, important contributors to the battle to free their nation.[72]

## NATIONALISTS AND WORKERS

The Nationalist Party was not a Marxist organization, but it did care about the plight of Puerto Rican workers, as indicated in the party's program. In response to the economic crisis of the 1930s, Nationalists linked their pro-independence agenda to workers' struggles, specifically those of the sugarcane workers and dockworkers, and the movement to lower the price of gasoline and basic foodstuffs.[73] In so doing, they filled a void left gaping when the Socialist Party formed the Coalición (Coalition) with the Republican Party in 1924 and virtually jettisoned workers for an alliance with a key component of the pro-U.S. Puerto Rican bourgeoisie.[74] Worker dissatisfaction with the Socialist Party and the Federación Libre de Trabajadores led sugarcane workers, who were demanding increased pay, an eight-hour workday, time and a half for overtime, and equal pay for women, to seek Albizu's leadership when they launched their strike in January 1934.[75] As they wrote to Albizu, "We, . . . workers in Gauyama, abandoned by our Socialist leaders . . . respectfully ask you . . . to lead our movement . . . we consider you the only man capable of leading our protest movement at the current time."[76] Albizu accepted the workers' request and traveled to Guayama the next day, where he addressed a huge crowd of 6,000 striking workers.[77] The workers solicited Albizu's aid precisely due to "the Nationalist Party's anti-imperialist character."[78] Indeed, according to El Imparcial, most striking sugar workers in Guánica "considered themselves Nationalists."[79] Albizu injected energy into the strike and traveled throughout the island meeting with workers and Nationalists to generate and coordinate support for the protest.[80] Although workers failed to obtain their demands, the strike, along with the generalized labor unrest that swept Puerto Rico in the early 1930s, convinced the Roosevelt administration it needed to improve conditions for workers and to send aid to the archipelago to prevent further turbulence.[81] The government enacted an eight-hour workday law and a bill to "provide payments for job-related injuries or deaths."[82]

Albizu was not the only Nationalist leader to back the sugarcane workers. José Lameiro, PNPR secretary general, wrote frequent columns about the strike, in which he simultaneously condemned the Socialist Party, upheld the demands of the workers, and argued that "the real problem is the lack of [national] independence that prevents people from . . . obtaining their sovereignty, [which would] make them the sole arbitrators of their interests."[83]

The Nationalists' differences with the Socialists and the FLT, which stemmed from the FLT's opposition to independence and failure to offer Puerto Rican workers a revolutionary path to winning, resurfaced during the 1938 dockworkers strike. Seven thousand dockworkers in Mayagüez, Ponce, and San Juan struck for higher wages, effectively shutting down the three ports.[84]

The Socialists and the FLT, working with the American Federation of Labor, were confident that the Roosevelt administration and its New Deal policies would ensure justice for the workers.[85] The PNPR, which viewed Roosevelt as the colonialist in chief, had no such expectations. As Nationalist leader Ramón Medina Ramírez astutely stated, "Roosevelt wants to save the capitalist system. . . . For that reason, he needs to support a serious organization [the AFL], which will boost his candidacy in the upcoming election."[86] Fortunately for the dock-workers, the Partido Comunista Puertorriqueño, which was active in the strike, had connections with the U.S.-based Congress of Industrial Organizations (CIO). The CIO galvanized its affiliate, the National Maritime Union (NMU), to support their Puerto Rican comrades, which contributed to the dockworkers' victory.[87] The strike also laid the groundwork for the emergence in 1940 of the more radical Confederación General de Trabajadores (General Confederation of Workers, CGT), which "by 1945 . . . had replaced the FLT as the dominant workers' representative." Puerto Rican Communist Party leaders played an important role in the foundation and flourishing of the CGT.[88]

### PUERTO RICAN COMMUNISTS AND NATIONALISTS

In 1934, the Communist International sent Alberto Sánchez, a former member of the PRNP and a member of the Communist Party USA (CPUSA) in New York City, to Puerto Rico to establish the Puerto Rican Communist Party.[89] The Communist Party, like the Nationalist Party, supported independence. In fact, it was founded on September 23, 1934, the anniversary of the Grito de Lares uprising in 1848.[90] The fledging party affiliated with the Comintern in 1935.[91] Unlike the Nationalist Party, the Communist Party considered the working class as the principal force capable of achieving first independence and then socialism. As César Andreu Iglesias, alternatively Communist Party president or secretary general from 1946 to 1953, stated, "The working class has the greatest interest in transforming society so as to obtain justice. The first stage of this transformation is to convert the ideals of the founding fathers of Lares into reality: conquer political sovereignty for the people."[92]

Communist Party relations with the Nationalists in the 1930s largely reflected Comintern and CPUSA directives. Confronted by the rising threat of fascism, the Comintern adopted Popular Front policies in 1935 and counseled Communist parties around the world to work with anti-fascist forces in their respective countries.[93] To that end, the Communist Party sought closer ties with the Nationalist Party. An exchange of letters between the two parties reveals that while each was quite willing to work with the other, they would do so only on their own terms. Thus, the Communist Party wrote the PNPR that it hoped to "create a popular, united, and anti-imperialist front" and asked the Nationalist Party to join it in forging "a unified struggle and a free Puerto Rico for Puerto Ricans."[94] The PNPR responded that while it welcomed Communist Party support, it insisted on maintaining its independence and, consequently, invited the Communists to join it.[95] Neither party accepted the other's requests.

Relations between the two parties improved over time, largely due to the close association that developed between the Nationalists and the Communist Party USA in New York City in the late 1930s and early 1940s (see chapter 7). The PCP consistently denounced U.S. government repression against the pro-independence organization. Like Communist parties throughout the hemisphere, the PCP called for the release of the Nationalist political prisoners, formed part of the Congreso Pro-Presos Políticos Nacionalistas (National Committee for the Freedom of the Political Prisoners), and condemned the Ponce Massacre.[96] In 1942, Puerto Rican Communists held a national assembly, in which they planned their work for the next two years. In addition to calling for the defeat of fascism, the strengthening of the workers' party, "a free people in a free world," they also advocated the freedom of "Albizu Campos and the Nationalists."[97] Connections between the two parties were so good that the PNPR invited the PCP to address its 1943 national assembly, despite their ongoing political differences. Communist Party president Juan Santos Rivera's speech reflected the party's emphasis on fighting fascism, which it linked to class politics and national sovereignty. As Santos Rivera proclaimed, the party was fighting for a "free and democratic republic," and by "defending the immediate interests of all the people, it would not only improve the economic [well-being] of the masses it would also . . . reinforce unity among the democratic nations against Hitlerism."[98]

The PNPR was not the only organization Puerto Rican Communists sought closer tie with as part of their efforts to advance the anti-fascist struggle. They also pursued a closer connection with the Popular Democratic Party of Luis Muñoz Marín, a relationship that benefitted the Popular Democrats more than it did the Communists. Backing from the CGT in the elections of 1940 contributed to Muñoz Marín's victory, and the Popular Democrats' populist politics attracted some leading Communists, including Alberto Sánchez, to its ranks. The CGT split in 1945, divided between those who supported the Popular Democrats and those who wanted to continue the union's radical politics.[99] The Communist Party lost its leadership role within the now splintered labor movement, and much of its base. By the early 1950s, the party was reduced to a shell of its former self, and the PPD became the dominant and dynamic force in Puerto Rican politics.[100]

## U.S. PLANS IN PUERTO RICO: IMPROVE THE
## ECONOMY AND ELIMINATE THE NATIONALISTS

The U.S. government considered the Nationalist Party's heightened militancy—as exemplified in Albizu's fiery calls for an immediate end to U.S. colonialism, the formation of the Enfermeras de la República and the Cadetes de la República, and Nationalist attacks on colonial officials, as I will go on to detail—as significant threats to its governance and its geopolitical interests in Latin America. These challenges undermined the Roosevelt administration's efforts to project itself as a good neighbor, one whose policy toward Latin America was distinct from that of its bellicose predecessors. To ease these dangers, Washington employed carrot-and-stick tactics: it extended New Deal–type policies to its Caribbean possession, assigned former military officers to rule the archipelago, and intensified surveillance and repression of the Nationalists.[101]

As part of its efforts to improve its image in the hemisphere, in 1934, the Roosevelt government transferred the administration of Puerto Rico and the Virgin Islands from the War Department to the Department of the Interior, headed by Harold Ickes, a civilian member of Roosevelt's inner circle. It appointed Ernest Gruening, a liberal specialist on Latin America, former editor of the *Nation*, and self-defined anti-imperialist, to head the newly created Department of Territories and Island Possessions.[102] A major task Gruening faced was improving the abysmal conditions in which the majority of Puerto Ricans lived.[103] He hoped to use Puerto Rico to showcase the benefits of U.S. rule and enhance the United States' standing in Latin America.[104] To accomplish this, conditions in Puerto Rico had to improve and the PNPR had to be eliminated.

Luis Muñoz Marín, the future governor of Puerto Rico and a key architect of the archipelago's transition to a Free Associated State in 1952, played a significant role in advancing New Deal policies in Puerto Rico. Muñoz had been a member of the pro-independence Liberal Party since 1931. When he was in Washington, D.C., in 1933, Ruby Black, a journalist and friend of Muna Lee, Muñoz Marín's first wife, secured an invitation for him to have tea in the White House with Eleanor Roosevelt.[105] During the visit, Franklin came into the room and the two men met; Muñoz Marín henceforth had the president's ear.[106] Muñoz Marín's friendship with the Roosevelts and his time in Washington convinced him that New Deal funds and reforms would simultaneously boost Puerto Rico's development and hasten its modernization, identify him as the politician responsible for bringing progress to the archipelago, and advance his political career. This realization contributed to his political evolution from a supporter of independence to an ally of the Roosevelts and, later, an opponent of the Nationalists.[107]

The Roosevelt administration established the Puerto Rican Reconstruction Administration in 1935, named Gruening its director, and mandated that it alleviate the severe economic and human crisis afflicting Puerto Rico. Gruening worked directly with Muñoz Marín and Carlos Chardón, an agronomist, chancellor of the University of Puerto Rico, and designer of the Chardón Plan, to accomplish these goals. The Chardón Plan aimed to build a "national base for development" that would "break out of the cycle of colonial underdevelopment" by ending the power of the absentee sugar monopolies, "permitting the growth of local capitalism," and retaining "the benefits of expanded production within the island economy."[108] Key to the project, and one reason why it failed, was its call to redistribute land to small or landless farmers and peasants. Sugar interests, which wielded great political weight, adamantly opposed the proposed breakup of their estates because their mode of production demanded large expanses of land. Political rivalry and infighting among Puerto Rican parties further undermined the agency's efforts.[109]

By 1939, it was clear that the plan had not fulfilled its promises. As Gordon Lewis summarizes, of the $57 million dispensed, "over 50 percent had been spent on labor or personnel services." The number of those who received relief fell far short of those in need. And of all the proposed infrastructure projects, only one, a hydroelectric program under the direction of a Puerto Rican engineer, succeeded.[110] The U.S. government's failure to alleviate the poverty that wracked the archipelago, and thereby lessen popular dissatisfaction and protest, convinced Washington that it needed to eliminate the Nationalists.

A range of U.S. officials and agencies, including the Justice Department, the FBI, and army and navy intelligence, worked with the Insular Police to infiltrate, surveil, imprison, and assassinate members of the Nationalist Party in the 1930s.[111] Their goal was to get rid of the Nationalist Party and end the most vociferous voice for independence. Between 1930 and 1939, at least forty-four Nationalists were arrested on a variety of charges, including intent to kill, explosives, conspiracy, traffic violations, or, in three cases, nothing at all. The police even arrested Nationalists who solicited funds for political prisoners.[112] Demonstrating the hemispheric reach of the U.S. justice system, Juan Antonio Corretjer, secretary general of the Nationalist Party, was arrested and jailed in Havana for three days in July 1935.[113]

In January 1936, Cecil Snyder, a U.S. federal judge in San Juan, wrote to FBI Director J. Edgar Hoover and asked him to "immediately" send an undercover agent to investigate the party. Two weeks later Hoover ordered the FBI to investigate the PNPR, and the agency created a file on party officers.[114] The bureau proceeded to establish "a regular and permanent presence" on the archipelago that initially consisted of two "G-men sent from the United States" and "a network of informers that started in the local police force itself."[115] From then until today, scores of FBI agents and informants, working in Puerto Rico, the United States, and across Latin America, have devoted countless hours and a variety of surveillance techniques and repressive tactics against the Nationalist Party—and other pro-independence forces.[116]

The FBI worked with other U.S. government officials to contain the independence movement. The appointment of Col. Francis E. Riggs as chief of police and Gen. Blanton Winship as governor in 1934 signaled that militarism and repression were central to Washington's rule in Puerto Rico.[117] As Luis Ferrao noted, "Winship was the closest Puerto Rico came to an authoritarian police state."[118] Their aggressive policies escalated politically charged violence on the archipelago and led to counterattacks by the Nationalists.

The first armed confrontation occurred at the University of Puerto Rico in Río Piedras. Tensions were high as some students sought to declare Albizu persona non grata on the campus while others, including the National Federation of Puerto Rican Students (Federación Nacional de Estudiantes Puertorriqueños), denounced their efforts as provocative and anti-Nationalist. On October 24, 1935, the day students assembled to vote on the issue, police stopped a car with four Nationalists driving in front of the university. A struggle ensued, and three Nationalists, one officer, and a passerby were killed.[119] The Nationalists declared their dead comrades "martyrs," and Albizu proclaimed no "impunity" for the murderers, who, he added, would not "last long in Puerto Rico."[120]

Retaliation was not long in coming. In February 23, 1936, Cadetes Hiram Rosado and Elías Beauchamp shot to death Police Chief Riggs, whom they held responsible for the killings in Río Piedras.[121] The police arrested the two men, took them to the station, and summarily executed them, an act that elicited widespread repudiation across Puerto Rico.[122] As further evidence of the support Puerto Ricans felt for the Nationalists, César Ayala and Rafael Bernabe point out that "while many lamented the assassination of Riggs, the killing of the Nationalists was widely condemned." Further, Gruening reported that Muñoz Marín would not utter "even a 'simple statement of sorrow' . . . regarding Rigg's death."[123] In March, the U.S. government seized on Riggs's killing as an opportunity to arrest and charge nine Nationalist leaders with seditious conspiracy to overthrow the U.S. government in Puerto Rico by force.[124]

The U.S. government was concerned about international support for the Nationalists, so before the trial against the Nationalist leaders began, the FBI issued a memo asking its agents in San Juan "to interview the consuls in Puerto Rico as to whether they called on [Albizu] Campos as representatives of their respective governments and whether [Albizu] Campos discussed with them the subject of revolution or a possible revolution."[125] The consulates in question were "Colombia, Mexico, Spain, Santo Domingo, Cuba, and Venezuela."[126] All denied "any contact with [Albizu] Campos or that he called on them."[127]

The first of two trials against the Nationalists began in July 1936. In an important indication of sentiment in the archipelago, the seven Puerto Rican jurors on the jury found the Nationalists not guilty, the five North American jurors found them guilty, and the judge declared a mistrial.[128] However, this ruling did not lessen the U.S. government's determination to see the Nationalists convicted. By coincidence, Rockwell Kent, a well-known U.S. author and artist, happened to be in Puerto Rico the day after the first trial. He attended a reception at La Fortaleza, the governor's mansion, where he was privy to conversations about the trial and plans to ensure a guilty verdict in the next one. Because he was from the United States, the partygoers assumed that he, like they, despised the Nationalists and agreed that they should be found guilty. Kent, however, was close to the CPUSA and opposed racism, imperialism, and colonialism.[129]

The day after the reception, Kent publicly reported what he had heard. According to him, a friend of his had introduced him to Cecil Snyder, "the prosecuting attorney in the Campos case." Snyder, who had urged the FBI to investigate the Nationalist Party, announced that "he had already received a dispatch from Washington telling him . . . that the Department of Justice would back him until he did get a conviction." According to Kent, "Mr. Snyder drew a paper from his pocket and handed it to my friend, saying, 'This is to be my next jury.'" In subsequent testimony to the U.S. Senate, Kent declared that most of the guests at Governor Winship's party had been "Americans . . . and upper-class Puerto Ricans." And, Kent added, "The jury of the second trial . . . contained several men whose connections were identical with those in the list."[130] Unsurprisingly, given the composition of the jury, eight of the Nationalists were found guilty and sentenced to jail terms of between six and ten years, to be served in Atlanta Federal Penitentiary. Juan Juarbe Juarbe, one of the original nine, had previously been absolved of the charges and was out of the country on a mission for the Nationalist Party.[131] Rafael Ortiz Pacheco, who was convicted, escaped and fled to the Dominican Republic.[132]

Kent was not the only North American to denounce the trial and act in solidarity with the Nationalists. Like Kent, U.S. congressman and attorney Vito Marcantonio opposed the imprisonment of the Nationalists and supported Puerto Rican independence, a cause he espoused the rest of his life. Marcantonio visited Puerto Rico shortly after the trial. He served as counsel on an unsuccessful appeal of the Nationalists' conviction and spoke at "mass meetings" in San Juan organized by the National Committee for the Freedom of the

Political Prisoners.[133] He returned to his district, El Barrio in upper Manhattan, the site of the largest number of Puerto Ricans in the United States, and spoke to a crowd of 10,000 Puerto Ricans who had "paraded for three hours through the streets of lower Harlem . . . to protest the attitudes and actions of 'Imperialistic America' in making 'slaves' of the natives of the island." Marcantonio denounced the "'political lynching' of Dr. Pedro Albizu Campos [and] said that the Puerto Rican's case 'will go down in history as another Tom Mooney or Scottsboro boys frame-up.'"[134] His remarks cemented the Nationalists' imprisonment in the twentieth-century history of U.S. repression against radicals and people of color and signaled the commitment of U.S. leftists to fight for their freedom along with Puerto Rico's.

The trial and imprisonment of the Nationalist leaders unleashed protests across the Americas. Activists, intellectuals, trade unions, politicians, and a range of anti-imperialist and leftist organizations and individuals throughout the hemisphere responded with outrage and protest, just as Kent and Marcantonio had done. The seeds of transnational solidarity that Albizu's tour in 1927–30 had planted blossomed into continentwide support for the political prisoners and the cause of independence. Expressions of solidarity flowed from New York City through the circum-Caribbean region and from Buenos Aires and Valparaíso, Chile. Although the U.S. government had hoped to silence the Nationalists by imprisoning them in Atlanta, the opposite occurred. The Nationalist political prisoners and the colonization of Puerto Rico became tangible representations of U.S. imperialism in the region.

# 6 PUERTO RICAN NATIONALISM, LATIN AMERICAN SOLIDARITY, AND THE 1930S HOW GOOD WAS THE GOOD NEIGHBOR POLICY?

In May 1936, U.S Ambassador to Costa Rica Leo R. Sack warned U.S. Secretary of State Cordell Hull of a "a concerted campaign which may become general throughout Latin America to utilize the cause of Puerto Rican independence as a weapon against the United States." He criticized the pro-independence coverage received in the "liberal or radical publications" *Repertorio Americano* and *Liberación* and the Communist Party newspaper *Trabajo*, which had its "usual fulminations against the State Department for what it characterizes as its . . . imperialistic policy in Puerto Rico." To emphasize his concern, Sack added that even the more mainstream *Diario de Costa Rica* carried a statement from Pedro Albizu Campos on his party's policy![1]

Although the ambassador stated that this publicity was of no "great importance," he nonetheless concluded, "The Latin American policy of the American Government which has been manifested in the withdrawal of the marines from Haiti and Nicaragua, the abrogation of the 'Platt Amendment,' and the negotiation of the treaty with Panama has apparently deprived anti-American radicals and 'intellectuals' of their most effective weapons, and they are now obliged to use the situation in Puerto Rico as a justification for continued agitation."[2] Ambassador Sack's prediction that "anti-American radicals and 'intellectuals'" would trumpet the cause of Puerto Rico was right, even though his assumptions about why they did so were wrong. He apparently considered their anti-Americanism the product of an unwarranted, negative attitude that willfully overlooked the merits of the Good Neighbor Policy and maliciously pursued issues that cast the United States in a negative light. He thus ignored Latin Americans' deeply rooted and long-fought struggles against European colonialism and foreign intervention and for nationhood and sovereignty. He equally failed to recognize that support for Puerto Rican independence across the region was neither new nor the latest fad; indeed, it stretched back to the early 1800s.

Discussions of the Good Neighbor Policy typically overlook Puerto Rico because the archipelago was not an independent Latin American nation.[3] Yet for many Latin Americans, Puerto Rico symbolized the unwelcome reality of U.S. domination of the region and exposed the hypocrisy of Washington's pledges of noninterference. Hemispheric opposition to U.S. colonialism in the archipelago and Latin Americans' impassioned demands for the release of the Nationalist political prisoners represent an important critique of the Good Neighbor Policy and evidence of significant hostility to U.S. intervention in the region. This chapter shifts the discussion of the Good Neighbor Policy from Washington and the U.S. officials who formulated it to Latin Americans who questioned both it and Washington's intentions for the region by denouncing U.S. colonialism in Puerto Rico. This offers a counterpoint to Max Paul Friedman's observation that Latin Americans' initial "skepticism in many quarters" to Washington's pledges of nonintervention yielded to trust won, in large part, by "the charismatic personality of FDR."[4]

Despite protests and requests from Latin Americans during the 1930s, the U.S. government did not grant Puerto Rico independence, nor did it release the Nationalist political prisoners. The U.S. government clearly exempted Puerto Rico from the Good Neighbor Policy's pledge not to intervene in the region. Indeed, U.S. interests, not the petitions of Latin Americans or the demands of anticolonial Puerto Ricans, determined U.S. policy toward the archipelago. Puerto Rico was essential to U.S. military defense plans for the Caribbean region given the impending and, after 1941, actual war with Germany and Italy. For that reason, the Nationalists' opposition to the United States' use of Puerto Rico as a military base, refusal to sign up for the draft after it was reinstated in 1940, and persistent calls for independence made conflict between the two inevitable.

## THE GOOD NEIGHBOR POLICY

Franklin Roosevelt set the tone for his administration's foreign policy toward Latin America in his inaugural address on March 4, 1933. He proclaimed, "I would dedicate this nation to the policy of the good neighbor—the neighbor who respects himself and because he does so respects the rights of others—the neighbor who respects his obligations and respects the sanctity of his agreements in and with a world of neighbors."[5] Over the next few years, this lofty but vague statement evolved into the Good Neighbor Policy, which defined the United States' relationship with Latin America for the next decade. The Good Neighbor Policy publicly eschewed unilateral military intervention and promoted cooperation with the region.[6]

The Good Neighbor Policy developed, in part, to ensure that Latin America would be a firm ally and provide a safe and reliable "backyard" in the upcoming war with Germany and Italy. As Justin Hart notes in reference to the Inter-American Peace Conference held in Buenos Aires in December 1936, at which Roosevelt reaffirmed the United States' commitment to nonintervention in

Latin America, "the specter of German rearmament and territorial expansion hung over the proceedings," a perception that sharpened Washington's determination to maintain good relations with governments throughout the hemisphere.[7] Furthermore, dictatorships friendly to the United States, such as Rafael Trujillo in the Dominican Republic and Anastasio Somoza in Nicaragua, ruled much of Latin America. They had strong economic ties to the United States, which reduced the need for U.S. military intervention. Finally, British and French imperial power in the region had fallen steadily since World War I, which made the moment a propitious one for the United States to proclaim a policy based on mutual respect.[8]

The Good Neighbor Policy not only reflected U.S. needs but also responded to the demands of Latin Americans to end foreign intervention in the region. At the Seventh International Conference of American States in Montevideo in 1933, every American nation, with the exception of Bolivia, agreed, "No state has the right to intervene in the internal or external affairs of another."[9] Delegates to the Inter-American Peace Conference in Buenos Aires extended and strengthened the nonintervention agreement of 1933 by pledging that their countries would resolve conflict with "pacific solutions."[10]

President Roosevelt attended the conference. He made the long journey to Buenos Aires by ship to assure Latin Americans that the U.S. government intended to fulfill its promises to respect regional sovereignty as set forth in the Good Neighbor Policy. Argentine president Augustín Justo went overboard to welcome the U.S. president. He decreed the day Roosevelt arrived a holiday and announced, "All the railroads will run special excursion trains to Buenos Aires for the occasion."[11] Roosevelt received a hero's greeting when he arrived; throngs of people lined the streets of the Argentine capital and cheered him as his car passed.[12]

Not all Argentines greeted Roosevelt so warmly. When he addressed the opening of the Inter-American Peace Conference, Liborio Justo, the son of President Justo, shouted, "Down with imperialism!"[13] Other Argentines also protested U.S. imperialism and called for Puerto Rican independence and the release of the imprisoned Nationalist leaders. Intellectuals, students, and politicians formed the Frente Unido Pro Constitución de la República de Puerto Rico (United Front in Favor of the Formation of the Republic of Puerto Rico). Students from the universities of Buenos Aires, Tucumán, El Litoral, and La Plata wrote to U.S. Secretary of State Cordell Hull "demanding the release of [jailed Nationalist] Juan Antonio Corretjer" and an end to the United States' "unjustified persecution . . . of the Nationalists."[14]

Manuel Ugarte, who had represented the Nationalist Party at the Brussels Congress in 1927, headed a group of intellectuals and politicians who sent a similar request to Hull.[15] Sixty-three members of the Argentine Congress, including the president and first and second vice presidents of the Chamber of Deputies, directed a letter to President Roosevelt "respectfully request[ing] of your Excellency the freedom of the Puerto Rican intellectuals, Pedro Albizu Campos, Juan Antonio Corretjer, Clemente Soto Velez, and their noble companions, leaders of the national movement for independence in our brother country."[16] Argentine writers organized authors in Europe, Australia, Asia, and Latin America to sign a petition to Roosevelt calling for the prisoners' freedom.[17] The Society of Journalists and Writers of Argentina penned a similar demand to Roosevelt, adding the Nationalists were imprisoned because they maintained "their traditions of race and language, so deeply rooted in the history of all peoples."[18]

A week before Roosevelt arrived in Buenos Aires, the Argentine Socialist Party held an alternative gathering, the Conferencia Popular por la Paz (People's Peace Conference). Differences of opinion appear to have been particularly strong in the presidential family. Not only did Liborio Justo heckle Roosevelt, but Argentine Socialist and feminist Alicia Moreau de Justo, who was married to the Argentine president, presided over the meeting.[19] At one point she announced, "Now is the time to talk about Puerto Rico," at which point she introduced José Peco, an eminent Argentine jurist who represented the Nationalist Party. Peco spoke of the "tragic history of this American nation" and extolled Albizu Campos, "imprisoned as the result of an order by North American authorities." The assembly then voted unanimously to call on the United States to "recognize the freedom of Puerto Rico."[20]

### NATIONALIST EMISSARIES GENERATE LATIN AMERICAN SOLIDARITY

Nationalist Party members were instrumental in bringing the colonial reality of Puerto Rico and Nationalist opposition to U.S rule to the attention of other Latin Americans. José Enamorado Cuesta, a Nationalist, traveled to the Dominican Republic by ship in 1933 to speak with the Asociación Nacional de Estudiantes de la República Dominicana (National Association of Students of the Dominican Republic) about Puerto Rico's colonial reality. When he arrived in Ciudad Trujillo (modern-day Santo Domingo), Dominican police arrested him. A U.S. Marine on the ship had reported Enamorado Cuesta to Dominican authorities, labeling him "dangerous." After his eventual release, Enamorado Cuesta spoke about Puerto Rico to audiences at the University of Santo Domingo and in San Pedro de Macorís.[21]

Juan Juarbe Juarbe, who had been found not guilty in the trial of the Nationalist Party leaders, became the Nationalist Party's secretary of foreign relations in 1936. He was born in Isabela, Puerto Rico, in 1910.[22] Unlike other Nationalists, Juarbe first made his name in the late 1920s as "one of Puerto Rico's most outstanding basketball players." Juarbe competed in the Second Central American and Caribbean Games in Havana in 1930 and studied for four years at the University of Puerto Rico.[23] He met Albizu following his return from Cuba and shortly thereafter became a Nationalist.[24] Juarbe spent much of the 1930s traveling throughout the Americas advocating a free Puerto Rico and an end to the imprisonment of the Nationalist leaders. He attended the Buenos Aires conference and delivered materials to delegates that, according to the *New York Times*, characterized U.S. rule as one based on "wicked and unjust exploitation."[25] The Nationalist Party also sent Marta Lomar, a Nationalist and president of the Women's Organization for Independence, to Buenos Aires. She represented the party in the peace conference that took place before the Inter-American Peace Conference.[26]

From Argentina, Juarbe traveled to Chile, where he worked with students from the leftist Federación de Estudiantes de Chile (FECH, Federation of Chilean Students) and student leaders from Colombia and Venezuela to plan the Congreso General de Estudiantes de America Latina (General Congress of Latin American Students), scheduled for August 1937. Juarbe served on the Organizing Committee for the conference (fig. 6.1).[27] Members of FECH published a lengthy interview with Juarbe in their newspaper and an article critical of the impact U.S. colonialism had on Puerto Rico's economy.[28] The president and secretary general of FECH wrote a letter to Roosevelt stating that when they had heard his proclamation of the Good Neighbor Policy in Buenos Aires, they had "trust[ed] in the sincerity of your words [and believed] that a new stage of higher understanding and solidarity between your country and Latin America was beginning." However, the Ponce Massacre and the "ignominious imprisonment of Dr. Albizu Campos and Juan Antonio Corretjer . . . sadly expose the falseness of your statement." Therefore, they asked him "to immediately put into practice your Good Neighbor statement and . . . respect the dignity of the men and countries of Latin America."[29]

Juarbe participated in the Pan American Press Conference in Valparaíso in 1937 as a Nationalist Party journalist.[30] There he delivered a "long impassioned speech" denouncing U.S. colonialism that "fired the delegates to a high pitch of intense emotion, a revival of their old antipathy for 'The Colossus of the North.'" Juarbe's powerful performance made him "the hero of the day." Delegates voted for a resolution asking the U.S. government to free the Nationalist prisoners and immediately recognize "the total independence of Puerto Rico." The attendees demonstrated their approval by "rising to their feet, clapping and cheering as they adopted it. Delegates embraced each other with joy." Alfonso

FIGURE 6.1. Juan Juarbe is seated at the end of the table to the left. He is at the 1937 planning meeting of the General Congress of Latin American Students in Santiago, Chile. Source: FECH newspaper, *Quincenario de la Federación de Estudiantes de Chile*, June 1937, 4.

Hernández-Catá, the Cuban minister to Chile, was so moved he "declared he was going to vote for the resolution even if it cost him his diplomatic career."[31] His words and the response they received attest to the Nationalists' ability to generate solidarity with their struggle, the strength of Cuban solidarity with the sister island of Puerto Rico, and the depth of Latin American anger at U.S. intervention in Puerto Rico.

Juarbe next attended a meeting of the Writers' Society of Chile, which convened a few months later. The society referenced Puerto Rico and the imprisoned Nationalist leaders and denounced the hypocrisy of U.S. policy toward the region.[32] It skewered President Roosevelt's advocacy of "permanent peace on this Western Continent"[33] and proclaimed that "this behavior [vis-à-vis Puerto Rico and the Nationalist prisoners] on the part of the powerful nation of North America is at odds with the pompous declarations of democracy President Roosevelt had made recently in the [1936] Peace Congress held in Buenos Aires." The society approved a resolution submitted by Juarbe requesting the release of the prisoners, the end of U.S. colonial rule, and that "all the governments, writers' societies, radio and press, of the Hispanic-American peoples . . . decisively join an energetic campaign in support of the immediate and absolute independence of Puerto Rico."[34] In so doing, the writers' organization added its voice to the chorus of anti-imperialist Latin Americans who condemned U.S. colonialism in the archipelago.

The Nobel Prize–winning author Gabriela Mistral joined with other Chilean writers to condemn the outcome of the Nationalist prisoners' trial. She was so appalled that she wrote a letter to the judge who had sentenced them: "The stature of the convicted Puerto Ricans corresponds, in terms of moral categories and civic significance, to San Martín, O'Higgins, and Artigas, who are [considered] heroes in [South America]. The attitude adopted by the North American authorities toward the Nationalist leaders of Puerto Rico is quite an extraordinary one for us."[35] Speaking as a Chilean and a Latin American, Mistral condemned the U.S. justice system's imprisonment of Albizu, whose stature she considered equal to that of the principal independence leaders of the early nineteenth-century struggle in the Southern Cone against Spanish colonialism.[36]

In order to ensure that Puerto Rico and the imprisoned Nationalists continued to garner the kind of international support Mistral exhibited, the Nationalist Party named Laura Meneses the party's "Plenipotentiary Delegate on a special mission" for Latin America in 1937.[37] Meneses was the ideal person to promote the Nationalist agenda across Latin America because she was highly educated and politically astute. As a Peruvian dedicated to the cause of Puerto Rican independence and the liberation of the Nationalist prisoners, one of whom was her husband, Albizu, she modeled the international solidarity she was tasked with generating. Meneses began her work in Cuba, where she joined Juarbe in 1939. The two lived and worked together in Cuba, Peru, and Mexico to promote support for Puerto Rican independence and the release of the Nationalist political prisoners and other anti-imperialist causes.[38] They joined with anti-imperialist Cubans to form the Cuban Committee to Free the Puerto Rican Patriots in 1939. Meneses was honorary president, Juarbe was secretary general, and the eminent historian Emilio Roig de Leuchsenring was president. Twenty-four other Cubans were vice presidents, four were secretaries, and eighty-five were council members. The group included leading scholars, writers, artists, journalists, lawyers, doctors, and labor leaders.[39]

The committee published "Manifesto a las naciones americanas" (Manifesto to American Nations), which condemned the "irregularities" of the Nationalist leaders' trial. It listed the names of three other Nationalist prisoners in the federal penitentiary in Leavenworth, Kansas, five more in Lewisburg,

Pennsylvania, and seven others in Puerto Rico.[40] The booklet denounced the "treatment that clearly violates the most elemental norms of justice and humanitarianism" to which the prisoners in Atlanta were subjected. The pamphlet stated prisoners could receive or send only one letter, written in English, a week. Their young children could neither visit nor write them. The prisoners had to destroy the letters as soon as they read them. They lacked medical care and were required to work outside in cold weather without adequate clothing.[41] When Gabriela Mistral traveled to Atlanta to visit "our Albizu . . . the prison [told me] he could only receive visits from family members. I was not allowed to see him! I could only look, with such sadness, at the massive prison that held the first Puerto Rican and, perhaps, the first Hispanic American."[42]

## LATIN AMERICANS RALLY BEHIND THE NATIONALISTS

Argentines, Chileans, and Cubans were not the only Latin Americans to advocate Puerto Rican independence and the release of the Nationalist prisoners; a variety of Latin Americans across the region issued similar calls. Three themes emerged in Latin Americans' statements on Puerto Rico. First, they contrasted the language and promises of the Good Neighbor Policy with the reality of U.S. colonialism in Puerto Rico, thereby exposing the hypocrisy of U.S. pledges to end intervention in the region. Second, they spoke of Puerto Rico as Latin American, despite almost forty years of U.S. rule and efforts to portray Puerto Rico as part of the United States. Third, they expressed concern about the imprisoned Nationalist Party leaders and repeatedly requested their release. For these Latin Americans, Puerto Rico became the symbol par excellence of U.S. imperialism in Latin America.

The similarity in language that Latin Americans across the region employed when they spoke about Puerto Rico and the Nationalists is striking; so, too are the number and range of Latin Americans who criticized the United States' treatment of Puerto Rico and Puerto Ricans. They included Argentine politicians, Chilean writers and students, and a variety of Cubans, as we have already seen. Members of the city council of Cartagena, Colombia; Costa Rican Communists and nationalists; a Haitian intellectual; and representatives of the Peruvian anti-imperialist organization the American Popular Revolutionary Alliance. Members of the Popular Front government in Chile also added their voices to those of other Latin Americans calling for an end to U.S. colonialism in Puerto Rico and/or the release of the Nationalist political prisoners. The geographic, national, and positional range of supporters illustrates the depth to which skepticism about the Good Neighbor Policy, opposition to U.S. colonialism in the archipelago, and anger about U.S. government repression of the Nationalists permeated the hemisphere.[43]

As I pointed out in the introduction, not all Latin Americans supported independence for Puerto Rico, nor did they all clamor for the release of the Nationalist prisoners, for reasons that lie beyond the scope of this book. However, those that did largely fell into two distinct but often overlapping categories. First, communist parties and organizations affiliated with them incorporated anticolonialism into their political platforms. Anticolonialism became a fundamental tenet of the Comintern in 1920 when Vladimir Lenin, M. N. Roy, and other colonial delegates pushed the international organization to adopt the policy at the body's second international congress.[44] For Latin American communists from the mid-1930s through the 1940s, anticolonialism and anti-imperialism merged and sharpened their shared commitment to a trans–Latin American identity, condemnation of U.S. intervention and political and economic domination of the region, and critique of that sector of the capitalist class (the non-national bourgeoisie), whose interests were intertwined with those of U.S. corporations and banks. In short, their anti-imperialist stance aligned with and reinforced their domestic program and contributed to their commitment to Puerto Rican independence.

For the second grouping, noncommunist nationalists such as Argentine Manuel Ugarte, Mexican José Vasconcelos, and Haitian Pierre-Moraviah Morpeau, defense of the nation coalesced with their repudiation of foreign intervention throughout the hemisphere, which from the 1920s on primarily meant the United States. Calls for an end to U.S. rule in Puerto Rico went hand in hand with their efforts to preserve their respective nations' language, culture, resources, and economic and political institutions and keep them independent of U.S. interference and control. Opposition to U.S. colonialism in Puerto Rico reflected these Latin Americans' political values and embrace of a trans–Latin American identity. And to the extent that an independent Puerto Rico would weaken U.S. imperialism in the region, as the Nationalist Party had argued since the 1920s, it advanced their work to protect and preserve their nation. The following paragraphs offer examples of Latin Americans who backed the Nationalist Party.

The city council of Cartagena, Colombia, sent a message to the U.S. State Department to convey their "most heated protest for the policy of terror and persecution that the U.S. authorities are carrying out against the people of Puerto Rico who are fighting for national liberation." Echoing the sentiments of many other Latin Americans, they stated, "We would like to make clear to the Department of State that the Good Neighbor Policy so praised by President Roosevelt . . . remains a beautiful concept, lacking any real content, as long as the United States continues to subjugate the weaker peoples in our continent."[45] When the chargé d'affaires in the U.S. legation in Bogota forwarded the council's statement to the secretary of state, he offered his opinion: "I understand that the Municipal Council of Cartagena consists entirely of colored persons, some of whom have questionable reputations. The Legation has replied to the council acknowledging receipt of the communication."[46] The chargé d'affaires' observation that members of the council were "colored persons" with "questionable reputations" likely influenced his decision not to pursue the matter. It also raises the question of whether the councilmen's race constituted the basis for the U.S. official's conclusion about their characters and suggests the power of Jim Crow attitudes to skew the perceptions and actions of the white men who made up the U.S. diplomatic corps in the 1930s.[47] Indeed, the fact that the city council of Cartagena was so angered by the U.S. "policy of terror and persecution . . . against the people of Puerto Rico" that it wrote to the State Department to condemn it and denounce the hollowness of the Good Neighbor Policy should have been of great concern to Washington. The council's outrage, like that of other Latin Americans, exemplifies the depth of anti-imperialist convictions and the breadth of continental solidarity with Puerto Rican independence and the Nationalist Party.

Other renowned individuals and important organizations across the Americas raised their voices in solidarity with the prisoners and Puerto Rico. One such individual was Pierre-Moraviah Morpeau, a Haitian poet, philosopher, nationalist, and close friend of Albizu and Corretjer.[48] He defended Puerto Rican independence and protested the Nationalist leaders' arrest in the press, on the radio, and in public events.[49] Morpeau, who was of African descent, organized a Grande Soirée Puertoricaine in Port-au-Prince in August 1936 and invited the American legation to attend, noting that he had "reserved a special place for them." Selden Chapin, the U.S. chargé d'affaires in Haiti, reported on the proposed event to the State Department. His message revealed a decidedly undiplomatic and racist attitude toward Morpeau that mirrors that of the U.S. chargé d'affaires in Colombia. Chapin wrote that Morpeau "had the effrontery to telephone me at the Legation and ask me if the Legation could lend him a portrait of President Roosevelt to place on the stage." Effrontery? The word suggests someone of inferior status, race, or nationality, displaying insolent or impertinent behavior to a superior. Is this how Chapin thought of Morpeau? Morpeau assured Chapin that "his lecture would not be unfriendly to the United States." However, Chapin responded that the legation could neither lend him the portrait nor attend the event. He would, he informed Washington, "endeavor to ascertain and report upon the substance of Dr. Morpeau's lecture." However, he added, "Port-au-Prince is such a small place . . . any representative of the Legation . . . would undoubtedly be noted and reported to Dr. Morpeau," an outcome Chapin apparently wished to avoid.[50]

FIGURE 6.2. Page in Aprista newspaper in support of a free Puerto Rico. Source: *Trinchera Aprista*, June 1938, 13.

Organizations also supported the Nationalist Party and denounced U.S. colonialism. One such group was APRA. Peruvian Haya de la Torre established APRA in Mexico after his exile from Peru in 1924. Influenced by both the Mexican Revolution and Marxism-Leninism, APRA promoted "anti-imperialist struggle in Latin America."[51] As the name suggests, the party considered itself a revolutionary organization and, at least through the 1930s, stood in solidarity with Puerto Rican independence. *Trinchera Aprista*, APRA's Mexican-based newspaper, published a series of articles about Puerto Rico and the Nationalists in 1938.[52] The first piece included an excerpt from Haya de la Torre's book *¿A dónde va Indoamérica?* (Where Is Indo-America Headed?), in which he defined Puerto Rico as "the only political colony of the United States." Pictures of Albizu, the "apostle of Puerto Rican independence," and

Juan Antonio Corretjer, "another great leader of Puerto Rican independence," followed.[53]

Trinchera Aprista dedicated an entire page titled "Apristas Support a Free Puerto Rico" to news about the U.S. colony (fig. 6.2). The page included a description of the Nationalists' commemoration of the late nineteenth- and early twentieth-century pro-independence figure José de Diego in San Juan, a summary of discussions in the U.S. Senate about Puerto Rico, and texts of telegrams that the Nationalist Party in New York City sent to Mexican president Lázaro Cárdenas congratulating him on his government's expropriation of U.S.-owned oil companies in 1938 and Cardenas's thanks to the Nationalists for their support. Another article reported on Congressman Vito Marcantonio's trip to the Atlanta Federal Penitentiary and his efforts to "obtain the freedom of Albizu Campos and his Puerto Rican prison companions."[54]

Concern about the plight of the Nationalist prisoners in Atlanta also galvanized Costa Rican Joaquín García Monge, the former minister of public education, director of the National Library, and editor of Repertorio Americano.[55] In 1939, García Monge was a Nationalist Party delegate to the meeting of the Ministers of Foreign Relations of the American Republics in Panama, where he spoke out in defense of the prisoners. He had received a letter from Meneses that described the horrible conditions her husband was enduring in the Atlanta Federal Penitentiary. Moved by her letter and his long friendship with and admiration for the Nationalist leaders, García urged the ministers meeting in Panama to solicit the U.S. government to "recognize the independence of Puerto Rico and [grant] the immediate and unconditional release of the Puerto Rican patriots, the hero Pedro Albizu Campos, the poet Juan Antonio Corretjer, and [the other] compañeros" in Atlanta.[56]

The Cuban Committee to Free the Puerto Rican Patriots also directed an appeal for the release of the Nationalist prisoners to the delegates in Panama. Roig de Leuchsenring sent an eighteen-page message from the Cuban committee to the conference. In it he outlined the history of Puerto Rico, the social, political, economic, and cultural impact of U.S. colonial rule, and the history of the independence movement. He concluded the lengthy missive asking the ministers to "request the United States government, as a contribution to the peace and democracy of America and as an act of reparation, immediately recognize the absolute independence of Puerto Rico and restore the freedom of Pedro Albizu Campos and the other Puerto Rican patriots." Narciso Garay, a Panamanian diplomat and the president of the meeting in Panama, did not directly refuse his petition; instead, he noted, "Your lengthy communication . . . was duly read and considered." However, he added, the conference could only address "subjects on the official agenda" since "time was limited."[57] Garay clearly had no intention of allowing such a controversial issue to disrupt the meeting over which he presided.

## LEFT-WING LATIN AMERICANS, PUERTO RICO, AND THE NATIONALIST PRISONERS

Left-wing parties across Latin America rallied in favor of Puerto Rican independence and the Puerto Rican Nationalists during the 1930s. Following the consolidation of fascist regimes in Italy and Germany and the banning of the Communist Party of Germany, the strongest outside the Soviet Union, the Comintern adopted the Popular Front policy in 1935.[58] The policy called on Communist parties globally to join with all prodemocracy forces to fight the principal enemy: fascism.[59] In response, Latin American Communist parties sought alliances and working relationships with antifascist parties across the hemisphere. The International Congress of American Democracies, an organization affiliated with the Communist Party, met in Montevideo, Uruguay, in 1939. Delegates from Argentina, Chile, Colombia, Cuba, Mexico, Peru, the United States, and Venezuela attended. The assembly backed labor rights, urged "President Roosevelt to free Puerto Rico," and called on Americans to fight fascism. According to the New York Times, the "projected international organization . . . has all the aspects of a Pan-American popular front."[60]

One of the most successful efforts to form such a front occurred in Chile, where the Communist, Socialist, and Radical parties, along with several smaller parties, united and won the presidential elections of 1937.[61] The Chilean government supported democratic means of governance and opposed the imprisonment of political opponents. Senator Marmaduke Grove, a Socialist and government leader, sent a telegram to Roosevelt in the name of the National Executive Committee of the Chilean government soliciting the release of Pedro Albizu Campos from the Atlanta Federal Penitentiary in 1939. Echoing earlier references to Roosevelt's avowals of goodwill, the text noted that the Chilean government had "faith in the President's spirit of justice."[62]

The Partido Vanguardia Popular (PVP, Popular Vanguard Party, the Costa Rican Communist Party) exhorted the "workers, intellectuals, students, and honorable men" of Costa Rica and the continent to "support the Puerto Rican people who fight to free themselves from the Yankees." It urged them to "ask for the freedom of Pedro Albizu Campos. Tell President Roosevelt that the Good Neighbor Policy should move from rhetoric to practice by freeing Puerto Rico."[63] The PVP, like the Popular Front government in Chile, called on the Roosevelt administration to square the promises of the Good Neighbor Policy with reality by ending its domination of Puerto Rico and releasing the Nationalist leaders.

*Claridad*, a left-wing Argentine magazine, published a special issue "dedicated to . . . the freedom and independence of Puerto Rico" in June 1939.[64] In it, Antonio Zamora, the editor, thundered against "Puerto Rico's continued domination by the United States," which he characterized as "a legacy of shame and political barbarism." Echoing the stance taken by other Latin Americans, he questioned the sincerity of Roosevelt's Good Neighbor Policy, given the "economic and political situation in which Puerto Rico finds itself." He added, "The cause of Puerto Rico does not just concern Puerto Ricans. It belongs to all the peoples of America. We all have a debt of solidarity with those people who fight for their independence and for the freedom of their apostles [the imprisoned Nationalists]."[65]

Latin Americans continued to protest the imprisonment and exile of the Nationalists into the 1940s. Alfredo Palacios, the Argentine Socialist, senator, and rector of the University of La Plata, was so outraged about their jailing that he wrote President Roosevelt in April 1942 to plea for the freedom of "Albizu Campos, the imprisoned liberator about whom Gabriela Mistral, the greatest poetess of America, has called the first Hispanic American." Palacios, like many other Latin Americans, called on Roosevelt to live up to the promises contained in the Good Neighbor Policy. He reminded Roosevelt that the U.S. president "had repudiated the tendency toward arbitrary imposition, proud exclusivism and isolation, which characterized dollar diplomacy." He lauded Roosevelt's "attitude in the face of the totalitarian danger" and pointed out that the positions he had proclaimed have "created serious responsibilities" with the "Ibero-American nations . . . whose sons love liberty as much as they love life." He proclaimed, "A leader for the independence of his country [Albizu] cannot be jailed in the country ruled by a president . . . who defends global democracy."[66] Palacios joined other Latin American individuals and organizations to demand in vain the United States live up to its image as a democratic nation and free both Puerto Rico and the Nationalist prisoners. As a result of its failure to do so, and as Ambassador Sack had predicted, U.S. colonial rule in Puerto Rico did indeed become a "weapon against the United States" for many Latin Americans. Nonetheless, the U.S. government was unwilling to resolve the issue by granting Puerto Rico independence and setting the Nationalist prisoners free.

## THE U.S. GOVERNMENT FAILS TO RESPOND TO LATIN AMERICAN DEMANDS

The Roosevelt administration was unmoved by Latin Americans' denunciations of U.S. colonial rule over Puerto Rico and failed to acquiesce to their demands to release the Nationalist prisoners primarily because U.S. military

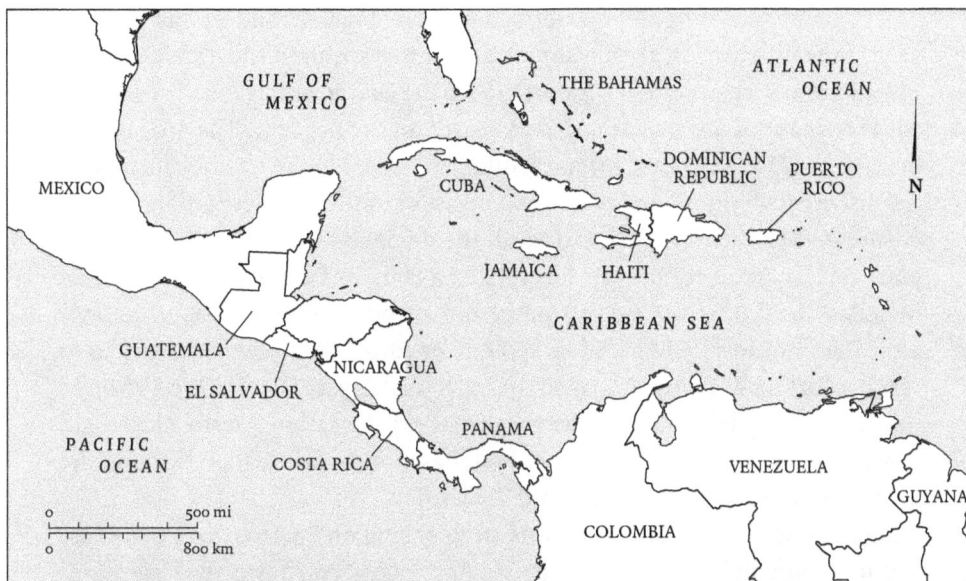

Map of the Caribbean showing Puerto Rico's strategic location as a source of U.S. control in the region. Source: Naomi Robles.

strategists considered Puerto Rico central to Washington's ability to control the Caribbean area against German Nazi incursions. In a 1943 message to the U.S. Senate, President Roosevelt made crystal clear how essential Puerto Rico was to U.S. war plans: "When the present war became imminent, . . . it was obvious that the chain of islands running in a great arc from Florida to the shoulder of South America, enclosing the Caribbean Sea, formed a vast natural shield for the Panama Canal. . . . And of this island shield, *Puerto Rico is the center. Its possession or control by any foreign power—or even the remote threat of such possession—would be repugnant to the most elementary principles of national defense.*"[67]

Roosevelt asserted Puerto Rico's importance to U.S. national defense even as he explained why he backed a congressional bill granting Puerto Ricans the right to elect their own governor.[68] Drawing on the discourse of rights and justice in which FDR often enveloped his policies, he declared, "The principles for which we are now fighting require that we should recognize the right of all our citizens—whether continental or overseas—to the greatest possible degree of home rule." Roosevelt then proceeded to undercut the pledge of sovereignty he appeared to be extending to Puerto Ricans when he added that he had no intention of ceding ultimate control to them. "The fiscal relationship of the insular government to the Federal Government would not be altered, nor would the ultimate power of the Congress to legislate for the Territory."[69]

U.S. military designs for Puerto Rico were not new; indeed, as we have seen, they were one of the reasons Washington acquired the archipelago in 1898. Puerto Rico's strategic importance to the United States increased as war with Germany and Italy loomed ever nearer on the horizon. The archipelago became the United States' primary military outpost in the Caribbean, and its defensive capabilities would soon extend as far as the southern Atlantic.[70] To ensure Puerto Rico's capacity to fulfill the demands the U.S. military would place on it, a naval committee formulated a plan for Puerto Rico in 1938 that included the "construction of a naval and air base in Puerto Rico." Shortly after Germany invaded Poland in September 1939, the U.S. military began to "expropriate land" in Aguadilla, on the northwest coast of Puerto Rico, to build the base, Borinquen Field.[71] The pattern of expropriating Puerto Rican land continued, as the U.S. armed forces built bases and other installations on the islands of Culebra, Puerto Rico, and Vieques.

Roosevelt Roads navy base, consisting of land on Puerto Rico's east coast and the island of Vieques, was massive. At 37,000 acres, it was the largest offshore U.S. Navy base in the western hemisphere, big enough to shelter the entire British navy, should such refuge be required.[72] As part of the project, the U.S. Navy acquired two-thirds of the inhabited island of Vieques and, after evicting the population from their homes, built a base in 1941.[73] The U.S. Army also beefed up its presence in Puerto Rico, constructing airfields and base facilities to support "the naval forces whose task it was to control the Caribbean Sea."[74] By 1945, the U.S. military operated more than thirty installations in Puerto Rico, including air fields, naval bases, forts, supply and storage stations, and camps.[75] The U.S. armed forces valued Puerto Rico's strategic position, and because the archipelago belonged to the United States, they could requisition the land they desired, regardless of the people who lived there and depended on it for their livelihood (fig. 6.3).[76]

Puerto Rico had one more resource the U.S. military appreciated: men who could be drafted to serve in its ranks. When the U.S. government made Puerto Ricans U.S. citizens in 1917, Puerto Rican men became eligible for the draft. In 1940, when the U.S. government reinstituted the draft—called "military training" at the time—as part of its mobilization for war, the Nationalist Party was forced to make a choice: how to respond to the draft?[77] Their opposition to it was not a given. In fact, as Ché Paralitici explains, Nationalist Party members did not agree on whether to reject the draft. Some Nationalists unequivocally opposed it, characterizing it as one more colonial imposition. Others argued that they should sign up, but only if Puerto Rico became independent. A third sector believed that it was their duty to fight fascism, a position they shared

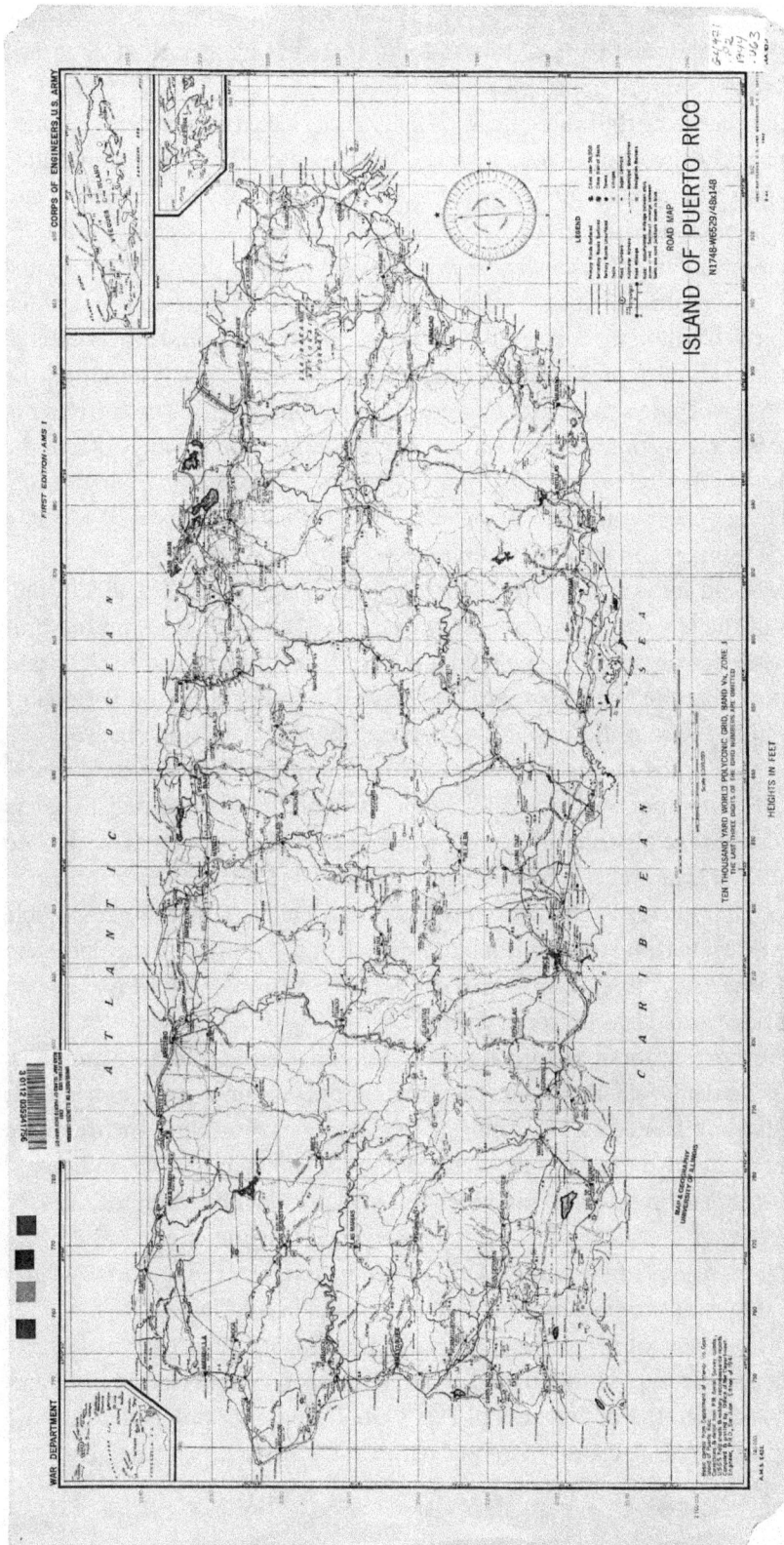

FIGURE 6.3. War Department map of Puerto Rico produced by the U.S. Army Corps of Engineers, 1944. Source: Digitization Services at the University Library, University of Illinois at Urbana-Champaign.

with the Communist Party of Puerto Rico; some even joined the U.S. armed forces to get military training.[78]

After debating the issue, the Nationalist Party leadership not only decided to oppose the draft but declared Puerto Rican men exempt from it and called on draft-age Nationalist men to evade it. Albizu drew on his training at Harvard Law School to build a legal and political case against conscription for Puerto Rican men and in defense of those arrested for violating the draft. He argued that conscription did not per se violate the Thirteenth Amendment, which prohibited involuntary servitude, because voters in the United States elected the senators and representatives who implemented the law. Therefore, the law had the people's mandate. However, Albizu contended, "The law was not applicable to Puerto Rico because none of the accused [of having violated the draft law] had voted to elect the Congress," since Puerto Ricans could not vote in any federal election.[79] In other words, drafting Puerto Rican men to fight in the U.S. military constituted involuntary servitude and was illegal.

It should come as no surprise that the party's legal and political interpretation of the law carried no weight with the U.S. government, and the pro-independence organization paid a high price for its opposition to the draft. Obeying either their conscience or the party's dictates or both, 100 Nationalist men refused to join the U.S. military during World War II and received sentences ranging from one to five years' imprisonment.[80] In the early 1940s, the U.S. government convicted four successive bodies of Nationalist leaders of "conspiring to obstruct the draft" and exiled them to prisons in the United States. After Nationalist Party vice president Julio de Santiago was imprisoned in 1942, Pedro Pérez Pagán, who was eighty years old and therefore ineligible for the draft, became the interim party president to ensure that the party had at least one leader free. Pérez Pagán remained vice president until 1944, when de Santiago was released from prison.[81]

The fate of Ramón Medina Ramírez, interim president of the Nationalist Party, is particularly heart-wrenching. Not only did Washington jail him in 1941, but it also imprisoned his five sons, including one who was blind and therefore exempt from the draft, because all six refused to enlist in the U.S. military.[82] This family's willingness to sacrifice their own personal freedom for the sake of that of their motherland, a quality shared by many members of the party, contributes to explaining why the U.S. government viewed the Nationalist Party as the single most important threat to its rule in Puerto Rico.

The U.S. government's occupation of Puerto Rico, its usurpation of Puerto Rican land to build military bases, and the imprisonment of Nationalist Party leaders exposed the hollowness of FDR's Good Neighbor proclamations and the hypocrisy of U.S. claims to uphold democracy. Instead, as Nationalist Party organizers and Latin American anti-imperialists asserted, they revealed that U.S. policy for the region remain rooted in protecting U.S. interests, not in establishing relations based on mutual respect and neighborliness. Further, Puerto Rico became a symbol of U.S. intervention in the region, and many Latin Americans considered the imprisoned Nationalists icons of anti-imperialist resistance. Solidarity with the Nationalist Party and Puerto Rican independence extended to the United States. After their release from the Atlanta Federal Penitentiary in the early 1940s, many of the Nationalist Party leaders traveled to New York City, where they worked closely with the Communist Party USA and members of the Harlem Ashram, a pacifist organization. It was also in New York that the American League for Puerto Rico's Independence, the first U.S.-based solidarity organization, formed in 1944.

# 7 PUERTO RICAN NATIONALISM IN NEW YORK CITY IN THE 1930S AND 1940S

When Pedro Albizu Campos and fellow Nationalist Luis F. Velázquez walked out of the Atlanta Federal Penitentiary in June 1943, several supporters were waiting. The welcoming committee included Juan Antonio Corretjer and Julio Pinto Gandía of the Nationalist Party and Samuel Neuberger, a Communist Party attorney sent by Congressman Vito Marcantonio and Earl Browder, secretary general of the Communist Party USA, to help them.[1] Neuberger's mission was to make sure Albizu got to New York City as swiftly and safely as possible. One major challenge Neuberger faced was how to travel with Albizu. Neuberger was white, and Albizu, according to U.S. racial constructions of the time, was Black. Since trains in the South were segregated, they could not travel together.

Neuberger quickly devised a plan. He reserved a compartment on the afternoon train and organized two other white people to join him. Neuberger recalled that he "advised each one to take Don Pedro under the arm," while he went on ahead. "When we got [to the train station], I screamed, 'Step aside, take that man aboard.' We [Albizu and the white men] walked right through [the station] . . . to the compartment. The psychology was simple. [H]earing this . . . authoritative voice that said step aside [and] had to be obeyed, [the crowd] did. We got into the compartment [and] closed the door. The porter was a Black man; he was obviously sympathetic. He acted like he saw and knew nothing, so we carried on."[2] Browder and Marcantonio met them at the station in New York City. According to FBI records, Browder and Marcantonio advised Albizu to "lie low."[3] Albizu, whose already poor health had greatly deteriorated during his five years of imprisonment, spent most of the next year and a half in Columbus Hospital in Manhattan.[4]

New York City in the 1940s was the headquarters of the CPUSA and the Nationalist Party, the site of a growing Puerto Rican community, and where Vito Marcantonio's congressional district was located.[5] It was where radical U.S. pacifists joined together in 1940 to form the Harlem Ashram, an organization that subsequently took up the cause of Puerto Rican independence. It was where North Americans organized the American League for Puerto Rico's Independence, a solidarity committee that called for an end to U.S. colonialism in the archipelago.

## THE NATIONALISTS AND NEW YORK CITY

Although Puerto Ricans had been immigrating to New York City since the late 1800s, they did so in greater numbers during the first three decades of the twentieth century. Even before the Jones Act made Puerto Ricans U.S. citizens in 1917, a Supreme Court ruling in 1904 declared that Puerto Ricans could "enter the [United States] without obstruction."[6] The relative facility with which they could travel to the United States, combined with the lack of jobs, even low-paying ones, in the archipelago pushed Puerto Ricans to seek work in New York. U.S. government restrictions on immigration in the 1920s resulted in a sharp decline in European immigrants, which increased the demand and opportunities for Puerto Rican laborers.[7] In 1910, roughly 2,000 Puerto Ricans lived in the United States; by 1940, that number had shot up to 69,967, primarily in New York City.[8] The center of the Puerto Rican community was East Harlem, in Upper Manhattan, although Puerto Ricans also lived in the Bronx, Brooklyn, and other parts of Manhattan.

Puerto Rican Nationalist organizations had existed in New York City since the early 1920s. In 1922, the Asociación Nacionalista (Nationalist Association), made up of Puerto Rican immigrants, sponsored a series of assemblies to stimulate community engagement with politics in Puerto Rico and the Antilles. Association members invited all those they considered "nuestra raza [Latin Americans, especially Dominicans, with whom they had close ties] living in New York City to come to discuss the future of our raza in América."[9] A number of "distinguished representatives of the Hispanic communities in New York answered the Borinquen society's call" and attended the meeting. Américo Lugo, the Dominican nationalist who welcomed Albizu to Santo Domingo in 1927 and subsequently led a Dominican committee in solidarity with Puerto Rican independence, spoke at the event. He "exalted Puerto Ricans' nationalist sentiment" and praised the spirit of the attendees, who "represented the patriotic feelings that beat in the hearts of Puerto Ricans."[10]

In 1930, New York Nationalists officially affiliated with the Puerto Rican Nationalist Party and became "an integral part of the nationalist movement in Puerto Rico."[11] The party had headquarters in Harlem and three sub-juntas, or branches, in Brooklyn, Bronx, and Washington Heights, Manhattan. According to party leaders, the pro-independence organization "had well over 8,000 members" and "a definite ideological influence over more than 50,000 Puerto Ricans" living in the five boroughs at the end of the decade.[12] The party enjoyed "friendly" relations with a plethora of Puerto Rican, Latin American, and leftist organizations, including the CPUSA, in New York.[13]

The Nationalist Party had deep roots in the Puerto Rican and Spanish-speaking communities of New York. Lydia Collazo, the daughter of Nationalist Party members Rosa and Oscar Collazo, grew up in a milieu imbued with patriotic sentiment and political activity.[14] In her memoirs she recalls the vibrant social and political life she led as a supporter of independence embedded in the Puerto Rican community in the 1940s. Because the party was chronically short of money, it dedicated much energy to fundraising. It held dances to raise money to cover the costs of maintaining party headquarters and to publish its monthly magazine, Revista Puerto Rico. After the Nationalist prisoners were released from the penitentiary, the party contributed money to their living expenses. Two or three times a year the party sponsored gala affairs with three orchestras that lasted into the early hours of the morning. Women wore evening dresses and men suits and ties or tuxedos. The dances were well organized. Members of the organizing committee greeted everyone who entered and "pinned a flower on the lapel of men's suits and handed a flower to every woman." Nationalist Party members responsible for security during the event were not allowed to "drink alcohol or dance until the end of the dance." As a result, the dances "were famous among the Spanish-speaking colony [of New York City]. People liked to go [to the dances] because they felt safe, [appreciated] the behavior of the Committee, and [supported] the goal of the fiesta." In fact, Collazo noted, "Some people donated more than the cost of the ticket because they knew it was to support Don Pedro [Albizu], thus for the Motherland."[15]

## THE NATIONALIST AND COMMUNIST PARTY ALLIANCE

The Nationalist Party in New York City worked with the Communist Party USA and various affiliated organizations beginning in the mid-1930s. Relations between the organizations had not always been congenial. In 1932, tensions between the two groups ran particularly high. At issue was the Nationalists' position that Puerto Ricans' political priority was to end U.S. colonial rule over the archipelago. The pro-independence party considered Puerto Ricans outside the archipelago "exiles" whose primary duty was to redeem "our native soil." The CPUSA, on the other hand, supported both independence and the fight against "exploitation being suffered by Puerto Ricans in New York." The differences between the two organizations escalated, and members of the two parties challenged each other at public rallies, which occasionally led to street fights and once culminated in the murder of a Nationalist, Angel Feliú. The "crime was attributed to Communists."[16]

Between 1933 and 1935, relations between the groups improved owing to the confluence of the two parties' political beliefs and interests and changes in the Communist International's politics and directives. The CPUSA, following the Comintern's lead, had opposed U.S. colonialism in Puerto Rico since its inception, so that was never a bone of contention. But in the late 1920s, in accordance with the Comintern, it adopted the class versus class political line and rejected alliances with any social democratic forces, which effectively precluded a relationship with the PNPR.[17] However, the rise and success of fascist parties in Europe radically altered the political scene and the Comintern's policies (discussed in chapter 6). Instead of calling for the unification of the Left on its terms, the CPUSA now sought alliances with all those who opposed fascism, which greatly contributed to the growing rapprochement between the CPUSA and the PNPR. The PNPR, for its part, was quite willing to work with the CPUSA because it was able to provide the Nationalists with money and resources, which it needed, and mobilize its cadres and sympathizers in support of causes dear to Nationalists' hearts.

The second reason relations between the two organizations improved centered on Vito Marcantonio, the U.S. congressman from East Harlem, whose district contained the highest concentration of Puerto Ricans in the United States.[18] Marcantonio not only spoke out and submitted bills in favor of Puerto Rican independence in the U.S. Congress but also advocated for the rights and needs of Puerto Ricans.[19] In addition to being one of Albizu's attorneys, he also pressed for better treatment for him and the other Nationalist prisoners in the penitentiary. Marcantonio became president of International Labor Defense (ILD), the U.S. branch of the Comintern's International Red Aid in 1937.[20] In that capacity, he made sure that the ILD sent monthly stipends of roughly five dollars to each of the Nationalist prisoners in the penitentiary.[21]

Although Marcantonio was not a member of the CPUSA, he was close to the party. His position as a congressman and commitment to using his public prominence to speak out on the local and national political stage in defense of progressive causes ranging from the decarceration of Tom Mooney, a political prisoner and labor and left-wing activist, to support for the Spanish Republic and the drive to end the poll tax that discriminated against poor people, especially Blacks, was invaluable to the Communist Party.[22]

Winning the votes of Puerto Ricans in his district was critical to Marcantonio's victory, and obtaining the political backing of the PNPR greatly contributed to his ability to do so. As Gilberto Concepción de Gracia and PNPR leaders observed, "In 1936, [the Nationalists] played an active part in the elections . . . by backing the candidacy of Vito Marcantonio. . . . Again in 1938 the organization threw its forces behind the candidacy of Marcantonio, *and its support was one of the deciding factors of his overwhelming victory.* In Marcantonio, they supported a great and proved friend of the Puerto Rican people and the national liberation movement, and their policy now is to pledge active support for any candidate who pledges himself to fight for Puerto Rican independence."[23] Thus, in addition to their joint support for Puerto Rican independence, the two parties benefited, albeit in different ways, from their mutual backing of each other.

Signs of their budding political alliance appeared in the mid-1930s when the Club Hostos (named for Eugenia María de Hostos, the famous nineteenth-century Puerto Rican independence leader), headed by Puerto Rican CPUSA member Bernardo Vega, invited Nationalist Filiberto Vázquez to speak on the "Foundations of the Nationalist Struggle in Puerto Rico."[24] The two organizations also joined with labor union federations and civic groups in January 1935 to support the dockworkers' strike then taking place in San Juan. According to Bernardo Vega, the joint activities "helped overcome the hostilities that Feliú's death had provoked between the nationalists and the Communists in New York."[25] It also paved the way for future political collaboration.

The two organizations jointly sponsored a large pro-independence march in September 1935 to commemorate the uprising against Spanish colonialism in Lares in 1868. The protest wound its way through East Harlem, the heart of the "Hispanic colony" in Manhattan. As one of the speakers said, "In the face of imperialism, we need a united front. The Communist Party is willing to unite with the Nationalists and the Revolutionary [Party] until we break the chains just as our ancestors joined together sixty-seven years ago to fight against Spanish oppression." Demonstrators carried banners bearing militant slogans such as "Any Puerto Rican who does not defend the freedom of his homeland is a traitor," "The Association for the Defense of Puerto Rico fights for the immediate and absolute independence of Puerto Rico!" and "Revolution will save Puerto Rico." The large crowd watched the parade from the sidewalk or their windows and rooftops, and many people joined in. Although most of the speakers were men, at least one woman, Ana López, a member of the Hijas de la Libertad (Daughters of Liberty), a Nationalist women's group, addressed the crowd.[26]

The relationship between the two organizations deepened in response to increased U.S. government repression of the Nationalist Party in Puerto Rico. Puerto Ricans in New York responded angrily to the conviction and sentencing of Nationalist Party leaders in San Juan in August 1936. A range of organizations, including the "Harlem Section of the Communist Party, the Centro Obrero Español, the International Cigarmakers' Union, and the Committee Against War and Fascism" rallied in support of the political prisoners.[27] Marcantonio, who had visited Albizu in jail in San Juan and conferred with him about his case, spoke to a large and angry crowd at one event in East Harlem.[28]

The opening sentence of a *New York Times* article captures the outrage Puerto Ricans felt at the impending imprisonment of the Nationalist leaders. It also attests to the radical, left-wing sentiments of many of the poor and working-class inhabitants of East Harlem. "Ten thousand Puerto Ricans, representing a score of political and social clubs in the city, paraded for three hours through the streets of Harlem yesterday afternoon to protest the attitude and actions of 'Imperialistic America' in making 'slaves' of the natives of the island." As they marched, they shouted, "Free Puerto Rico!" and "Down With Yankee Imperialism!" Their chants sparked a responding chord among residents in the area, "populated mostly by Negroes and Spaniards," who "leaned out of windows and over the edges of roof-tops and added their protests to those of the demonstrators." When Marcantonio spoke to the crowd, he simultaneously racialized and politicized the conviction of the Nationalists and linked it to past cases in which the CPUSA had been involved. He characterized their imprisonment as a "political lynching" that "will go down in history as another Tom Mooney or Scottsboro Boys frame-up."[29] His comparison implies that Blacks, Puerto Ricans, and Communists had a common history and reality of oppression, whether this be due to racism or politics or both. Marcantonio's comments also suggested that a shared history of attacks provided the basis for unity among these diverse targets of government and popular violence.

The Ponce Massacre in March 1937, when Insular Police acting under the orders of U.S.-appointed Governor Winship shot and killed nineteen and wounded over 150 unarmed marchers at a Nationalist Party rally, unleashed a wave of anger among Puerto Ricans in New York City. Nationalists, Communists, and Marcantonio decried the violence at a community meeting in Harlem.[30] The CPUSA joined a protest sponsored by the local branch of the PNPR. Forty picketers marched on Fifth Avenue for four hours to protest the assault on Puerto Ricans. One demonstrator carried a sign that read, "Governor Winship Is Responsible for the Attack of the Police Against the People of Puerto Rico."[31]

The PNPR and CPUSA then called for the formation of the American Committee for the Defense of Puerto Rican Political Prisoners. The preliminary meeting of the group was held in the PNPR's office and included representatives from the CPUSA and affiliated organizations, including the "American League Against War and Fascism, the International Workers Order, the International Labor Defense, the Communist Party, the Young Communist League, and organizers in Lower Harlem." The committee announced plans to canvass "liberals and educators in the United States for the purpose of forming a committee of

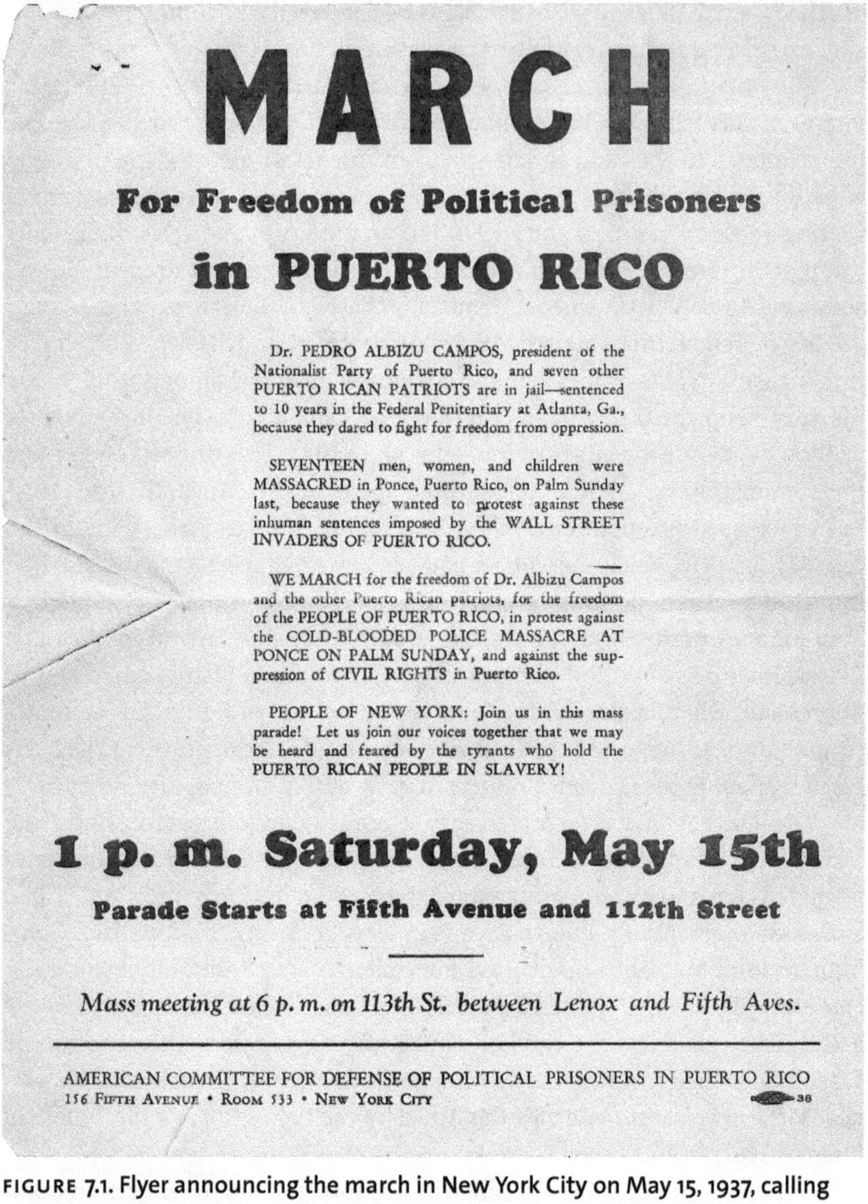

# MARCH

## For Freedom of Political Prisoners

## in PUERTO RICO

Dr. PEDRO ALBIZU CAMPOS, president of the Nationalist Party of Puerto Rico, and seven other PUERTO RICAN PATRIOTS are in jail—sentenced to 10 years in the Federal Penitentiary at Atlanta, Ga., because they dared to fight for freedom from oppression.

SEVENTEEN men, women, and children were MASSACRED in Ponce, Puerto Rico, on Palm Sunday last, because they wanted to protest against these inhuman sentences imposed by the WALL STREET INVADERS OF PUERTO RICO.

WE MARCH for the freedom of Dr. Albizu Campos and the other Puerto Rican patriots, for the freedom of the PEOPLE OF PUERTO RICO, in protest against the COLD-BLOODED POLICE MASSACRE AT PONCE ON PALM SUNDAY, and against the suppression of CIVIL RIGHTS in Puerto Rico.

PEOPLE OF NEW YORK: Join us in this mass parade! Let us join our voices together that we may be heard and feared by the tyrants who hold the PUERTO RICAN PEOPLE IN SLAVERY!

## 1 p. m. Saturday, May 15th

### Parade Starts at Fifth Avenue and 112th Street

Mass meeting at 6 p.m. on 113th St. between Lenox and Fifth Aves.

AMERICAN COMMITTEE FOR DEFENSE OF POLITICAL PRISONERS IN PUERTO RICO
156 FIFTH AVENUE • ROOM 533 • NEW YORK CITY                    36

FIGURE 7.1. Flyer announcing the march in New York City on May 15, 1937, calling for the freedom of Puerto Rican political prisoners and protesting the Ponce Massacre and the suppression of civil liberties. Source: Earl Browder Papers, Special Collections Research Center, Syracuse University Libraries.

inquiry into the conditions in Puerto Rico." It urged people to send "resolutions to President Roosevelt calling for a congressional investigation of the American administration of the island of Puerto Rico."[32]

## THE NATIONALIST PARTY IN PUERTO RICO
## FACES A CHALLENGING REALITY

One reason the Nationalist Party leadership established itself in New York City had to do with the difficult situation the party faced in Puerto Rico. All the Nationalist Party leaders who had been imprisoned in the Atlanta Federal Penitentiary were released by 1943, and like Albizu, several of them—including Corretjer, Luis F. Velázquez, and Clemente Soto Vélez—took up residence in New York City. In effect, the leadership of the Nationalist Party relocated there, which made a lot of sense.[33] The Ponce Massacre, the exile of the party leadership, and heightened levels of repression had weakened the PNPR in Puerto Rico. The Insular Police's attack in Ponce angered Puerto Ricans across the island; it also traumatized some of the participants and scared some party members and supporters in the archipelago. Dominga de la Cruz's story offers insight into how deeply disturbing the shootings in Ponce were.[34] De la Cruz was the Nationalist who picked up the Puerto Rican flag after the woman carrying it was shot in the Ponce Massacre. Years later, de la Cruz recalled how much the shootings tore her up emotionally. After that day, she said, "I kept on working, but I wasn't the same. I was exhausted, nervous, deeply affected. I had to leave [the party]. They [the party leadership] recommended I see a psychologist," who suggested she "get involved in the theater." She followed his advice and began to perform in public. Laura Meneses saw her perform and encouraged her to go to Cuba for training. De la Cruz lived in Cuba from 1942 to 1944. She returned to Puerto Rico seven years after the Ponce Massacre but was still so distraught that she had to leave. She lived in Mexico for the next sixteen years but maintained contact with the party and remained committed to Puerto Rican independence. Sometime after 1943, she traveled to New York City to visit Albizu following his release from prison, but she was no longer psychologically able to be the party activist she had been.[35]

Colonial officials continued to harass the party, most likely hoping to achieve its demise. As José Manuel Dávila points out, Governor Winship "pressured mayors in Puerto Rico to prevent the Cadetes and the Enfermeras from carrying out their traditional parades and military practices under any and all circumstances."[36] Thus, when the Nationalists wanted to hold their annual pilgrimage to Lares in September 1937, the town mayor authorized them to hold their morning activities, which largely consisted of "a mass and the placing a floral offering in the Plaza de la Revolución." However, "he denied the party permission to conduct its political activities in the afternoon."[37] This is in stark contrast to the warm reception the mayor and other city officials extended to the Nationalists in 1930. The president of a local social club courageously invited the party to use his club's headquarters to carry out its afternoon program, an offer the party accepted. Armed police surrounded the gathering, "continually threatening to repeat the crimes of the other massacre [in Ponce]," in an obvious effort to intimidate participants.[38]

Indisputably, people left the party in response to the repression, threats, and harassment.[39] As one Nationalists told Dávila, after the massacre, "we never saw [a large number of cadetes and enfermeras] again." Or, as another confided to him, "a lot of the young people withdrew [from the party], whether out of fear or for some other reason."[40] Nationalist Party membership continued to decline over the next decade.[41] This, in turn, led to fewer resources to support the party, precisely when the imprisonment of so many of its members required more funds to defend and support them and provide for their families.

The problems that beset the party explain, in part, why the leadership was open to new approaches and allies. When the Nationalists were imprisoned in Atlanta, they developed a friendship and camaraderie with Earl Browder, the secretary general of the Communist Party, who was also jailed there.[42] Through conversations with him, they became convinced that it was not only possible but necessary to "create in the United States a powerful solidarity movement with the independence of Puerto Rico." Further, they understood that the CPUSA "had committed itself to financially and organizational[ly] support the undertaking."[43] The CPUSA had already made its support for the Nationalist Party very clear when, for example, Earl Browder met with Under Secretary of State Sumner Welles to urge him to convince President Roosevelt that "Albizu Campos be released from Atlanta without the probationary restriction."[44]

One other reason why the Nationalists established party headquarters in the United States was that the Communist Party and the Puerto Rican and Latino communities in New York City offered them the resources and backing they needed to rebuild and expand. And on a pragmatic level, Albizu had to complete four more years of probation in the United States before he was legally able to return to Puerto Rico. What better place to recuperate and rebuild in than New York?[45]

### THE HARLEM ASHRAM: U.S. PACIFISTS AND SOLIDARITY

Albizu, who emerged from prison in poor health, spent the next seventeen months in Columbus Hospital in Manhattan. He turned his hospital room into a receiving area where he met with Puerto Rican comrades, U.S. supporters, and international visitors. Albizu's hospital sojourn not only improved his health but also afforded the Nationalist Party the opportunity to strengthen its local organization, establish relations with new and important people and organizations in the New York area and beyond, and develop enduring bonds of solidarity with a group of pacifists organized in the Harlem Ashram.

Two U.S. Methodist missionaries, Ralph Templin and Jay Holmes Smith, began the Harlem Ashram in 1940. Both Templin and Smith had served in India at a time when Britain ruled the country and brooked no questioning of its power. Missionaries "could remain in India only as long as they were loyal to the British Raj."[46] Templin and other missionaries were expelled from India because they criticized Britain's unilateral declaration, in 1939, that India, like its colonial ruler, was at war with Germany despite Britain's failure to consult with the Indian people before issuing this statement.[47]

Following their return to the United States, the two men established the Harlem Ashram, whose members committed themselves to principles of nonviolence, a life of "voluntary poverty," and the practice of direct action in pursuit of social and racial justice and "inter-racial reconciliation."[48] Because they considered "racial justice as America's No. 1 problem . . . and most of [their] work concern[ed] the Negro-white aspect of this problem," they established their project in Harlem, which they characterized as "the Negro capital of the new nation." They added, "Living here makes it easy for us to contact Negro leaders." They added a presumably well-intentioned declaration that nonetheless betrays a profound lack of understanding of what it means to be Black in the United States. "Living here helps us who are white to get something of the 'feel' of being a Negro in America."[49]

The Harlem Ashram worked with other pacifist organizations such as the Fellowship of Reconciliation (FOR), founded in the United States in 1915 by A. J. Muste and Jane Addams, among others.[50] Members of the ashram initially focused on India and were arrested for peacefully protesting at the British embassy in Washington in favor of a free India. Templin and Smith also undertook an eight-day fast to protest "the refusal of the British Government to release Mahatma Gandhi."[51] Three other people had joined the ashram by 1941. One of them was Ruth Reynolds, an antiracist pacifist.

As Andrea Friedman writes, Reynolds was a committed pacifist and, therefore, "an unlikely convert to the cause of militant nationalism."[52] However, Reynolds, like other members of the ashram, was profoundly antiracist and believed passionately in social justice. Reynolds grew up in South Dakota in a Methodist family. One day her father took her to meet a chief of the Oglala Sioux. Afterward, she asked her father about the Sioux and, upon learning their history, told him that "this place where we live should belong to the Indians." As she commented years later, "This was the first time I consciously understood that there was great injustice in this country."[53] While studying at Northwestern University she came into contact with the Fellowship of Reconciliation and later attended FOR training at the Harlem Ashram, which is how she became involved with the pacifist group.

Reynolds and other members of the ashram learned about Puerto Rico through a Puerto Rican Baptist minister they had met doing community work in the neighborhood. They invited him over for dinner and, after talking for a while, "pressed him for his opinions on our work." The minister told them that "he found it difficult to understand how people living in a Puerto Rican community, demonstrating for the independence of India, . . . seemed to have no similar concern for what our own government was doing in Puerto Rico." His comment fell like "a bombshell" because the group had "never thought about it." It also pushed Reynolds and the rest of the ashram to learn more about Puerto Rico and, presumably, to challenge both their relationship to their government and their privileged position as white people in an imperialist nation.[54]

Reynolds and other members of the ashram next met Nationalist Party leader Julio Pinto Gandía, who educated them about Puerto Rico. Their discussions deepened their understanding of the extent of injustice committed by the United States. As a result, in January 1944 the ashram organized a protest calling for India's independence, and for "the first time we joined the Puerto Rico issue with our demonstration."[55] Reynolds was arrested that day, and pictures in the newspaper showed her getting into the paddy wagon with, she said, a "great big grin on my face." Albizu liked that Reynolds smiled while being hauled away by the police so much that "he asked Pinto to bring me to see him," and the two got along famously. "I was very close to him from that time til his death."[56]

## THE AMERICAN LEAGUE FOR PUERTO RICO'S INDEPENDENCE

Members of the Harlem Ashram quickly developed a close relationship with Albizu and he with them. By 1945, Albizu was listed on the Harlem Ashram's stationery as one of its advisers.[57] The ashram members' meeting with Albizu sparked what I judge to be the birth of the U.S. movement in solidarity with Puerto Rican independence. By that I mean that they were the first North Americans to form an organization committed to ending their nation's colonial rule in Puerto Rico and to freeing those Puerto Rican political prisoners their government labeled terrorists.

Solidarity work, like all political endeavors, is seldom free of conflict.[58] Given that this was the first organization dedicated solely to the cause of Puerto Rico, it is not surprising that the group's positions on the status of Puerto Rico were subject to debate. A clear division emerged in the incipient stages of the league's formation between those members who worked with, and took leadership from, the Nationalist Party and those who did not. These disagreements came to light when the group first discussed its statement of purpose. The main debate was whether they should support independence, which is what the Nationalist Party espoused, or self-determination, which was more amorphous. As one proponent of the latter position stated, "We can not [sic] tell the Puerto Rican people what to ask for." Thelma Mielke, who later represented the Nationalist Party at the United Nations, urged the body to call for independence. She "asked us [participants in the meeting] to face this problem as Americans interested in liberty, and felt there was a tendency to dodge this issue among us."[59] The issues Mielke thought people were dodging was that Puerto Rico was a U.S. colony and should be a free nation.

Two members put forward a motion that clarified how the two positions diverged. Instead of demanding an end to U.S. rule, they advocated reforms that were predicated on the continued colonial relationship between Puerto Rico and the United States. The motion had three points regarding what the group should do: "(1) Work for self-determination; (2) Awaken this country to the economic misrule, and bad health and educational conditions for which our people are responsible in Puerto Rico; and (3) Urge the [U.S.] government to increase industry and . . . provide adequate immediate relief for the desperate poverty of the people of Puerto Rico." Six people voted in favor and five against, at which point the chairman ruled that "so close a vote could not be considered decisive" and put the matter on the agenda for the next meeting.[60] However, members of the Harlem Ashram did not support halfway measures when fundamental rights and social justice were at stake. They supported independence, not the less specific self-determination. As a result, they parted ways with their more conciliatory friends, and Reynolds and Jay Holmes Smith formed the American League for Puerto Rico's Independence in December 1944.[61] They worked with Richard Walsh, the husband of Pearl Buck and editor of the *Asia* journal, and Thelma Mielke to get the organization off the ground.[62]

Mielke became politically active in 1933 when she went to Elmhurst College, a Lutheran school outside of Chicago where the German student body was decidedly antifascist. She was vice president of the Student Christian Association in 1935–36 and chairman of the Social Justice Committee in 1936–37, and on Armistice Day 1936, she participated in a picket for peace.[63] After moving to New York City to attend graduate school at Columbia University, Mielke got involved with pacifist and civil rights groups such as the Fellowship of Reconciliation, the War Resisters League, and the American Civil Liberties Union and, through them, the Harlem Ashram, where she learned about Puerto Rico. Because she opposed colonialism, she decided that she wanted to meet Albizu;

according to her, she went to his hospital room and introduced herself to him. The meeting cemented her commitment to solidarity work with Puerto Rico.[64]

One of the first challenges the newly formed group faced was how to increase its membership. The league began by sending personalized letters to a number of "prominent people" across the United States. They targeted select individuals because "we feel before we have a large membership drive we should have the backing of as many well-known American people as possible."[65] Many of the letters stated, "As you may know, there is being formed a group to work for the freedom of Puerto Rico," and then asked the recipient of the letter to join.[66] When Pearl Buck, the Nobel Prize–winning author of *The Good Earth*, wrote to potential members about the new organization, she didn't beat around the bush. She asked people to join because "we can no longer be silent about the fact of American imperialism."[67]

According to Reynolds, "The response to this letter has been very encouraging. Men and women representatives of the best in labor, religion, education, and sociology have already joined our ranks." Some of the supporters were Eleanor Copenhaver Anderson, widow of Sherwood Anderson, the well-known author, labor organizer, and a member of the YMCA national staff; Devere Allen, editor of Worldview Press and a prominent pacifist and Socialist; Carleton Beals, who made his name when he interviewed Augusto César Sandino in Nicaragua in 1928 and was later recognized as an expert on Latin America; Mary McLeod Bethune, the well-known educator, civil rights activist, and adviser to Franklin Roosevelt; Rockwell Kent, the left-wing artist who exposed U.S. government manipulations during the trial of the Nationalist Party leaders in 1936; and A. Philip Randolph, president of the Brotherhood of Sleeping Car Porters.[68]

In one of the first public activities the league engaged in, Ruth Reynolds testified before the U.S. Senate on the Tydings Bill of 1936. The bill, which bore Senator Millard Tydings's name, called for the U.S. government to withdraw from Puerto Rico and recognize its independence. Tydings had been a close friend of Colonel Riggs, the U.S.-appointed chief of the Puerto Rican police force who had been killed by two members of the Nationalist Party in 1935. Riggs's death so enraged Tydings that he introduced the bill in 1936 to punish Puerto Ricans by severing U.S. ties with the archipelago, not out of genuine opposition to U.S. colonialism.[69]

Reynolds's testimony established the league's position on Puerto Rico. Above all, it signaled the organization's belief that the United States "owe[s] independence to Puerto Rico" and that Americans have the duty to "rectify the mistakes of their fathers." Reynolds ended her testimony stating, "It is our sacred and patriotic duty in this period of history to see to it that our Government withdraws from Puerto Rico, so that that nation may take its place as a sovereign American republic, and so that our nation may stand before the world free of any suggestion of imperialistic ambition."[70] However, the bill had no chance of passing. The Nationalist Party initially built on the momentum the bill's apparent support for independence created and called for the organization of a constituent assembly. The Liberal Party, which supported independence, was reluctant to endorse a bill that would damage the Puerto Rican economy by likely closing the U.S. market for Puerto Rican goods and ending U.S. aid to the archipelago.[71] Marcantonio denounced the bill, which he referred to as "the Tydings Bill for fictitious independence," and introduced his own legislation calling for "real" independence.[72] In the face of the unanticipated response, Tydings "announced his plan for a committee . . . to study conditions in Puerto Rico to determine the feasibility of early independence" and the bill died a quiet death.[73]

### PUERTO RICO AND THE UNITED NATIONS

Even as it built a solid relationship with U.S. anti-imperialists, the Nationalist Party continued its efforts to garner international support for Puerto Rican independence. One focus of their work, as well as that of the American League for Puerto Rico's Independence, was the United Nations. The United Nations formed in San Francisco in 1945, at the end of World War II and the beginning of the Cold War. As historian Stephen Wertheim argues, the United States sponsored the United Nations' development as part of its plan to ensure "US political-military preeminence in global affairs." The international body would "legitimate the American *domination* of power politics like no lone nationalism or limited alliance could."[74] Although anticolonial movements in Asia and Africa surged following the defeat of the Axis powers and the weakening of Britain and France, they had not yet achieved independence and were thus not full voting members of the United Nations.[75] Their absence allowed the United States and Western Europe to dominate the United Nations in the 1940s.[76] As a result, the United Nations did not take a firm position against colonialism. Indeed, colonized peoples of the "*established* colonies were awarded only one thing, a pledge in Chapter XI . . . that the colonial powers would transmit regular reports to the Secretary General of the United Nations on . . . 'conditions' in their colonies. . . . The first reports on Puerto Rico and the Virgin Islands [both U.S. colonies] . . . submitted to the United Nations by the United States in August 1946, were simply previously published annual reports of the governors."[77]

Reflecting the power the United States exerted within the international body, U.N. files described Puerto Rico as a "nonautonomous territory" and allowed Washington simply to "submit an annual report on social and economic conditions to the secretary general."[78] To counter the United States' denial that it held Puerto Rico as a colony, the Nationalist Party solicited and received admission to the United Nations in 1947 as a nongovernmental organization.[79] According to Thelma Mielke, she told Albizu Campos that the Nationalist Party should seek membership in the United Nations' special committee on non-self-governing territories, which she had just read about in the *New York Times*. Albizu agreed and asked Mielke to represent the party before the international body, which she did until 1950.[80] In 1946, the American League for Puerto Rico's Independence submitted a petition to Trygve Lie, the Norwegian secretary general of the United Nations, calling on the body to end U.S. rule over the Caribbean nation. The league, working in close concert with the Nationalist Party, appealed to the United Nations because it did not believe the U.S. government would free Puerto Rico unless international pressure forced it to do so. In his cover letter to Lie, Jay Holmes Smith, chairman of the league, boldly stated, "This is perhaps the first instance of citizens of a greater power appealing to the United Nations to take action critical of the domination of their own nation over another."[81] The league's petition charged that "the treatment of Puerto Rico by the Congress of the United States is in violation of the *United Nations Charter*" and that "the continued subjugation of the people of Puerto Rico violates the 'Declaration Regarding Non-Self-Governing Territories' set forth in Chapter 11, Article 73 of the Charter."[82]

The league's eleven-page brief consisted of a carefully argued exposé of the multiple ways in which the United States violated the U.N. Charter, according to the solidarity organization. It included one of the fundamental legal arguments advanced by Albizu: Spain had granted Puerto Rico autonomy in 1897 and therefore "had no legal right to transfer Puerto Rico to any other power." The change in political relationship "could [not] be made without the approval of the Parliament of Puerto Rico."[83] Thus, the United States' acquisition of Puerto Rico was illegal and should be abrogated. The document further charged the United States with "Tyranny and Terrorism," "Cultural and Economic Imperialism," "Broken Pledges," and "deceiving Puerto Rican war veterans." It next detailed the league's unsuccessful plan, which it titled "Efforts to Move Congress," to act on Puerto Rico as well as the other work the organization has engaged in to further the cause of Puerto Rican independence. Illustrating how important the Nationalist Party, and therefore the league, considered hemispheric solidarity, the brief lists fourteen petitions sent to the United States from "responsible bodies of Latin America" calling "for the independence of Puerto Rico and the liberation of her Nationalist leaders."[84] The Nationalist Party and American League for Puerto Rico's Independence anticipated that their call would fall on receptive ears. The 1940s were years of rising anticolonial sentiment and successful national liberation movements around the world. Latin American nations held twenty out of fifty-one seats in the U.N. General Assembly, making the region "the most important single voting bloc."[85] However, the Nationalists failed to appreciate the extent of U.S. power over the region and the United Nations and the U.S. government's adamant refusal to let the United Nations or any international body dictate terms or interfere with its political agenda.

In 1947 the Nationalist Party sent a letter to Secretary General Lie in which it defined itself as "the only Puerto Rican organization with observer status" in the United Nations. It solicited a meeting with Lie for Nationalist representatives to "present him with the true picture of the economic, social, and economic conditions in Puerto Rico." It also asked Lie to share this information with other bodies and U.N. members.[86] Although Lie did not grant the Nationalist Party its request for a meeting, the Ad Hoc Commission of the United Nations did discuss Puerto Rico on the urging of the Philippines and the Soviet Union. The Soviet delegate denounced the conditions many workers in Puerto Rico faced, such as low salaries and the lack of food and health care. The United States, France, Belgium, and Great Britain rejected his criticisms. On the fourth day of discussions, the Soviet delegate demanded that the United Nations "investigate all the subjugated countries . . . with specific reference to Puerto Rico," a proposal that China, India, Egypt, and the Philippines backed. However, when the proposal came before the General Assembly, it resulted in a tie vote and did not pass.[87]

His period of probation completed, Albizu was able to leave New York in December 1947 and return to Puerto Rico, where he received a hero's welcome. Hundreds, perhaps thousands (the newspapers describe "a multitude"), waited at the docks to greet him when he stepped off the ship that brought him home after ten years of exile in the United States. Delegations representing the Unión General de Trabajadores, the Communist Party, the Confederación General de Trabajadores, the Puerto Rican Independence Party, students from the University of Puerto Rico, and the insular leadership of the Nationalist Party waited to greet him. When he stepped off the ship, he uttered some of his most famous and moving words, "The laws of love and sacrifice do not allow separation. . . . I never felt absent, I was never absent because I knew I was in the hearts and thoughts of all my disciples."[88]

The ten years away had taken their toll, but they had also offered the Nationalist Party new, important, and enduring relationships. The Nationalists' ties with the Communist Party had strengthened. For the first time a U.S.-based solidarity organization, the American League for Puerto Rico's Independence, developed, and it would stand by the Nationalist Party over the challenging next decade and beyond, albeit with different names and members.

However, the political situation in Puerto Rico was profoundly different in 1947 from what it had been in 1937. First and foremost, the Partido Popular Demócrata, led by Luis Muñoz Marín, the largest party in the archipelago, was poised to win the upcoming gubernatorial elections. The upsurge in support for the PPD not only signaled the decline in backing for the Nationalists and independence but also foreshadowed the seismic political shift that would occur in the early 1950s, when Muñoz Marín, who had formerly advocated independence, ushered in the process that resulted in Puerto Rico becoming a Free Associated State—and propelled the Nationalist Party to launch an unsuccessful islandwide revolt calling for an end to colonial rule on October 30, 1950.

# 8

# THE NATIONALIST PARTY AND THE COLD WAR
## 1940S–1950S

In May 1948, Alejandrina Gotay, a member of the Fajardo Junta of the Nationalist Party, wrote to Julio de Santiago, the party's national treasurer. Her letter contained a neatly written list of names with the amount of dues each member had donated to the party that month. Only nine names appeared on the list, all women's. Each had donated between $0.50 and $2.00, for a grand total of $9.75. According to party arrangements, local branches kept 25 percent of the money raised for their own use and sent the remainder to the national office. Thus, the Fajardo branch kept $2.43 and, after deducting $0.12 for postage, forwarded $7.20.[1]

Gotay explained why she was late in sending the money and why some members had failed to contribute. Although "there are many more members [in the junta]" than the nine who had paid, the others "have not been able to find work" and were unable to pay their dues. She noted that since the local leader died, "the organization has not worked with the members, and, as a result, we have not collected dues."[2]

This letter offers insight into the state of the Nationalist Party at the end of the 1940s. The party continued to suffer the negative repercussions of U.S. and Puerto Rican government repression unleashed against it in the 1930s and early 1940s: the Ponce Massacre, the imprisonment and exile of its leadership, the negative propaganda that led to members losing their jobs or fearing they would, and the apprehension and reality that party members or people associated with it would fall victim to government harassment or oppression. Still, the party maintained itself, although its organizational capacity was greatly weakened. Though most Nationalist Party members were poor, they gave what they could. Some managed to donate $2.00, others could only give $0.50, and many couldn't contribute anything at all. Their willingness to give what they could is emblematic of their and other Nationalist Party members' dedication and loyalty to the party that, against great odds, struggled for a free Puerto Rico.

The interplay between domestic Puerto Rican politics and U.S. global politics exacerbated the challenges Nationalists faced in their struggle for independence. After World War II, the United States expanded its already extensive control in Latin America as its rivalry with the Soviet Union for global domination intensified. But to win the public relations war for moral and political supremacy, a battle that multiple levels of the U.S. government engaged in, it had to change the optics regarding its relationship with Puerto Rico. How could the U.S. government proclaim itself the champion of democracy and freedom and continue to colonize Puerto Rico? To resolve this problem, U.S. officials worked with Luis Muñoz Marín and the Partido Popular Demócrata ostensibly to end U.S. colonial rule. This process culminated in the establishment in 1952 of the Estado Libre Asociado (ELA, Free Associated State) or Commonwealth of Puerto Rico. The launching of the ELA both reflected and engendered decreased support for independence and the Nationalist Party.

The domestic setbacks the Nationalists suffered were mirrored in similar losses in two international bodies dominated by the United States, the Organization of American States (OAS) and the United Nations. Although some members of these organizations supported the Nationalist Party and Puerto Rican independence, U.S. officials convinced a majority of representatives in both bodies to vote in line with U.S. wishes. The issues under consideration were whether Puerto Rico was a U.S. colony and, if so, whether it should attain independence. Representatives who aligned with the United States did so either because their political and economic interests dovetailed or because they were unable or unwilling to resist the pressure Washington brought to bear on them. Still, several nations, such as Guatemala under progressive presidents Juan José Arévalo and Jacobo Arbenz, defied the United States and backed independence for Puerto Rico.

The Nationalist Party denounced all attempts to convince Puerto Ricans and the world that U.S. colonialism was over. However, internal disorganization as well as declining membership and resources, which Gotay's letter attests to, greatly limited the party's efforts, as did the PPD's growing appeal and many Puerto Ricans' improved standard of living. Nonetheless, the Nationalists refused to give up. They continued their work, which included appealing to Latin Americans and North Americans to back their call for an independent nation. And, as we will see, a surprising number did.

## LUIS MUÑOZ MARÍN AND THE POPULAR DEMOCRATIC PARTY'S ASCENSION TO POWER

The Luis Muñoz Marín and PPD juggernaut dominated Puerto Rican politics during the 1940s and 1950s. Muñoz Marín started the PPD with like-minded colleagues in 1938, after the Liberal Party expelled him due to his rejection of the pro-independence Tydings Bill, which party president Antonio Barceló supported.[3] Once a critic of U.S. colonialism, by the mid-1940s Muñoz Marín had abandoned his previous support for independence. Instead, he favored social reforms and a continued relationship with the United States.[4] Far from challenging U.S. rule in Puerto Rico, Muñoz Marín and other PPD leaders explicitly and repeatedly stated that Puerto Rico's status was not an issue in the elections of 1940.[5]

Electoral support for the PPD skyrocketed from 38 percent in 1938 to 65 percent in 1940. Muñoz Marín easily won the gubernatorial race in 1948, the first time the United States allowed Puerto Ricans to elect their governor, with 61 percent of the vote.[6] He was reelected governor in the next three elections and stepped down in 1964 after serving sixteen years. Muñoz Marín shepherded Puerto Rico's transition from a direct U.S. colony to a more camouflaged one. The process established him as the political leader who improved Puerto Ricans' lives and obtained greater political freedom for them, a carefully cultivated image that helps explain why he stayed in power for so long.[7]

Many Puerto Ricans embraced the PPD platform, which, as Eileen Suárez Findlay explains, pledged to deliver social justice, specifically, "higher wages, redistribution of land, [and] legislation of social equality" to the people. It also promised to achieve "productive modernity" in Puerto Rico through "the attraction of U.S. governmental and private capital for rapid industrialization, construction of infrastructure, and provision of social services." The PPD programs, which enjoyed U.S. backing and financing, were so effective that "in the space of two decades, the entire island effectively transformed from a largely rural, agricultural society to an overwhelmingly urban, industrial one."[8]

Muñoz Marín's speech at a PPD leadership meeting in 1947 captures his vision of how the party had made and would make Puerto Ricans' lives better and, in the process, lessen the archipelago's dependency on the United States and achieve freedom. He began by pointing out one concrete example of how the Popular Democrats had benefited Puerto Ricans. There are now "a quarter of a million more Puerto Ricans than there were in 1940 . . . not because more people are being born but because fewer people are dying." In 1940, "eighteen people out of 1,000 died; now only twelve out of 1,000 do." And the reason fewer people died, he stated, was "the benefits given" by the PPD. Furthermore, "production has increased," but "light industry must increase even more so that federal aid—about which we should feel no shame—will no longer be needed and we can be free since people are not free as long as their economic survival depends on another [people]." He concluded on a rousing note. "Our will and integrity are huge; we are ready to win freedom."[9]

The Popular Democrats offered people hope that their lives would improve under their leadership. And many did. Its campaign slogan for 1952, "Pan, Tierra y Libertad" (Bread, Land, and Liberty), encapsulated the vision of the better life the party represented.[10] And indeed, during the 1940s more and better-paying jobs helped lift many out of the desperate poverty that had engulfed Puerto Ricans in the 1930s. Per capita income in 1940 averaged $122; by 1950, it had more than doubled to $279.[11] These economic advances, combined with the dynamic and optimistic manner in which the PPD projected itself and the future, stood in sharp contrast to the suffering and sacrifice the Nationalists embodied. The juxtaposition of these two visions contributed to many Puerto Ricans backing the Popular Democrats and renouncing the dream of a truly free nation.

The Nationalists were not the only Puerto Ricans who favored independence. Some members of the PPD abandoned the party and formed the Partido Independentista Puertorriqueño in 1946 after the PPD removed independence from its platform. Prominent among their numbers was Gilberto Concepción de Gracia, who had been one of Pedro Albizu Campos's lawyers and a member of the Nationalist Party junta in New York City, as we saw in chapter 7. Some Nationalists also joined the PIP, primarily for tactical reasons: they did not believe that independence would be achieved through armed struggle.[12] The PIP, unlike the PNPR, condemned the use of violence and pursued an electoral path to victory, a tactic the Nationalists had abandoned in the 1930s.[13] The PIP initially did very well, which demonstrated that a significant number of Puerto Ricans supported independence. It garnered 19 percent of the vote in the election of 1952, a sum it never again obtained. In 1960, it received only 3 percent of the vote.[14]

## THE NATIONALIST PARTY'S EFFORTS TO REBUILD THE ORGANIZATION

One of the Nationalist Party's main tasks after Pedro Albizu Campos and other party leaders returned from exile in 1947 was to rebuild the organization and recover its influence in Puerto Rican politics. The party had indeed declined in terms of numbers and resources, as well as internal cohesion and public projection, in the more than ten years since the leadership was first imprisoned in the Atlanta Federal Penitentiary. The party engaged in several measures to reconstitute its base, grow its membership, enhance its public presence, and regain the influence it had held in the 1930s. On the most basic level, the leadership encouraged members who had left or been expelled from the party to rejoin.[15] Paulino Castro, PNPR general secretary, wrote to all the presidents of the local party juntas, instructing them to "extend all assistance and courtesies for reentry into the liberation movement to everyone who meets the conditions stated in the resolution [approved in the party's national meeting]; the only requirement is they pledge to commit life and property [vida y hacienda] to the cause of Puerto Rican independence."[16] The response was positive. Leaders of local juntas across the island, from Río Piedras to San Germán to Naguabo and Cayey, even the far-flung junta in Indian Head, Indiana, wrote to Castro to inform him that they had held meetings, elected new officers, and rebuilt the local organization.[17]

The party also held public events to publicize its presence, attract and hold members, and project its politics. It had been the party's practice to organize activities and issue statements to commemorate key dates in Puerto Rico's anticolonial political calendar since the early 1930s.[18] To protest "half a century of foreign intervention in the destiny of the Puerto Rican nation," in July 1948, the Nationalist Party organized a public meeting in Guánica, where U.S. troops had invaded the archipelago in 1898. Participants would meet in the plaza and march to the bay, where "Yankee military forces disembarked." The event included a reading of the PNPR's proclamation for the day, a message from an unnamed Venezuelan, and final remarks by Albizu. Since the party was unable to secure a telephone line to broadcast the program live, Albizu would later "deliver his speech in the studios of the WPRP radio station in Ponce . . . [and] it will be retransmitted on radio stations in Arecibo and Mayaquez [sic]."[19] Continuing their tradition, Nationalists organized a "Solemn Commemoration" of the Grito de Lares on September 23, 1948. Activities would begin with a march to the cathedral in Lares, where Mass would be celebrated, and continue with two floral offerings, one on the tombs of the "heroes and martyrs of the historic day" and one at the foot of the obelisk in the Plaza de la Revolución. Pierre-Moraviah Morpeau, the Haitian nationalist and Nationalist Party supporter, would attend. He was bringing with him "a mixture of Puerto Rican and Haitian soil from the tombs of the heroes and martyrs of the sister republic [of Haiti]."[20]

In addition to holding public events, the Nationalist Party denounced U.S. militarism. It condemned the U.S. Navy's use of the Puerto Rican island of Vieques for target practice and opposed its use of atomic weapons.[21] Albizu was so concerned about the situation in Vieques that he addressed it when he spoke to the crowd gathered to welcome him home from the United States in December 1947. He declared, "What is happening today with the Island of Vieques, with the U.S. Navy trying to expropriate most of the land for its use, is a concrete example of what could happen in all of Puerto Rico."[22] As Laura Meneses pointed out, the Nationalist Party opposed the U.S. military's expropriation and use of 12 percent of Puerto Rico's land because it stripped Puerto Ricans of access to the land and converted Puerto Rico into a potential target "of atomic reprisal should the United States attack any atomic power." Puerto

Ricans had absolutely no say in the U.S. armed forces' confiscation of their land or use of their waters to construct military bases or carry out trainings.[23]

The party also called on Puerto Ricans not to enlist in the U.S. military. In 1948, the U.S. government established the first postwar draft in U.S. history.[24] The PNPR urged its members to reject the draft and refuse to be part of the U.S. imperialist military. "Naturally, the demand to *kill or die* in defense of the empire is considered the most hateful demand the United States government makes on Puerto Ricans."[25] In keeping with its opposition to U.S. imperialism, the party condemned U.S. aggression in Korea, which it defined as a "criminal maneuver to spark war" in Asia, and announced in banner headlines, "Korea Expels [the] Yankees."[26]

Six male members of the Nationalist Party refused to register for the draft and spurned offers by the United States government to avoid prosecution by signing up for the U.S. military. They were tried, found guilty of violating the Selective Service Act, and sentenced to between one to two years, to be served in U.S. prisons. All six men were cadetes, and the two who received a two-year sentence were both sons of prominent Nationalists.[27] By the 1950s, the party, realizing that their legal appeals to overturn the sentences were futile, changed tactics. Instead of challenging the draft in court, Nationalists evaded it by going underground in Puerto Rico or fleeing to Cuba.[28]

Rafael Cancel Miranda, who along with Ramón Medina Maisonave received a two-year sentence for refusing to register, exemplifies the party's evolving tactics regarding the draft. He returned to Puerto Rico in 1950 after he was released from the Atlanta Federal Penitentiary. When he realized the U.S. government would try him again on the same charges, he changed his name and went to live in Cuba in 1951.[29] He arrived penniless, but fortunately Laura Meneses and Juan Juarbe, who had been living in Cuba since 1950, helped him and found him a place to live.[30] He recounted, "I lived there for fourteen months. I labored in Public Works . . . until [President Fulgencio] Batista imprisoned me and kicked me out [in August 1952], obviously following orders from the U.S. Embassy."[31]

The imprisonment of Nationalist draft resisters was not the only form of repression the U.S. government employed against independence supporters. The Puerto Rican police and FBI intensified their surveillance, harassment, arrests, and imprisonment of anticolonial Puerto Ricans after Albizu's return in 1947.[32] In 1948 Laura Meneses and the couple's three children returned to Puerto Rico and lived with Albizu until 1950, first in the Hotel Normandie and then in Old San Juan.[33] Surveillance of the family was intense and unremitting. Meneses recalled, "Police detachments were always stationed in front of the Hotel Normandie. . . . They followed my husband, me, and my daughter Rosa, who accompanied me wherever we went. Persecution and provocation were constant."[34] They were not the only Nationalists subjected to such intense scrutiny.

Indeed, as the Puerto Rican media reported in 1987, "For many decades, the police of Puerto Rico had compiled dossiers [carpetas] with information on the legal political activities of thousands of individuals and organizations, mostly advocates of independence."[35] The carpetas are a treasure trove of information, some of it accurate, some of it not. They reveal the intense scrutiny to which the police, through their minute recounting of the daily activities of independentistas, subjected the Nationalists. Agents recorded where Nationalists went, with whom they met, what car they drove, what they said in meetings, where they lived, and what they looked like.[36] By detailing the sizable resources, time, personnel, and energy the FBI and the Puerto Rican police devoted to pursuing the anticolonial organization, the carpetas testify to the concern and fear the Nationalists inspired in these repressive forces.

In addition to keeping close tabs on individual Nationalists, the Muñoz Marín government passed the Ley de Mordaza, the Gag Law or Law 53, in 1948. The Gag Law was modeled on the U.S. Alien Registration Act, known as the Smith Act, of 1940.[37] The Puerto Rican version criminalized anyone who supported "the need, desirability, or convenience of overturning, destroying, or paralyzing the Insular Government." The law was "a copy, a direct translation of . . . the 'Smith Law.'"[38] Although passed in 1948, it was first used in 1950 to convict Nationalists who participated in the anticolonial uprising that year.

In defiance of the repressive measures directed against it, the Nationalist Party continued its policy of retraimiento and called on Puerto Ricans to refrain from participating in the upcoming gubernatorial elections, which it characterized as promoting "war among brothers." Shortly before the elections of November 1948, it issued a proclamation "exhorting Puerto Ricans not to vote." Pointing out that the United States had invaded Puerto Rico fifty years earlier, it stated, "What can we expect from this struggle [voting]? The same as usual: poverty and misery, which will increase and force us to leave our country or die of hunger in our own land."[39] However, most Puerto Ricans did not heed their call and, instead, participated in the elections.

## THE CREATION OF THE ESTADO LIBRE ASOCIADO
## OR COMMONWEALTH OF PUERTO RICO

The electoral process that led to the 1952 establishment of the Estado Libre Asociado began in July 1951, when 76.5 percent of Puerto Ricans who cast their ballots (35 percent abstained) voted in favor of Public Law 600, which sanctioned the election of a constitutional assembly. The assembly was charged with drafting a constitution for Puerto Rico, which would then be submitted to a vote. In March 1952, 374,649 Puerto Ricans voted in favor of the constitution and 83,923 opposed it.[40] However, only 49.8 percent of eligible voters, less than a majority, voted, for reasons that are not clear. Both the PNPR and the PIP called on their members to boycott the voting, which accounts for some, but not all, of the abstentions.[41] "The constitution," as César Ayala and Rafael Bernabe point out, "was to deal only with the structure of the insular government, not with any aspect of the relation with the United States."[42] In reality, as President Truman stated in his address to Congress, when Puerto Ricans backed the constitutional assembly and, by extension the new constitution, they "reaffirm[ed] their union with the United States on the terms proposed by the [U.S.] Congress."[43]

Muñoz Marín's popularity, people's faith in him and his pledges of greater self-rule, and their improved standard of living explain why a large number of Puerto Ricans voted to become a Free Associated State. ELA, which remains in force to this day, promised to devolve political power over the archipelago to Puerto Ricans and end U.S. colonialism. However, the Nationalist Party warned, prophetically, this was not going to happen. Instead, Albizu charged, ELA represented "the new theory of colonialism by consent."[44] Indeed, although Puerto Rico gained control over some aspects of local government, Washington continued and continues to exercise control over all key decisions that affect Puerto Rico's status, economy, political structures, and relations with other countries.

One other reason Puerto Ricans supported ELA was the increased Americanization of the archipelago. By the 1950s, U.S. capital had penetrated most economic enterprises across the archipelago, and the PPD depended on it to finance its programs.[45] Along with the expansion of U.S. capital came dependency on U.S. products, a consumer culture, and the sense that "American" products were better than Puerto Rican ones. José E. López, director of the Puerto Rican Cultural Center in Chicago, tells a story that illustrates this point well. When he grew up in San Sebastián, Puerto Rico, white eggs were referred to as "American" eggs and brown eggs were called Puerto Rican eggs. Both were produced in Puerto Rico, often on the same farm. But the message was that brown eggs were not as good as white eggs, and that Puerto Ricans, who are "brown," are not as good as "Americans," who are "white."[46]

In addition, Puerto Ricans' frequent *vaivén*, back-and-forth travel between New York City and San Juan in the *guagua aérea* (literally air bus or airplane), what Jorge Duany characterizes as "circular migration," expanded the Puerto Rican diaspora in the United States since the population flow was greater to the United States than back to Puerto Rico. It also generated Americanization, growing familiarity with and, in many but not all cases, acceptance of U.S. products, way of doing things, and lifestyle.[47] Americanization symbolized progress and modernity for many Puerto Ricans, as Antonio Sotomayor points out. "Modernization comprised a project of political dignity and economic industrialization that lifted Puerto Ricans from centuries of colonial exploitation." However, he adds, "Puerto Rican modernization actually consolidated colonialism and increased economic dependence within the U.S. economic system."[48]

The United States needed to maintain control over the archipelago because Puerto Rico's position in the Caribbean, draftable population, and accessible military bases leveraged Washington's goal of regional and global dominance. This was true during World War II, as we have seen, and it was true after the war, when communism replaced fascism as the United States' primary global enemy. The U.S. military, particularly the navy, needed to retain control of its bases, training grounds, and target-practice areas in the archipelago in order to have the capability to deploy its troops rapidly and effectively to those areas and against those forces Washington deemed a threat to U.S. control. Washington understood that maintaining control over Puerto Rico facilitated its quest for global power, whereas being identified as a colonial power in the postwar world undermined this goal. The creation of the ELA addressed both concerns. Washington preserved power over Puerto Rico, and the archipelago, apparently, was no longer a U.S. colony.

The United States, unlike Europe, the Soviet Union, or Japan, emerged from World War II with its economy not only intact but booming, armed to the teeth, and determined to become the number one superpower in the world and win the Cold War. To do this, it needed to convince the world that it, unlike the Soviet Union, represented democracy and freedom. But that would be a tough image to sell as long as it held Puerto Rico as its colony. To win global hearts and minds, the United States had to present itself as a country whose practices and policies mirrored its promises. To achieve this, it worked with the PPD to develop the ELA, which discursively allowed it to declare an end to U.S. rule over the archipelago. The following discussion of the U.S. government's role in the formation of the ELA sheds light on how Washington maneuvered to convince the world it was no longer a colonial power.

U.S. government documents establish two important points. First, U.S. officials were highly cognizant of how important Washington's relation to Puerto Rico was to its global image. Second, they were intimately involved in the process that led to the creation of the ELA. In 1945, Rexford Tugwell, whom FDR had appointed governor of Puerto Rico, announced he was resigning his position to become a professor at the University of Chicago. The White House began discussions to determine who should replace him and concluded that the next governor should be Puerto Rican. Political considerations, inflected by Cold War politics, heavily influenced this decision, as a White House report from 1946 makes clear: "The strongest reasons of national policy support the selection of a native Puerto Rican to be the governor of that territory." These reasons were, in order of importance, that "to the dependent people of the world and to all of Latin America, Puerto Rico is 'the window' through which the United States is viewed. . . . The appointment of a native Puerto Rican as governor will be acclaimed by the dependent peoples of the world, including the Orient." Another important factor stemmed from the U.S. rivalry with the USSR for global popular backing: "As is well known, ever since the San Francisco conference [to establish the United Nations in 1945], the Soviet Union has waged an aggressive and successful campaign to assume leadership in this field [of world opinion]. An opportunity [that is, the change in Puerto Rico's status] is now afforded for the United States dramatically to reassert its leadership."[49]

In 1947, the State Department published a study titled "Puerto Rico: Interest and Attitude of Foreign Countries." The report focused on Latin America because "comment on the Puerto Rican policy of the United State is found to chiefly center" there.[50] It analyzes Puerto Rico's relations with other Caribbean and Latin American nations and regional press coverage of Puerto Rico, particularly of the Nationalist Party and independence. Reflecting the United States' obsession with communism, it devotes a special section to examining Communist parties' support for the Nationalists and independence. The report echoes U.S. Ambassador to Costa Rica Leo Sacks's warnings in 1936 of "a concerted campaign which may become general throughout Latin America to utilize the cause of Puerto Rican independence as a weapon against the United States," in addition to the concerns raised in the White House report discussed above.[51] Because the State Department report so clearly articulates U.S. government officials' thinking about Puerto Rico and Latin America, I quote from it at length.

> The fact that many Latin Americans are conscious of their fundamental racial and cultural kinship with the Puerto Ricans and recall that Puerto Rico was annexed to the United States in an imperialistic phase of the latter's history means that as long as Puerto Ricans are generally dissatisfied with the existing conditions[,] the relations of the United States with the other American republics are to some extent jeopardized. Criticism of the policy of the United States, although not a constant interest, has been sufficiently widespread to justify the assumption that at least those in the other American republics who, for nationalist, ideological, or other reasons, are inclined to oppose the policies of this government will in the future take advantage of

any opportunity to criticize American policy in Puerto Rico. This, together with some genuine concern for a dependent neighbor, tends to undermine good relations between this country and the other American republics.[52]

The conclusions asserted in these two reports convinced U.S. officials they had to take steps to transform the optics of the United States' relationship with Puerto Rico. They determined that naming a Puerto Rican as governor of the archipelago would improve Americans' perceptions of the United States. Thus, the U.S. government chose Jesús Piñero, a PPD stalwart whom Muñoz Marín backed, to be the governor. In a calculated, if highly ironic move, Truman appointed Piñero governor on July 25, 1946, the forty-eighth anniversary of the U.S. invasion in 1898. The date simultaneously established U.S. control over Puerto Rico and projected the "benevolent" nature of that rule by naming a Puerto Rican to run the local government. The next step was to allow Puerto Ricans to vote for their own governor for the first time since 1898. Luis Muñoz Marín was the hands-down favorite; he sailed to victory with 61 percent of the vote. In addition, the Popular Democratic Party won control of the position of resident commissioner as well as all but one of the seventy-seven municipalities, the political jurisdictions into which Puerto Rico is divided.[53]

Although Muñoz Marín and the party claimed credit for the new constitution and the end to U.S. colonial rule they said it heralded, Congress had to approve every step in the process, from Public Law 600 to, as we have seen, the new constitution, which many might consider evidence of Puerto Rico's ongoing subordinate status. After many discussions between U.S. officials, Muñoz Marín and Resident Commissioner Antonio Fernós-Isern, Congress approved the new Puerto Rican constitution on July 3, 1952.[54] However, in an act that clarifies to what extent the United States did not plan to relinquish its power in Puerto Rico, Truman declared the existence of the Commonwealth of Puerto Rico on July 25, 1952, more than three months before Puerto Ricans actually voted on it and, once again, on the day when the United States invaded Puerto Rico in 1898.[55] When he presented the new constitution to Congress in 1952, Truman took the opportunity to trumpet U.S. virtues and respect for democracy, proclaiming, "The United States gives evidence once more of its adherence to the principle of self-determination and its devotion to the ideals of freedom and democracy."[56]

The U.S. government then seized on Puerto Rico's supposed change in status to proclaim to the world that the days of U.S. colonial rule were over. As Henry Cabot Lodge, the patrician U.S. representative to the United Nations, declared to the international body in 1953, "In light of the change in the constitutional position and status of Puerto Rico, the United States Government considers that it is no longer necessary or appropriate for the United States to continue to transmit information on Puerto Rico under article 73 (e).[57] Therefore, the United States Government has decided that with the submission of information for the period July 1, 1951 to June 30, 1952, it will cease to transmit information on Puerto Rico."[58]

Both the PNPR and the PIP contested U.S. assertions that Puerto Rico should be taken off the United Nations' list.[59] Members of Americans for Puerto Rico's Independence—the new name for the American League for Puerto Rico's Independence, the North American committee in solidarity with Puerto Rico—sharply challenged U.S. government claims that the United States no longer needed to report Puerto Rico's status to the United Nations. They, along with their attorney Conrad Lynn, issued a number of statements directed at both the U.N. General Assembly and the U.S. public denying the U.S. government's assertion that Puerto Rico had achieved self-governance. Ruth Reynolds penned a powerful and lengthy denunciation of U.S. government attempts to deceive the world into thinking that Puerto Rico was now free. As she wrote, there were two ways a colony could achieve a "full measure of self-government": either by "the attainment of complete independence" or "through the free union or association of a territory with other component parts of the administering power." And neither of these two options had occurred in Puerto Rico. However, as Reynolds concludes, the United Nations "is not to be trifled with," and the attainment of one of these two conditions "must precede any thought of removal of Puerto Rico from the list of non-self-governing territories on which it is required to render information."[60]

Despite independence supporters' passionate and well-founded arguments attesting to Puerto Rico's status as a U.S. colony, the U.N. General Assembly passed Resolution 748 (VIII), which stated that the United States no longer needed to submit reports on Puerto Rico to the United Nations. Of the fifty-one U.N. member states, twenty-six voted in favor of the U.S.-backed resolution, sixteen against it, among which was India, whose representative forcefully rejected it, and eighteen abstained.[61] The vote offers a snapshot of U.S. sites of power in the world in 1953.

Puerto Rico was effectively off the United Nations' agenda until 1972. It was taken up only after the balance of power in the United Nations shifted in the 1960s following the admission of revolutionary Cuba, which has long championed independence for Puerto Rico, and sixteen newly independent African countries. These countries' anticolonial position led the United Nations to adopt Resolution 1514 in 1960. The resolution, "Declaration on the Granting of Independence to Colonial Countries and People," passed and a Special

Decolonization Committee was created. In 1972, twenty-two years after the Nationalist Party's status as an observer was rescinded (the United States forced the resignation of PNPR representative Thelma Mielke after the party's 1950 uprising and assault on President Truman, as we shall see in chapter 9), the committee "called for Puerto Rico's case to be reconsidered," which has happened periodically ever since.[62]

## THE NATIONALIST PARTY'S INTERNATIONAL WORK

The United Nations was not the only arena in which the Nationalists and their supporters sought support for independence. During the 1940s, activists attended conferences and worked with solidarity committees, influential individuals, and supportive organizations across Latin America to generate regional solidarity with their struggle. So successful were they that the State Department noted in the report discussed above: "There is ample evidence that much of the interest in Puerto Rico expressed in the other American republics has been the result of a very active campaign conducted by certain Puerto Ricans."[63]

Communist parties and groups and individuals they worked with throughout the hemisphere consistently rallied in defense of Puerto Rican independence, as they had done since the 1930s. Mexican labor leader Vicente Toledano Lombardo exemplifies such support. According to Patrick Iber, Toledano "never joined a Communist party, [but he] had been recruited by the Soviet Union in 1935."[64] In other words, he was a Comintern agent, but not a militant of the Communist Party of Mexico. Toledano Lombardo was, however, the principal leader of the left-wing Confederación de Trabajadores de América Latina (CTAL, Workers Confederation of Latin America), which he had helped establish in 1938. By 1944, CTAL "claimed to represent some 3.3 million workers in sixteen countries."[65]

Toledano Lombardo had a long history of calling for Puerto Rican independence and working with the Nationalist Party. In 1938, CTAL held a conference in Mexico. According to a State Department report, Juarbe attended the conference and "asked permission to speak [on] behalf of the independence of Puerto Rico." Permission was denied, presumably because he was not a labor delegate. However, the assembly passed a resolution "urging moral support for the independence of Puerto Rico and the liberation of Pedro Albizu Campos and other Nationalists serving sentences in the Atlanta Penitentiary." The report added, "Vicente Lombardo Toledano . . . has advocated for Puerto Rico on several occasions."[66]

Members of the Nationalist Party greatly appreciated Toledano's efforts on behalf of Puerto Rico, as Nationalist Party leader Juan Antonio Corretjer publicly acknowledged. In 1943, the Nationalists held an event to celebrate the Grito de Lares in New York City. Corretjer spoke at the event, as did Earl Browder, secretary general of the CPUSA, and Charles Collins from the Negro Labor Victory Committee. When Corretjer addressed the crowd, which numbered somewhere between 500 and 600 people, he said, "Through the leadership of Vicente Toledano Lombardo, four million Spanish-Americans [Latin Americans] have been recruited for the independence of Puerto Rico."[67] Corretjer also called for the creation of a commission to survey all the capitals of the hemisphere, "from Buenos Aires to Washington," on the question of support for Puerto Rican independence. His friendship with Toledano and the backing of the CTAL convinced him that such an ambitious undertaking was possible. Corretjer optimistically concluded that the undertaking "will end in Washington, where they [the Nationalists] will have the support of all the Spanish-speaking chancelleries."[68]

Concrete expressions of solidarity manifested throughout the continent. The Comité Cubano pro Libertad de Patriotas Puertorriqueños (Cuban Committee for Liberty of the Puerto Rican Patriots) called for the release of the Nationalist political prisoners and the freedom of Puerto Rico in 1940.[69] In 1943, the Cuban House of Representatives "unanimously declared that Cuba was morally and materially obligated to work for Puerto Rican independence . . . [because] this had been a prime article . . . of the Cuban Revolutionary Party founded by José Martí in 1892." Three years later, Cuban parties "organized a parliamentary committee to promote Puerto Rican independence."[70] A Mexican and a Cuban communist established the Mexican Committee for the Independence of Puerto Rico in Mexico City in 1943.[71] Juarbe organized the Venezuelan Committee for the Independence of Puerto Rico in Caracas in 1948.[72] When Juarbe and Meneses lived in Peru in the late 1940s, they worked with the American Popular Revolutionary Alliance, led by Haya de la Torre, to promote solidarity with the Nationalist Party.[73] According to Meneses, they presented several "solidarity events together with APRA" and "inaugurated [APRA's] Pedro Albizu Campos library" in 1947.[74]

Members of the Nationalist Party and their supporters also participated in regional gatherings, agitating in favor of Puerto Rican independence. For example, two members of the Nationalist Party, Juarbe and José Enamorado Cuesta, attended the Ninth International Conference of American States in Bogota in 1948. The seventeen-point resolution they presented to the conference ended by asking the participants to "invite the United States, as a practical reaffirmation of nations' right to be independent, and as a demonstration before the world of the respect that exists among American nations regarding their reciprocal rights, to immediately end its half-century of intervention in Puerto Rico and to restore the Republic of Puerto Rico."[75]

The U.S. delegation, headed by Secretary of State George C. Marshall, had a very different, even antagonistic agenda for the meeting. The United States sought to ensure its hemispheric hegemony by establishing an anti-Soviet and anti-Communist bloc, promoting capitalist development, and "bringing about an inter-American collective security system."[76] As Marshall announced somewhat more diplomatically to the assembly, the United States saw the meeting as an opportunity to obtain "the understanding and cooperation of other nations whose objectives are the same as ours."[77]

In response to Latin American diplomats' requests for greater economic support, Marshall promised that the United States would increase aid to the region but counseled Latin Americans to rely on "private sources, both domestic and foreign," for the infusion of capital they needed. Because Europe's reconstruction took priority, the United States would contribute only a "small portion" of the capital Latin America expected and needed to develop.[78] Marshall made no mention of Puerto Rico and ignored the Nationalists' calls for independence in his speech.

Latin American diplomats were not all as compliant as the United States wished. Venezuelan president Rómulo Betancourt, who spoke at the closing of the congress, unequivocally backed the demand for a sovereign Puerto Rico. In a section of his speech titled "Colonialism Must Be Eradicated in the Americas," he proclaimed, "A close link exists between . . . freedom in the Americas and the irritating persistence of colonialism in our continent, to use an expression adopted unanimously by the National Congress of Venezuela. The fact that colonial powers have been allowed to dominate vast portions of this hemisphere undermines our collective faith in the efficacy of the inter-American system. . . . We hope that Puerto Ricans will be able to attend the next conference as representatives of a sovereign state."[79] The Guatemalan delegate, who represented the democratic and nationalist government of Juan José Arévalo, backed Betancourt's condemnation of colonialism embodied in what became Resolution 33. So did Antonio Parra Velasco, the Ecuadorian representative who, in addition to supporting Puerto Rican independence, was Juarbe's close friend. The final text of the resolution included Argentina's call for an end to British rule of the Falklands/Malvinas and Guatemala's demand that Britain withdraw its troops from Belize.[80]

Despite the sympathy Puerto Rico evoked in many Latin Americans, the United States emerged victorious from the conference, as nations acquiesced to its wishes due to pressure from Washington or because their interests aligned or both. Delegates unanimously approved the U.S.-proposed anticommunist Resolution 32, titled "The Preservation and Defense of Democracy in America." The resolution "condemn[ed] the methods of every system tending to suppress political and civil rights and liberties, and in particular the action of international Communism or any totalitarian doctrine."[81] Delegates also agreed to establish the Organization of American States, a decision the U.S government ratified.[82]

One agreement that did not meet with U.S. approval was Resolution 33, which established the American Committee on Dependent Territories.[83] The resolution passed because Argentina, Cuba, Guatemala, and Venezuela fully backed it and anticolonial sentiment prevailed throughout the hemisphere. By December 1948, the only countries that had failed to appoint representatives to the committee were Bolivia, Brazil, Chile, the Dominican Republic, Nicaragua, Uruguay, and, of course, the United States.[84] There can be no doubt that the United States' reluctance to endorse the resolution and name a representative to the committee stemmed from its determination to prevent hemispheric discussion on Puerto Rico. Robert Lovett, the acting secretary of state who has been described as George Marshall's "alter ego," made U.S. concerns very clear when he wrote in December 1948 that the efforts of the "Committee to obtain information from inside a non-self-governing territory [Puerto Rico] would almost inevitably be regarded by the controlling country [the United States] as intervention in its domestic affairs, violating a principle to which the American republics have given special devotion."[85] Ironically, the wording of the resolution revealed certain limitations in the extent of the committee's reach, which should have allayed U.S. fears: "It is a just aspiration of the American Republics that colonialism and the occupation of American territories by extra-continental countries should be brought to an end."[86] In other words, the committee's mandate did not include American colonization of American territories. This restriction effectively hampered the efforts of Nationalists and their supporters to place the status of Puerto Rico on the OAS's agenda.

The first meeting of the American Committee on Dependent Territories took place in Havana on March 15, 1949. Thirteen American nations participated; the United States was not among them.[87] Delegates discussed whether Puerto Rico's situation fell under the OAS's purview. Representatives from Argentina, Cuba, Guatemala, and Mexico argued that it did, and the committee unanimously voted to send "all the background and reports presented . . . about Puerto Rico" to the OAS Council so that it could "determine the course [of action] that should be followed" regarding Puerto Rico.[88] The council would then ask the member states to determine whether the committee could judge the issue. In April 1949, the Puerto Rican Senate censured the committee's recommendation, declaring, "Puerto Rico would make its own decision on the question of its future relationship with the United States."[89] By July 1949, only Costa Rica, Cuba, Ecuador, and Guatemala had affirmed the committee's competence to assess if it should judge Puerto Rico's status, while Bolivia, Brazil, Colombia, the Dominican Republic, El Salvador, Haiti, Honduras, Mexico, Nicaragua, Panama, Paraguay, Peru, the United States, and Venezuela announced their opposition."[90] The issue of Puerto Rican independence was effectively eliminated from the OAS.

Political tides were not flowing in favor of Puerto Rican independence or the Nationalist Party at the end of the 1940s and the beginning of the 1950s. Instead, many Puerto Ricans gravitated toward Luis Muñoz Marín and the Popular Democratic Party, and their promises of a better economic future and greater political autonomy. The United States, which sought to project itself globally as the defender of democracy and progress and the opponent of colonialism and totalitarianism, skillfully worked with the PPD to convince many in the archipelago and around the world that it had effectively ended its colonial rule of Puerto Rico. U.S. power in the United Nations and Organization of American States was so great that it succeeded in removing the status of Puerto Rico as an issue of discussion in both bodies.

Despite these huge setbacks, the highly committed if numerically reduced members of the Nationalist Party persisted in their efforts to convince Puerto Ricans that they should strive for independence. They also continued to seek international, particularly Latin American, solidarity with their struggle. The fairly bleak, even desperate, situation in which they found themselves, combined with their fervent determination to end U.S. colonial rule and their continued faith in their ability to generate support in Puerto Rico and across the region, convinced them to launch the uprising of October 30, 1950, in Puerto Rico, along with the attempt of November 1 to assassinate President Truman in Washington, D.C.[91] I explore the impact these two attacks and the Nationalists' 1954 assault on Congress had on the party and solidarity with it and Puerto Rican independence in chapter 9.

# 9

## THE 1950S
## ARMED STRUGGLE, REPRESSION, EXILE, AND SOLIDARITY

On October 30, 1950, armed units of the Ejército Libertador (Liberation Army) of the Nationalist Party launched an islandwide rebellion against U.S. colonial rule. In Jayuya, a mountainous town of 1,500 in the interior of Puerto Rico, Nationalist leader Blanca Canales climbed to the balcony of the Palace Hotel, unfurled the Puerto Rican flag, shouted, "¡Viva Puerto Rico Libre!" and declared the Republic of Puerto Rico.[1] The Nationalists held the town for three days. National Guard planes strafed the city, and the Insular Police and National Guard deployed tanks, machine guns, and troops to capture it. By November 2, the joint forces had suppressed the uprising and arrested more than a thousand Puerto Ricans, including Canales.[2]

The Nationalists launched their assaults during the height of the Cold War, at a time when U.S. hegemony reigned almost supreme in Latin America. Not only did they attack U.S. colonial institutions in Puerto Rico, but two members of the Nationalist Party attempted to assassinate President Harry Truman on November 1, 1950, in Washington. Then on March 1, 1954, four members of the Nationalist Party opened fire in the U.S. Congress.

The Nationalists carried out these armed actions because they believed it was their patriotic and moral duty to denounce and expose as false Muñoz Marín's and the U.S. government's claims that Puerto Rico was no longer a U.S. colony. They paid a heavy price for their deeds. Nationalist leaders and members spent decades in prison, subjected to cruel conditions and inhumane treatment, often in isolation. They were denied visits due to regulations or their families and friends' inability to cover travel costs. Their absence, combined with the generalized repression against the party and its supporters, contributed to the party's decline, from which it never really recovered.

Much of what people know about the Nationalist Party is this part of their story. But the continentwide scope of solidarity with the party and Puerto Rican independence has been largely ignored. Despite U.S. hegemony across the region, support for the Nationalist Party and prisoners and demands for an end to U.S. colonialism persisted. Individual, organizational, and institutional appeals saved the life of Oscar Collazo, the Nationalist who survived the attack on President Truman. Nationalist organizers worked in Cuba, joined revolutionary exile communities in Guatemala and Mexico, built close ties with Fidel Castro's 26th of July Movement, and traveled throughout the Americas to bring attention to and build solidarity with colonized Puerto Rico and the imprisoned Nationalists. Their victories were partial. Collazo was not executed and the prisoners were eventually released, but Puerto Rico remains a U.S. colony. Nonetheless, their story reveals much about the heretofore unrecognized breadth and depth of anti-imperialist trans-American solidarity with those Puerto Ricans who risked their lives to establish a free homeland.

**THE UPRISING OF OCTOBER 1950**

Three factors propelled the Nationalist Party to initiate the rebellion on October 30, 1950. First, Nationalists feared that the government of Muñoz Marín, working in conjunction with Washington, was implementing a plan to arrest and/or assassinate them, beginning with Pedro Albizu Campos.[3] Two years earlier, in March 1948, the FBI had declared the Nationalist Party a "subversive organization," thus both a designated and a legitimate target of governmental repression.[4] Nationalists knew that the Gag Law enacted that year was designed specifically to be used against them and they wanted to act while they still could. Furthermore, the party understood that Law 600, which Truman had signed on July 13, 1950, approved the organization of a constituent convention that would pave the way to the writing of a new constitution.[5] The new constitution would allow both the Muñoz Marín and U.S. governments to claim that U.S. colonial rule in Puerto Rico was over. As scholar Carlos Zapata notes, the Nationalists worried that Muñoz Marín and the Popular Democrats' project would succeed and that "if they didn't do something quickly their beloved ideas of independence would be forever destroyed."[6]

Finally, the Nationalists conceived their actions as a message, a kind of SOS to the international community and a call to continental solidarity. They acted to alert the world that the U.S. and Muñoz Marín governments aimed to destroy the independence movement and convert Puerto Rico into a permanent, if disguised, U.S. colony. They understood that they were up against the full, unbridled muscle of the United States, the most powerful country in the world. They risked their lives in a singularly unequal battle to let the world know that there were Puerto Ricans willing to die in pursuit of an independent nation. In a clear statement as to whom they considered the enemy, they attacked institutions representing U.S. colonialism, such as police stations and post offices, in seven towns across Puerto Rico, and La Fortaleza, the governor's mansion,

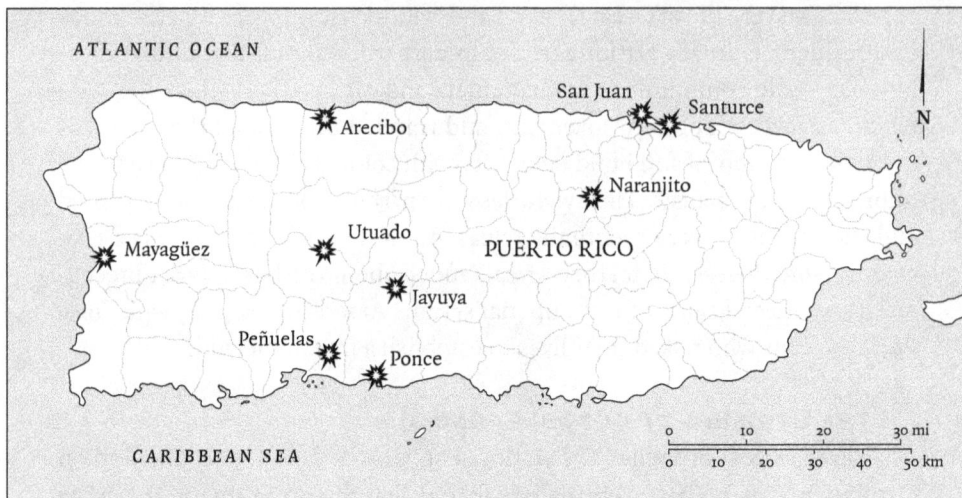

Sites of Nationalist Party attacks during the October 1950 uprising.
Source: Naomi Robles.

in San Juan. And on November 1, two Nationalists attempted to assassinate the U.S. president.[7]

The combatants planned to first take over Utuado and "hold it for a month," according to Elio Torresola, a Nationalist Party leader in Jayuya and Blanca Canales's cousin.[8] They chose Utuado because, as the president of the Junta Nacionalista in Utuado explained, the town's location in the central mountain range made it relatively inaccessible and geographically strategic. Once they cut off access to Utuado, Nationalists anticipated they could hold it and nearby Jayuya for some time.[9] "The goal . . . was to get the world, the United Nations, to act on the issue. [Controlling Utuado for a month] would allow time for foreign intervention."[10] However, very little went according to plan. Although the participants were brave, dedicated, and determined, willing to sacrifice their lives to achieve a free Puerto Rico, many of them lacked training, high-quality weapons, critical logistical assistance, and sufficient understanding of the proposed actions. And the world did not intervene on their behalf.

The revolt got off on the wrong foot. Only 140 Nationalists took part; some who had promised to participate failed to appear.[11] Furthermore, according to Tomás López de Victoria, the supreme commander of the Ejército Libertador, they "had not set a firm date for the revolution" to take place. It only began when it did because, as he explained, "we found out the police had started to search . . . Nationalists' houses in Ponce . . . so we moved up the date [and] didn't have enough time to organize it well across the Island."[12] The element of surprise was nonexistent, since the police already knew about the revolt in advance thanks to informers in the party, while coordination across the island was weak to nonexistent, with units launching the uprising at different times. As Elio Torresola recounted, "We were preparing the arms and the molotovs when Blanca [Canales] said, 'Listen! Listen!' [The news is reporting that] Nationalists have attacked in Arecibo and many police are dead!" Once the news was announced, they "went to Jayuya about half an hour earlier than the time agreed upon."[13] Nonetheless, the Jayuya team successfully took over the town and held it until aerial strafing and heavily armed troops forced them to surrender on November 1.

Carlos Padilla was a university student in October 1950. He joined a small group of Nationalists in Río Piedras that planned to attack a police station in San Juan. But by the time they got to their target, "the police were lined up in front of the station," so their driver "suddenly sped up and flew out of there, leaving [the rest of us] disoriented." The police shot and then detained the fleeing Nationalists. They arrested Padilla and took him "to the very same police station [they] had been planning to attack."[14]

That afternoon police assaulted Albizu Campos's home in Old San Juan, which doubled as Nationalist Party headquarters. Nationalists Doris Torresola (Elio's sister), Carmen Pérez, and Juan José Muñoz, who were in the office, fought back against the police, as did Albizu. A police bullet hit Torresola in the neck, so Pérez and Muñoz carried her outside for medical care. Police promptly arrested all three and continued firing into the apartment. Alvaro Rivera Walker, a Nationalist, somehow evaded police scrutiny, entered the building, and fought alongside Albizu. A barrage of teargas fired by the police rendered Albizu unconscious. Rivera carried him outside and the police arrested them and took them to police headquarters on November 2.[15]

But the fighting was not entirely over. Angry that the U.S. media portrayed the fighting as an intra–Puerto Rican struggle, not an anticolonial struggle, and outraged at the world's ignorance of the repression the U.S. and Muñoz Marín governments had unleashed against Nationalists, two New York City members of the Nationalist Party, Oscar Collazo and Griselio Torresola (Elio and Doris's brother), traveled to Washington, D.C., "to draw the attention of the North American people and the world to the suffering" taking place in Puerto Rico.[16] Convinced they would not survive the attack, they purchased one-way tickets.[17] Once in Washington, they went to Blair House, the temporary residence of President Truman, and attempted to kill him.[18] Guards intercepted them, and in the ensuing gun battle, Lesley Coffet, a Washington, D.C., police officer, and Griselio Torresola were killed and Oscar Collazo was severely wounded. President Truman emerged unscathed.[19]

## THE REPRESSIVE AFTERMATH

Both the U.S. and Muñoz Marín governments knew that to convince the world that Washington no longer colonized Puerto Rico, they had to repress the Nationalists and ensure that voter registration, scheduled for November 4 and 5, 1950, proceed unimpeded. To that end, the police began the large-scale arrest of Puerto Ricans they deemed dangerous. Those arrested extended beyond the Nationalists and included members of the Puerto Rican Communist Party, the Puerto Rican Independence Party, labor leaders, and even some members of Muñoz Marín's Popular Democratic Party.[20] The detention of Puerto Ricans who had not participated in the insurrection reflected Cold War hysteria and fear of communism. Muñoz Marín labeled the uprising a "conspiracy against democracy helped by the Communists."[21] He portrayed himself as the defender of "freedom and democracy," courageously protecting "my people" against conspiratorial attacks conducted by "fascists and Communists."[22] By November 7, voting registration concluded, at least 800 of the more than 1,000 arrested were released.[23]

Arrests and detentions were not limited to Puerto Rico. The FBI also questioned and arrested several dozen members or supporters of the Nationalist Party in New York City.[24] Carmen Dolores Torresola, Griselio's partner, and Rosa Collazo, Oscar's wife and treasurer of the Nationalist Party in New York City, were both arrested on November 1. Charged with conspiring to "harm a member of the Government," Rosa was held for two months in the Women's House of Detention in Manhattan, where her cellmate and soon-to-be friend was Ethel Rosenberg.[25] The FBI also arrested the three Collazo girls, Lydia, Iris, and Zoraida, and interrogated them all night.[26] They repeatedly asked Lydia, "Who gave the orders?"[27] At 6:30 the next morning, when it was clear the three knew nothing about the attack, the FBI released the girls, who returned home to "an empty nest."[28]

Repression was not limited to arrests, nor did it end once the detainees were incarcerated. As scholar Yvonne Acosta points out, the police conducted unwarranted searches of Nationalists' homes and violated their habeas corpus rights.[29] Most of the 180 Nationalists brought to trial were convicted, and many of them received extrordinarily high sentences. Fifty-three Nationalists were condemned to life imprisonment.[30] Many were held in subhuman conditions while others were subjected to torture and, allegedly, illegal medical experiments designed to disorient and damage them.

Nationalist Heriberto Marín Torres was twenty-two years old when he was convicted of murder, arson, and carrying arms. He was sentenced to "life in prison at hard labor plus forty-five years, to be served consecutively." He spent most of the next nine years in jail in Arecibo in a six-by-ten-foot cell.

According to Marín, the food had worms in it, the prisoners were allowed to bathe only once every twenty-two days, and their cells were lit up twenty-four hours a day. For the first year neither he nor the other political prisoners were allowed any contact with the outside world, no visits, except with their lawyers, and no letters.[31]

The prisoners called the horrific treatment they suffered torture. In 1952, the Nationalist Party presented to the Organization of American States and the United Nations the testimonies of Nationalists Pedro Albizu Campos, Carlos Padilla, Carmen Pérez, Doris Torresola, and Ruth Reynolds, the North American leader of the American League for Puerto Rico's Independence, all of whom were imprisoned in Puerto Rican jails after the revolt of 1950.[32] The women revealed that they had experienced painful vibrations emanating from an unknown source. In her testimony, Doris Torresola reported that one night, "the vibrations were stronger than ever; the beds shook. . . . I stood up and it felt like something electric shot up my legs. . . . My head was so heavy because the vibrations penetrated my ears as if my entire head was wrapped in a spider's web."[33] Ruth Reynolds related that "the electric shocks, or whatever they were, were especially strong at the base of my head and in my wrists and ankles." She also heard voices coming from under her cell speaking about her in English and making lewd comments about her relationship with Albizu and her attorney, Conrad Lynn, who was Black.[34] After Lynn visited her, he described her cell as "windowless, there was no bed, and an overflowing pail served as a latrine. The stench was horrible, not sharp and pungent like a stockyard but heavy and pervasive. There seemed to be no air to breathe."[35]

The best-known case of torture is that of Albizu Campos. Carlos Padilla, the university student introduced above, was Albizu's cellmate from November 1951 until May 1952, when he was released. In his statement, he wrote that he witnessed Albizu's hands and ankles swelling, though he did not know the cause. By January 1951, he wrote, "The pain in [Albizu's] left shoulder was so terrible that he couldn't move his arm. . . . He couldn't get out of bed, nor could he stand up or sit down."[36] Albizu described how the tortures he experienced at that time affected him: "I felt a terrible coldness, as if my stomach were breaking down, frequent urination, and a general state of weakness that led to a feeling of prostration. I lost my voice. . . . I realized I was the victim of electronic experiments being carried out by the armed forces of the United States."[37] Both the U.S. and Puerto Rican governments dismissed these accusations as the mad ramblings of a crazy person.

Not content with imprisoning the Nationalists, the U.S. and Muñoz Marín governments also attempted to discredit the Nationalist Party and the independence movement. They disparaged Nationalists, especially Albizu Campos, by labeling them crazy and fanatics. If they succeeded in convincing people in Puerto Rico and across the Americas that Albizu, the leader of the Nationalist Party, was nuts, they would undermine the party's credibility.[38] Thus, they dismissed Albizu's accusations of torture by laser beams or nuclear rays as the unfounded ravings of a lunatic. A U.S. congressional report called the Nationalists a "band of mad radicals."[39] Muñoz Marín, covering two very divergent political bases, called the Nationalists "Communists and Fascists" and characterized the uprising as "a criminal conspiracy committed by a group of fanatics," nothing more than a "lunatic movement."[40] As Andrea Friedman notes, "By labeling Albizu Campos crazy . . . Muñoz Marín sought to cement the portrayal of Nationalism as irrational, terroristic, and undemocratic, and the Commonwealth as the defender of civil liberties and democracy."[41] What exactly caused the Nationalist prisoners' health problems has never been fully established. However, supporters are certain that the prisoners were the victims of U.S. medical and scientific tortures. To determine the cause of her husbands' burns and swellings, Laura Meneses had Dr. Orlando Duamy, president of the Cuban Cancer Association and an expert on radiation, examine Albizu after his release in 1953. According to his report, "Albizu Campos' injuries were produced by radiation."[42] Indeed, as Friedman points out, the belief that their afflictions may have been the result of "illicit experimentation . . . may be more comprehensible in light of recent evidence of [U.S.] government-sanctioned experimentation on prisoners and others during these years, including the use of both irradiation and psychotropic drugs."[43]

## LATIN AMERICAN SOLIDARITY WITH THE NATIONALIST PRISONERS

The Latin American political panorama in the early 1950s was radically different than it had been just five years before. Whereas progressive and democratic governments were the norm in the mid-1940s, by the early 1950s rightwing dictatorships, allied with and backed by the United States, dominated the continent.[44] These regimes willingly adopted the Cold War positions and anti-Communist discourses and policies the United States expected of them because it served their interests to do so. They gladly repressed labor unions and Communist parties; sought private U.S. capital; sent their militaries to receive training and indoctrination from the U.S. armed forces at the School of the Americas in Panama; signed military pacts with the United States, such as the Rio Pact of 1947, by which signatories pledged to defend each other should they come under attack; and largely ceded control of the Organization of American States to Washington. The U.S. government, for its part, preached U.S. diplomat George F. Kennan's "containment" of communism policy and followed the Truman Doctrine, which promised to "provide political, military and economic assistance to all democratic nations under threat from external or internal authoritarian forces."[45] This was the context in which the Nationalist Party rose up against the world's greatest superpower. The pro-independence forces did not, could not, have triumphed militarily against the United States and the Muñoz Marín government, but remarkably, they did win some political victories.

Although the deck was stacked against them, the Nationalists pursued Latin American solidarity, as they had done since the 1920s. To facilitate this work, the party charged Juan Juarbe, Laura Meneses, Carlos Padilla, and Lydia Collazo with generating hemispheric support for Puerto Rican independence and freedom for Nationalist political prisoners. Padilla was released from La Princesa prison in San Juan in May 1952 and went to Cuba in June.[46] Both Laura Meneses, who had traveled to Cuba in 1950, and Juan Juarbe were already there.[47] Lydia Collazo promoted local and continental solidarity from her home in New York City.[48]

Cuban support for the Nationalists flourished from 1950 to 1952. President Carlos Prío Socarrás welcomed the Nationalist exiles, ten of whom had found refuge on the sister island.[49] The prestigious and well-connected members of the Junta Nacional Cubana Pro Independencia de Puerto Rico, whose president was Emilio Roig de Leuchsenring, ensured that the cause of Puerto Rican independence received widespread support on the island. When they learned of the repression the Muñoz Marín and U.S. governments had unleashed following the uprising of October 1950, a number of Cubans took action. A House of Representatives delegation made up of representatives from across the Cuban political spectrum attempted to travel to San Juan "to intervene in the Nationalist conflict," but the U.S. government refused to let the flight proceed from Miami to Puerto Rico.[50]

President Prío Socarrás hastily dashed off a cable to Muñoz Marín. He conveyed his position in two courteous but frank lines: "The Cuban government, inspired by our peoples' traditional generosity and human rights principles, begs you to use your position to guarantee the lives of Albizu Campos and his comrades and thus avoid continental anger. I thank you for your humane mediation and express to you my highest consideration."[51] After evoking the long-standing connection between Cubans and Puerto Ricans and extolling their mutual generosity and respect for human rights, Prío Socarrás called on Muñoz Marín to safeguard the lives of Albizu Campos and other Nationalist prisoners. Evoking a shared regional identity and anticipating continental solidarity with the prisoners, he warned that Latin Americans would be aroused should any harm befall the Nationalists.

No such diplomatic niceties constrained Roig de Leuchsenring, who did not mince words in his angry missive to Muñoz Marín. "Knowing that I interpret the feelings of the Cuban people, I send you and your gang, all accomplices of Yankee barbarism, my energetic protest of the assassination of patriotic Nationalists and the persecution of Dr. Pedro Albizu Campos, brothers in the ideals of freedom and democracy of Martí and Hostos."[52] University students, who had previously organized the Committee for the Independence of Puerto Rico and displayed the Nationalist Party flag in the assembly hall of the student federation, attempted unsuccessfully to hoist the Puerto Rican flag on their campus. Thwarted, they marched through the streets of Havana in support of the Nationalists until police broke up the demonstration.[53] Fidel Castro organized a program in the University of Havana advocating Puerto Rican independence and led a demonstration in front of the U.S. embassy.[54] Cubans were not alone in expressing their support for the Nationalists following the 1950 uprising, as the continental mobilization to save Oscar Collazo's life illustrates.

## A TRANSNATIONAL CAMPAIGN

Oscar Collazo's trial took eight days. Government attorneys portrayed him as a criminal and member of a conspiratorial, subversive movement whose goal was to "sew terror and bring disorder and anarchy to the nation's capital." The defense attorney, in consultation with Collazo, sought to establish the political nature of his actions by recounting the history of "abuse and humiliation the people of Puerto Rico had suffered" since the United States invaded in 1898. In a by-now-familiar attempt to paint the Nationalists as a bunch of lunatics, the judge called a recess and asked Collazo if he would be willing to plead insanity. Collazo rejected the request and the insinuation that "only crazy people fight for the independence of Puerto Rico."[55] The jury, which was composed exclusively of white men, found Collazo guilty of first-degree murder, assault on the home of the president, and the illegal possession of weapons. The judge sentenced him on April 6, 1951, to death in the electric chair.[56]

Instead of distancing themselves from the man who tried to kill Truman, some members of the Latino community in New York rallied to his defense. Luisa Quintero, a reporter for the Spanish-language newspaper La Prensa, who was considered the "grande dame of Puerto Rican journalism," Isabel Cuchi Coll, a well-known author and niece of José Coll y Cuchi, one of the founders of the Nationalist Party, and other members of the Latino community in New York City formed the Pro-Oscar Collazo Defense Committee.[57] After Rosa Collazo and Carmen Dolores Torresola were released from the Women's House of Detention due to insufficient evidence in December 1950, Rosa joined the committee, as did Lydia Collazo.[58]

What is most notable about the committee is that it was successful. The campaign for Collazo mushroomed from a small group of Puerto Ricans in New York City to a global campaign that mobilized hundreds of thousands of people to write petitions, letters, telegrams, and articles. They stimulated sufficient pressure to convince Truman that he should commute Collazo's sentence to life imprisonment. The odds against this outcome were formidable. Not only did the campaign take place during the height of the Cold War, but it sought to save the life of the man convicted of attempting to assassinate the president, the so-called leader of the free world.

Why were Collazo's supporters victorious? I attribute their success to three interrelated factors. First, the organizers built a strong base in New York City, the site of the largest Puerto Rican population outside the archipelago and the place where Oscar Collazo had lived, worked, raised his family, and conducted his political work. From this stronghold they generated domestic and international support for Collazo that extended beyond New York to cities such as Chicago as well as to Latin America and other parts of the world.[59] Second, the basic message of the campaign was simple: Collazo does not deserve to die because he is a patriot fighting for the freedom of his nation. This language allowed people from a variety of political backgrounds, ranging from pacifists to Communists to the general public, to back the campaign's basic, humanitarian demand to save Collazo's life.[60] Third, many Latin Americans responded positively to the campaign because they supported the Nationalists and opposed the death penalty. Furthermore, rallying to save Collazo's life allowed them to express opposition to U.S. hegemony in Latin America in a politically safe way, since the call was couched in the language of humanitarianism.[61] Indeed, opposition from Puerto Rico and Latin America had a significant impact on Truman's decision to commute Collazo's sentence.[62]

The Pro-Oscar Collazo Defense Committee effectively mobilized the Latino community of New York by bringing together the visibility and stature of prominent Puerto Ricans such as Luisa Quintero with grassroots efforts to inform and involve the public. Lydia Collazo recounted that she, Iris, and Zoraida traversed New York City asking people to sign petitions calling on Truman to spare Collazo's life. One site they frequented was the Teatro Puerto Rico in the Bronx, an entertainment venue that presented "the best films and live shows with Latino artists from all of South and North America." Carlos Montalbán, the brother of Hollywood film star Ricardo Montalbán, managed the theater and supported the work to save Collazo. According to Lydia, most people they spoke with supported their efforts, which allowed them to collect thousands of signatures.[63]

The Pro-Oscar Collazo Defense Committee evolved into the Committee to Save the Life of Oscar Collazo and, in the process, expanded its base beyond the Latino community to include leading U.S. pacifists as well as Congressman Vito Marcantonio and attorneys Conrad Lynn and Abraham Unger, a prominent member of the Communist Party USA. Ralph Templin, the Methodist minister who helped form the Harlem Ashram, and A. J. Muste, the preeminent U.S. pacifist and a leader of Peacemakers, worked to prevent Collazo's execution. The committee's petition characterized signers as loyal Americans who were appealing to Truman on humanitarian and patriotic grounds. It defined Oscar Collazo as a political prisoner, a designation the U.S. government has never accorded to detainees held in U.S. prisons.[64] The petition, directed to President Harry S. Truman, read, "The undersigned, good and loyal citizens and legal residents of the United States, respectfully request from your Excellency to commute the sentence of Mr. Oscar Collazo, political prisoner now awaiting execution at a Federal prison. May justice be tempered with mercy and may this country show other countries the real meaning of its great heritage of democracy, tolerance and human understanding."[65]

In the weeks preceding August 1, 1952, the date set for Collazo's execution, Peacemakers sent a letter to Truman clarifying why it, a "group of Americans scattered across the country and opposing the use of violence in all its forms," called on the president to commute Collazo's sentence. The letter recalled that the founding of the United States occurred because "our forefathers rose up and overthrew with force and violence the tyrannical yoke which they felt intolerable upon them." It framed the attack at Blair House as an act "against what the participants regarded as intolerable tyranny in their native country, Puerto Rico." It pointed out the nondemocratic nature of U.S. rule in Puerto Rico by asking why it is that "Puerto Ricans have no real representation" in Washington. "How much control do Puerto Ricans have over their economy?" "Is it just that their youths are conscripted under a Selective Service Act in the adoption of which they had no voice?"—a question that hearkens back to the Nationalists' arguments against the imposition of the draft in Puerto Rico. The letter concluded by urging Truman "to exercise the power granted to you by the people and to exercise immediate executive clemency to forestall the execution of Oscar Collazo."[66]

On July 10, the committee held a well-attended event in New York City, the "Conferencia Pro-Vida de Oscar Collazo," to mobilize support for Collazo, raise funds for his defense, and announce the group's next steps.[67] Vito Marcantonio and Luisa Quintero spoke at the program and Abraham Unger presided over it. Ralph Templin gave the keynote speech in which he declared, "The true American spirit . . . is to recognize and admire the patriot, those who are willing to sacrifice their lives for their people. . . . The moral imperative emanates from the democratic nature [of our government] and makes it impossible for this nation to steal the life of an American patriot, Oscar Collazo." The activity raised $168 for the campaign. The committee announced it planned to send one delegation to meet with Truman and deliver 500,000 signed petitions. Another delegation would submit the remaining 500,000 signatures to the United Nations and ask the international body to intercede with Truman. Unger closed the program explaining that whereas Collazo could not ask for clemency for political reasons (he refused to beg the government that colonized his nation to save his life), Truman had the constitutional power to pardon him.[68]

Committee members sought to broaden support for Collazo by calling on Latin Americans to back their cause. Building on work conducted and relations established in previous decades, they contacted official representatives of Latin American governments stationed in the United States, wrote to sympathetic individuals and organizations throughout the hemisphere, and communicated with journalists about the case.[69] They made personal appeals to prominent individuals to support Collazo. Luisa Quintero wrote to President Getúlio Vargas of Brazil asking him to "repudiate the death penalty" for Oscar Collazo "in the name of the highest principles of justice and [in light of] Christians' repudiation of the death penalty that reigns in our continent."[70] However, Vargas apparently heeded the advice of his secretary, who counseled him, "This is an internal matter of the United States. We can't question their democratic process. . . . I suggest we file the letter and do nothing."[71]

Luckily for Collazo, other governments responded more favorably. The Guatemalan government of Juan José Arévalo, a progressive nationalist and anti-imperialist, was "in the forefront of the anti-colonialism movement in the Hemisphere" and offered "tacit support for Puerto Rican independence."[72] The Guatemalan, Argentine, and Uruguayan congresses all passed resolutions backing Collazo.[73] Uruguayans formed the Grupo Uruguayo Pro Libertad de Puerto Rico (Uruguayan Group in Support of Puerto Rican Freedom). A lengthy article by the organization appeared in the left-wing newspaper Marcha. It recounted the history of Albizu's political development from Harvard to his imprisonment in 1937 through his return to Puerto Rico in 1947 and his subsequent imprisonment following the uprising of 1950. Drawing on a press bulletin released by Juarbe in Havana in June 1950, the article expressed sympathy for the Nationalists, empathized with the uprising, and condemned U.S. imperialism in Puerto Rico.[74] In July 1952, believing that Collazo's execution was imminent, the Grupo Uruguayo wrote to Rosa Collazo to express "our deepest solidarity . . . on the eve of this painful event that will add a new name to the list of those sacrificed for the cause of a dignified and free Indoamérica."[75]

Student organizations across the hemisphere expressed their support for the Nationalists and their opposition to the execution of Collazo. They employed many of the same appeals to humanitarianism and patriotism that U.S. pacifists and the Pro-Oscar Collazo Defense Committee did. The Alianza Universitaria Pro Federación Latinoamericana (University Alliance in Support of Latin American Federation) of Uruguay issued a declaration of solidarity in response to the October revolt.[76] The Federación de Estudiantes Universitarios (Federation of University Students) in Cuba called on the United States to not "execute a man who fights for the same liberatory ideas as the North American patriot Nathan Hale" had. When the Congreso Interamericano de Estudiantes (InterAmerican Student Congress) met in Brazil in 1952, it, too, drew on similar concepts to express the organization's condemnation of the "imposition of the death penalty on the Puerto Rican patriot Oscar Collazo."[77]

On July 24, 1952, a week before Collazo's scheduled execution, President Truman issued a presidential order to "commute the sentence of . . . Oscar Collazo" to life imprisonment. Neither Truman nor his press secretary, who announced the decision, offered an explanation. The *New York Times* speculated, "The motives for the President's action today were compassion and the desire to make a gesture to the people of Puerto Rico . . . when they were implementing the new Constitution." Rosa Collazo acknowledged that Truman "made a grand gesture," but her thanks went to "all our American friends and those people and institutions from Central and South America who helped us in our cause."[78] The most likely explanation is that political pressure emanating from Puerto Rico and Latin America encouraged Truman to make this decision. Dean Acheson, U.S. secretary of state, encouraged Truman to commute Collazo's sentence, noting that "it would make a very good impression in Latin America." He pointed out that both "the Uruguayan and Guatemalan legislatures had passed memorials in favor of commutation and the Uruguayan Ambassador had made unofficial representations on behalf of Collazo." He offered two explanations for their position. First, "In most Latin American countries capital punishment is forbidden," and second, "Most people in those countries believe that political crimes ought not to be treated the way ordinary crimes are treated." He added that "Puerto Ricans also share these views" and that Muñoz Marín had sent Truman a telegram "urging commutation of Collazzzo's [*sic*] sentence."[79] Indeed, Muñoz Marín had written to Acheson and Interior Secretary Douglas Chapman "recommending the commutation to avoid a 'misunderstanding' by Latin America in general and the Puerto Rican people in particular."[80]

The campaign to save Collazo's life scored a tremendous victory. Vicente Cubillos, a writer for the Cuban magazine *Bohemia*, captured the popular euphoria it created in New York City's Puerto Rican–Latino community. On hearing the good news, he raced to congratulate Rosa, who declared, "This is the happiest day of my life!" Cubillos recounted, "Supporters crowded into the Collazo's tiny apartment in the Bronx . . . cheered from their windows . . . and poured into the street to celebrate." In addition, "a truck with a loudspeaker drove through the area announcing the news." When it reached the Collazos' apartment, "two hundred people were following behind." The joyful demonstrators marched for miles from the Bronx to the Latino community in the Upper East Side, with more and more people joining along the way.[81]

Despite this remarkable victory, support for the Nationalist Party plunged. The leadership and much of the membership were imprisoned. The prisoners received lengthy sentences and had little to no contact with the outside world, except for occasional visits from their attorneys and, nearly a year after their arrest, some family members. Membership in the party shriveled. Many supporters, friends, and even some family members wanted nothing to do with the party since association with it resulted in repression, loss of work, shunning, and potential jail time.[82]

## FOUR NATIONALISTS ATTACK THE U.S. CONGRESS

On March 1, 1954, Lolita Lebrón led Andrés Figueroa Cordero, Irvin Flores, and Rafael Cancel Miranda into the Ladies' Gallery of the U.S. House of Representatives. The Nationalists whipped out their pistols and fired, Lebrón at the cupola, the three men at the congressmen on the floor below. Lebrón shouted, "¡Viva Puerto Rico Libre!" and attempted to unfurl the Puerto Rican flag.[83] Before she could do so, guards, spectators, even one congressman "overcame and disarmed" the Nationalists, who were arrested and booked on charges of "assault with intent to kill." Figueroa managed to slip away but was soon apprehended at the Washington bus station.[84]

The Nationalists timed their action to coincide with the opening of the Tenth Inter-American Conference in Caracas. Ever mindful of how important Latin America was to their struggle, they wanted delegates and other Latin Americans to know that, despite claims to the contrary, Puerto Rico was still a U.S. colony and some Puerto Ricans were willing to sacrifice their lives to free it.[85] Unsurprisingly, the Puerto Rican Senate, pro-statehood and PPD politicians, organizations, and individuals across Puerto Rico roundly condemned the action. The five PIP senators abstained from the Senate vote condemning the attack.[86] Arturo Morales Carrión, Puerto Rico's undersecretary of state and part of the U.S. delegation in Caracas, denounced the action as a "desperate attempt" by a group of "fanatics [seeking] to destroy the free, intimate, and voluntary association that the people of Puerto Rico have established with the United States."[87] Muñoz Marín hurriedly jumped on a plane to Washington to assure U.S. politicians and the public that he repudiated the shooting and earnestly desired to maintain "good relations" with the United States. To demonstrate his loyalty, he visited President Eisenhower and four of the wounded congressmen (the fifth was in critical condition and receiving family visits only). In a reciprocal gesture, the wives of the five wounded congressmen invited Inés Mendoza, Muñoz Marín's wife and a former Nationalist, to a luncheon to demonstrate that they "bore no grudge against Puerto Rico."[88] In a further display of goodwill, the U.S. Congress gave Muñoz Marín and Antonio Fernós-Isern, Puerto Rico's resident commissioner, a standing ovation when they visited Congress.[89]

Because the shooting took place during the Cold War, the Puerto Rican and U.S. governments immediately linked the incident to Communists. Fernós-Isern defined it as a "Communist Plot" and declared that some Puerto Ricans in New York were "being used as dupes by Communists."[90] Muñoz Marín offered to help the House Un-American Activities Committee investigate communism and its connection with the Nationalists in Puerto Rico.[91] The FBI sought to "clarify if communism had something to do with the conspiracy."[92] Secretary of State John Foster Dulles, who led the U.S. delegation in Caracas, proclaimed that the "Reds had influenced the Nationalists."[93]

By connecting the nefarious "Reds" with the "fanatical" Nationalists, Popular Democratic Party officials could link their battle against the Nationalists with the U.S.'s global anti-Communist crusade. Tying the Nationalists to the Communists also allowed both the U.S. and Puerto Rican governments to dismiss the Nationalists' claims that Puerto Rico remained a U.S. colony as nothing more than anti-U.S. Communist propaganda. Conflating the violence of the Nationalists with the alleged machinations of the Communists, and portraying them both as devious forces that would use any means to achieve their goals, served Dulles's key objective in Caracas: convince Latin American nations that they had to adopt the United States' Cold War agenda and reject communism.[94]

Linking the Nationalists to the Communists served another purpose. It reinforced the idea that neither group was really "American"; indeed, they were foreign, the enemy Other. Puerto Ricans may have been "domestic" (part of the United States) by virtue of being made U.S. citizens in 1917, but only in a foreign sense, because for most "Americans" Puerto Ricans weren't really "American."[95] Nor were Communists, many of whom were Jewish in a nation that was deeply anti-Semitic.[96] Many in the United States believed that Communists' primary allegiance was to the Soviet Union, no matter what their birth certificate said.[97] Merging Nationalists with Communists made both groups appear more dangerous, foreign, and untrustworthy, which justified the intense repression unleashed against them in the 1950s.[98]

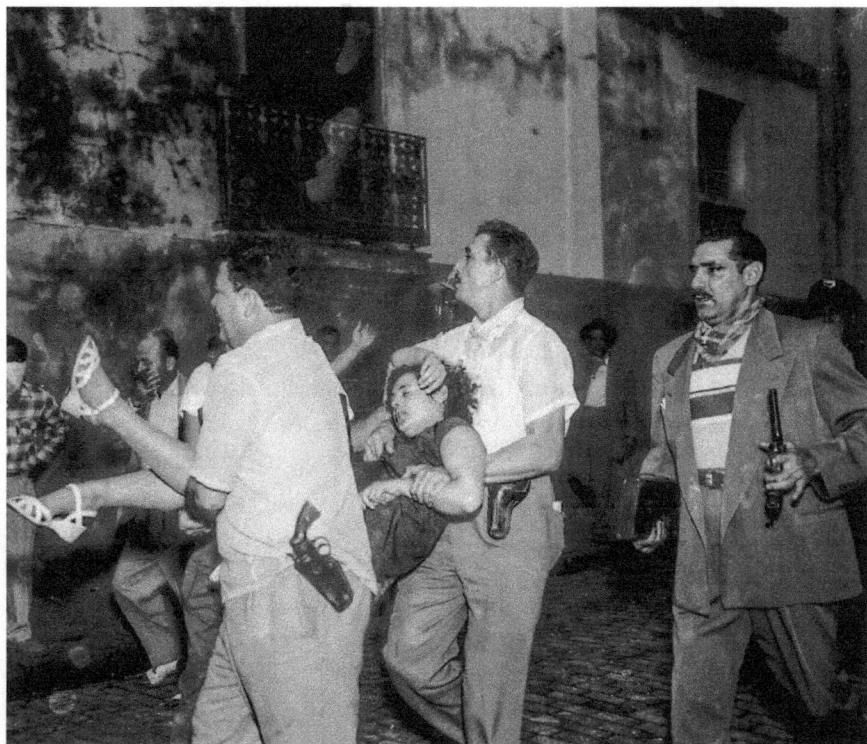

FIGURE 9.1. Puerto Rican police carrying Doris Torresola after their assault on Nationalist Party headquarters in San Juan in March 1954. Source: Archivo General de Puerto Rico.

Indeed, persecution of Nationalists was swift. Party leaders across the island were arrested, as were scores of Nationalists in New York and Chicago. In a déjà vu of 1950, a gun battle ensued after police opened fire on Nationalist Party headquarters in Old San Juan, where Albizu Campos, Carmen Pérez, José Rivera, Isabel Rosado, and Doris Torresola were ensconced. Again, police lobbed so much tear gas into the offices that the occupants were rendered unconscious and had to be carried to the waiting ambulances (fig. 9.1).[99] In the trials that followed, twenty-six Puerto Ricans living on the island were convicted of violating Law 53, or attempting to overthrow the insular government by force. Most were sentenced to seven to ten years' imprisonment. Carmen Pérez was sentenced to sixty years. Isabel Rosado, who was with her in the Nationalist Party headquarters, received two sentences totaling two to twenty years. Doris Torresola received from nine to seventeen years.[100] Seven Nationalists from New York, including Rosa Collazo, and three from Chicago were convicted of seditious conspiracy and sentenced to six years.[101] The three men who attacked the U.S. Congress were sentenced to twenty-five to seventy-five years, and Lebrón received a sentence of sixteen years and eight months to fifty years.[102] Eleven Communist Party leaders in Puerto Rico were also arrested.[103]

## THE PUERTO RICAN COMMUNIST PARTY'S AND COMMUNIST PARTY USA'S RESPONSE

The Puerto Rican Communist Party and the Communist Party USA were caught between a rock and a hard place. To disavow their long-standing support for Puerto Rican independence and their lengthy relationship with the Nationalist Party would have violated their political principles, contradicted their public statements, and strained credibility.[104] Yet their tactical and political differences with the Nationalist Party and their desire to minimize government repression against themselves meant they had to distinguish themselves from the organization that had just shot up Congress and tried to assassinate Truman less than four years earlier.[105]

To clarify its relationship to and position on the Nationalists' 1954 assault, the PCP issued a statement, which the CPUSA subsequently translated and published in its newspaper, the *Daily Worker*. The statement opened by characterizing the assault as "the unfortunate incident," then pivoted to criticize the "U.S. government and fascists' use [of the attack] as a pretext to intensify the terror and persecution they are employing in the United States, Puerto Rico, and Latin America against any progressive, democratic, or national liberation movement." To distinguish how its ideology and tactics differed from those of the Nationalists, the PCP clarified that "scientific socialism" guided its work, so "terrorist acts are contrary to its methods of struggle." It characterized efforts to link the PCP to the shooting as an "infamous calumny" that was both "false and ridiculous," denounced colonialism, and accused the United States of trying to make "the peoples of the world believe that the Free Associated State ended our country's enslavement." The declaration ended by calling for "the establishment of a free and independent homeland."[106]

The *Daily Worker* published a series of articles over the next two weeks that established the CPUSA's opposition to U.S. colonialism, concern for Puerto Ricans, and political sympathy for and distance from the Nationalist Party. In large letters on the paper's first page, the *Daily Worker* boldly, even courageously, proclaimed, "Puerto Rican Independence Still the Issue," two days after the attack on Congress.[107] One article quoted Lebrón to buttress CPUSA claims that it had no relationship to the action: "Miss Lebron was pressed by reporters to tell whether there were Communists behind the attack. She said there was no connection and denied knowing anything about Communists or communism except that 'it is bad. . . . I like my own movement better.'"[108] Another article derided Dulles for "spouting at the Caracas Conference about the 'beacons of freedom in the Western Hemisphere,'" while "the FBI was handing out subpoenas to nearly 100 Puerto Ricans in New York's big-ghetto for Spanish-speaking people."[109]

### PACIFISTS AND ANTI-IMPERIALIST SOLIDARITY

Communists were not the only people to stand up for Puerto Rican independence. So, too, did a remarkable group of pacifists and anti-imperialists whose commitment to Puerto Rican independence and Puerto Rican political prisoners has gone largely unrecognized.[110] They formed or participated in organizations such as Peacemakers, the Ruth Reynolds Defense Committee (RRDC), and the Committee for Justice to Puerto Ricans. Peacemakers formed in Chicago in April 1948 when a group of pacifist men pledged to refuse military service, registration, or conscription, to make or transport weapons, and "to spread the idea of peacemaking and to develop non-violent methods of opposing war through various forms of non-cooperation and to advocate unilateral disarmament and economic democracy."[111] The Ruth Reynolds Defense Committee formed in 1951 after the demise of the American League for Puerto Rico's Independence. Its goal was to secure Reynolds's release from prison in Puerto Rico. Ruth Reynolds disagreed with the decision to end the league. She claimed that Jay Holmes Smith "decided it was best to dissolve the League" because "we had not been very successful in our efforts," which, she noted, made her "so angry."[112] In fact, some members quit the league because they opposed the Nationalist Party's use of armed struggle in October and November 1950.[113]

Members of the Committee for Justice to Puerto Ricans included leading pacifists such as A. J. Muste and Dave Dellinger, longtime advocates of Puerto Rican independence such as Thelma Mielke, Ruth Reynolds (once she got out of prison on bond pending appeal in June 1952), and Ralph Templin, and notable authors such as Norman Mailer and Waldo Frank.[114] The committee had four immediate goals: "prevent the violation of civil rights" in Puerto Rico and New York City; educate people about "the history and economic and political conditions of Puerto Rico"; secure "the best possible defense for the Washington defendants [the four Nationalists who attacked Congress] and related cases"; and "raise and administer funds" for their defense.[115]

Although membership in the three committees overlapped, participants were not all cut from the same political cloth. Some, such as Ruth Reynolds, Thelma Mielke, and Ralph Templin, forged close bonds with the Nationalists, even though they disagreed with the party's use of violence. Others, such as

Congress on Racial Equality

Fellowship of Reconciliation

Catholic Worker

War Resisters League

Peacemakers

Ruth Reynolds Defense Committee

Committee for Justice to Puerto Ricans

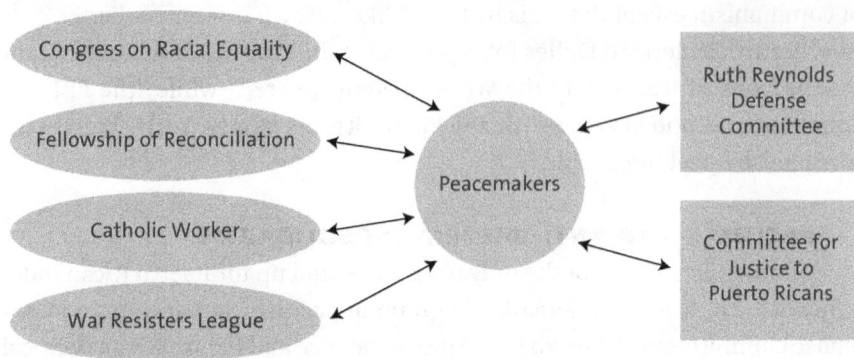

Connections among pacifist and Puerto Rican solidarity organizations in New York City in the 1950s. Source: Roberto Villaseñor.

Jay Holmes Smith, supported independence for Puerto Rico and freedom for the prisoners but distanced himself from the PNPR. Despite these differences, they shared a common commitment to justice and opposed U.S. colonialism. Given the climate of fear, suspicion, and conformity that reigned in the United States in the 1950s, critics of U.S. government policies and those who stood up for "terrorists" who attacked the United States faced being castigated as threats to national security who lacked patriotic fiber.[116] Nonetheless, these solidarity activists persisted in demanding justice for Puerto Rico, the release of the political prisoners, and respect for civil liberties.

Despite the high-profile supporters, pacifist and progressive communities did not uniformly support Puerto Rican independence, the Nationalist Party, or the political prisoners. One stumbling block for some pacifists was that the best-known proponents of independence were the Nationalists, who both espoused and engaged in armed actions. Other pacifists disliked what they perceived to be the Nationalist Party's internal politics. Jim Peck, a well-known civil rights activist, thought that the party's "set up [was] thoroughly anti-democratic and . . . completely fascist" and didn't think that Peacemakers should affiliate with it.[117] Muste challenged Peck's assertion. He recognized that the Peacemakers should endeavor to "search for the truth" about the Nationalist Party. At the same time, he argued that the U.S. military's exploitation of Puerto Rico was dangerous and that pacifists should oppose it because "the use the US makes of Puerto Rico as a naval and air base which probably would be terribly blasted if there should be a war, and in US conscription of Puerto Ricans for war, there is an evil that we do not need to investigate further."[118]

Some pacifists refused to support Ruth Reynolds, an avowed pacifist, because they believed her advocacy of independence and association with the Nationalist Party meant that she condoned violence.[119] Further, some in the pacifist community opposed independence altogether and supported the PPD and the Free Associated State. As A. J. Muste noted, "A good many well-disposed persons contend that Puerto Rico is much better off as part of the United States than it could possibly be separately."[120] Nonetheless, radical pacifists, including members of the New York City chapters of Catholic Worker, Mt. Morris House, Peacemakers, Fellowship of Reconciliation, and the War Resisters League, supported Reynolds and attended meetings of the RRDC, wrote and distributed flyers or articles about her, and marched in her defense.[121] Thus, a small but significant number of pacifists believed that solidarity with Puerto Rico and the political prisoners should be high on pacifists' and progressive North Americans' political agenda and acted on their beliefs.

A. J. Muste, for example, helped form the RRDC and urged "pacifists and other advocates of civil liberties" to make "a more careful study of the Puerto Rican situation and especially . . . what is happening there to civil liberties involving the Nationalist Party members."[122] He flew to Puerto Rico in June 1951 to learn about conditions and to meet with Reynolds, whom he described as "a U.S. pacifist who has for a good many years been interested in Puerto Rican matters, an advocate of Puerto Rican independence, and sympathetic to the Nationalist Party led by Pedro Albizu Campos."[123] He returned to the United States convinced that the pacifist movement needed "to step up the support" of the RRDC.[124]

Because Muste opposed violence, he found the Nationalists' 1954 attack on the U.S. Congress "particularly shocking and horrible." Yet instead of condemning the action, he considered it a wake-up call to people in the United States to "see recent Puerto Rican events as part of the whole problem of [U.S.] relations with Latin America." As a result, he urged Americans to engage in a "serious attempt . . . to understand the Puerto Rican situation and to put an end to every form of control over the Puerto Rican people . . . by the U.S. or U.S. interests—not least to put an end to the use of Puerto Rico as a military base by the U.S. armed forces."[125]

Ralph Templin expressed no doubt about the need to end U.S. rule in Puerto Rico and release the political prisoners. Nor did other members of Peacemakers. As one of their leaflets stated following the failed assassination attempt against Truman, "The method was wrong. But the goal is right. Free Puerto Rico."[126] Templin, Ernest Bromley, and Wallace Nelson traveled to Puerto Rico in August 1951 as a Peacemakers delegation to "show that one group of Americans is now

FIGURE 9.2. Ralph Templin, leader of the pacifist group the Peacemakers and supporter of Puerto Rican independence and Puerto Rican political prisoners, circa 1950. Source: Lawrence Templin.

shoulder to shoulder in resisting all imperialism, beginning at home."[127] The three confronted the issue of violence head-on by asking, "Can [Peacemakers] lead their fellow Americans to feel with them that the beginning of ending the violence lies with their own repentance and repudiation of all the inequalities and injustices inherent in the very nature of the imperialism which the United States fosters [in Puerto Rico]?"[128]

The three Peacemakers attended the first day of Reynolds's trial, traveled widely across the island and to Vieques, spoke with a range of Puerto Ricans, and studied the economic and political conditions closely.[129] Their visit reinforced their opposition to U.S. colonialism and increased their admiration for the Nationalist Party, as they noted in their report. "There is among the Nationalists, however, a degree of unique courage which is respected even by opponents. There is also among them a loyalty, of an unusual kind, to what they have come to believe in. These are traits which cannot help but be developed in people who belong to a minority group which opposes the status quo and the strong arm of the government."[130]

As people of faith, the Peacemakers were guided by their ethical commitment and determination to gain justice, their willingness to pay a high personal cost for their beliefs, as the imprisonment of Ruth Reynolds amply demonstrates, and their commitment to persevere despite difficult conditions. Two actions they carried out exemplify these qualities. The first focused on the United States' stationing of intercontinental ballistic missiles in Puerto Rico, the dangers the U.S. military presence posed to Puerto Ricans, and the need for nonmilitaristic solutions to world problems. To call attention to these threats, nine Peacemakers walked from Guánica Bay, where U.S. troops invaded Puerto Rico in 1898, to San Juan, a distance of 150 miles, between December 25, 1958, and January 5, 1959. During the walk, which they called "a mission of peace and good will," they handed out leaflets in English and Spanish and spoke with people about the Muñoz Marín government, his economic policies, and the U.S. military presence. They made no mention of the Nationalist Party prisoners or independence. Seymour Eichel, a pacificist who had gone to jail as a conscientious objector, was one of the marchers. He remembers that the "Insular police followed us openly until [journalists from the newspaper] El Imparcial took pictures of them. . . . Then they became more discrete and followed us at a distance." The security forces did what they could to undermine the march. "When we got to one town, a fellow . . . said, you know we'd be very happy to put you up. Then his parents were visited by the [police] and he said, 'I am sorry you wouldn't be welcome, there would be too many problems for my parents.' So that was the kind of atmosphere that there was at that time."[131] The local radio and press covered their progress. The PIP passed a resolution of solidarity with them, and the pro-independence Federación Universitaria Pro Independencia (Federation of Pro Independence University Students) endorsed the walk, as did the Nationalist Party.[132] After they returned to the United States, the Peacemaker Walkers, as they called themselves, sent a cablegram to President Eisenhower and Gen. Maxwell Taylor that expressed their demands. "Walking from Guanica [sic] to Casa Blanca [the U.S. military headquarters in Puerto Rico], we encountered widespread popular apprehension of annihilation by atomic bombardment due to intercontinental ballistic missile base. We urge immediate ending of this threat to the people of Puerto Rico and the world, and the removal of all United States military establishments."[133]

In the second action, Ralph Templin and Al Uhrie from Peacemakers and Nationalist Lydia Collazo began a five-day fast in San Juan in December 1960, "call[ing] for [Albizu's] release and for that of the other Nationalists in prison."[134] Roughly fifty Puerto Rican Nationalist Party prisoners, including Albizu, remained in prison in the United States and Puerto Rico in 1960.[135] Since his return to prison in 1954, Albizu had suffered "two paralytic strokes that left him mute and completely paralyzed on his right side." He was being treated in the Presbyterian Hospital in San Juan, where armed guards watched him twenty-four hours a day. The three activists began their fast "on the side-walk

FIGURE 9.3. Ruth Reynolds leads Peacemakers on a walk in Puerto Rico. Her sign reads, "We pacifists are walking from Guanica to San Juan." Directly behind her is Wallace Nelson. The next sign reads, "We oppose U.S. military and congressional domination in Puerto Rico." Source: Ruth M. Reynolds Papers, 1915–1989, Center for Puerto Rican Studies Library and Archives, Hunter College, City University of New York.

of a narrow side street just under the third story window of the room in which . . . Dr. Pedro Albizu Campos is a prisoner of the Government" on December 23, 1960.[136] Although the only news coverage they garnered was an article in the *San Juan Star*, the U.S. government was clearly paying attention. When Lydia Collazo arrived at the San Juan airport, en route to New York City once the fast ended, the FBI was waiting for her. They searched her luggage and threw her clothes all over the place but found nothing suspicious or incriminating.[137]

## BUILDING SOLIDARITY AND AN ANTI-IMPERIALIST COMMUNITY OF LATIN AMERICAN EXILES

Latin American communist parties were the primary target of U.S. government repression during the Cold War. These attacks, combined with the legacy of Browderism, which had led many communists to seek alliances and accommodation, not conflict, with their ruling classes and the United States, meant that most communist parties were largely incapable of offering either inspirational programs or meaningful proposals for substantial changes.[138] The political vacuum their weakness created left the terrain open for new voices, platforms, and initiatives, the most successful of which was the 26th of July Movement, which culminated in the Cuban Revolution in 1959.

In the early 1950s, Nationalist Party exiles Carlos Padilla, Laura Meneses, and Juan Juarbe worked with revolutionary forces in Cuba, Guatemala, and Mexico, where the 26th of July Movement organized its ultimately triumphal return to Cuba.[139] Their experiences and relationships with revolutionary forces made them more open to Marxism, a political evolution occurring simultaneously in Puerto Rico among some supporters of independence.[140] Exile also increased their awareness of their "pan-Latin American identity."[141]

The Prío Socarras government (1948–52) had offered Juarbe, Meneses, Padilla, and about seven other Nationalist exiles refuge in Cuba.[142] However, Fulgencio Batista's military coup of March 1952 radically altered Cuba's political landscape and subsequently forced the Nationalists to leave. Cuban revolutionary forces, with whom the Nationalists worked, moved into armed opposition and, on July 26, 1953, attacked La Moncada military barracks. The failed assault led to the death of many of the attackers and the imprisonment of others, followed by the exile of some revolutionaries, including Fidel Castro.[143]

The Batista government embraced Cold War anticommunism, became a U.S. ally in the region, and worked with U.S. officials.[144] Cuban military officers, presumably following U.S. government directives, picked up Juarbe and Padilla in Havana after the Nationalists attacked the U.S. Congress.[145] Padilla was held in El Principe jail for two months and tortured by Cuban intelligence officers, who hoped to connect him with the shooting in Congress. This was absurd since, Padilla explained to me, "I had not moved [from Havana] and they knew it. The U.S. Embassy had people following me." Padilla is convinced the U.S. government was involved in his arrest because when Cuban police interrogated him, "the FBI were outside in the corridor. They never came in, but they were there listening and they spoke perfect Spanish."[146]

The court found Padilla not guilty, a verdict that Padilla believes reflected the U.S. government's goal of having him released so that he could be detained as an illegal immigrant, turned over to the FBI, and returned to the United States.[147] Luckily, Padilla's cellmates were revolutionary students and trade-union leaders who helped him escape from jail and connect with comrades who communicated his situation to the Guatemalan embassy. Embassy staff smuggled him onto a Guatemalan plane that was in Cuba to refuel and pick up supplies. With their aid, Padilla clandestinely escaped Cuba and landed in

Guatemala in April 1954, where the government of Jacobo Arbenz welcomed him.[148]

The Arbenz government's domestic and foreign policies complemented each other: both reflected a progressive, nationalist, and anti-imperialist politic. The government's efforts to nationalize the U.S.-based United Fruit company's massive landholdings in Guatemala and thereby promote agrarian reform and improve peasants' standard of living, went hand in hand with its anticolonial and anti-imperialist positions in the United Nations and the Organization of American States.[149] The governments of both Juan José Arevalo (1945–51) and Arbenz in Guatemala publicly advocated an end to U.S. colonial rule in Puerto Rico. Not only did the Arevalo government urge President Truman to commute Oscar Collazo's death sentence to life imprisonment, but it also repeatedly "agitated" for Puerto Rican independence. The Guatemalan military band even played "La Borinqueña" (which the government newspaper called "the Nationalist hymn") not "The Star-Spangled Banner" when the Puerto Rican team lined up at the opening ceremony of the Central American Games in Guatemala City in 1950.[150] And in 1953, Guatemala voted against the United States' successful proposal that the United Nations remove Puerto Rico from the list of non-self-governing territories in recognition of its status as a commonwealth.[151]

In line with its progressive policies, Guatemala offered refuge to Latin American exiles and activists, including Hilda Gadea, a Peruvian affiliated with APRA, and Ernesto Guevara, who were a couple.[152] Guevara and Padilla became friends, drawn together by their shared anti-imperialist politics. The CIA-directed overthrow of the Arbenz administration in June 1954 abruptly ended the democratic government's attempts to ameliorate the lives of millions of Guatemalans and eliminated the safe space for Latin American exiles. Fearing for his life, Padilla joined some 400 equally threatened Guatemalans and Latin Americans who sought refuge in the Argentine embassy. As historian Ernesto Semán writes, the asylum seekers included "poets, artists, intellectuals, leaders, and activists; their names dot the struggles that shaped the region during the twentieth century."[153] Padilla stayed in the embassy for two to three months until President Juan Perón sent planes to evacuate him and other refugees to Argentina.[154]

In Argentina, Padilla continued his mission to mobilize Latin Americans in solidarity with Puerto Rican independence and Nationalist prisoners. Ernesto Guevara put him in touch with Enrique V. Corominas, the diplomat who had served as Argentina's representative in the United Nations and the Organization of American States and was the author of a number of well-regarded books, including *Puerto Rico libre*.[155] Corominas gave him both political and material support. Padilla wrote anonymous articles in the Argentine newspaper *Clarín* about Puerto Rico and worked with a young Argentine, Rito D. Luna, to set up the Asociación de Amigos Pro Libertad de Puerto Rico (Association of Friends in Support of Puerto Rican Freedom) on August 4, 1955.[156] After Perón was overthrown in 1955, Padilla went to Uruguay, where Argentine Socialist Alfredo Palacios was the ambassador. Palacios, like many progressive Argentines, had long supported Puerto Rican independence. From Uruguay, Padilla continued his peripatetic mission to generate solidarity.[157] He spent the next decade traveling in South America. In Chile he worked with students and distributed literature about Puerto Rico.[158] He worked with members of the Ecuadorian congress, who in 1957 passed the Solidarity Agreement with the Peoples of Algeria and Puerto Rico discussed in the introduction.[159] The agreement proclaimed the "right of the Puerto Rican nation to join the continental family of sovereign nations" and called on the international community to "fulfill its commitments with the UN Charter" and ensure that the Puerto Rican people achieve "their future sovereignty."[160]

After Padilla left Argentina, Luna and María Santander, the association's new secretary, wrote to Ruth Reynolds and Lydia Collazo to establish regular exchanges with them.[161] The organization declared its intent "to fight for the independence of Puerto Rico"; "study and diffuse the political, economic, social and cultural reality of Puerto Rico"; and "fight against any form of imperialist intervention, in any part of the world."[162] During the next few years, the Argentine association regularly informed Collazo and Reynolds of their work, which included communicating their support for independence to Puerto Ricans who visited Buenos Aires; holding public events, such as one in which Carlos Padilla spoke; writing to Dag Hammarskjöld, U.N. secretary general, stating their support for Puerto Rican independence; congratulating Peacemakers on their walk in Puerto Rico; and publishing *Puerto Rico Libre*.[163]

Unlike Padilla, Laura Meneses was not arrested in March 1954, but the Cuban Military Intelligence Service interrogated her. Facing increased repression and told by the Cuban government that she had to leave, Meneses obtained a tourist visa from the Mexican consulate in Havana. She relocated to Mexico, where Juarbe had moved in January for health reasons.[164] There they worked with other Latin American political exiles, especially Cubans in the 26th of July Movement, and became close with Ernesto Guevara and Hilda Gadea, who had sought refuge in Mexico after the overthrow of Arbenz.[165]

Gadea introduced them to Che Guevara, and according to Juarbe, they "hit it off so well that from then on we went [to Meneses' house] once a week, and . . . [discussed] problems and events in Latin America."[166] Meneses and Juarbe reunited with Fidel Castro and became part of the Cuban revolutionaries' inner circle of confidantes.[167] The level of trust between them was so high that Meneses and Juarbe accompanied members of the 26th of July Movement into the countryside for target practice under the direction of Gen. Alberto Bayo.[168] When Guevara left Mexico on the yacht *Granma* to initiate the Cuban revolution, Gadea went to live with Meneses.[169]

The Cubans and Puerto Ricans formed part of an anti-imperialist community of Latin American exiles. They held political events and supported each other and the struggles they were part of.[170] On October 18, 1955, for example, they gathered in Chapultepec Park in Mexico City to commemorate Mexico's Grito de Dolores and call for an end to U.S.-backed dictatorships in the Americas. Speakers and attendees included Guatemalan and Colombian exiles, Mexicans representing diverse organizations, and Meneses, Juarbe, and Fidel Castro. The Guatemalan speaker lauded the "advantages of freedom for which they had fought." Juarbe proclaimed that "it was essential to end all existing dictatorships." Castro, the final speaker, castigated the "United States as the protector of dictatorships in the Americas."[171]

Meneses and Juarbe worked in other arenas to generate support for Puerto Rican independence and the Nationalist prisoners among Mexicans, the exile community, and across Latin America. They formed the Comité Mexicano Pro Independencia de Puerto Rico (Mexican Committee for the Independence of Puerto Rico) and wrote about Puerto Rico's colonial situation. The committee published Juarbe's book, *El derecho de Puerto Rico a su independencia*, in 1954. The book reproduced two Nationalist documents, one given at the conference in Bogota of 1948 and the other to the American Commission of Dependent Territories in 1949.[172] The committee concluded its short introduction to the book by proclaiming its members' solidarity with Puerto Rico and declaring that Puerto Rico's independence was critical to Latin America: "We are on the side of Puerto Rico in its amazing fight. There is no such thing as a small enemy. The power of force can only be transitory. 'Whether force or law will triumph in América will be determined in Puerto Rico,' as Albizu Campos so clearly stated."[173]

Juarbe and Meneses also wrote for the Mexican publication *Humanismo, Revista Mensual de Cultura*.[174] The journal's editorial committee included representatives from Mexico, Central America, the Antilles, South America, and Spain in exile. To justify the Nationalists' attempt to assassinate President Truman and their attack on the U.S. Congress, Juarbe wrote a lengthy treatise on the history and reality of U.S. colonialism in Puerto Rico.[175] Meneses, who also contributed to the magazine, took a very different approach, one that appealed to the readers' emotions. She noted that she and Pedro Albizu Campos had been married for thirty-three years, fifteen of which he had spent in jail. She told the story of Olga Viscal, a young Puerto Rican Nationalist student, who had developed tuberculosis as a result of the horrendous conditions she was subjected to following her imprisonment in 1950. Meneses recounted that Francisco Matos Paoli, Puerto Rico's premier poet and essayist and a Nationalist, had been a prisoner since the 1950 uprising. His situation was so physically and mentally damaging that it "broke his health to the point where he can no longer write."[176] Meneses ended her powerful indictment of U.S. colonialism and the imprisonment of Nationalist prisoners with a ringing endorsement of Puerto Ricans' right to fight and a reminder that Latin America is one. "Fighting for independence is not a crime, it is a duty. And for Hispanic Americans, the patria is the entire continent."[177]

From one perspective, the history of the Nationalist Party in the 1950s is the story of defeat. The party suffered three successive military failures, the death of important cadre, the imprisonment of scores of leaders and militants, the decline of popular support and membership, and an inability to achieve its political goals. Puerto Rico became a free associated state, a change that a majority of Puerto Ricans appeared to support, and the United Nations removed the archipelago from its list of dependent territories.

There is nothing surprising about these defeats. What is amazing, though, is the audacity of the Nationalists, who dared to attack the most powerful nation in the world. Yet these reverses, the depths and negative consequences of which cannot be overestimated, fail to convey the whole picture. They overlook the courage and solidarity of countless Latin Americans who acted in support of Puerto Rican independence and in defense of the Nationalist prisoners. They ignore those North Americans who challenged the psychological, emotional, and political clampdown and repression that McCarthyism, then at its height, engendered. They disregard the ability of people, acting in solidarity, to save the life of Oscar Collazo, spirit Carlos Padilla out of Cuba to safety in Guatemala, and endure a hunger strike or prison to secure an independent Puerto Rico and the release of Nationalist political prisoners. And they fail to consider the impact of time and changing conditions.

Lolita Lebrón spent twenty-five years in U.S. prisons, many of them in isolation. Prison guards raped her. For years she had few, if any, visits. Once considered a terrorist, she is now viewed as a national heroine by many in Puerto Rico, the United States, and around the world. I asked her how she felt about the attack on the U.S. Congress. Although she had become a pacifist, she responded that the actions "were necessary." "We do not regret them," she told me. "If people had not been willing to give their lives for the patria or there had been no political prisoners, then we would be nothing, and we would not have accomplished anything. These things inspire and sustain a cause. They are necessary."[178]

# CONCLUSION

Pedro Albizu Campos died on April 21, 1965, a few months after Governor Luis Muñoz Marín pardoned him in November 1964.[1] Albizu's body lay in state in the Ateneo Puertorriqueño in San Juan, and thousands of people from all walks of life and across the political spectrum came to pay their respects. The flow of mourners was so great that "within twenty-four hours, twelve thousand memorial ribbons had been distributed and thousands of mourners left without them because they could not be prepared fast enough to keep up with the demand."[2]

Albizu's funeral procession took place on April 25. It wound its way from the Ateneo through Old San Juan to San Juan Bautista Cathedral and from there to the cemetery. Music played, people threw flowers on the coffin, and participants carried pictures of Ramón Emeterio Betances and Albizu, as well as the flags of Lares, Puerto Rico, and the Nationalist Party. Women and men dressed in the uniforms of the enfermeras and cadetes marched in front of and around Albizu's coffin.[3] One hundred thousand people jammed the streets to share their grief and bid farewell to the man former secretary general of the Puerto Rican Communist Party César Andreu Iglesias declared "the conscience of Puerto Rico."[4] The crowd was so thick that it took three hours and fifteen minutes to proceed from the Ateneo to the cathedral, a distance of less than a mile. Nationalists from Chicago, Los Angeles, and New York joined the crowd, as did dignitaries and supporters from Cuba, Mexico, and South America. The Venezuelan parliament observed five minutes of silence in honor of Albizu, and hundreds of "cables, letters, cards, and notes of condolences from Latin American workers' congresses and from artists and professionals from around the world" were sent.[5]

Laura Meneses had not seen her husband since 1950 because the U.S. government routinely denied her requests to visit him. Washington only allowed her to see him less than two weeks before he died. Meneses had become a Cuban citizen and first secretary of the Cuban mission at the United Nations, so she traveled on a Cuban diplomatic visa.[6] She organized and spoke at the graveyard ceremony, denouncing the U.S. government's ill treatment of Albizu: "The assassination has been consummated." She then summarized Albizu's life and legacy. "Albizu Campos lived for his people and he died for them—the sacrifice imposed on him by the enemy of his nation's freedom and independence."[7] Other speakers included José Antonio Otero, interim president of the Puerto Rican Nationalist Party; Laura Albizu Campos de Meneses, the couple's youngest daughter, who lived in Peru; and José Herrera Oropeza, a member of the Venezuelan Congress, committed anti-imperialist, and supporter of human rights.[8] In his speech, Herrera explained what Albizu meant to Venezuelans and Latin Americans more broadly. "We in Venezuela love and admire him because we know he represented part of the Latin American people's ceaseless process to achieve independence from North American imperialism. Pedro Albizu Campos is not only Puerto Rican, he is Latin American."[9]

I end with this story because it encapsulates the main arguments of the book. For many Puerto Rican and Latin American anticolonialists and revolutionaries across the nineteenth and twentieth centuries, as well as for U.S.-based progressives and leftists, nationalism was integrally linked to anti-imperialism, internationalism, and transnational relations of solidarity. The PNPR was deeply rooted in Puerto Rico and profoundly committed to securing the national independence of the archipelago. At the same time, it identified Puerto Rico as part of Latin America, much of which shared its language, religion, culture, and history. The Nationalists sought to establish a sovereign republic and end U.S. rule, not to distance Puerto Rico from its neighbors and sister nations of the Americas, but to rejoin them on equal footing. Most of all, the Nationalist Party wanted to end decades of U.S. colonialism so that Puerto Ricans could rule themselves, instead of being dictated to by Washington.

The events, speakers, and attendees at Albizu's funeral reflect the links between and among nationalism, internationalism, transnationalism, and anti-imperialism that characterized the party's politics. They clearly refute the idea that nationalism is inevitably and necessarily xenophobic and reestablish the vision of anticolonialism as a liberatory force shared by many revolutionary forces across the Global South. Albizu's body lay in state at the Ateneo, one of Puerto Rico's oldest and most respected cultural institutes. Although it is not known how many of the 100,000 mourners supported independence, their attendance unmistakably signaled their respect for Albizu and the Nationalist Party. The presence of thousands and thousands of mourners was simultaneously a massive outpouring of sorrow and an affirmation of their *puertorrique-ñidad*, Puertoricanness.

Although she was not Puerto Rican, Laura Meneses embodied these multiple connections. In addition to being a grieving widow, she was a Peruvian woman who, after marrying Albizu, dedicated her life to building solidarity with the Nationalist cause throughout the hemisphere. Her words at his burial attest to her anger and her anguish even as they assert that Albizu died for his people and attribute his death to the United States. For Meneses, as for other Nationalists, solidarity was a two-way street. Cuban governments and people had supported her and other Nationalists since the 1920s and repeatedly backed Puerto Rican independence in national and international forums. When she could, she reciprocated their solidarity. As a committed anti-imperialist, she drew on her diplomatic skills, years of traveling and living in Cuba, Peru, and Mexico, and profound gratitude to Cubans, most especially the revolutionary forces, to represent the sister republic in the United Nations after 1959.

Herrera Oropeza's funeral address echoed the words spoken by countless Latin Americans from the 1920s through the early 1950s, only a small portion of which have made their way into this book. His testimony simultaneously paid homage to Albizu as a fighter for Puerto Rican independence and situated him in the more general fight of Latin Americans to end U.S. imperialism in the continent. Speaking in the name of the Venezuelan people, Herrera affirmed both their and Latin Americans' solidarity with the occupied colony of Puerto Rico.[10]

Manifestations of Latin American solidarity with Puerto Rican independence and the Nationalists continued through the late 1950s and early 1960s, although they occurred less frequently than in earlier decades. In addition to Albizu, thirty-five other Nationalist political prisoners, whose sentences ranged from twelve to 485 years, were still being held in Puerto Rican or U.S. jails in 1962.[11] Ché Paralitici calculated that their combined sentences totaled 7,000 years and the average sentence was 175 years.[12] These prisoners' health declined during these years, due to a combination of unhygienic conditions, the lack of nutritious food, and the absence of good, in some cases any, health care. Supporters in Latin America and the United States blamed the U.S. government for the miserable conditions in which the prisoners were held and, consequently, their poor health. I cited the letter Chilean politicians wrote to President Eisenhower in September 1957 in the introduction. In addition to demanding freedom for Albizu and all the prisoners, the letter made clear that the signers believed Albizu's situation was so grave that his imprisonment in "colonial jails . . . will shortly lead to his death" and counseled Eisenhower to free him.[13] The Argentine Asociación de Amigos Pro Libertad de Puerto Rico wrote to Governor Muñoz Marín urging him to release Albizu.[14] In December 1957, a delegation of Ecuadorian politicians visited Puerto Rico and Albizu, who was confined to the Presbyterian Hospital in San Juan. They found him in such poor health, "a human ruin," that four of the delegates broke down in tears; one of the delegates was so upset that he suffered a heart attack, from which he recovered.[15]

### FREE THE NATIONALIST PRISONERS!

In 1957, the Puerto Rican legislature unanimously repealed the infamous Law 53 of 1948, the Gag Law that most of the Nationalist prisoners had been convicted of violating.[16] This led to the release of some prisoners, but several dozen remained incarcerated. By the late 1960s, many of them had been released. But it was not until 1972 that the last Nationalist prisoner in Puerto Rico, Bernardo Díaz y Díaz, was freed.[17] He, however, refused to leave his cell as long as five Nationalists (Lolita Lebrón in Alderson, West Virginia; Rafael Cancel Miranda, in Marion, Illinois; and Oscar Collazo, Andrés Figueroa Cordero, and Irvin Flores in Leavenworth, Kansas) remained incarcerated in U.S. federal penitentiaries. It took the combined efforts of four police officers to remove him.[18]

The odds against securing the release of one Puerto Rican prisoner convicted of attempting to kill a U.S. president and four others convicted of attacking the U.S. Congress and wounding five congressmen in the midst of the Cold War were pretty high. It took the joint work of individuals, organizations, and governments to achieve it. By the time the five Nationalists imprisoned in U.S. jails were released in the late 1970s, Figueroa Cordero had been in jail twenty-three years, Cancel Miranda, Flores, and Lebrón twenty-five, and Collazo twenty-nine.

The first sign of success the campaign to free the five Nationalist prisoners enjoyed occurred in October 1977, when President Jimmy Carter freed Figueroa Cordero, who suffered terminal cancer. Before he died in March 1979, Figueroa Cordero reaffirmed his commitment to a free Puerto Rico.[19] Referring to the attack on the U.S. Congress in 1954, he said, "I would do it half a million times if I had to. To save your country, there is no other recourse than to give your life."[20]

By 1979, domestic, Puerto Rican, and international pressure on Carter to release the four other Nationalist prisoners had grown exponentially. The multilayered work, which ranged from petitions to bombs and was carried out in the United States, Puerto Rico, Latin America, and around the world, contributed to creating a climate in which it was not only possible but expedient for Carter to free them. A number of Puerto Rican institutions and individuals, including both legislative houses, the Episcopal, Methodist, and Catholic churches, "labor unions, professional organizations, student councils, cultural groups, and four former governors," demanded their freedom.[21] One clear manifestation of the power the movement exerted was the growing list of organizations and individuals that advocated their freedom. Both the World Peace Council and the U.S. National Council of Churches did, as did a family member of one of the congressmen who had been shot in 1954.[22] Congressional representatives publicly called on Carter to let the prisoners go. In 1978, four Black U.S. representatives, Shirley Chisholm (D-N.Y.), Ronald Dellums (D-Calif.), John Conyers (D-Mich.), and Parren Mitchell (D-Md.) wrote a letter to Carter "requesting that the release take place before Christmas to reaffirm 'our country's commitment to human rights, in the name of Christian charity and in the spirit of brotherly love.'"[23] Robert García, the only congressman of Puerto Rican descent, urged Carter to commutate their sentence. He had grown up next door to Oscar Collazo and stated, "It's a chapter in the history of Puerto Rico that should be over. They've already paid the price."[24]

On September 6, 1979, Carter granted the Nationalist prisoners unconditional release. The four walked through their respective prison gates to freedom on September 10. Members of the National Committee to Free the Nationalist Prisoners, a Chicago-based organization active in the campaign to free them, and the Nationalists' attorneys and family members met them and escorted them to a heroes' welcome in Chicago.[25] From Chicago the four Nationalists traveled to New York City. There they addressed 3,000 to 4,000 supporters at Saint Paul the Apostle Church in Manhattan and held a press conference at the United Nations organized by the Cuban chargé d'affaires.[26]

From New York the four flew to Puerto Rico, along with friends, family, supporters, and reporters. During the flight Lebrón "distributed copies of 'La Borinqueña' (the island's national anthem) to all on board and led the singing when they landed in San Juan's airport."[27] At the airport, "You looked out at a sea of Puerto Rican flags and people were going crazy. It was amazing!"[28] Six thousand supporters waited to welcome the Nationalists home, greeting them with chants of "Viva Puerto Rico Libre!" and "Jíbaros sí, Yankis no!" The Nationalists spoke to the adoring crowd from a "makeshift speakers' platform." Lebrón, her spirit unquenched, shouted, "The United States will repress anyone that tries to assert their birthright on nationhood." And Collazo, with tears streaming down his face, announced, "I am so happy to be in a place where I am not afraid to express my emotions."[29] Thousands of cheering Puerto Ricans lined the road as the entourage made its way to its first stop: the cemetery in Old San Juan where Albizu was buried.[30] When she arrived, Lebrón kissed Albizu's tomb and "prayed to God to grant independence to the island."[31]

These four Nationalists, like all but two of the Nationalists I interviewed for this book, have since died. They all remained, or in the two cases remain, committed to independence for Puerto Rico and were, or are, active in the anticolonial and social justice struggles that have occurred on the archipelago in the past four decades. They called for the release of Puerto Rican freedom fighters who went to jail as a result of their participation in armed actions in Puerto Rico or the United States to protest U.S. colonialism.[32] They participated in the fight to stop the U.S. Navy's use of the Puerto Rican island of Vieques for target practice. Lebrón, for example, joined other protestors who "trespassed" on U.S. Navy land in Vieques, for which she and thirty others were arrested and jailed on May 1, 2003.[33] They repeatedly exerted their moral and political authority to call for unity among those who seek an independent Puerto Rico, but their pleas went unheeded. Today, the independence movement is small and divided, even as dissatisfaction with Puerto Rico's status as a U.S. colony has increased. Its growth has been spurred since 2008 by the deepening economic crisis; the widespread outrage many Puerto Ricans felt following the U.S. Congress' unilateral passage and imposition of PROMESA (Puerto Rican Oversight, Management, and Economic Stability Act) in 2016; the devastation Hurricanes Irma and Maria unleashed in September 2017; the glaring indifference the U.S. government demonstrated to the subsequent suffering of Puerto Ricans, most graphically revealed when President Trump threw paper towels to Puerto Ricans on his visit to the island; and the financial and economic depredations U.S. financiers and entrepreneurs have wreaked on the archipelago.[34]

The Nationalist Party exists today. Ironically, its current influence and membership are sharply reduced, but an appreciation of its historic impact and legacy continues to expand. Indeed, awareness of, interest in, and respect for the Nationalist Party among Puerto Ricans in Puerto Rico and the United States have greatly expanded in recent years. Calle 13, the award-winning musical group, has sung about them; murals on walls in San Juan, Ponce, Mayagüez, New York City, Chicago, and elsewhere portray them as both suffering and heroic figures; buildings and streets are named after them.[35] Pedro Albizu Campos, Rafael Cancel Miranda, and Lolita Lebrón, along with other Nationalists, form part of Puerto Rico's heroic and patriotic pantheon, as do Ramón Emeterio Betances, Eugenio María de Hostos, and Lola Rodríguez de Tió. Many of the rituals and principles the Nationalists initiated and stood for have been adopted not only by independentistas but by much of the Puerto Rican population. Every year the independence movement celebrates the uprising of September 23, 1868, against the Spanish in Lares. Members of the Fuerzas Armadas de Liberación Nacional refused to recognize the right of the U.S. government to try them and declared themselves prisoners of war after their arrest in Chicago in April 1980.[36] On a more mass, even quotidian level, waving the Puerto Rican flag is a commonplace feature of many demonstrations in Puerto Rico and in diasporic communities in the United States. The symbol of the flag is stamped on countless tee-shirts, mugs, and knickknacks and an integral part of street art across the archipelago.[37] What makes this even more significant is that the blue used in the flag is increasingly a light blue, indicating support for nationalism, as opposed to the darker blue, which has long signaled acceptance of the status quo or statehood.[38] In addition, feeling and asserting pride in being Puerto Rican is central to many Puerto Ricans' most basic sense of who they are as a people and as individuals. That, too, is a legacy of the Nationalist Party, which consistently affirmed Puerto Ricans' dignity, history, and right to rule themselves.

# ACKNOWLEDGMENTS

I began thinking about this book in 2004, when I interviewed Lolita Lebrón. In the intervening years so many people have helped me. I give a great big thank you to all those who have been so generous with their time, thoughts, insights, and encouragement.

I thank the members of the Puerto Rican Nationalist Party (PNPR) who shared their thoughts and experiences with me. I learned so much from them, and I greatly admire their *valor y sacrificio* (courage and sacrifice) and dedication to an independent Puerto Rico. I also thank those courageous North American activists who recounted their inspiring stories of working in solidarity with the PNPR. One of my deepest regrets is that most of those I interviewed are no longer with us so I can't give them a copy of this book, my deepest thanks, and *un abrazo de corazón*.

It's hard for me to imagine how I could have written this book without the support, suggestions, and insights of José E. López, a person I think of as a walking encyclopedia of Puerto Rican history. Thank you for your feedback and for telling me why you thought it was important to write this book.

I am very grateful to former political prisoners Alicia Rodríguez and Luis Rosa for helping me conduct research on the PNPR. It was a real joy to talk with Alicia, Fifo (her mother), and Isabel Rodríguez, who was roughly ninety-eight at the time. I'll never forget the nighttime drive down the sharply windy mountainous roads from Adjuntas to Cayey after Fifo and I spoke with Nationalist Antonio Cruz.

Olga Jiménez de Wagenheim is not only a great historian but also a wonderful colleague and friend. She generously read almost every chapter of this book, pointed out my mistakes, and offered me constructive advice.

Anita Grisales read and edited an earlier draft of this manuscript. She is an excellent editor. She helped me clarify some rather messy thinking and writing to produce a clearer manuscript. Many thanks to Jim O'Brien, friend and number one indexer.

Luckily, I met José Manuel Dávila at the University of Puerto Rico library in 2008. He both writes and produces films about the Nationalist Party and has helped me in so many ways. I also had the opportunity to conduct research and interviews with Janine Santiago. I thank the Torresola family (Angelina, Ana María, Elio, and Luis) for their exuberant welcome of me and Janine and my subsequent communications with them. Antonio Sotomayor is a good friend and colleague! He has generously shared materials and thoughts about Puerto Rican history, the Nationalists, and Juan Juarbe Juarbe (who appears in both of our books!).

I am deeply grateful to members of the Windy City Writing Group (Ben Johnson, Andrae Marak, Teresa Prados-Torreira, Mike Staudenmeier, Ellie Walsh, Neici Zeller). Over the years, they have read some version of every chapter in this book and provided me with constructive feedback about how to make them better. Although I often thought, I can't possibly make those changes, can't they just think it's wonderful the way it is, I realized that their suggestions were not only necessary but doable. Their comments have made this manuscript so much better! Many other people have read multiple chapters, one chapter, or part of a chapter and offered suggestions about how to improve the text. Others have connected me with people to speak with or sources to consult. Some people have buoyed my spirits when I felt unsure about how to proceed or whether the project was going in the right direction. Each and every one of them took time out of their busy schedules to help me. I really appreciate it and want them to know they made a difference. I wish I could describe what each person did, but space doesn't allow me. However, I hope each of you knows how grateful I am. Thank you, Myriem Aboutaher, Alvita Akiboh, Mercedes Fernández-Asenjo, Sara Awartani, César Ayala, John Bartlett, Marc Becker, Martín Bergal, Andrés Bisso, Ashley Black, Chris Boyer, Lina Britto, Laura Browder, Julia Buck, Antoinette Burton, Barry Carr, Eladio Cancel, Michelle Chase, Robert Curley, Michael Deutsch, Phil Devon, Barbara Duhl, Rebecca Earle, Rusti Eisenberg, Howie Emmer, Chris Erick, Isabel Farias, Elisa Fernández, Luis Angel Ferrao, Thomas Field, Eileen Finlay, Andrea Friedman, Elizabeth Friedman, Humberto García Muñiz, Romina Akemi Green, Tanya Harmer, Patti Harms, Anna Henger, Daniel Immerwahr, Jane Juffer, Temma Kaplan, Laurence La Fountain-Stokes, Raymond Laureano, Victoria Langland, Marisol LeBrón, Michelle Liffick, Hugo Vallenas Málaga, Vania Markarian, Claude Marks, Cruz Bonlarron Martínez, Lisa Materson, Rob McBride, Emily Meehan, Jorell Meléndez-Badillo Gerald Meyer, Jessica Stites Mor, Marisel Moreno, Arlen Muller, Pamela Murray, Jorge Nállim, Eugenia Palieraki, Ché Paralitici, Ricardo Parvex, Amanda Power, Sandra Pujals, Margaret Randall, Harri Franqui Rivera, Eugenia Rodríguez, Michael Rodríguez-Muñiz, Ileana Rodríguez-Silva, Virginia Sanchez-Korrol, Rachell Sánchez-Rivera, José Enrique Ayoroa Santaliz, Aldo Lauria Santiago, Juan Pablo Scarfi, Ernesto Semán, Mara Siegal, Andor Skotnes, Randy Sowell, Peter Staudenmeier, Jan Susler, Lawrence Templin, Lorrin Thomas, Miguel Tinker-Salas, Xavier Totti, Mary Kay Vaughan, Jill Vickers, Kevin Young, and Jacob Zumoff.

Special thanks to three longtime friends and colleagues whom I have worked with since I was a graduate student in the 1990s: Lisa Baldez, Sandy Deutsch, and Neici Zeller. Each in her own way has offered me amazing support, mental stimulation, insights, and plenty of Yes You Can Do It morale boosters along the way. I am particularly grateful to Neici for her help with translations and sharing her understanding of Dominican, Puerto Rican, and Caribbean history.

Aaron Coy Moulton is a researcher par excellence whose skills are matched only by his generosity. I know all the places he went to conduct research, because wherever he went, he sent me documents he found related to the Nationalists. Mara Dodge encouraged me to go to grad school and has been a constant source of good advice, friendship, insightful conversations, and fun ever since. I particularly thank her for helping me recover from my recent surgery. Thanks to Van Gosse, my co-chair in Historians for Peace and Democracy, for his comments on my work and encouragement to create positive political change in this country.

For the first two years of the pandemic, my friend Ji-Yeon Yuh and I worked together via Skype, she at her desk in Evanston, I at mine in Chicago. Knowing that I had a "work date" and check-in with her every weekday helped keep me on my toes and writing.

I would also like to thank four IIT students. Elnaz Moshfeghian and Ashley Snyder researched U.S. newspapers for coverage of the Nationalists. Roberto Villaseñor and Naomi Robles designed many of the images in the book.

The Franklin Research Grant from the American Philosophical Society allowed me to visit several U.S.-based archives. Support from Humberto García Muñiz and the Instituto de Estudios del Caribe at the University of Puerto Rico, Río Piedras, made my first research trip to Puerto Rico possible and introduced me to multiple resources available at the university. I thank Dean Chris Himes at the Illinois Institute of Technology for funds to travel to Mexico and Peru. I thank her and Matt Bauer for granting me a paid leave of absence to write the manuscript. That made all the difference!

Debbie Gershenowitz was the first editor I spoke with about my project. Though it has taken many years to complete, she has enthusiastically backed it and offered me the guidance I needed to improve the book. As I often say to friends and colleagues (who always agree with me), I am so lucky to have the best editor out there! And thank you to Erin Granville, Elizabeth Orange, Carol Seigler, Lindsay Starr, and the efficient, knowledgeable, and skilled team at the University of North Carolina Press. It has been a real pleasure working with you.

My deepest thanks go to my (twin) sister, Melinda. Through thick and thin, and despite occasional arguments (I don't think any of them could possibly be my fault!), she is always there for me. She is often the first person to read what I have written and always generous with her comments. It's nice to know that the person I have known all my life (regardless of when you think life begins) is a true friend who is often willing to put aside her work to read or discuss mine and, when necessary, engage in a discussion about what I have written and ways to improve it.

# NOTES

## Abbreviations

AGPR    Archivos Generales de Puerto Rico, Departamento de Justicia
NARA    National Archives and Records Administration
RG    Record Group
RRP    Ruth M. Reynolds Papers, Centro de Estudios Puertorriqueõs
RTC    Ralph T. Templin Collection, United Methodist Church Archives

## Introduction

1. Lolita Lebrón, interview with author, September 4, 2004, Chicago.
2. Lebrón interview.
3. Jiménez de Wagenheim, *Nationalist Heroines*, 262, 264.
4. For an annotated version of this interview, see Power, "If People Had Not Been Willing."
5. I thank Amanda Power for helping me formulate some of the ideas expressed here.
6. Maldonado Denis, "Perspectivas," 800; Zepeda Cortés, *Cambios y adaptaciones*, 71.
7. Palacios, *Nuestra América*, 1.
8. Shaffer, "Havana Hub," 49; Meléndez-Badillo, *Voces libertarias*, 139–41; Shaffer, *Anarchists of the Caribbean*.
9. Pujals, "¡Embarcados!"; Pujals, "'Soviet Caribbean'"; Carr, "Pioneering Transnational Solidarity"; Melgar Bao, "Anti-imperialist League."
10. Putnam, *Radical Moves*, 17.
11. James, *Holding Aloft the Banner*, 15.
12. Putnam, *Radical Moves*, 17. Although powerful labor movements developed in the French colonies of Martinique and Guadalupe, they sought "full political and economic equality with mainland France," not independence. Bonilla, *Non-Sovereign Futures*, 4. On Guadalupeans' push for assimilation with France, see Jenkins, *Vichy in the Tropics*, 7, 82–83. Guadalupe and Martinique became overseas departments, not independent nations, in 1946.
13. James, *Holding Aloft the Banner*, 56–66.
14. James, *Holding Aloft the Banner*, 136.
15. Carrión, "Two Variants of Caribbean Nationalism," 36. Carrión's article dissects the differences between Garvey and Albizu. Whereas Garvey identified Black oppression as the problem and global Black unity as the solution, Albizu defined U.S. colonial rule as the problem and independence as the solution. Although the Nationalists and the UNIA apparently had no relations with each other, one of the most prominent Puerto Ricans in New York City, Arturo Schomburg, "was a strong supporter of Marcus Garvey," although he "never believed in the idea of a return to Africa." James, *Holding Aloft the Banner*, 211.
16. For example, Nationalist leaders wrote courteous messages to President Warren G. Harding and to Congress announcing the party's formation in 1922, as I discuss in chapter 3.
17. The Nationalist Party fared poorly in the 1932 elections, winning only 5,257 votes out of 380,000 votes cast. Nolla-Acosta, *Puerto Rico Election Results*, 63. However, that was not the primary reason the pro-independence organization unanimously agreed to "abstain" after participating in the 1932 National Assembly elections. *El Mundo*, December 15, 1933. The decision, instead, corresponded to the party's belief that Puerto Ricans had to organize and fight to achieve independence because the United States would never willingly grant it freedom. Further, the party argued, electoral participation perpetuated Puerto Ricans' dependence on the U.S. government and faith in its promises to respect the wishes of the

Puerto Rican people. "La jefatura nacionalista llama a sus correligionarios a la abstención electoral," *El Mundo*, October 29, 1936. For a helpful discussion of *retraimiento*, see Jiménez Aponte, "*La Urna como sepulcro*."

18. A poll conducted shortly after Hurricane Maria devastated Puerto Rico in September 2017 revealed the disquieting truth: only 54 percent of U.S. residents knew that Puerto Ricans are U.S. citizens. Kyle Dropp and Brendan Nyyhan, "Nearly Half of Americans Don't Know Puerto Ricans Are Fellow Citizens," *New York Times*, September 26, 2017. For an analysis of what leading U.S. textbooks write about Puerto Rico, see Gosse, "United States Textbooks." I capitalize "Nationalists" to refer specifically to members of the Puerto Rican Nationalist Party; otherwise, I refer to people who espouse a nationalist point of view as "nationalists."

19. The five had been New York City–based members of the Nationalist Party. They were Oscar Collazo, jailed in 1950 for his attempted assassination of President Harry S. Truman, and Lolita Lebrón, Andrés Figueroa, Irvin Flores, and Rafael Cancel Miranda, jailed in 1954 following their attack on Congress.

20. "Commutations Granted by President Jimmy Carter (1977–1981)," U.S. Department of Justice, www.justice.gov/pardon/commutations-granted-president-jimmy-carter-1977 -1981; "Ailing Puerto Rican in 1954 Attack on Congress Is Freed by Carter," *New York Times*, October 7, 1977.

21. The FALN was a clandestine Puerto Rican organization that carried out armed actions in the United States from 1974 to roughly 1981. The group called for Puerto Rican independence and the release of the Puerto Rican Nationalist prisoners, among other issues. For a collection of their communiqués, see Committee in Solidarity, *Towards People's War for Independence*. Between 1980 and 1983, fifteen Puerto Ricans were arrested, tried, and convicted of various charges linked to their alleged involvement in the FALN. In August 1999, President Bill Clinton granted twelve of the pro-independence activists conditional clemency. Power, "From Freedom Fighters to Patriots," 147. Two more prisoners, Haydée Torres and Carlo Alberto Torres, were released in 2009 and 2010, respectively. Oscar López Rivera, the last of the FALN prisoners, was freed in May 2017. Carlos Rivera Giusti and David McFadden," Puerto Rican Militant Oscar Lopez Rivera Freed from Custody after 36 years," *Chicago Tribune*, May 17, 2017.

22. I use "American" to refer to the Americas: North, Central, and South America and the Caribbean or the people who live there. I call the United States of America "the United States."

23. For the history and ideology of the PIP, see Berrios Martínez, *Tierra prometida*; and Concepción de Gracia, *Nombre de la verdad*.

24. I use "archipelago" to refer to the main island and the island municipalities of Culebra and Vieques. I use "Island" or "Puerto Rico" to refer to the main island. I thank Marisol Lebrón for her thoughts on this nomenclature. In an interview in *Los Quijotes* in 1926, Albizu Campos described Puerto Rico and the Antilles as "an archipelago" where a battle between "Yankee imperialism and Ibero-americanismo" was taking place. His merging of Puerto Rico and the Antilles speaks to the essentially transnational nature of his concept of nationalism. Reprinted in Castro, *Historia sinóptica*, 69.

25. Coll y Cuchí, *Nacionalismo en Puerto Rico*, 144. The Nationalist Party used Ibero-América, referring to Spain and Portugal's former colonies and Hispano-América, Spain's former colonies, interchangeably during the 1920s and 1930s.

26. Allende Gossens, "Homenaje a la memoria de Latcham," 2159–62.

27. One of the earlier books on white nationalism is Swain, *New White Nationalism*. See also Anderson, *White Rage*. Fascism has been and is grounded in nationalism. It exalts both the defense of the nation in opposition to the dangerous "Other," whose identity varies depending on the historical context and political exigencies. It also proclaims the restoration of a mythical past, when the nation was pure, undefiled by the threatening intruders or internal

enemies. On the first point, see Durham, *Women and Fascism*, 3. On the second, see Paxton, *Anatomy of Fascism*; and Griffin, *Nature of Fascism*, chaps. 1, 2.

28. Vijay Prasad conveys the power and utopian vision of anti-imperialist leaders and movements across the Third World in the twentieth century in *The Darker Nations*. Partha Chatterjee analyzes changing attitudes toward nationalism in the latter part of the twentieth century in *The Nation and Its Fragments*, 3–7. For an overview of anticolonial movements, which unfortunately does not include Puerto Rico, see Westad, *Global Cold War*, 79–109. For a positive assessment of national liberation struggles, see Nzongola-Ntalaja, "Amílcar Cabral."

29. On South-South solidarity, see Stites Mor, *Human Rights and Transnational Solidarity*.

30. Ashley Currier explores how Namibian feminists and LGBT activists have challenged post-independence misogyny and homophobia in Namibia by advancing what they refer to as "sexual decolonization" in "Aftermath of Decolonization," 443. For women's gendered critique of the Nicaraguan revolution, see Randall, *Sandino's Daughters Revisited*. A similar critique of the Puerto Rican independence movement and/or Left remains to be written.

31. For a discussion of Cuba's role in supporting the liberation of Angola and Namibia, see Gleijeses, *Visions of Freedom*; Hatzky, "Cuba's Concept of 'International Solidarity'"; and Hatzky, *Cubans in Angola*.

32. Chatterjee, *Nation and Its Fragments*, 3.

33. Lewis, *Puerto Rico*, 81. Lewis does not say what the incident was. By "Americans," Lewis meant inhabitants of the United States, not the population of the Americas. Other sources, including an article in *Life* in 1954, attributed Albizu's "hatred" of the United States to the treatment he received in the U.S. military. According to this version, Albizu voluntarily joined the U.S. Army in World War I. The army assigned him to a segregated Black unit, despite his protestations that he was white. Immerwahr, *How to Hide*, 118. (According to Harry Franqui-Rivera, "Race and the Myth," Albizu served in a segregated Black Puerto Rican unit in Puerto Rico.) The humiliating episode and racist treatment he received in the army were so degrading, so the story runs, that resentment and loathing replaced Albizu's admiration and love for the United States and turned him into the fanatical terrorist who hated the United States. For insights into the gendered and racial tropes this assessment of what happened reveals, see Friedman, *Citizenship in Cold War America*, 146. This interpretation reduces Albizu's desire to secure an independent homeland to a personal slight he received while ignoring both the negative impact of racism in the U.S. military and the fundamental problems of Washington's colonial rule in Puerto Rico.

34. Lewis, *Puerto Rico*, 81.

35. Lewis, *Puerto Rico*, 81.

36. Ferrao, *Pedro Albizu Campos*, 317.

37. Ferrao, *Pedro Albizu Campos*, 317.

38. Ferrao, *Pedro Albizu Campos*, 303–7.

39. Taller de Formación Política, *Pedro Albizu Campos*, 49–61.

40. "Albizu Campos contra el fascismo y el comunismo," *La Democracia*, May 3, 1938; *El Mundo*, May 4, 1938.

41. Taller de Formación Política, *Pedro Albizu Campos*, 49.

42. Taller de Formación Política, *Pedro Albizu Campos*, 54–55. I revisit the issue of the Cadetes' uniforms in chapter 5.

43. Taller de Formación Política, *Pedro Albizu Campos*, 60–61.

44. Gluckstein, *People's History*, 167.

45. Gluckstein, *People's History*, 169. For a description of the various positions taken by Indian political forces on India's involvement in World War II, see Gluckstein, *People's History*, 167–68.

46. Simón Arce, "*Volverán banderas victoriosas*," 518.

47. Simón Arce, *"Volverán banderas victoriosas,"* 519.

48. Rafael Ángel Simón Arce, personal communication, September 4, 2020. The two individuals are Elpidio de Mier and Federico Tilen. Simón Arce, *"Volverán banderas victoriosas,"* 97–98, 275.

49. Rodríguez Beruff, "Prologue," xii. During his tenure, Winship unleashed a series of attacks against the Nationalist Party, including the Ponce Massacre of 1937, which resulted in the death of nineteen Puerto Ricans. See chapter 5.

50. Aponte Vázquez, *Albizu*; Manuel Carrión, Garcia Ruiz, and Rodríguez Fraticelli, *Nación puertorriqueña*; Ferrao, *Pedro Albizu Campos*; Ribes Tovar, *Albizu Campos*; Rosado, *Pedro Albizu Campos*; Rosario Natal, *Albizu Campos*; Silén, *Nosotros solos*; Torres, *Pedro Albizu Campos*.

51. A wealth of studies has focused on women's participation in parties and movements and reshaped how we understand them. For a small sampling, see Harmer, *Beatriz Allende*; McGuire, *Dark End of the Street*; and Ransby, *Ella Baker*. For a study of Peronism that does not focus on Juan Perón, see Karush, *New Cultural History*.

52. For the view that nationalism and nation building are masculine projects, see Pateman, *Disorder of Women*; Connell, *Masculinities*; Albanese, *Mothers of the Nation*; and Nagel, "Masculinity and Nationalism." For challenges to this perspective that focus on women's interpretations of their relationship to nationalism, see Power, "Women, Gender"; Dirik, "Overcoming the Nation-State"; and West, *Feminist Nationalism*.

53. As Jane Juffer pointed out to me, the lack of sources on and by women is a gendered problem, which reflects the lack of gender equality within the party and the public.

54. Bosque-Pérez and Colón Morera, *Puerto Rico under Colonial Rule*; Paralitici, *Sentencia impuesta*.

55. Bosque-Pérez, "Political Persecution," 20, 14.

56. Seijo Bruno, *Insurrección nacionalista*.

57. Seijo Bruno, *Insurrección nacionalista*, 243.

58. Dávila Marichal, "¡Atención!"; Dávila Marichal, "'Mujer no debe,'" 56; Dávila Marichal, "Estudio del nacionalismo revolucionario."

59. Jiménez-Muñoz, "'Race' and Class among *Nacionalista* Women."

60. For two examples of works that place Puerto Rico in the Caribbean context, see Morales Carrión, *Puerto Rico and the Non Hispanic Caribbean*; and García Passalacqua, "Ariadne's Thread."

61. On solidarity networks in Latin America, see Melgar Bao, "Anti-imperialist League"; Carr, "Pioneering Transnational Solidarity;" and Shaffer, *Anarchists of the Caribbean*.

62. Padilla Pérez, *Puerto Rico*, 102–4.

63. Algeria was then fighting to end French colonial rule, which it achieved in 1962. As Eugenia Palieraki points out, Algeria was "an emblematic case of anticolonial struggle" internationally. Palieraki, "Chile, Algeria, and the Third World," 277. Since Puerto Rico occupied that same position in Latin America, it makes sense that Ecuadorian politicians would join the two. I thank Andres Bisso for making me aware of Padilla Pérez's book and Marc Becker for explaining who the Ecuadorian politicians were.

64. Padilla Pérez, *Puerto Rico*, 103.

65. Latin American activists and politicians across the political spectrum have drawn on family references to justify and advance their struggles. See Chase, *Revolution within the Revolution*; and Thomas, *Contesting Legitimacy in Chile*.

66. Padilla Pérez, *Puerto Rico*, 105–6, 131, 104.

67. *El Siglo*, September 14, 1957, cited in Padilla Pérez, *Puerto Rico*, 139; letter to President Dwight D. Eisenhower, September 12, 1957, reprinted in Medina Rámirez, *Movimiento libertador*, 2:758–59. For a discussion of ties between the National Liberation Front of Algeria and the Chilean Left, see Palieraki, "Chile, Algeria, and the Third World."

68. I thank Neici Zeller for pointing out the problems with "flattening" Latin America or Latin Americans.

69. Sánchez, *Testimonio personal*, 175.

70. Only one of the Nationalists and none of the U.S. solidarity activists I interviewed for this book is alive today. I also interviewed ten children of the Nationalists, all of whom retained vivid memories of their parents and the party. Happily, all are in good health.

71. Uruguayan José Enrique Rodó drew on Shakespeare's play *The Tempest* when he wrote the poem "Ariel" in 1900. Arielismo, as the movement came to be known in Latin America, propounded the idea that although the United States was materially superior, Latin America was spiritually superior. Miller, *Shadow of the State*, 178. *Hispanismo*, which emerged in the latter part of the 1800s, was an ideology that promoted a common heritage and identity for Latin Americans, especially those of Spanish descent. Sepúlveda, *Sueño*, 13.

## Chapter One

1. Her desire for a free nation was so strong that she named her daughter Patria (motherland or homeland). Azize Vargas, *Mujer en la lucha*, 26. For an excellent biography of her, see Acosta-Belén, "Lola Rodríguez de Tió."

2. On the lack of educational opportunities for women in the 1800s, see Azize Vargas, *Mujer en la lucha*, 17–24.

3. Acosta-Belén, "Lola Rodríguez de Tió," 89.

4. Acosta-Belén, "Lola Rodríguez de Tió," 90–96; "Lola Rodríguez de Tió," The World of 1898: The Spanish-American War, Hispanic Division, Library of Congress, www.loc.gov/rr/hispanic/1898/lola.html. In 1896, she became vice president of the Hermanas de Rius Rivera, a women's group affiliated with the Puerto Rican Section of the Cuban Revolutionary Party in New York City. Toledo, "Ramón Emeterio Betances," 20; Ojeda Reyes, *Peregrinos de la libertad*, 101–5.

5. Romero-Cesaro, "Whose Legacy?," 773.

6. For a concise history of the song, see J. E. Cuesta, "'La Borinquena': Porto Ricans Regard Native Song as a National Hymn," *New York Times*, July 10, 1929. José Enamorado Cuesta was a member of the Puerto Rican Nationalist Party. In 1952, the commonwealth government of Puerto Rico, headed by Luis Muñoz Marín of the Popular Democratic Party, made a very different version of "La Borinqueña" the hymn of the Free Associated State. Stripped of its revolutionary content, this version begins, "The land of Borinquen, where I was born, is a flowery garden of magical beauty." "Himno de Puerto Rico," Portal Oficial del Gobierno de Puerto Rico, https://pr.gov/SobrePuertoRico/Pages/Himnos-Oficiales.aspx.

7. Rodríguez wrote "La Borinqueña" to be sung to the tune of a popular song, hoping to build on people's familiarity with the melody to boost support for independence. Ojeda Reyes, *Peregrinos de la libertad*, 98.

8. Zepeda Cortés, *Cambios y adaptaciones*, 71.

9. Rodríguez was not the only pro-independence figure who advocated women's political participation. Hostos and Betances also promoted the education and emancipation of women. Azize Vargas, *Mujer en la lucha*, 20–22.

10. Rodríguez de Tió, *Mi libro de Cuba*, translation mine.

11. Acosta-Belén, "Lola Rodríguez de Tió," 84.

12. As Manuel Maldonado Denis notes, "One other common characteristic of Puerto Rican nationalism in the nineteenth century is its internationalism, the belief that the liberation of Puerto Rico was tightly linked to the liberation of the Antilles and of Latin America in general." Maldonado Denis, "Aproximación crítica al fenómeno," 285.

13. Bolívar, *El Libertador*, 14.

14. Bolívar, *El Libertador*, 15.

15. Scarano, "Jíbaro Masquerade," 1406.

16. Franqui-Rivera, *Soldiers of the Nation*, 13–15. For a historiographical overview of the development of a distinct Puerto Rican identity during the nineteenth century, see Morris, *Puerto Rico*, 21–22.

17. Castillo Morales, "'Movimiento libertador,'" 2. Bernabé was not the only Puerto Rican who opposed Spanish rule. For example, when a Spanish commission asked authorities in San Juan to send the local militia to reinforce royalist troops fighting rebels in Caracas in 1810, members refused to go, saying they would not battle their "Caracas brothers." And in 1811, some landowners around San Germán, a town in southwestern Puerto Rico, plotted against Spanish rule for reasons that are not clear. In any case, the conspiracy was quashed. Santana, "Puerto Rico in a Revolutionary World," 73.

18. Jiménez de Wagenheim, *Puerto Rico's Revolt*, 3.

19. Jiménez de Wagenheim, *Puerto Rico's Revolt*, 2–3.

20. For an insightful analysis of the role creole elites played in the independence movements, the tensions that emerged between them and the popular sectors, and the elites' appropriation of nationalism to legitimize their break with Spain and justify their rule, see Hamnett, "Process and Pattern."

21. Domínguez, *Insurrection or Loyalty*, 161; Foner, *History of Cuba*, 63.

22. Scarano, "Jíbaro Masquerade," 1426. Nonetheless, as Scarano points out, their apprehensions did not prevent liberals from pushing for reforms in trade, politics, the church, and such rights as freedom of speech and greater "representation in the Spanish *Cortes*." Scarano, "Jíbaro Masquerade," 1427.

23. Jiménez de Wagenheim, *Puerto Rico's Revolt*, 4; Kinsbruner, *Independence in Spanish America*, 103.

24. Santana, "Puerto Rico in a Revolutionary World," 73.

25. Kinsbruner, *Independence in Spanish America*, 103.

26. Liberal creoles supported progressive measures such as the establishment of a constitution and the separation of church and military power, which challenged Spanish rule and suggested the existence of a distinct, Puerto Rican national identity. Scarano, "Jíbaro Masquerade," 1429–30, 1431.

27. Emeterio Betances, "A los puertorriqueños," 61.

28. Emeterio Betances, "A los puertorriqueños," 61.

29. The Puerto Rican revolt was originally timed to occur jointly with the anticolonial uprising in Cuba, which had been planned for late October. However, documents discussing plans for the uprising in Puerto Rico fell into Spanish hands, forcing the revolutionaries to initiate the fighting early, which contributed to the uprising's failure. For two excellent discussions of the uprising and subsequent political and historiographical understandings of it, see Franqui-Rivera, *Soldiers of the Nation*, 6–15; and Jiménez de Wagenheim, *Puerto Rico's Revolt*.

30. Dietz, *Economic History*, 16–17; Jiménez de Wagenheim, *Puerto Rico's Revolt*, 4–7.

31. Jiménez de Wagenheim, *Puerto Rico's Revolt*, 24. For a concise explanation of the complex factors that led Puerto Ricans first to question, then to oppose Spanish rule, see Jiménez de Wagenheim, *Puerto Rico's Revolt*, 5–24.

32. Ojeda Reyes and Estrade, "Los diez mandamientos," 69–70.

33. Ruiz Belvis, who was also of Afro descent, was a vocal reformist, abolitionist, and supporter of independence. Spanish officials banished him from Puerto Rico as well. Martínez-Fernández, "Political Change in the Spanish Caribbean," 42–43, 50, 59n22. He traveled with Betances to New York City in 1867, where they founded the Revolutionary Committee of Puerto Rico. They wrote a manifesto considered "the programmatic basis for the Lares uprising." Meléndez, *Patria*, 72. Ruiz Belvis then sailed to Chile to obtain support for Puerto Rican independence, where he died of unknown causes.

34. Estrade, "Remarques sur le caractère tardif," 108–9.

35. Indeed, Betances was one of the period's foremost proponents of women's political and educational rights. Azize Vargas, *Mujer en la lucha*, 20–22.

36. Estrade, "Remarques sur le caractère tardif," 108.

37. Jiménez de Wagenheim, *Puerto Rico's Revolt*, 61–62; Meléndez, *Patria*, 68.

38. Meléndez, *Patria*, 24, 39–40. Paris was a center of Cuban exiles, which is why the PRC was established there. Meléndez, *Patria*, 18.

39. Arroyo, *Writing Secrecy*, 74.

40. Maldonado Denis, "Perspectivas del nacionalismo," 800; Zepeda Cortés, *Cambios y adaptaciones*, 71.

41. Ojeda Reyes, "Ramón Emeterio Betances," 33.

42. Smith, *Grant*, 449, 500–501.

43. Reyes-Santos, "Pan-Antillean Politics," 142. Both men opposed monarchial rule and advocated the creation of republics. In the early 1870s, the two Antilleans founded the Liga de las Antillas in Paris, whose goal was to ensure that Cuba, Puerto Rico, Santo Domingo (as the Dominican Republic was then called), and Haiti remained "outside the reach of any foreign domination." Ojeda Reyes, "Ramón Emeterio Betances," 34. Betances became a Dominican citizen and one of that country's diplomatic representatives in France in the 1880s.

44. Emeterio Betances, "Patria, justicia, libertad," 59.

45. Pike, *Hispanismo*, 64. Anti-U.S. sentiment was particularly strong in Argentina. One general announced he wanted to go to Cuba to fight the United States. The Buenos Aires newspaper *El Tiempo* published a letter from a professor that stated, "If Hispanic Americans took the side of the United States, they would be aligning themselves against the Hispanic raza and community." Pike, *Hispanismo*, 65.

46. Michel Gobat locates the "largest [anti-imperialist] alliance in Latin American history" in protests against U.S. filibuster William Walker's invasion of Nicaragua in 1856. He argues that the widespread adoption of Latin America as a geopolitical entity, a concept that persists to this day, "resulted from the transnational mobilization of an imperial concept—the Latin race—for anti-imperialist ends." Gobat, "Invention of Latin America," 1346, 1348.

47. Martí, "Nuestra América." Cemís were the gods of the Taino people, the original inhabitants of many Caribbean islands. They represented the islands, just as the condor symbolized the Andean peoples. For Martí and Cuban revolutionaries' ideas of race, see de la Fuente, *Nation for All*, 26–39. Although Martí repudiated white racial superiority, he apparently clung to ideas about male superiority, as Teresa Prados-Torreira points out. He disapproved of what he perceived to be U.S. women's "equality" and thought that women working outside the home would lead to a "disintegration of domestic happiness and society's moral fiber." He did, however, support "both women's education and their right to vote." Prados-Torreira, *Rebel Women*, 133–34.

48. Gonzalo Marín was a poet and committed anti-imperialist. Like his brother, he fought and died fighting to liberate Cuba from Spain. Lomas, "Migration and Decolonial Politics," 155. Sotero Figueroa, like Gonzalo Marín, was an artisan and liberal who included the struggle for social equality into his fight to end Spanish rule and slavery. For more on them, see Hoffnung-Garskof, "To Abolish the Law of Castes."

49. Hoffnung-Garskof, *Racial Migrations*, 192. Jesse Hoffnung-Garskof draws these quotations from their manifesto "Al pueblo puertorriqueño," published in *Patria*, March 14, 1892.

50. Sepúlveda, *Sueño*, 13.

51. Muller, *Cuban Emigrés*, 180.

52. Rodríguez, *Celebración de "La Raza,"* 31–32.

53. Pike, *Hispanismo*, 41.

54. Faber, "'Hora ha llegado,'" 89–90. I thank Jorell Meléndez-Badillo for pointing out this source and for encouraging me to be more critical of Hispanismo.

55. Pineda Buitrago, "Entre el desprecio y la admiración," 132.

56. For example, the Honduran Froylán Turcios published the *Revista Ariel*, which in 1927 became the official voice of the Sandinista army then fighting the U.S. Marines in Nicaragua. Galicia Martínez, "Sandino en Ariel," 146.

57. Miller, *Shadow of the State*, 178.

58. Kozol, "Estaciones del antiimperialismo rioplatenses," 27.

59. Darío, *Selected Writings*, 119.

60. Devés Valdés, *Del "Ariel" de Rodó*, 163.

61. Devés Valdés, *Del "Ariel" de Rodó*, 164–73.

62. Devés Valdés, *Del "Ariel" de Rodó*, 101. For an insightful discussion of Vasconcelos's thoughts and policies on education, see Vaughan, *State, Education, and Social Class*, 135–36, 140–42; for his contributions to cultural nationalism, see chap. 8.

63. Quijada, "Latinos y anglosajones," 602. Manuel Ugarte, a confirmed anti-imperialist, traveled throughout Latin America in the early 1900s. When in Cuba, he met Lola Rodríguez de Tió. He attempted to visit Puerto Rico, but as he later found out, the cablegrams he sent from Havana and Santo Domingo concerning his trip never arrived in San Juan. Ugarte, *Destino de un continente*, 66, 79–80.

64. Ugarte, *Destino de un continente*, 66, 79–80.

65. Whitney, "War and Nation Building," 364.

## Chapter Two

1. The Nationalist Party venerated de Diego as the principal advocate for Puerto Rico independence in the late 1800s and early 1900s. A member of the creole elite and an attorney and poet, he led the Autonomy Party, which called for autonomy from Spain. After 1898, he advocated independence from the United States. The party apparently ignored de Diego's role as lawyer for the Central Guánica, the U.S.-owned "largest refinery of sugar in Puerto Rico and one of the foremost exploiters of the Puerto Rican working class." Campos and Flores, "Migración y cultura puertorriqueñas," 306, 308.

2. Rosado, *Pedro Albizu Campos*, 107.

3. Rosado, *Pedro Albizu Campos*, 107.

4. Rosado, *Pedro Albizu Campos*, 107; Torres, "Albizu Campos," 40. I thank José Davíla Marichal for this latter reference and Neici Zeller for help with the translation.

5. Rosado, *Pedro Albizu Campos*, 108; Julio Artiaga, "Gran mitin nacionalista en San Juan," *El Nacionalista de Ponce*, July 24, 1926, 7, cited in Tirado Avilés, "Forja de un líder," 72.

6. José Fusté notes that Miles "was known as the most accomplished Indian-fighting commander in the US Army. He led forces during the Ghost Dance War against the Lakota and . . . defeated Chief Joseph during the Nez Perce War." Fusté, "Repeating Islands of Debt," 112n24.

7. Ayala and Bernabe, *Puerto Rico in the American Century*, 15. For an alternative view that emphasizes Puerto Rican resistance to the United States, see González-Cruz, Marquez Sola, and Terando, "U.S. Invasion of Puerto Rico," 9–11.

8. Drafters of the Foraker Act mistakenly spelled Puerto Rico as Porto Rico, which remained the official spelling until 1930. Morris, *Puerto Rico*, 27.

9. Dietz, *Economic History*, 87. Under the Autonomy Charter of 1897 from Spain, all men, without restriction, could vote.

10. Ayala and Bernabe, *Puerto Rico in the American Century*, 28; Cabán, *Constructing a Colonial People*, 115.

11. Ayala and Bernabe, *Puerto Rico in the American Century*, 28.

12. Ayala and Bernabe, *Puerto Rico in the American Century*, 161.

13. Morris, *Puerto Rico*, 31; Ayala and Bernabe, *Puerto Rico in the American Century*, 157. Although all persons born in Puerto Rico became U.S. citizens, the act allowed Puerto Ricans to retain Spanish or Puerto Rican citizenship. As of 1930, 6,248 people "retained their allegiance to Spain," and five men declared themselves citizens of Puerto Rico. U.S. Bureau of the Census, *Fifteenth Census of the United States*, 134. Historian Harry Franqui-Rivera takes pains to establish the United States did not impose citizenship to draft Puerto Rican men into the U.S. military during World War I. Instead, the U.S. government believed that making Puerto Ricans U.S. citizens would "ensure their loyalty" to the United States in the face of possible German incursions. Franqui-Rivera, *Soldiers of the Nation*, 70–71.

14. Dietz, *Economic History*, 86–89.

15. Ayala and Bernabe, *Puerto Rico in the American Century*, 26.

16. Neither the Philippines nor Cuba ever became a state. Hawai'i did in 1959, after the native population lost numeric superiority on the island. As of 2022, the Commonwealth of the Northern Mariana Islands, Guam, the U.S. Virgin Islands, and American Samoa are unincorporated territories.

17. For a fascinating discussion of how ideas about race informed both imperialists and anti-imperialists, see Love, *Race over Empire*. Love notes that for many in the United States, climate, which was also linked to racial notions, defined territorial boundaries as well: "There were hot and tropical places, points beyond which it was believed that members of the white race could not occupy, settle, develop, or transplant their institutions without suffering some moral or physical calamity" (24).

18. Weiner, "Teutonic Constitutionalism," 59. Weiner explains "ethno-juridical discourse" as "a way of characterizing the proper boundaries of civic life in which the concepts of race and law were mutually constitutive" (48).

19. Weiner, "Teutonic Constitutionalism," 60.

20. Beisner, *Twelve against Empire*.

21. For a copy of the league's platform see, "Platform of the Anti-imperialist League," n. 1. Beisner, *Twelve against Empire*, 27.

22. "Anti-imperialist League Protest," *New York Times*, November 26, 1898. The league opposed the U.S. conquest of all the island territories, but it focused particularly on the Philippines.

23. Anti-imperialist League, *Protest against the Philippine Policy*.

24. Roughly 8 million people inhabited the newly acquired overseas territories of the United States in 1900; 1,118,012 of them lived in Puerto Rico. Gannett, *Statistical Atlas*, 36. I thank Daniel Immerwahr for this reference.

25. Massachusetts senator George Hoar and Mark Twain sided with those the United States invaded. Hoar praised the Filipinos, believed them fully capable of running their country, and castigated the United States for its treatment of them. Beisner, *Twelve against Empire*, 160–62. Twain opposed U.S. imperialism, stating, "I am opposed to having the eagle put its talons on any other land." Excerpt from the *New York Herald*, October 15, 1900, in "Mark Twain," The World of 1898: The Spanish-American War, Hispanic Division, Library of Congress, www.loc.gov/rr/hispanic/1898/twain.html.

26. Burnett and Marshall, "Between Foreign and Domestic," 4.

27. "McKinley Re-Elected," *New York Times*, November 7, 1900.

28. Fusté, "Repeating Islands of Debt," 96.

29. Downes v. Bidwell, 182 U.S. 244 (1901) at 287, 190; Balzac v. Porto Rico 258 U.S. 298 (1922). In *Puerto Rico v. Sanchez Valle* (2016), the Supreme Court reaffirmed the findings of the Insular Cases that Puerto Rico is a U.S. territory and lacks independent sovereignty, which effectively undermined claims of autonomy or self-rule made by Puerto Rican governments since 1952. Jiménez, "Looking for a Way Forward."

30. As historian James G. Whitman points out, the Nazi Party drew lessons from the U.S. policy of classifying Puerto Ricans, Filipinos, Chinese, Blacks, and Native Americans as second-class citizens when it designed its own racial laws. Whitman, *Hitler's American Model*, 43, 59.

31. *Annual Report of the War Department*, 342.

32. *Annual Report of the War Department*, 342.

33. *Annual Report of the War Department*, 342, emphasis added. I thank Pedro Cabán for pointing me to Hathi Trust, where I located this and other documents.

34. Gates, "George Whitfield Davis," 279.

35. As cited in Cabán, *Constructing a Colonial People*, 122, emphasis added.

36. In 1815, 80 percent of the U.S. population "lived and worked on farms." Between 1820 and 1860, the nation transformed into an increasingly urbanized society whose most dynamic sector was manufacturing. Barney, *Passage of the Republic*, 9–11.

37. Mahan, *Influence of Sea Power*, 33–34.

38. Mahan, *Influence of Sea Power*, 33–34.

39. Cabán, *Constructing a Colonial People*, 25.

40. Cabán, *Constructing a Colonial People*, 27.

41. Cabán, *Constructing a Colonial People*, 15–17.

42. For a discussion of U.S. military installations in Puerto Rico, see García Muñiz, "U.S. Military Installations"; and Estades-Font, "Critical Year," 50. For a discussion of how critical U.S. policymakers considered control of Puerto Rico to their plans to build a canal through Central America, see Ayala and Bernabe, *Puerto Rico in the American Century*, 14.

43. Ayala and Bernabe, *Puerto Rico in the American Century*, 231.

44. García Muñiz, "U.S. Military Installations, 82.

45. McCaffrey, *Military Power*, 87–88.

46. Dietz, *Economic History*, 109.

47. Pérez Velasco, "Condición obrera," 157.

48. Dietz, *Economic History*, 102.

49. For the text of the Foraker Act, Pub. L. 56-191, see https://govtrackus.s3.amazonaws.com/legislink/pdf/stat/31/STATUTE-31-Pg77.pdf. Ayala and Bernabe, *Puerto Rico in the American Century*, 36–37. The Jones Act also established the Leyes de Cabotaje (Cabotaje Laws), which decreed that all goods entering Puerto Rico be carried on U.S. ships. This law, which persists today, effectively prevented other countries from sending aid to a devastated Puerto Rico following Hurricanes Irma and María in September 2017.

50. Baldoz and Ayala, "Bordering of America," 10n15.

51. Dietz, *Economic History*, 109; Ayala and Bernabe, *Puerto Rico in the American Century*, 38.

52. Ayala and Bergad, *Agrarian Puerto Rico*, 72.

53. César Ayala and Laird Bergad argue that land ownership was already concentrated before the United States took over in 1898. They point out that as U.S.-imposed taxes increased, landowners found it more profitable to sell uncultivated land. As a result, the number of farmers grew during the first two decades of U.S. rule, and the average farm size decreased. Ayala and Bergad, "Rural Puerto Rico," 70–71.

54. Dietz, *Economic History*, 104, 110.

55. Levy, *Puerto Ricans in the Empire*, 3.

56. Weekly income for families in 1936 was $8.60 in the tobacco regions, $10.07 in the coffee regions, and $16.20 in the sugar regions. Levy, *Puerto Ricans in the Empire*, 48.

57. *Twenty-Second Annual Report of the Governor of Porto Rico*, 30.

58. Pérez Velasco, "Condición obrera," 159.

59. Pérez Velasco, "Condición obrera," 163.

60. Silvestrini-Pacheco, "Women as Workers," 248–49. Colón, Mergal, and Torres, *Participación de la mujer*, 17.

61. *Twenty-Second Annual Report of the Governor of Porto Rico*, 48.

62. *Twenty-Second Annual Report of the Governor of Porto Rico*, 30.

63. Valle-Ferrer, *Luisa Capetillo*, 34.

64. Meléndez-Badillo, "Mateo and Juana," 109.

65. Meléndez-Badillo, "Party of Ex-convicts."

66. For a detailed analysis of the different political forces involved in the strike, see Taller de Formación Politica, *¡Huelga en la caña!*

67. For an insightful discussion of women and the organized labor movement see Rodríguez-Silva, *Silencing Race*, 112, 171–74.

68. Valle-Ferrer, *Luisa Capetillo*, 26, 46.

69. Randall, *Pueblo*, 17–23.

70. Randall, *Pueblo*, 25.

71. Randall, *Pueblo*, 27–28.

72. The women workers hired readers to break the monotony of rolling cigars and to educate and politicize them. Randall, *Pueblo*, 29; Tinajero, *Lector*, 123–24.

73. Randall, *Pueblo*, 30–33, 34.

74. Del Moral, *Negotiating Empire*, 8–9.

75. Morris, *Puerto Rico*, 26.

76. Dietz, *Economic History*, 84.

77. U.S. Bureau of Insular Affairs, *Report*, 16.

78. U.S. Bureau of the Census, *Fifteenth Census*, 134, 140.

79. U.S. Bureau of the Census, *Fourteenth Census*, 1203. I have rounded off all the figures for easier reading.

80. For a discussion of "male honor," see Suárez Findlay, *Imposing Decency*, 27–30. However, as she points out, the public-private dichotomy did not operate for "plebian" women since they had to work in the public sphere. Whereas wealthy men could isolate women in their homes or rely on the courts to rule in their favor should a dispute arise, "plebian" men more frequently resorted to violence to control women. Suárez Findlay, *Imposing Decency*, 29.

81. Del Moral, *Negotiating Empire*, 65–66.

82. U.S. Bureau of the Census, *Fourteenth Census*, 1205.

83. U.S. Bureau of the Census, *Fifteenth Census*, 141.

84. A study by Columbia University's International Institute of Teacher's College found that the use of English in the classroom was ineffective and recommended that students be taught in Spanish up to the third grade. Morris, *Puerto Rico*, 35. U.S. educational officials ignored the institute's findings.

85. U.S. Bureau of the Census, *Fourteenth Census*, 1207.

86. U.S. Bureau of the Census, *Fifteenth Census*, iv, 143.

87. Alejandrina Torres, interview with author, November 18, 2018, Chicago. The Spanish was: "Yo nunca dije una mentira pues quiero imitar a Jorge Washington." After Alejandrina Torres moved to Chicago in the early 1960s, she became active in social justice projects through the United Congregational Church, located in the Puerto Rican community, as well as in organizations to support the independence of Puerto Rico and freedom for the Nationalist Party political prisoners. In 1985, she was arrested, accused of being a member of the Armed Forces of National Liberation, and convicted of seditious conspiracy, serving sixteen years in U.S. prisons.

88. Torres interview.

89. Rodríguez-Silva, *Silencing Race*, 202. However, as Rodríguez-Silva points out, "U.S. colonizers did not always . . . [distinguish] between . . . creole elites, urban workers, and the large mass of rural inhabitants. To them, the Puerto Rican signified a racially inferior, weak, ill, impoverished, and consequently feminized body" (202).

90. Suárez Findlay, *Imposing Decency*, 111.

91. Walsh, "'Advancing the Kingdom,'" 9.

92. Walsh, "'Advancing the Kingdom,'" 10.

93. For a description of the former's life and an example of the latter, see Ayala and Bergad, *Agrarian Puerto Rico*, 70–71, 71–78.

94. Del Moral, *Negotiating Empire*, 9, 19.

95. Suárez Findlay, *Imposing Decency*, 112.

96. Walsh, "Not-So-Docile," 148–71.

97. Negrón de Montilla, *Americanización*, 135, 237, 240.

98. Torres interview.

99. Jiménez de Wagenheim, *Puerto Rico*, 243.

100. The bomba was originally an Afro–Puerto Rican music and dance that developed on sugar plantations along the southern coast. Mintz, "Culture History," 246.

101. For background on Rafael Hernández, see Quintero Rivera, *Salsa, sabor y control!*, 308–10.

102. Go, *American Empire*, chap. 2. The chapter includes a helpful history of the Autonomist movement and points out that the elite leaders of the early 1900s hoped to replicate the success of the 1800s movement for Puerto Rican autonomy from Spain. In 1898, Spain granted Puerto Rico autonomy, and the liberal Autonomist Party, led by Luis Muñoz Rivera, Luis Muñoz Marín's father, governed the archipelago until the U.S. invasion in July of that year. Go, *American Empire*, 71–80.

103. Hoffnung-Garskof, *Racial Migrations*, 16–21. Suárez Findlay, *Imposing Decency*, 23. As the author notes, *pardo* designated someone who was "light brown," while *moreno* was "a more respectful way to describe someone perceived to be dark brown," and *negro* was a less respectful way. Hoffnung-Garskof, *Racial Migrations*, 20.

104. Suárez Findlay, *Imposing Decency*, 23. For an excellent discussion of the categories and mutability of race in the Spanish Caribbean more broadly, see Twinam, *Purchasing Whiteness*.

105. The composition of one's blood was, of course, impossible to detect, given the lack of knowledge about or ability to test for DNA until the 1950s. Further, the concept of race is spurious to begin with. See Omi and Winant, *Racial Formation*.

106. U.S. scholars have produced a wealth of materials on this issue. Some of my favorites for the U.S. colonial period include Brown, *Good Wives, Nasty Wenches*; Hudson, "From 'Nation' to 'Race'"; and Spear, *Race, Sex, and Social Order*.

107. U.S. Bureau of the Census, *Fifteenth Census*, 136.

108. Loveman and Muñiz, "How Puerto Rico Became White," 935.

109. Loveman and Muñiz, "How Puerto Rico Became White," 935.

110. Loveman, "U.S. Census," 95, 96, 102.

111. Duany, *Puerto Rican Nation*, 238, 247, 249.

112. See Fanon, *Black Skin, White Masks*.

### Chapter Three

1. Canales, *Constitución*. Shortly after Blanca Canales died in 1996, three members of the pro-independence Congreso Nacional Hostosiano (National Hostos Congress) published her biography based on notes Canales had written about her childhood and youth, her membership in the Nationalist Party, and her role in the 1950 uprising against U.S. colonialism. Canales, *Constitución*, v.

2. Canales, *Constitución*, 4.

3. Canales, *Constitución*, 5.

4. Canales, *Constitución*, 11.

5. Jiménez de Wagenheim, *Nationalist Heroines*, 66.

6. Canales, *Constitución*, 52.

7. I thank Mike Staudenmaier for his help on formulating these ideas.

8. Colón, Mergal, and Torres, *Participación de la mujer*, 44.

9. Ayala and Bernabe, *Puerto Rico in the American Century*, 53–54.

10. Pagán, *Historia de los partidos*, 506.

11. Suárez Findlay, *Imposing Decency*, 102.

12. Cabán, *Constructing a Colonial People*, 6, 163.

13. Morris, *Puerto Rico*, 24.

14. Suárez Findlay, *Imposing Decency*, 142, 102; Ayala and Bernabe, *Puerto Rico in the American Century*, 54.

15. Bhana, *United States*, 8.

16. Ayala and Bernabe, *Puerto Rico in the American Century*, 17.

17. Ayala and Bernabe, *Puerto Rico in the American Century*, 61–62; Dietz, *Economic History*, 85.

18. Dietz, *Economic History*, 94.

19. Mary White Ovington, "The United States in Puerto Rico," *Nation*, July 15, 1916, 272.

20. Clark, "Prohibition in Puerto Rico," 84.

21. Meléndez-Badillo, "Imagining Resistance," 47.

22. Meléndez-Badillo, "Party of Ex-convicts," 79.

23. Meléndez-Badillo, "Party of Ex-convicts," 79.

24. Acosta-Belén, "Puerto Rican Women," 9.

25. Silvestrini-Pacheco, "Women as Workers," 250.

26. Augustín Laó-Montes describes both women as early twentieth century "anarchist and socialist Afrodescendant labor leaders." Laó-Montes, "Afro-Latin American Feminisms," 13.

27. Meléndez-Badillo, "Party of Ex-convicts," 87.

28. Colón, Mergal, and Torres, *Participación de la mujer*, 32. Apparently, other parties agreed with this calculation, which is one reason they opposed granting women the right to vote. Colón, Mergal, and Torres, *Participación de la mujer*, 42.

29. Morris, *Puerto Rico*, 29.

30. Santiago-Valles, "'Our Race Today,'" 111.

31. Ferrao, *Pedro Albizu Campos*, 40–41, 48–53.

32. Coll y Cuchí, *Nacionalismo*, 5. The book is a rich but untapped source of the Nationalist Party's early history; in addition to Coll y Cuchí's writings, it contains transcriptions of relevant articles and letters. The book won the Academia Española de la Lengua best book of the year award in 1923. "José Coll," Biografías, https://web.archive.org/web/20110911212842/http://www.zonai.com:80/promociones/biografias/0101/josecoll.asp.

33. "Existe una lista de nombres de empleados del gbo. que por sus ideas políticas se consideran enemigos del gbo.," *El Mundo*, August 24, 1921, 1.

34. Coll y Cuchí, *Nacionalismo*, 6.

35. Ayala and Bernabe, *Puerto Rico in the American Century*, 58–59. Reily scornfully referred to the Puerto Rican flag as "a dirty rag." Morris, *Puerto Rico*, 34.

36. Coll y Cuchí, *Nacionalismo*, 5.

37. Coll y Cuchí, *Nacionalismo*, 137–39. Puerto Rico had seventy-seven municipalities in 1930.

38. "En la Asamblea celebrada ayer en el pueblo de Río Piedras, quedó formalmente constituido el Partido Nacionalista y aprobada su declaración de Principios," *El Mundo*, September 8, 1922, 1, 3; Coll y Cuchí, *Nacionalismo*, 140.

39. I thank Neici Zeller for clarifying what "Licenciado" meant in Puerto Rico in these years.

40. Rosado, *Pedro Albizu Campos*, 93.

41. "Antonio Ayuso, Publisher, Dies; Built San Juan's El Imparcial," *New York Times*, April 27, 1970. The FBI kept tabs on him at least until 1957, perhaps beyond. FBI, *Nationalist Party of Puerto Rico (NPPR)*, SJ-100-3_64_064_207.pdf, 209.

42. According to Ernest Gruening, director of the Division of Territories and Islands Possessions from 1934 to 1939, when Ayuso Valdivieso was its editor, *Imparcial* "was an indefatigable spewer of distortion and hate against Americans." Gruening, *Many Battles*, 205.

43. Castro, *Historia sinóptica*, 12–14.

44. Several of these men formed part of the Club Borinquen, which issued the manifesto to the Puerto Rican people mentioned in chapter 1 and published *Patria*. Hoffnung-Garskof, *Racial Migrations*, 191.

45. Ayoroa Santaliz, *Contracanto*, 67.

46. *El Nacionalista* began publication on September 25, 1922, eight days after the founding of the Nationalist Party, and ceased publication in 1931. Coll y Cuchí, *Nacionalismo*, 158; Rosado, *Pedro Albizu Campos*, 148.

47. Rosado, *Pedro Albizu Campos*, 341–42. In the early 1920s, Albizu referred to himself as Mayoral Barnés's lieutenant. Ayoroa Santaliz, "Don Ramón Mayoral Barnés." For Albizu's statement why he joined then quit the Union Party, see Bernal Díaz del Caney, "Pedro Albizu Campos," *Los Quijotes*, June 11, 1927, in Torres, *Pedro Albizu Campos*, 42–43.

48. The U.S. Democratic Party viewed Coll y Cuchí so favorably that it invited him to give speeches in Spanish across the United States in favor of (Catholic) presidential candidate Al Smith. According to news reports, this was the first national political campaign in the United States that included Spanish. "El Lcdo. Jose Coll y Cuchí recorrerá los Estados Unidos pronunciando discursos en defensa de Al Smith," *El Mundo*, October 12, 1928, 2.

49. The party participated in the 1932 elections and lost by a landslide. Vivas Maldonado, *Historia de Puerto Rico*, 210; Castro, *Historia Sinóptica*, 13.

50. "Bienvenidos a la docta casa de la cultura puertorriqueña!," El Ateneo, https://ateneopr.org.

51. Puerto Rican newspapers *La Democracia, La Correspondencia, La Estrella de Puerto Rico*, and *El Mundo* all expressed their support for Coll y Cuchí and their indignation at Mont Reily's "despotic abuse" of his power. For copies of what they wrote see, Coll y Cuchí, *Nacionalismo*, 38–41.

52. According to Ileana Rodríguez-Silva, Puerto Rican elites, of which Coll y Cuchí was a member, employed virility "in reference to the strength of character of the ideal liberal Puerto Rican man." The word "entailed morality, sexual restraint, physical strength, and scientific rationality," qualities Reily and other U.S. officials apparently believed Puerto Rican men lacked but ones that Coll y Cuchí used to define himself. Rodríguez-Silva, *Silencing Race*, 140.

53. Coll y Cuchí, *Nacionalismo*, 37. In her discussion of gender and the Cuban revolution, Michelle Chase points to a similar construction of masculinity among city-based men involved in the anti-Batista resistance. Unlike the fighting men in the Sierra Maestra who epitomized "warrior masculinity," the urban men grounded their radical politics in "familiar notions of masculine honor, paternal responsibility, and sexual propriety." Chase, *Revolution within the Revolution*, 46.

54. Coll y Cuchí, *Nacionalismo*, 36–38.

55. Coll y Cuchí, *Nacionalismo*, 144.

56. Coll y Cuchí, *Nacionalismo*, 145–46.

57. Coll y Cuchí, *Nacionalismo*, 145.

58. Coll y Cuchí, *Nacionalismo*, 46.

59. As Cynthia Enloe points out, "Nationalism typically has sprung from masculinized memory, masculinized humiliation, and masculinized hope." Enloe, *Bananas, Beaches, and Bases*, 44. Joane Nagel argues that men and masculinity were central to nationalism and the construction of the nation-state. Nagel, "Masculinity and Nationalism." See also Stoler, *Carnal Knowledge*, 46.

60. Stoler, *Carnal Knowledge*, 46.

61. "Porto Ricans Demand Removal of Gov. Reily," *New York Times*, September 5, 1921.

62. "Porto Ricans Demand Removal of Gov. Reily."

63. Clark, *Porto Rico and Its Problems*, 60. Reily was subsequently convicted on charges of payroll padding at his job in the Kansas Department of Public Works and paroled six months into his sentence due to ill health. "E. M. Reily Indicted in Kansas City Graft," *New York Times*, July 16, 1939; "E. Mont Reily, Ill, Is Paroled," *New York Times*, June 3, 1940.

64. Coll y Cuchí, *Nacionalismo*, 26.

65. For a discussion of these practices by the Puerto Rican elite, see Rodríguez-Silva, *Silencing Race*.

66. Puerto Rican organizations approached race in different ways. The Republican Party "accused" the Union Party of "race hatred." The FLT, which included many Afro-Puerto Ricans in its ranks, "simultaneously spoke about racial differences within the working classes and minimized their importance." Suárez Findlay, *Imposing Decency*, 142, 143.

67. Rodríguez-Silva, *Silencing Race*, 6.

68. Coll y Cuchí, *Nacionalismo*, 25.

69. As Eileen Suárez Findlay notes, "Colonial officials . . . generally represented island elite men as either too ineffectual . . . or too contaminated with the despotic political practices of their former Spanish master to govern properly. . . . they clearly needed U.S. imperial tutelage." Findlay, *Left without a Father*, 29.

70. Rosado, *Pedro Albizu Campos*, 4–5, 13.

71. Vasconcelos, *Indología*, xxv.

72. See Rodríguez Cancel, "Conflictos ideólogicos," 19.

73. Albizu was not alone in denouncing white supremacy in the United States while ignoring or minimizing it in Puerto Rico, a phenomenon Hilda Lloréns dissects in "'Racialization Works Differently Here."

74. Albizu Campos, "Concepto de la raza," 26.

75. Ilan Rachum notes that for much of the Spanish-speaking world in the Americas in the early twentieth century, *raza* "carrie[d] the meaning of an extended community bound by cultural ties in addition to that of a people belonging to the same stock and carrying similar physical traits." Rachum, "Origins," 21.

76. Albizu Campos, "Concepto de la raza," 26.

77. Bernand, "Colón y la modernidad," 341. On Yrigoyen's role, see Bernand, "Colón y la modernidad," 44–45. For a history of Día de la Raza, see Rodríguez, *Celebración de la raza*, esp. chap. 1. I thank Michael Staudenmaier for telling me about this book.

78. For a history and conceptualization of the links between raza and Spanish identity in Puerto Rico, see Rodríguez, *Celebración de la raza*, chap. 8.

79. Albizu Campos, "Discurso," 30.

80. Albizu Campos, "Discurso," 31–32.

81. Albizu Campos, "Discurso," 32.

82. A number of scholars have criticized constructions of Puerto Rican identity that privilege Spanish heritage and obscure or deny African influence as well as the ongoing reality of racism. A particular target has been the idea that Puerto Ricans are one "gran familia," the product of the happy blending of the African, the Indigenous, and the Spanish, because

it ignores racial, class, and sexual differences. See Acosta Cruz, *Dream Nation*, 39, 43, 75, 123; Duany, "Nation on the Move"; Godreau, *Scripts of Blackness*; Lloréns, *Imagining the Great Puerto Rican Family*; and Rivera-Rideau, *Remixing Reggaetón*.

83. José de Diego was the leader of the Puerto Rican Autonomist Party, which called on the Spanish government to grant Puerto Rico greater self-rule and reforms, but not necessarily independence. He later joined the Union Party and called for independence from the United States. Ayala and Bernabe, *Puerto Rico in the American Century*, 23, 57.

84. Coll y Cuchí, *Nacionalismo*, 287.

85. On the Nationalists and feminization of the flag, *nuestra bandera* in Spanish, see Arroyo, "Living the Political, 135.

86. Albizu Campos, "Discurso," 289. On the conflation of women and the nation, see Yuval-Davis and Anthias, *Woman-Nation-State*, 26–28.

87. Coll y Cuchí, *Nacionalismo*, 289.

88. Coll y Cuchí reprinted the article from *El Corresponsal* but did not provide the date or title. Coll y Cuchí, *Nacionalismo*, 261–63.

89. On Puerto Rican women's involvement with the hemispheric suffrage movement, see Marino, *Feminism for the Americas*, 36, 65, 149.

90. Azize Vargas, *Mujer en la lucha*, 101–2, 108.

91. Archivo Digital Nacional de Puerto Rico, Periódicos Históricos, http://adnpr.net/colecciones-digitales/.

92. "Los actos nacionalistas de Vieques y Naguabo," *El Mundo*, November 15, 1930.

93. "Una junta nacionalista de damas," *El Mundo*, September 19, 1981.

94. Barceló Miller, "Halfhearted Solidarity," 129, 131. For a critical assessment of how Padilla's upper-class position, whiteness, and gender affected her role in the party and politics more generally, see Jiménez-Muñoz, "'Race' and Class among *Nacionalista* Women," esp. 177–80.

95. "Una sección femenina de la Junta Nacionalista," *El Mundo*, October 3, 1931. Puerto Rican newspapers routinely covered Nationalist Party events. The push for women's suffrage likely generated increased interest in women's activism.

96. "Grandioso Mítin Nacionalista en Río Piedras," *La Nación*, December 30, 1932.

97. "Los actos nacionalistas de Vieques y Naguabo."

98. "Los actos nacionalistas de Vieques y Naguabo." Pro-independence forces employ the "flag of Lares" to indicate their opposition to U.S. rule. I chose this representative quotation both because he gave it at the ceremony for the first *sección femenina* and because Joan of Arc was a potent symbol for many Nationalists, especially women. Joan was a Catholic woman who sacrificed her life for the freedom of her nation. See Power, "Women, Gender," 138.

99. Yuval-Davis and Anthias, *Woman-Nation-State*, 26–28.

100. More work remains to be done to fully understand the Nationalist Party's gender politics. However, as I point out here and in Power, "Women, Gender," to do this we must move beyond quoting Albizu and incorporate the thoughts of other men and especially women members and leaders.

101. "Paraceres," *El Mundo*, December 1, 1930.

102. For examples of how U.S. women used ideas of gender differences and women's moral superiority to justify their political activism in the temperance and abolition movements of the early 1800s, see Welter, "Cult of True Womanhood," and during the woman's suffrage movement in the late 1800s and early 1900s, see Baker, "Domestication of Politics."

103. "Adhesión femenina al Partido Nacionalista," *El Mundo*, May 25, 1931. The figure of the self-sacrificing woman is common in patriarchal, Catholic societies. For the classic discussion of Marianismo, the belief that the Virgin Mary is the appropriate role model for women because women are spiritually and morally superior to men and should accept the

abuse men mete out to them, see Stevens, "Marianismo." For a refutation of Stevens's claims, see Navarro, "Against *Marianismo*."

104. Jiménez-Muñoz, "'Race' and Class among *Nacionalista* Women," 180; Ferrao, *Pedro Albizu Campos*, 342–43.

105. "El Movimiento Nacionalista en todo el país," *La Nación*, August 14, 1931; "Los Nacionalistas de Barranquitas," *El Mundo*, May 20, 1932; "Candidaturas del Partido Nacionalista," *El Mundo*, September 20, 1932; "Candidaturas del Partido Nacionalista," *El Mundo*, September 22, 1932. I thank Luis Ferrao for sharing these sources with me.

106. Colón, Mergal, and Torres, *Participación de la mujer*, 42; Suárez Findlay, *Imposing Decency*, 156.

107. Colón, Mergal, and Torres, *Participación de la mujer*, 93.

108. For discussion of these groups, see Colón, Mergal, and Torres, *Participación de la mujer*, 42–43; Azize Vargas, "Emergence of Feminism," 180–81.

109. Isabelle Picó argues that upper- and middle-class women's participation in the suffrage movement stemmed from economic dislocations their families suffered due to U.S. colonialism that resulted in small and middle-sized landowners losing their land and moving to cities. The landowners' daughter received more education, "respectable jobs" opened up, and women entered the professions, which heightened their independence and increased their desire and capacity to be politically active. Picó, "History of Women's Struggle," 54. For a discussion of how elite women's interests conflicted with those of elite men and the former's recourse to the U.S. Congress to pressure the male colonial elite to grant them suffrage, see Jiménez-Muñoz, "'So We Decided to Come."

110. Colón, Mergal, and Torres, *Participación de la mujer*, 44.

111. Albizu Campos, "Sufragio," 2–3.

112. Albizu Campos, "Feminismo y la independencia."

113. Albizu Campos, "Mujer libertadora."

114. Abreu de Aguilar and Ana Roque de Duprey, who spoke out for women's rights in the late 1800s, had fought for the extension of the vote to all women, including illiterate ones. Colón, Mergal, and Torres, *Participación de la mujer*, 43.

115. Albizu Campos, "Mujer libertadora."

116. Albizu Campos, "Mujer libertadora."

117. Albizu Campos, "Feminismo y la independencia." After the 1932 election, the Nationalist Party adopted the position of *retraimiento*, which means to withdraw from any colonial institutions, and refused to participate in any elections so long as Puerto Rico remained a colony of the United States.

118. "Si las mujeres en Puerto Rico son verdaderas patriotas," *El Mundo*, May 4, 1931, 2; 33. Torregosa was referring to Adams's famous admonition to her husband, John Adams, one of the framers of the U.S. Constitution, to "Remember the Ladies!"

119. In an interview conducted in 1965, she stated that she was never a member of the Nationalist Party but that she sympathized with it in the 1930s and donated money to it. Notes from interview with Robert J. Alexander, June 9, 1965, folder 41, box 9, Robert J. Alexander Papers, Special Collections and University Archives, Rutgers University Libraries. She was then married to Luis Muñoz Marín, the leader of the Popular Democratic Party and the first elected governor of Puerto Rico.

120. Angela Negrón Muñiz, "Conversando con las principales feministas del país," *El Mundo*, August 23, 1931.

121. "Programa de los actos que celebrara mañana," *El Mundo*, September 22, 1931. Padilla parted ways with the Nationalist Party in 1936 because she opposed violence and disagreed with Albizu's call for retaliation against the Insular Police. Fernández Sanz, *Trina Padilla de Sanz*, 162.

122. Jiménez-Muñoz connects Padilla's politics to her patrician background and membership in Puerto Rico's creole elite. She provides her biography and a critical appraisal of her politics in "'Race' and Class among *Nacionalista* Women."

123. Negrón Muñiz, "Conversando con las principales feministas del país."

124. Ileana Rodríguez-Silva points out that both the Partido Unión and the short-lived Party for Independence (1912–14) identified Puerto Ricans as members of the *raza iberoamericana*, in acknowledgment of the population's African, Indian (Taino), and Iberian ethnic origins. However, they emphasized European contributions, which they believed "overrode any negative trait inherited from those supposedly racially inferior groups." Rodríguez-Silva, *Silencing Race*, 187.

125. Walsh, "'Advancing the Kingdom,'" esp. 56, 65, 114.

126. "En la Asamblea celebrada ayer," *El Mundo*, September 8, 1922; Coll y Cuchí, *Nacionalismo*, 144.

127. Again, the Nationalists' focus on the archipelago's Hispanic legacy privileged the history and reality of the creole and mestizo elite and their descendants, overlooked the genocidal impact Spain had on the indigenous Taíno and the brutal treatment enslaved Africans endured, assumed the existence of a homogenous *raza*, and ignored the radically distinct treatment and experiences of Puerto Ricans of Afro descent.

128. Coll y Cuchí, *Nacionalismo*, 273.

129. Coll y Cuchí, *Nacionalismo*, 273.

130. Vivas Maldonado, *Historia de Puerto Rico*, 210.

131. *El Mundo*, August 4, 1927, 5.

132. *El Mundo*, August 4, 1927, 5.

133. "El Lcdo Acosta Velarde renuncia la presidencia del Partido Nacionalista," *El Mundo*, December 14, 1927. He retired because of poor health in 1928 but remained loyal to the party.

134. "El Lcdo Acosta Velarde renuncia la presidencia del Partido Nacionalista."

135. "En la República de Colombia se prepara una campaña por la independencia de Pto. Rico," *El Mundo*, July 7, 1926, 3. Unfortunately, I have not been able to find any further information about this committee.

136. "En Bogotá se constituye un Comité Pro Independencia de Puerto Rico," *El Mundo*, February 18, 1927.

137. In his book *El Señor Don Samuel Zemurray y la soberanía de Honduras* (1926), Alfredo Trejo Castillo expressed his opposition to U.S. economic and political incursions into Honduras.

138. Andrew and Cleven, "Pan American Centennial Congress," 184.

139. Andrew and Cleven, "Pan American Centennial Congress," 188.

140. "Partido Nacionalista extiende gratitud al Fdo. Trejo Castillo," *El Mundo*, August 18, 1926, 3.

141. "Que debo contarme en el número de los que decididamente engrosan las filas del Partido Nacionalista de Puerto Rico," *El Mundo*, October 9, 1926, 1.

142. "Ninguna causa tan conmovedora como la de ustedes; ninguna más alta ni más digna de cooperación y ayuda," *El Mundo*, October 18, 1926, 3.

143. *El Mundo*, April 30, 1926, 1; Vasconcelos, *Indología*, xxii. Vasconcelos's book consists of a lengthy prologue in which he recounts how he came to speak in Puerto Rico and his thoughts on Puerto Rico. One purpose of the prologue was to refute charges that he spoke at the university for financial gain and to advance U.S. imperialist interests in the region.

144. Vasconcelos, *Indología*, xxiii; *El Mundo*, November 26, 1926, 1; Tirado Avilés, "Forja de un líder," 74.

145. Vasconcelos, *Indología*, xxiv. Unfortunately, he does not share more details of what they talked about, nor have I been able to discover Albizu's memories of or thoughts on the conversation.

146. "Puerto Rico before the International Anti-Colonial Congress," *El Nacionalista de Ponce*, April 9, 1927, 1, 5–6; *El Mundo*, November 26, 1926, 1; Rodríguez-Fraticelli, "Pedro Albizu Campos," 29.

147. Jones, *League against Imperialism*, 5–7.

148. The party lacked the funds to send any of its members to represent it.

149. League against Colonial Oppression, *List of Organizations and Delegates Attending the Congress against Colonial Oppression and Imperialism*, 3, League against Imperialism Archives, International Institute of Social History.

150. Vasconcelos, "Text of the Speech," 1.

151. Vasconcelos, "Text of the Speech," 1.

152. Vasconcelos, "Text of the Speech," 2.

153. *Kundgebung der Nationalen Partei Porto Ricos*, League against Imperialism Archives, International Institute of Social History. I thank Peter Staudenmeier for translating the document and Michael Staudenmaier for putting me in contact with his brother.

154. Mella, *Documentos y artículos*, 640. I thank Hugo Vallenas Málaga for sharing this document with me.

## Chapter Four

1. For a copy of the telegram, see Rosado, *Pedro Albizu Campos*, 539. Enriquillo was the son of Nationalist Federico Henríquez, whose brother, Francisco, had been the Dominican president in 1916, before the imposition of U.S. rule.

2. The three sources I have drawn on to construct what Albizu did in Haiti are de Albizu Campos, *Albizu Campos y la independencia*, 43–45; Medina Ramírez, *Movimiento libertador*, 1:88; and Rosado, *Pedro Albizu Campos*, 130–31. For background on Jolibois and Haitian efforts to generate international solidarity, see Hector, "Solidarité et luttes politiques."

3. McPherson, *Invaded*, 2.

4. This is not to say that any single voice captured the range of perspectives on these issues. Individuals and organizations in both the United States and Puerto Rico held a variety of opinions regarding U.S. foreign policy and the desired relationship between Puerto Rico and the United States. This chapter focuses on those of anti-imperialist nationalists.

5. I thank Felice Batlan for this formulation.

6. "Acosta Velarde cree que Coolidge dejará de ser silencioso cuando hable Albizu Campos en America," *La Democracia*, June 21, 1927, 13. The paper reprinted his speech in full. Acosta Valerde's comments reflect the sense of continental unity that José Martí expressed in "Nuestra América," *La Revista Ilustrada de Nueva York*, January 10, 1891.

7. On Paris as a center of anti-imperialist activity, see Goebel, *Anti-imperial Metropolis*.

8. Yankelevich, "En la retaguardia de la Revolución Mexicana," 37–38.

9. The PNPR condemned the murder of Sandino, whom it defined as "the beating heart of Nuestra América," and blamed his death on the United States. Albizu Campos, "Proclama ante la muerte de Sandino," 295.

10. Smith, *Talons of the Eagle*, 87. Sandino led a guerrilla army composed primarily of peasants against the U.S. occupation between 1927 and 1933, the year Franklin Roosevelt withdrew U.S. troops. Smith, *Talons of the Eagle*, 87.

11. McPherson, *Invaded*, 197–207. Alan McPherson charts the rise and fall of Latin American support for Sandino (see pp. 217–27) and the impact the decline had on Sandino's characterization and vision of the battle for national liberation.

12. Carr, "Pioneering Transnational Solidarity," 142.

13. Ribes Tovar, *Albizu Campos*, 36.

14. Rosado, *Pedro Albizu Campos*, 459–60. I thank Neici Zeller for explaining to me what proper protocol was needed for visiting dignitaries.

15. "Transcript of Laura Meneses," reel 1, MM-7 RG XUU Series 2, Registrar Records, Graduate School of Arts and Sciences, Radcliffe, Schlesinger Library, Harvard Radcliffe Institute. Meneses received her PhD in Natural Sciences from San Marcos University in Lima, Peru, in 1918. De Albizu Campos, *Albizu Campos y la independencia*, 19–21, 33. According to Peruvian law, a Peruvian woman who married a foreigner ceased to be a Peruvian citizen. See Hill, "Citizenship of Married Women," 728. In 1948, the U.S. government stripped her of her U.S. citizenship. De Albizu Campos, *Albizu Campos y la independencia*, 137. The U.S. government allowed Meneses to visit Albizu only once during the six years he was in the Atlanta Federal Penitentiary. Meneses Albizu Campos and Lora Gamarra, *Vida de amor*, 25, 34.

16. Ribes Tovar, *Albizu Campos*, 35; Medina Ramirez, *Movimiento libertador*, 1:100.

17. "El banquete de la capital," *El Nacionalista de Ponce*, June 25, 1927, 5; "La Cruzada Nacionalista," *El Nacionalista de Ponce*, June 24, 1927, 1.

18. "El homenaje al Lcdo. Albizu Campos en el Hotel Palace," *El Nacionalista de Ponce*, June 25, 1927, 3.

19. *El Mundo*, July 26, 1927, cited in Rosado, *Pedro Albizu Campos*, 121. Before Albizu's arrival, the Puerto Rican and Dominican Nationalists had exchanged cablegrams about his appearance. In one, Dominican Nationalists said they would receive Albizu, "as their guest." "La cruzada nacionalista en Ibero-América," *El Nacionalista de Ponce*, June 25, 1927, 9.

20. Torres, *Pedro Albizu Campos*, 9.

21. According to Bruce Calder, "Puerto Ricans . . . arrived in the late nineteenth and early twentieth centuries . . . and . . . tended to join the lower middle sector, working as artisans and small merchants." Calder, *Impact of Intervention*, xxvi–xxvii. By the end of the nineteenth century, Puerto Rico had "an overabundance of labor," and some immigrated to the Dominican Republic in search of work. "In 1894, eight hundred and eighty-eight Puerto Ricans were reported to have migrated to San Pedro de Macorís to work in the sugar mills." Ayala, *American Sugar Kingdom*, 163–64.

22. Medina Ramírez, *Movimiento libertador*, 1:85.

23. "Las conferencias del Dr. Albizu Campos," *Listín Diario*, July 5, 1927, 1.

24. "Por Puerto Rico libre!," *Listín Diario*, August 20, 1927, 4. "Lic." is short for Licenciado, an honorific title.

25. *El Nacionalista de Ponce*, July 2, 1927, 4.

26. "Los Nacionalistas de Puerto Rico envían un patriótico mensaje al pueblo Dominicano," *El Mundo*, July 7, 1924, 6. President Vásquez responded the next day thanking the party for its support and adding, "Please transmit to the Puerto Rican Nationalist Party my sympathies with your aspirations in favor of the destiny of the American peoples." "El Presidente de Santo Domingo contesta el mensaje del Partido Nacionalista," *El Mundo*, July 15, 1924, 1.

27. "La conferencia del Doctor Campos fue un bello acto cultural," *Listín Diario*, July 1, 1927, 1.

28. "Un mitin pro-independencia de Pto. Rico en Santo Domingo," *El Mundo*, June 7, 1927, 3.

29. Henríquez and Lugo were founding members of the Dominican Nationalist Party, created during the U.S. occupation. Lugo, "perhaps the foremost anti-American Dominican," had been jailed by the United States in 1922 for his antioccupation activities. McPherson, *Invaded*, 127; Calder, *Impact of Intervention*, 197.

30. "Se constituyó la 'Junta Nacional Pro Independencia de Puerto Rico,'" *El Mundo*, August 8, 1927, 1.

31. "Tres juntas pro independencia de Puerto Rico se han constituido en Santo Domingo," *El Mundo*, July 16, 1927, 3.

32. "A los puertorriqueños y demás interesados en las cuestiones patrias," *El Nacionalista de Ponce*, January 7, 1928, 3.

33. "Los federacionistas dominicanos se unen al movimiento pro-independencia de Puerto Rico," *El Mundo*, August 25, 1927, 3.

34. Calder, *Impact of Intervention*, 204; McPherson, *Invaded*, 163–64.

35. According to Bruce Calder, the president of Brazil did not meet with them, while Alan McPherson writes that the president of Peru declined to do so. Calder, *Impact of Intervention*, 204; McPherson, *Invaded*, 164.

36. Calder, *Impact of Intervention*, 188, 199, 204; McPherson, *Invaded*, 159–68.

37. Rosado, *Pedro Albizu Campos*, 577.

38. For examples of these letters, see Rosado, *Pedro Albizu Campos*, 529–34.

39. Renda, *Taking Haiti*, 10. The NAACP was so concerned about conditions in Haiti that it sent James Weldon Johnson to investigate them in 1920. He concluded that during the first five years of the U.S. occupation the marines had killed 5,000 Haitians, tortured Haitian men and women, and reinstituted forced labor (slavery). For a summary of his report, see Johnson, "Haitian Investigation," 9–11.

40. McPherson, *Invaded*, 238. For a discussion of Johnson's investigation, the impact it had on him, and his work to end the U.S. occupation of Haiti, see Renda, *Taking Haiti*, 188–96.

41. "Haitian Republic Bars Senator as 'Undesirable,'" *New York Times*, March 13, 1927. Borno, understandably, did not look favorably on a visit from the senator and refused to let him enter the country.

42. McPherson, *Invaded*, 137. McPherson, "Joseph Jolibois Fils," 145, disparages Jolibois's contributions to the antioccupation movement. In contrast, Devés Valdés, *Del Ariel de Rodó*, 175, characterizes him as a respected member of transnational intellectual and leftist Latin American networks.

43. Smith, *Red and Black*, 33.

44. The Patriotic Union began in 1915, dissolved a few months later, and was revived in 1920. It called for the restoration of Haitian territory to Haitians and denounced "the abuse and authoritarianism of the occupation." McPherson, *Invaded*, 139–40.

45. "Miembros del nacionalismo y de la prensa de Haití son encarcelados," *Listín Diario*, July 1, 1927.

46. *El Mundo*, July 25, 1927, 1.

47. Although Roman Catholicism was the official religion, the practice of vodou was widespread and remains so today. For a discussion of the African origins of Haitian vodou, see Fernández-Olmos and Paravisini-Gebert, *Creole Religions*, 109–17. Albizu's dreams of an Antillean Confederation persisted after his trip. Former secretary general of the PNPR Juan Antonio Corretjer recounted that in 1934 Albizu "was still thinking about the Antillean ideal . . . Albizu instructed [him] to move to Haiti and meet with Pierre Paul, Christián, and Pierre Moraviah Morpeau." Juan Antonio Corretjer, "Albizu Campos y la Lucha de las Antillas," *El Mundo*, October 24, 1961, 25.

48. Santiago-Valles, "'Our Race Today," 118–19.

49. "Albizu Campos estuvo algunas horas en Puerto Principe, Haiti," *El Mundo*, October 1, 1927, 17.

50. *Le Temps*, October 12, 1927, reprinted and translated in Spanish in *El Nacionalista de Ponce*, October 15, 1927, 10.

51. *Le Temps*, October 12, 1927.

52. Rosado, *Pedro Albizu Campos*, 35.

53. See Lang, "Primer."

54. My thanks to Ben Johnson for helping me formulate this critique.

55. "La Junta Nacionalista de Puerto Rico se constituye un 'Comité Pro-Independencia de Haiti,'" *El Mundo*, October 7, 1927. To date, I have not been able to find how long this committee existed or what it did.

56. A condition for the withdrawal of U.S. troops from Cuba was the Cuban government's signing the Platt Amendment in 1901. One provision allowed the U.S. military to intervene in Cuba when it deemed it necessary; another ceded Cuban land for the construction of U.S. bases, which is why the United States has Guantánamo to this day. See Meade, *History*, 130; Stoner, *From the House*, 65; and Hatzky, *Juan Antonio Mella*, 142.

57. Rosado, *Pedro Albizu Campos*, 133.

58. Rubén Martínez Villena was a high-ranking member of the Cuban Communist Party and a delegate of the Comintern. Alejo Carpentier was the noted intellectual and writer, credited with initiating magical realism, and the author of *The Kingdom of This World*, among other novels. Jeifets and Jeifets, *América Latina*, 399–401, 131–32. On Francisco Ichaso and his work with *Revista de Avance*, see Ripoll, "*Revista de Avance*," 263.

59. Roa, *Fuego*, 196–97.

60. Roa, *Fuego*, 196–97. Members of its editorial staff joined the Junta Nacional Cubana Pro Independencia de Puerto Rico.

61. "Se constituye la 'Junta Nacional Cubana Pro-Independencia de Pto. Rico,'" *El Mundo*, October 7, 1927, 5. Enrique José Varona was one of the founders of the Junta Revolucionaria Pro Independencia de Cuba y Puerto Rico in New York, along with José Martí and Ramón Emeterio Betances. He was director of the magazine *Revista de Cuba* and linked to the leadership of the Partido Autonomista; Roig de Leuchsenring was an eminent Cuban historian who was named "Historian of the City of Havana." Torres, *Pedro Albizu Campos*, 46–48. Medina Ramírez, *Movimiento libertador*, 1:78–79. Enrique Gay Galbo was the founder, editor, and journalist of several Cuban newspapers, a historian, and an internationally connected and recognized intellectual. Juan Marinello Vidaorreta was a leftist intellectual with links to the Cuban Communist Party. Jeifets and Jeifets, *América Latina*, 64, 132, 242.

62. Hatzky, *Juan Antonio Mella*, 78–80.

63. Hatzky, *Juan Antonio Mella*, 20.

64. Mañach, "Recuerdos de Albizu Campos," 6; "El Lcdo. Albizu Campos objeto de un homenaje en La Habana," *El Mundo*, November 8, 1927, 3, in Rosado, *Pedro Albizu Campos*, 546.

65. "El caso de Puerto Rico es el atentado más grave que ha hecho Estados Unidos contra Ibero América," *El Mundo*, November 26, 1927.

66. I only know that she was on the council because I came across a picture of her seated with other members of the junta. Rosado, *Pedro Albizu Campos*, 536.

67. Stoner, *From the House*, 56, 57.

68. Cuban women were significant political actors, as K. Lynn Stoner makes abundantly clear in *From the House*. On the important role Dominican women played during this period, see Zeller, *Discursos y espacios*. On Puerto Rican women and suffrage, see Azize Vargas, *Mujer en la lucha*; and Barceló Miller, *Lucha por el sufragio*.

69. For examples of these letters, see Rosado, *Pedro Albizu Campos*, 500–535. One exception to the man-to-man correspondence was when Federico Acosta Velarde, president of the PRNP, wrote to Panamanian Julia Palau de Gámez to thank her for her work in the 1926 Inter-American Congress on Women. Paula de Gámez had called for Puerto Rico's "independence and absolute sovereignty, without which continental peace cannot be ensured." Federico Acosta Velarde to Julia Palau de Gámez, July 27, 1927, in Rosado, *Pedro Albizu Campos*, 512.

70. Meneses had their third child in Peru.

71. To date, I have only located one letter from Albizu to Meneses: Pedro Albizu Campos to Laura Meneses de Albizu, Mexico City, January 16, 1928, reprinted in Rosado, *Pedro Albizu Campos*, 486–92.

72. Meyer, *Cristero Rebellion*, 21.

73. Revolutionary leaders sought to secularize Mexico by eliminating the power of the Catholic Church. A number of constitutional articles stripped the church of its control

and influence. Article 3 said that the state, not the church, will run the education system. Article 27 said that churches may not "acquire, hold or administer real property." Article 130 declared that anyone who "propagate[es] a religious creed" cannot educate "laborers or field workers," in other words, the vast majority of the Mexican population. "1917 Constitution of Mexico," Latin American Studies Association, www.latinamericanstudies.org/mexico /1917-Constitution.htm.

74. Jean Meyer characterizes it as a conflict between "the men who were administering the state in order to modernize it and those perhaps two-thirds of the population in 1920, who constituted traditional Mexico." Meyer, "Revolution and Reconstruction," 202.

75. Meyer, *Cristero Rebellion*, 54. I thank María Teresa Fernández for explaining to me how critical this period was.

76. Rosado, *Pedro Albizu Campos*, 136–37.

77. Vasconcelos's opposition to Calles was so pronounced that he contacted leaders of the Cristero Revolt and ran against him in the 1929 elections, which he lost. Legrás, "Voluntad revolucionaria," 73.

78. Rosado, *Pedro Albizu Campos*, 136.

79. Albizu Campos to Meneses, January 16, 1928, 486.

80. Berbusse, "Unofficial Intervention," 45–46; Meyer and Sherman, *Course of Mexican History*, 585–87.

81. For a history of the league, see Kersffeld, *Contra el imperio*; Melgar Bao, "Anti-imperialist League;" Pujals, "¡Embarcados!"; and Pujals, "'La Brigada Móvil.'"

82. Jeifets and Jeifets, "Jaime Nevarez y la fundación del movimiento comunista;" Pujals, "¡Embarcados!," 2–3.

83. Hatzky, *Julio Antonio Mella*.

84. Hatzky, *Julio Antonio Mella*, 167, 170–71.

85. Fray Mario Rodríguez León, "#788 Pedro Albizu Campos en México (1927–1928)," interview with Ángel Collado Schwarz, May 13, 2018, La Voz del Centro, http://www .vozdelcentro.org/2018/05/13/788-pedro-albizu-campos-en-mexico-1927-1928/; Meneses Albizu Campos and Lora Gamarra, *Vida de amor*, 31–32.

86. Blanca Canales, who led the uprising of 1950 in Jayuya, attended the lecture. It was the first time she heard Albizu speak. She remembered, "He spoke about the Aztec and Mayan cultures. In short, he made us see a world we had never seen before." Canales, *Constitución*, 6.

87. "La conferencia de Albizu en la universidad," *El Mundo*, March 21, 1930, 6, reprinted in Torres, *Pedro Albizu Campos*, 75–76.

88. It is reasonable to suggest that Albizu's inability to establish meaningful contacts in Mexico contributed to his misunderstanding of the Mexican reality and complexity. I thank Mike Staudenmaier for this insight.

89. Rosado, *Pedro Albizu Campos*, appendixes, 547. Medina Ramírez, *Movimiento libertador*, 1:106–7.

90. "Congreso de la Prensa Latina," *Heraldo de Cuba*, reprinted in El Nacionalista de Puerto Rico, April 17, 1928, 9.

91. "Congreso de la Prensa Latina." "Riotous Outbreaks Mark Latin Press Parley When French Oppose Censure of Us [sic] at Havana," *New York Times*, March 9, 1928.

92. Jorge Mañach to Federico Acosto Velarde, April 25, 1928, Havana, printed in El Nacionalista, May 26, 1928, 3.

93. Rosado, *Pedro Albizu Campos*, 141.

94. Rivas Tovar, *Albizu Campos*, 38.

95. Haya de la Torre, *Construyendo el aprismo*, 44, 57–60.

96. Stein, *Populism in Peru*, 147–49. It fell to APRA members outside Peru to maintain connections with Puerto Rico and the Nationalists. In 1929, APRA leader and writer Magda

Portal visited Puerto Rico, Cuba, and the Dominican Republic, "the countries that most suffered the cruel yoke of the invader." Haya de la Torre, *Construyendo el aprismo*, 44. She spoke at the University of Puerto Rico, delivering one talk titled "Latin America Confronting Imperialism" and another defending the Mexican Revolution. Moving beyond the university, she participated in "anti-U.S. demonstrations, distribut[ed] fliers and vehemently embrac[ed] the cause of the Puerto Rican nationalists." Weaver, *Peruvian Rebel*, 75. Portal was subsequently deported from Puerto Rico "for speaking against the United States." Sara Beatriz Guardia, "Magda Portal: La poesía combative," *Yumpu*, May 7, 2013, www.yumpu.com/es/document /read/14118665/entrevistas-a-magda-portal-y-angela-ramos.

97. Rosado, *Pedro Albizu Campos*, 147; De Albizu Campos, *Albizu Campos y la independencia*, 53, 55.

98. Rosado, *Pedro Albizu Campos*, 161.

99. Foreign, usually British or U.S., monopolies owned the cable companies used to send communications from one Latin American country to another. As a result, the U.S. government had access to the messages exchanged among Albizu, the PNPR, and the various people involved in his trip. McGreery, "Wireless Empire," 24. I thank Enrique Ayoroa Santilez, José Giusti, and Ben Johnson for helping me to locate this article.

100. Memorandum for the Secretary of War from General Frank McIntyre, October 12, 1927, Folder: Albizu y Campos, Pedro, Box 13, Personal Name and Information File, 1914–1945, NARA. "Declares Porto Rico Business Is Favorable," *New York Times*, December 12, 1925. Ironically, Albizu and McIntyre had met previously. Albizu volunteered his services to McIntyre in 1917 "on the condition he would serve with Puerto Rican troops." Instead, McIntyre "recommended that he stay at Harvard," and when Albizu enlisted in 1918, he was assigned to the "Black-Puerto Rican 375th Regiment." Franqui-Rivera, *Soldiers of the Nation*, 254n45.

101. "A Pro-Independence of Porto Rico Meeting in Santo Domingo," Entry 21, Folder: Albizu y Campos, Pedro, Box 13, Personal Name and Information File, 1914–1945, NARA. I thank Mónica Jiménez for sending me these documents.

102. Francis White to the Secretary of War, September 19, 1927, Entry 21, Folder: Albizu y Campos, Pedro, Box 13, Personal Name and Information File, 1914–1945, NARA.

### Chapter Five

1. The cadetes and enfermeras were Nationalist Party organizations for men and women, respectively.

2. This section draws on Dávila Marichal, "¡Atención!," 136–45; and Randall, *Pueblo*.

3. Randall, *Pueblo*, 52.

4. Fortuño Janeiro, *Album histórico de Ponce*, 293.

5. José A. Lanauze, one of the founders of the Puerto Rican Communist Party, also addressed the crowd and called for the formation of "a popular front to defend the Puerto Rican cause." Fortuño Janeiro, *Album histórico de Ponce*, 293.

6. Ayala and Bernabe, *Puerto Rico in the American Century*, 116.

7. For a detailed and authoritative analysis of the event, see Hays, *Report of the Commission*.

8. Clark, *Porto Rico and Its Problems*, vii.

9. Clark, *Porto Rico and Its Problems*, xix.

10. Estimates range from 225 to 392 or more dead and between $30 and $85 million in property damage. See Palm and Hodgson, "Natural Hazards," 283; and Dietz, *Economic History*, 137.

11. Dietz, *Economic History*, 137.

12. Levy, *Puerto Ricans in the Empire*, 31–32.

13. Levy, *Puerto Ricans in the Empire*, 32.

14. Bergad, "Agrarian History of Puerto Rico," 85.

15. Ayala and Bernabe, *Puerto Rico in the American Century*, 95–96; Dietz, *Economic History*, 137–39. Nonetheless, 1933's crop of 785,000 tons was 21 percent lower than the previous crop of 992,000 tons. "Puerto Rico's Sugar Crop," *New York Times*, June 15, 1933.

16. César Ayala and Laird Bergad argue that most land and mills did not pass into U.S. hands: "Puerto Rican mill owners were pervasive and major owners of sugar estates." Puerto Ricans were able to retain ownership to a greater extent than their Dominican and Cuban counterparts because Puerto Rico was included "within the tariff wall of the United States [which] provided Puerto Rican sugar producers with distinct advantages." Ayala and Bergad, *Agrarian Puerto Rico*, 71.

17. The Jones Act of 1917 ruled that only ships built and registered in the United States could transport goods to Puerto Rico, which effectively led to higher prices. "Ley de Cabotaje asfixia la economía de Puerto Rico, según estudios," *Noticel*, March 27, 2014, www.noticel.com /economia/ley-de-cabotaje-asfixia-la-econma-de-puerto-rico-segn-estudios/610980495.

18. "Puerto Rico Seeks Share in New Deal," *New York Times*, November 19, 1933.

19. "Puerto Rico Seeks Share in New Deal."

20. Dietz, *Economic History*, 139.

21. Silvestrini-Pacheco, "Women as Workers," 252.

22. Dietz, *Economic History*, 139–41.

23. No polls on these issues were taken in Puerto Rico in the 1930s, and after 1932 the Nationalists did not participate in elections.

24. Antonio Barceló, previously of the Union Party, formed the pro-independence Liberal Party in 1932. Carr, *Puerto Rico*, 55.

25. Medina Ramírez, *Movimiento libertador*, 1:110–11; Rosado, *Pedro Albizu Campos*, 144.

26. "Una asamblea general para reorganizer el Partido Nacionalista," *El Mundo*, April 1, 1930, 3. It is not clear which invitees attended. Reporters from Puerto Rican newspapers and the Associated Press were there. "Lo que contesta el presidente del Partido Nacionalista a las manifestaciones de Don José Coll Cuchi," *El Mundo*, May 14, 1930, 1, reprinted in Torres, *Pedro Albizu Campos*, 89. Romain Rolland was a left-wing French writer who won the Nobel Prize in literature in 1915. Both he and Henri Barbusse, a French writer and Communist, attended the Brussels Congress in 1927, as did Vasconcelos and Ugarte. See chapter 3; and Jones, *League against Imperialism*, 7. *La Rábida* was published between 1911 and 1933 and distributed on both sides of the Atlantic. Márquez Macias, *Huelva y América*.

27. "Asamblea General Nacionalista," *Puerto Rico Ilustrado*, May 17, 1930.

28. He ended saying that he had more to report about Mexico and Peru, but the hour was late. "La Asamblea General Nacionalista de ayer," *El Mundo*, May 12, 1930, 1, 7, 11, reprinted in Torres, *Pedro Albizu Campos*, 82–84.

29. "El Lcdo. Pedro Albizu Campos fue electo presidente del Partido Nacionalista de Puerto Rico," *El Mundo*, May 13, 1930, 1, reprinted in Torres, *Pedro Albizu Campos*, 86. José Coll y Cuchí, one of the founders, and Antonio Ayuso Valdivieso, the former president, subsequently quit the party because they disagreed with its newly formulated antagonism toward the United States. Rosado, *Pedro Albizu Campos*, 161.

30. "El Lcdo. Pedro Albizu Campos fue electo," 86, emphasis added. The Nationalist Party participated in the 1932 elections and suffered a disastrous defeat. It received only 5,257 of the 380,000 votes cast. Albizu received 11,634 in his senator-at-large bid, coming in last out of eight candidates. Nolla-Acosta, *Puerto Rico Election Results*, 63. This loss influenced the party's rejection of electoral participation and the adoption of more militant policies.

31. "El Lcdo. Pedro Albizu Campos fue electo," 86. Import-substitution theory proposes that a nation should foster national production and eliminate foreign imports to overcome dependency on foreign powers and build its economy. Dependency theory posits that wealthy foreign nations control the economies of poor nations, which results in the wealthy nations'

extraction of money from the poor nations owing to their ability to control the prices of imports and exports.

32. "El Lcdo. Pedro Albizu Campos fue electo," 86.

33. "El Lcdo. Pedro Albizu Campos fue electo," 86.

34. "El Lcdo. Pedro Albizu Campos fue electo," 87.

35. "El Lcdo. Pedro Albizu Campos fue electo," 87.

36. On politics and performance, see Taylor, *Archive and Repertoire*, esp. chap. 6.

37. As Miranda Joseph discusses, nations develop "myths of origins" to "restore some imagined historical community." Joseph, *Romance of Community*, xx.

38. The independence movement continues to commemorate the rebellion of 1868 in Lares.

39. "Resolución declarando huéspedes de honor del pueblo de Lares," *El Nacionalista de Puerto Rico*, September 20, 1930, 15.

40. Puerto Rican poet Luis Lloréns Torres wrote the patriotic poem that recounts the history of the 1868 uprising. Morrero, *Luis Llorrens Torres*.

41. "Programa para la peregrinación a Lares," *El Nacionalista de Puerto Rico*, September 20, 1930, 1.

42. Dávila Dávila, "Bonos," 33, 35. Albizu probably got the idea of selling bonds from Irish Republicans. Dávila Dávila, "Bonos," 33. The FBI, which avidly sought information on Nationalist Party activities throughout the Americas, reported that it had "received information that Pedro Albizu Campos has been successful in distributing a substantial number of the so-called bonds of the Republic of Puerto Rico through Mexico, Central and South America." May 1, 1936, 811C.00/34, RG 59, Department of State Central Files, NARA. In 1937, the left-leaning Federation of Students of Chile bought a bond to support "the emancipatory movement of Puerto Rico." "Bono a Favor de Puerto Rico."

43. Corretjer and Tapia Lee, "Mariana Bracetti y Albizu Campos," 8.

44. Dávila Dávila, "Bonos," 39.

45. Lamia Azize Mawad learned about nationalism when she was twelve or thirteen years old. Dávila Marichal, "'Mujer no debe,'" 56.

46. Dávila Marichal, "'Mujer no debe,'" 56

47. Dávila Marichal, "'Mujer no debe,'" 57–58. I have not been able to find more information about these organizations. However, pro-independence Caribbean women's groups calling themselves Las Hijas date back to the late 1800s. For information on the nineteenth-century La Liga de las Hijas de Cuba, see Casanova de Villaverde, *Biográficos*, esp. 103, 115, 117. I thank Mercedes Fernández-Asenjo for locating this book for me. Connections continued among nationalist women in Cuba, the Dominican Republic, and Puerto Rico in the twentieth century. In 1922, women in the Dominican Republic started *Fémina*, which, among other issues, encouraged women's participation in the "national struggle" and established connections with "anti-imperialist women in Puerto Rico and Cuba." Zeller, *Discursos y espacios*, 68.

48. Antonio Cruz, interview with author, March 14, 2006, Adjuntas, P.R. Cruz was a former cadete. Dávila Marichal, "Mujer no debe," 58. The enfermeras functioned as a women's auxiliary of the Nationalist Party, as did the Black Cross Nurses of the United Negro Improvement Association, led by Marcus Garvey. Both organizations gave women opportunities to publicly participate in and lead groups that formed part of their respective nationalist movements. Unlike the enfermeras, the Black Cross nurses provided direct and ongoing medical services to their communities. See Duncan, "'Efficient Womanhood," chap. 4; and James, *Holding Aloft the Banner*, 137, 139–40.

49. The Torresolas were a prominent Nationalist family. One of Angelina's brothers, Elio, led the Jayuya uprising in 1950. Another brother, Griselio, participated in the attempt to kill

President Truman on November 1, 1950. Her sister, Doris, worked very closely with Albizu and was wounded when the Puerto Rican police attacked PRNP headquarters in 1950. Angelina Torresola, interview with author and Janine Santiago, October 26, 2013, Guaynabo, P.R.

50. Torresola interview.

51. Canales, *Constitución*, 12.

52. Torresola interview.

53. "Puerto Rican Nationalists Honor 'Martyr,' Marking First Anniversary of Flag Riot," *New York Times*, April 17, 1933.

54. Pérez Marchand, *Reminiscencia Histórica*, 89. I thank José Manuel Dávila for this reference.

55. "El Partido Nacionalista se reune en asemblea," *Puerto Rico Ilustrado*, October 8, 1932, 5.

56. Isabel Rosado, interview with author, May 16, 2008, Ceiba, P.R.

57. Jiménez de Wagenheim, *Nationalist Heroines*, 161–81.

58. Dávila Marichal, "¡Atención!," 20–27.

59. Estanislao Lugo, interview with author, May 21, 2008, Carolina, P.R.

60. Heriberto Marín, interview with author, May 20, 2008, San Juan, P.R.

61. On fascism and racism, see Bock, "Racism and Sexism"; Mosse, *Nazi Culture*, esp. chap. 3; and Durham, *Women and Fascism*, esp. chap. 5. Acão Integralista Brasileira, the fascist Brazilian organization, included people of African, indigenous, and mestizo descent among its members. Deutsch, *Derechas*, 280–81.

62. He received his law degree from Harvard in 1922. For information on Albizu's time at Harvard, see Rosado, *Pedro Albizu Campos*, 36–57; Stevens-Arroyo, "Catholic Worldview"; and De Jesús, "I Have Endeavored."

63. "International Night Observed," *Harvard Crimson*, March 31, 1916. John Reed, the author of *Ten Days That Shook the World*, founded the club in 1908 and served as its president. Laura E. Hatt, "You Say You Want a Revolution," *Harvard Crimson*, March 31, 2016, www.thecrimson.com/article/2016/3/31/john-reed-scrut/.

64. "Alumnus Held in Plot on President," *Harvard Crimson*, November 30, 1950.

65. Go, "Anti-imperialism," 86; De Jesús, "I Have Endeavored," 481.

66. Anthony M. Stevens-Arroyo argues that the Catalan priest Jaime Balmes introduced Albizu to the hypocrisy of British Protestant claims that they had "brought . . . democracy while they gave Ireland its freedom." Instead, Balmes "emphasized that Catholic civilization respected local culture" and "preserved the diversity of even small nations," arguments that became part of Albizu's discourse. Stevens-Arroyo, "Catholic Worldview," 62, 63.

67. Luis A. Ferrao agrees that Albizu's contact with Irish Republicans had a deep impact on him but questions the religious comparison between Puerto Rico and Ireland. He notes that Catholicism has been integral to the Irish national identity for over 1,500 years, whereas Catholicism had existed in Puerto Rico for only 400 years and was always linked to the Spanish state. Ferrao, *Pedro Albizu*, 266–69. While this is true, it's important to note the Nationalists understood and used the connection between religion and colonialism to explain and further their pro-independence agenda, as I discuss below. For a discussion of the parallels between the Irish and Puerto Rican struggles, see Silén, *Nosotros solos*. Colonel Riggs informed the FBI that Albizu used tactics that Éamon de Valera had employed during the Easter Rising in 1916. Ferrao, *Pedro Albizu*, 184.

68. Metscher, *James Connolly*; Nevin, *James Connolly*.

69. The notion of physical sacrifice runs through twentieth-century Irish Republican thinking and practice, from the prisoners tortured following the Easter Rising to the ten hunger strikers who died in 1981. On martyrdom and the Irish struggle, see Aretxaga, *Shattering Silence*, 45–49; and Sweeney, "Irish Hunger Strikes."

70. "Los actos nacionalistas de Vieques y Naguabo," *El Mundo*, November 15, 1930.

71. Ayoroa Santalíz, "Insurrección nacionalista," 26. For a discussion of Joan of Arc's gender transgressions, see Feinberg, *Transgender Warriors*, 31–35.

72. Feinberg, *Transgender Warriors*, 31–35. For a fuller discussion of these ideas, see Power, "Women, Gender."

73. Corretjer, "Albizu Campos." According to Juan Antonio Corretjer, Albizu denounced the "monstrous oil monopolies" and the high price of gasoline on the radio. Instead of building roads, relying on cars, and buying gasoline, Albizu favored the use of hydroelectric power and the construction of a good railroad system in Puerto Rico. Corretjer claims that Albizu's speech "ignited the massive protest in Puerto Rico" that halted private and public transportation as drivers joined the protest. Corretjer, "Albizu Campos," 134–35.

74. Although the parties represented different classes, they both advocated statehood for Puerto Rico and denounced independence.

75. Dietz, *Economic History*, 166.

76. "Obreros de Guayama se dirigen, al líder nationalista Albizu Campos," *El Mundo*, January 13, 1934.

77. "Obreros de Guayama se dirigen." Previous FLT rallies had attracted 500 workers at most. The authors of ¡Huelga en la caña! attribute the sizable growth in attendance at the Guayama protest to Albizu's presence. Taller de Formación Política, ¡Huelga en la caña!, 123.

78. Taller de Formación Política, ¡Huelga en la caña!, 14. Workers throughout the island sent similar letters to Albizu asking for his guidance.

79. Taller de Formación Política, ¡Huelga en la caña!, 167.

80. "El presidente del nacionalismo recorre los centros huelgarios," *El Mundo*, February 5, 1934.

81. Ayala and Bernabe, *Puerto Rico in the American Century*, 96–97.

82. Dietz, *Economic History*, 167.

83. José Lameiro, "Lo que dice de la huelga," *El Mundo*, January 24, 1934.

84. Taller de Formación Política, *No estamos pidiendo*, 22.

85. Taller de Formación Política, ¡Huelga en la caña!, 184.

86. Taller de Formación Política, ¡Huelga en la caña!, 180.

87. Both the PCP and the PNPR favored the CIO and NMU's more militant politics and tactics. Taller de Formación Política, ¡Huelga en la caña!, 180. The PNPR and CPUSA spoke together at events in New York City to generate support for the strike, as I discuss in chapter 7. For different forces and politics at play, see Taller de Formación Política, *No estamos pidiendo*.

88. Ayala and Bernabe, *Puerto Rico in the American Century*, 95, 145–46.

89. The Comintern's first attempt to set up a communist party in Puerto Rico in the early 1920s failed. Pujals, "Presencia de Internacional Comunista"; Díaz, "Partido Comunista," chap. 3.

90. Andreu Iglesias, *Independencia y socialismo*, 43.

91. Díaz, "Partido Comunista," chaps. 4, 5.

92. Díaz, "Partido Comunista," chaps. 4, 5. Andreu Iglesias joined the PCP in 1936 and rose to prominence in its Trade Union Secretariat. In 1939 he studied in the CPUSA's National School in New York City. After his return to Puerto Rico, he was elected to the executive committee of the Confederación General de Trabajadores (CGT). Fromm, *Cesar Andreu Iglesias*, 145–46.

93. Dimitrov, "Fascist Offensive."

94. "Un mensaje comunista," *El Mundo*, November 7, 1935.

95. "Correspondencia de hombres," *La Palabra*, November 18, 1935.

96. Díaz, "Partido Comunista," chap. 4: 8, 20.

97. Díaz, "Partido Comunista," chap. 5: 11–12.

98. "El Partido Comunista Puertorriqueño pide la independencia de la isla," *Pueblos Hispanos*, April 3, 1943.

99. Dietz, *Economic History*, 225; Ayala and Bernabe, *Puerto Rico in the American Century*, 154.

100. Pujals, "Soviet Caribbean," 263; Ayala and Bernabe, *Puerto Rico in the American Century*, 154–56.

101. See Bosque-Pérez and Colón Morera, *Puerto Rico under Colonial Rule*; and Paralitici, *Sentencia impuesta*. Repression extended beyond the Nationalists. U.S. rulers considered flying the Puerto Rican flag subversive and illegal. Paralitici, *Sentencia impuesta*, 72.

102. Gruening's liberal, anti-imperialist credentials crumbled when faced with the Nationalists' demand for independence. As James Dietz writes, "Gruening quickly shed his liberal image when colonial authority was challenged by the Puerto Rican Nationalist party." Dietz, *Economic History*, 148.

103. Johnson, "Anti-imperialism."

104. Gruening, *Many Battles*, 262.

105. Fernós López-Cepero, *Correspondencia secreta*, 43–45. I thank Dr. Fernós for generously giving me a copy of his book. Fernós claims that Ruby Black served as adviser and confidante on U.S.-Puerto Rican relations for Luis Muñoz Marín.

106. Fernós López-Cepero, *Correspondencia secreta*, 84; Zepeda Cortés, *Cambios y adaptaciones*, 183. On Muñoz Marín and the Liberal Party, see Ayala and Bernabe, *Puerto Rico in the American Century*, 100.

107. Antonio Fernós López-Cepero states that Black urged Muñoz Marín to make this change. See Fernós López-Cepero, *Correspondencia secreta*, 49–51, 160–63. This political evolution explains why the pro-independence Liberal Party expelled him in 1937 and he organized the Popular Democratic Party in 1938. See Zepeda Cortés, *Cambios y adaptaciones*, 183–94; and Ayala and Bernabe, *Puerto Rico in the American Century*, 97–101.

108. Dietz, *Economic History*, 149; Johnson, "Anti-imperialism," 90–92, 96; Lewis, *Puerto Rico*, 69–70; Ayala and Bernabe, *Puerto Rico in the American Century*, 102–3.

109. Ayala and Bernabe, *Puerto Rico in the American Century*, 103–4; Carr, *Puerto Rico*, 59–61.

110. Lewis, *Puerto Rico*, 73.

111. Estades-Font, "Critical Year." Following the assassination of Riggs, U.S. military intelligence sent weekly reports on Puerto Rico to the War Department. Estades-Font, "Critical Year," 51.

112. Paralitici, *Sentencia impuesta*, 75.

113. For a description and chart of these cases, see Paralitici, *Sentencia impuesta*, 61–78, 413–16. Corretjer traveled to Cuba to reaffirm the island's solidarity with Puerto Rican independence. "Regresa mañana a Puerto Rico," *El Mundo*, July 6, 1935.

114. Cecil Snyder to J. Edgar Hoover, January 15, 1936, 1–3, in FBI, "Subject: Pedro Albizu Campos"; Aponte Vázquez, *Albizu*, 10–13; Bosque-Pérez, "Political Persecution," 20–21.

115. Bosque-Pérez, *FBI and Puerto Rico*, 6; Bosque-Pérez, "Political Persecution," 21.

116. For sources on repression, see Paralitici, *Sentencia impuesta*; Bosque-Pérez and Colón Morera, *Puerto Rico under Colonial Rule*; and Nieves Falcón, *Siglo de represión*.

117. Governor Blanton Winship gained notoriety for his role in the Ponce massacre of 1937.

118. Ferrao, *Pedro Albizu Campos*, 153.

119. "Cinco muertos y varios heridos en los sucesos de ayer," *El Mundo*, October 25, 1935, 1; "Cuatro muertos y varios heridos en un espectacular tiroteo ocurrido ayer en Río Piedras," *La Democracia*, October 25, 1935, 1. For background on the shooting, see Rosado, *Pedro Albizu Campos*, 204–11.

120. "Honor a los mártires," *La Palabra*, November 4, 1935. *La Palabra* was the Nationalist Party's newspaper. Not all Nationalists supported the use of violence. See Rodríguez Cancel, "Conflictos ideológicos," 14–15.

121. They chose the date to commemorate the murder of Nicaraguan anti-imperialist August César Sandino two years earlier. Rosado, *El nacionalismo*, 65–73.

122. "Coronel de la Policía muerto a balazos," *El Mundo*, February 24, 1936 1; Ayala and Bernabe, *Puerto Rico in the American Century*, 110. The PCP denounced the "bloody action" and called for the formation of an "anti-imperialist united front of Communists, Nationalists, Liberals, and *independentistas.*" "Hasta los policías decentes y enteros se sienten avergonzados de las últimas matanzas," *El Imparcial*, February 2, 1936.

123. Ayala and Bernabe, *Puerto Rico in the American Century*, 110.

124. This was the first time the U.S. government charged pro-independence Puerto Ricans with seditious conspiracy but not the last. It applied the same charge against Nationalists arrested in the 1950s and against members of the Armed Forces of National Liberation (FALN) in the 1980s.

125. "Memo from E. A. Tamm to J. Edgar Hoover," April 8, 1936, in FBI, *Nationalist Party of Puerto Rico (NPPR)*, 23:94.

126. FBI, *Nationalist Party of Puerto Rico*, 23:100.

127. "Telegram from San Juan to FBI, Washington, D.C.," n.d., in FBI, *Nationalist Party of Puerto Rico*, 23:105.

128. Rosado, *Pedro Albizu Campos*, 233–37.

129. On Kent's life, see "The Man Who Was Rockwell Kent," *Daily World*, May 11, 1977, 8; "Rockwell Kent, Artist, Is Dead; Championed Left-Wing Causes," *New York Times*, March 14, 1971, 1.

130. Rockwell's testimony is cited in Latin American Task Force, *Vito Marcantonio*, 19. Elmer Ellsworth, a North American living in Puerto Rico, served on the second jury, which he later criticized. He wrote President Roosevelt in support of a petition for clemency for the Nationalist prisoners because "my associates on the jury all seemed to be motivated by strong if not violent prejudice against the Nationalists and were prepared to convict them regardless of the evidence. . . . It was evident . . . that the Nationalists did not and could not get a free trial." Rosario Natal, *Albizu Campos*, 65. Ellsworth later served as special assistant to Jesus Piñero, the first Puerto Rican governor of Puerto Rico (1946–48). Collado-Schwarz, *Truman y Puerto Rico*, 390.

131. Juarbe Juarbe, "Autobiografía," 1. I thank Antonio Sotomayor for sending me a copy.

132. Paralitici, *Sentencia impuesta*, 67. Ortiz Pacheco returned to Puerto Rico after three years and denounced the Nationalist Party. Charges against him were dropped. Dávila Marichal, "¡Atención!," 131n39; "Puerto Rican Fugitive Finds U.S Rule Is Best," *New York Times*, January 4, 1939.

133. Meyer, *Vito Marcantonio*, 154.

134. "10,000 Parade Here for Puerto Ricans," *New York Times*, August 30, 1936. Tom Mooney was a left-wing labor leader who was imprisoned from 1916 to 1939 on what many considered "a famed-up bombing charge." The CPUSA campaigned vigorously for his release. See Healey and Isserman, *California Red*, 77.

### Chapter Six

1. Leo R. Sack to Secretary of State, "Puerto Rican Independence Movement," Folder 9-8-68, Box 864, Central Files Puerto Rico, RG 126 Office of Territories, NARA. I thank Alvita Akiboh for this citation information.

2. Sack to Secretary of State.

3. See Friedman, *Nazis and Good Neighbors*; Gilderhus, *Second Century*; Gilderhus, LaFevor, and LaRosa, *Third Century*; and Schoultz, *Their Own Best Interest*, chap. 5.

4. Friedman, *Nazis and Good Neighbors*, 77. One notable exception is Johnson, "Anti-imperialism," which argues that "initially, [President] Roosevelt, [sic] treated Puerto

Rico separately from his overall Latin America agenda" (93). However, after the Montevideo Conference affirmed its position on nonintervention, Roosevelt "began incorporating Puerto Rico into his revised inter-American agenda." He appointed Ernest Gruening, an avowed anti-imperialist, to head the Division of Territories and Island Possessions, under whose jurisdiction Puerto Rico fell. See Friedman, *Nazis and Good Neighbors*, 93, 89, 94. See chapter 3 in this volume for U.S. government policies in Puerto Rico during the 1930s.

5. Franklin D. Roosevelt's First Inaugural Address, March 4, 1933, 6, First Carbon Files, Speeches of President Franklin D. Roosevelt, 1933–1945, Franklin Delano Roosevelt, Papers as President, President's Personal File, 1933–1945, NARA.

6. For a concise discussion of the Good Neighbor Policy, see Friedman, "Good Neighbor Policy."

7. Hart, *Empire of Ideas*, 20.

8. Smith, *Talons of the Eagle*, 92–93.

9. "Convention on Rights and Duties of States (Inter-American), December 26, 1933," 4, The Avalon Project, http://avalon.law.yale.edu/20th_century/intam03.asp. Thomas Field and Kevin Young informed me that Bolivia probably opposed the resolution because President Daniel Salamanca had provoked a war with Paraguay and feared that the resolution would be invoked against him.

10. "Anti-War Treaty of Non-Aggression and Conciliation (Saavedra Lamas Treaty); October 10, 1933," The Avalon Project, http://avalon.law.yale.edu/20th_century/intam01.asp.

11. "Roosevelt Yields to Argentine Plea," *New York Times*, November 25, 1936.

12. "Roosevelt Yields to Argentine Plea." See coverage of Roosevelt's visit in *La Vanguardia*, especially "Fue grandioso el recibimiento a Roosevelt" and "Flores, muchas flores," December 1, 1936, 2. Jorge Nállim explains Roosevelt's popularity by pointing out that his New Deal policy served as "a [respected] reference point" for politicians and parties across the political spectrum in Argentina, although they emphasized and promoted different aspects of it. Nallím, *Transformations and Crisis*, 103.

13. Liberio was "rumored to be a Communist." "President Justo's Son Seized as the Heckler of Roosevelt," *New York Times*, December 2, 1936.

14. "La Federación Universitaria Argentina solicita," *El Mundo*, May 20, 1936, 4.

15. "La Federación Universitaria Argentina solicita."

16. "Petition from the Congress of Buenos Aires, Argentina Republic, to Hon. Franklin D. Roosevelt," September 22, 1936, folder 7, box 27, RRP.

17. Signatories hailed from Argentina, Australia, Belgium, Bolivia, Brazil, Catalonia, Chile, Colombia, Egypt, France, India, Italy, Palestine, Santo Domingo (Dominican Republic), Spain, Switzerland, Uruguay. "Letter to Hon. President of the United States of America," September 15, 1936, folder 7, box 27, RRP.

18. "Letter from the Society of Journalists and Writers of Argentina to Hon. Franklin D. Roosevelt," October 5, 1936, folder 7, box 27, RRP.

19. Merino, *Feminism for the Americas*, 134–35. I thank Sandra Deutsch for telling me about the conference.

20. "Inauguróse ayer la Conferencia Popular por la paz," *La Vanguardia*, November 23, 1936, 2.

21. Ortiz-Carrión and Torres-Rivera, *Voluntarios de la libertad*, 65.

22. Juarbe Juarbe, "Autobiografía," 1.

23. Ayoroa Santaliz, "¿Quién es Juarbe?," 2, 8. Juarbe Juarbe, "Autobiografía," 1. In 1985, Juarbe was inducted into the Puerto Rican Sports Hall of Fame. Sotomayor, *Sovereign Colony*, 84.

24. Ayoroa Santaliz, "¿Quién es Juarbe Juarbe?," 2.

25. "Puerto Ricans Appeal for Peace Parley Aid," *New York Times*, December 2, 1936. To counter Nationalist efforts, Roosevelt appoint Emilio del Toro, a Puerto Rican member of

the insular Supreme Court and a firm supporter of U.S. rule, as legal counselor to the U.S. delegation. Juarbe Juarbe, "Autobiografía," 1.

26. "Seek Place in Conference," *New York Times*, November 18, 1936; "Information Regarding the Questioning of Don Juan Juarbe y Juarbe," 3, file 7, box 27, RRP.

27. "Algunos Miembros de la Comisión Organizadora del COSO," FECH, June 1937, 4.

28. "Juan Juarbe y Juarbe habla para la FECH," FECH, July 1937, 1; "Roosevelt en Puerto Rico," FECH, September 1937, 13.

29. "Carta de la FECH al presidente de los EE.UU," FECH, September 1937, 13.

30. Juarbe Juarbe, "Autobiografía," 1.

31. "U.S. 'Imperialism' Target at Parley; The Press Conference in Chile Demands Puerto Rico's Immediate Freedom," *New York Times*, January 10, 1937.

32. For a history of the society, see Nállim, "Culture, Politics and the Cold War." Members of the Sociedad de Escritores de Chile included prominent Chilean writers and intellectuals who had "connections with the University of Chile and other academic and cultural institution in Chile." In addition, "its public declarations and voice were widely circulated in the press and radio," thus increasing the number of Chileans who were familiar with the situation in Puerto Rico and the incarceration of the Nationalists. Jorge Nállim, personal communication, October 15, 2019.

33. "President Roosevelt to the President of Argentina (Justo)," in Axton et al., *Foreign Relations of the United States Diplomatic Papers, 1936*, 3–5.

34. "Primer Congreso de Escritores," SECH, *Boletín de la Sociedad de Escritores de Chile*, May 1936, 53–54. I thank Jorge Nállim for sending me a copy of this publication.

35. As cited in Juarbe Juarbe, "Puerto Rico lucha," 41.

36. José Artigas, José de San Martín, and Bernardo O'Higgins led the armies that liberated what became Uruguay, Argentina, and Chile, respectively.

37. "Pedro Albizu Campos Released from Atlanta, 1943," 13, in FBI Documents, reel 19, "Pedro Albizu Campos and Nationalist Party."

38. "Falleció Doña Laura Meneses," *Granma*, April 16, 1973; "Falleció el luchador Puertorriqueño Juan Juarbe," *Granma*, December 22, 1992. There has been much speculation as to whether they were a couple. What is known is that she remained married to Albizu Campos and Juarbe never married. Her children lived with Meneses and Juarbe in Peru, Mexico, and Cuba.

39. Comité Cubano Pro Libertad de Patriotas Puertorriqueños, "Comité Cubano Pro Libertad de Patriotas Puertorriqueños," in *Por la independencia*, 11–14.

40. Comité Cubano Pro Libertad de Patriotas Puertorriqueños, "Manifesto a las naciones americanas," in *Por la independencia*, 17. U.S. repression and imprisonment against the Nationalist Party extended beyond the leadership. Ché Paralitici points out that from 1935 to 1939, forty-five Nationalists were convicted on various charges and imprisoned, mainly in Puerto Rico. Paralitici, *Sentencia impuesta*, 66–78.

41. Comité Cubano Pro Libertad de Patriotas Puertorriqueños, "Manifesto a las naciones americanas," in *Por la independencia*, 19–20.

42. Torres, *Hablan sobre Albizu Campos*, i.

43. I thank Ashley Black for helping me with this formulation.

44. Riddell, Prasad, and Mollah, "Theses on the National and Colonial Questions," in *Liberate the Colonies!*, 94–99.

45. Secretaria de Concejo, May 26, 1936, enclosure no. 1 to dispatch no. 801 of May 29, 1936, from the Legation at Bogotá, 811C.01/39, Decimal file 1930–39, RG 59, Department of State Central Files, NARA.

46. "Communication from Cartagena City Council concerning Puerto Rico," May 29, 1936, 811C.01/39, Decimal file 1930–39, RG 59, Department of State Central Files, NARA. The

chargé d'affaires's description of the council members echoes that of a U.S. official in Cuba who characterized a group of boys and young men "chanting 'Down with Yankee imperialism!" as being "coloured and of the peon type." Sullivan, "'For the Liberty,'" 3. According to Francisco Flórez Bolívar, a Colombian historian who is an expert on Blacks and Mulattos in Colombian political and intellectual life, several members of the Municipal Council of Cartagena were important figures in the labor movement, the Partido Socialista Revolucionario (Revolutionary Socialist Party), and the Communist Party, which explains their willingness to condemn the imprisonment of the Nationalist Party leaders. Flórez Bolívar, email communication, November 19, 2019. I thank Lina Britto for putting me in touch with Flórez Bolívar.

47. For a discussion of how Jim Crow influenced U.S. corporate and political officials in Guatemala in these years, see Colby, "Banana Growing," esp. 604–5, 605n18, 611–12. One example of a top U.S. official's perspectives on Blacks in Latin America is Secretary of State Henry Stimson, who labeled Haitians "niggers" in his diary and advocated "giving back at them as hard as they gave [U.S. representatives]." McPherson, Invaded, 257.

48. For background on him, see Casey, "Anti-Occupation Collaborations."

49. "El Dr. Moraviah Morpeau toma la palabra en defense del nacionalismo," La Palabra, April 6, 1936, 1. Morpeau was a lifelong supporter of Puerto Rican independence.

50. "Activities of Representative," Port-au-Prince, Haiti, August 1, 1936, 811C.01/43, Decimal file 1930–39, RG 59, Department of State Central Files, NARA.

51. García-Bryce, Haya de la Torre, chap. 1. Iñigo García-Bryce describes Haya de la Torre's exile, the people and influences he was in touch with, and the ideological and political goals of APRA during the 1920s and 1930s in this chapter.

52. APRA started in Mexico in either 1926 or 1928. See García-Bryce, Haya de la Torre, 36, on APRA's early years in Mexico.

53. "Los Apristas estamos con Puerto Rico libre," Trinchera Aprista, June 1938, 13. I thank Martín Bergal for sending me copies of the newspaper. Because most active Apristas were in exile in the 1930s, the paper was published in Mexico.

54. "Los Apristas estamos con Puerto Rico libre," 15.

55. Repertorio Americano was a weekly newspaper that wrote about "Hispanic Culture" and anti-imperialism. It included news, analysis, and commentary on Latin America by Latin Americans and was published between 1919 and 1958. "Repertorio Americano," Universidad Nacional, Costa Rica, www.repositorio.una.ac.cr/handle/11056/2923.

56. García Carrillo, Cartas selectas, 7–8, 119.

57. García Carrillo, Cartas selectas, 41–42.

58. The goal of the Comintern, which formed in 1919 under the direction of Vladimir Lenin, was to "establish and coordinate the activities of the communist parties around the world." Pujals, "'Brigada Móvil,'" 216.

59. Georgi Dimitrov led the Comintern from 1934 to 1943. He called for the formation of a "broad people's anti-fascist front on the basis of the proletarian united front" at the Seventh Comintern Congress. See Dimitrov, Report of the Seventh World Congress, 31; and Degras, Communist International, 346–49.

60. "Anti-Fascist Front Set Up in Americas," New York Times, March 23, 1939; Jack O'Donohue, "Uruguay Confab Helps Strengthen Democracy throughout the Americas," CIO News, April 17, 1939, 8.

61. Spain (1936–39) and France (1936–38) were the only other countries with Popular Front governments. On the Popular Front government in Chile, see Drake, Socialism and Populism in Chile, chaps. 7, 8.

62. "Position of Vanguardista (ex-Nacista) Party and its leader, González von Marées," December 20, 1939, 811C.01/96, 811C.01/97, Decimal file 1930–39, RG 59, Department of State Central Files, NARA.

63. "Hombres Honrados del Continente!," *Trabajo*, reprinted as "La Fraternidad Iberoamericana en acción," in *La Palabra*, June 6, 1936. For information on *Trabajo* and the Vanguardia Popular, see Molina Jiménez, "Comunistas y la publicidad." I thank Eugenia Rodríguez for sharing this and related articles with me.

64. *Claridad* was published from 1930 to 1941 by Editorial Claridad, which brought together Socialists and Communists, left-wing writers, and "the intelligentsia in aid of the Spanish Republic and against fascism." Bethell and Roxborough, *Latin America*, 103.

65. Ferreira de Cassone, *Claridad y el internacionalismo americano*, 19; "Unidad y Libertad de América," *Claridad*, June 1939, 2–3. I thank Sandy Deutsch for telling me about this issue of *Claridad*.

66. Palacios, *Nuestra América*, 275–76. The book also contains Roosevelt's response to Palacios in May 1942 and Palacios's response to Roosevelt.

67. Senate Subcommittee of the Committee on Territories and Insular Affairs, "Bill to Amend the Organic Act of Puerto Rico," 7, emphasis added.

68. Senate Bill 1407 sought to amend the Organic Act of Puerto Rico of 1917. Roosevelt set up committee that prepared the bill, named Harold Ickes, secretary of the Interior, to head it, and appointed Luis Muñoz Marín, the future first elected governor of Puerto Rico, as one of four Puerto Ricans on it. Senate, "Bill to Amend the Organic Act of Puerto Rico," 1, 310.

69. Senate, "Bill to Amend the Organic Act of Puerto Rico," 7.

70. Piñero Cádiz, "Base Aeronaval," 296.

71. Rodríguez Beruff and Bolívar Fresneda, *Puerto Rico*, 13.

72. García Muñiz, "U.S. Military Installations," 55.

73. McCaffrey, "Social Struggle," 87. Vieques acquired even greater importance as a site for U.S. military training during the Cold War.

74. Conn, Engelman, and Fairchild, *Guarding the United States*, 3.

75. Collado-Schwarz, *Truman y Puerto Rico*, 302–3.

76. I thank Alyssa Bralower, from Digitization Services at the University Library, University of Illinois Urbana-Champaign, for her help in locating and sending me a copy of this map, and Jenny Marie Johnson, Map and Geography Librarian, at the University Library, University of Illinois Urbana-Champaign for explaining to me that since the map is a federal government publication, it is in the public domain.

77. Paralitici, *Sentencia impuesta*, 81.

78. Paralitici, *Represión*, 74.

79. Medina Ramírez, *Movimiento libertador*, 1:209.

80. Paralitici, *Sentencia impuesta*, 80.

81. Medina Ramírez, *Movimiento libertador*, 1:209–10; Paralitici, *Sentencia impuesta*, 85, 418.

82. Medina Ramírez, *Movimiento libertador*, 1:210; Paralitici, *Sentencia impuesta*, 420–21.

## Chapter Seven

1. Corretjer had been released from the Atlanta Federal Penitentiary in June 1942. "General Intelligence Survey," May 1943, Decimal file 1930–39, RG 59, NARA.

2. Samuel Neuberger interviewed by Mary Licht, December 16, 1982, cassette 3, box 1, Communist Party of the United States of America Oral History Collection, OH.065, Tamiment Library and Robert F. Wagner Labor Archives, New York University.

3. Memo, May 11, 1954, 2, in FBI, "Subject: Pedro Albizu Campos."

4. The CPUSA paid Albizu's bills while he was confined in the hospital. For copies of those bills, see "Albizu Campos, Pedro, 1936–1944," box 2, Earl Browder Papers, Special Collections Research Center, Syracuse University Libraries.

5. According to Van Gosse, by the end of the 1930s, the CPUSA "had a small but well organized mass base, with a membership of 100,000 and an active periphery five or perhaps

ten times greater. New York was the heart of Communist strength." Gosse, *Where the Boys Are*, 20.

6. Falcón, "Migration and Development," 153.

7. Grosfoguel, "Puerto Ricans in the USA," 236.

8. Acosta-Belén, *Puerto Ricans in the United States*, 13.

9. "La asociación nacionalista portorriqueña discutirá el Proyecto de Estado Libre," *La Prensa*, February 2, 1922, 1. I thank Lorrin Thomas for sharing copies of *La Prensa* with me.

10. "La asociación nacionalista portorriqueña celebró ayer su asamblea extraordinaria," *La Prensa*, February 6, 1922, 1.

11. Mary Testa, "The Puerto Rican Nationalist Movement in New York City," January 4, 1939, *Spanish Book*, reel 269, folder 9, WPA Federal Writers' Project, New York City Municipal Archive. I thank Lorrin Thomas for sharing copies of the *Spanish Book* with me.

12. Testa, "Puerto Rican Nationalist Movement," 1.

13. Mary Testa, "Sociedades amigas que cooperan con la causa," January 4, 1939, *Spanish Book*, WPA Federal Writers' Project, New York City Municipal Archive. For example, it worked with the Hijos de Juauco (Puerto Rico), the Vanguardia Puertorriqueña, the Mutualista Obrera Mexicana, the Club de Muchachos Mexicanos, the Frente Popular Español de Queens, and the Club Obrero Español.

14. Collazo has very fond memories of these years because she loved growing up in a Nationalist community and because, "my parents did everything to make us [Lydia and her sister Iris] happy." Collazo Cortés, *Entre dos paréntesis*, 57.

15. All preceding quotations in this paragraph are from Collazo, *Entre dos paréntesis*, 53–56.

16. Andreu Iglesias, *Memoirs of Bernardo Vega*, 171.

17. Eley, *Forging Democracy*, 228.

18. Meyer, "Pedro Albizu Campos," 97; Schaffer, *Vito Marcantonio*, 57. For an excellent biography of Marcantonio, see Meyer, *Vito Marcantonio*. For a collection of his speeches and writings, see Rubenstein, *I Vote My Conscience*.

19. Marcantonio's papers, which are housed at the New York Public Library, contain numerous examples of Puerto Ricans asking him to intercede on their behalf on a number of issues and his responses to the petitioners. For examples of his efforts to improve the lives of his Puerto Rican constituents, see Andreu Iglesias, *Memoirs of Bernardo Vega*, 184–85.

20. Meyer, *Vito Marcantonio*; Rubenstein, *I Vote My Conscience*.

21. The ILD's monetary support of the Nationalist prisoners alerted the FBI to the budding relationship between the PNPR and the CPUSA. In one of the agency's first memos on the issue, an FBI agent informed J. Edgar Hoover in 1939, the "International Labor Defense in New York sent an air mail to the [Atlanta] prison enclosing $5.00 to each one of the seven Nationalists saying to use this money for cigarettes and to keep their spirits up." Memo from Special Agent to J. Edgar Hoover, December 5, 1939, in FBI, *Nationalist Party of Puerto Rico* (NPPR), 23:185–86. Vito Marcantonio to Corretjer, July 21, 1939, Correspondence of Juan Antonio Corretjer, box 46, Vito Marcantonio Papers, New York Public Library.

22. Rubenstein, *I Vote My Conscience*.

23. Testa, "Puerto Rican Nationalist Movement," 2, emphasis added.

24. Andreu Iglesias, *Memoirs of Bernardo Vega*, 173.

25. Andreu Iglesias, *Memoirs of Bernardo Vega*, 179–80. When dockworkers struck in 1938, members of the CPUSA and Nationalists again joined to form a solidarity committee with the strikers. Ayala and Bernabe, *Puerto Rico in the American Century*, 141.

26. "El desfile pro independencia de Puerto Rico," *El Mundo*, September 23, 1935. The article is reprinted from the New York City newspaper *La Prensa*. Bernardo Vega wrote that the "massive turnout" also included the Centro Obrero Español and the Seventh-Day Adventist church, among others. Andreu Iglesias, *Memoirs of Bernardo Vega*, 180. The Hijas de la Libertad

formed in Puerto Rico in the early 1930s and evolved into the Enfermeras de la República, discussed in chapter 5.

27. Andreu Iglesias, *Memoirs of Bernardo Vega*, 186–87.

28. "Marcantonio Sees Albizu," *New York Times*, August 3, 1936.

29. "10,000 Parade Here for Puerto Ricans," *New York Times*, August 30, 1936. Tom Mooney was a left labor leader who was imprisoned from 1916 to 1939 on what many considered "a framed-up bombing charge." The CPUSA campaigned vigorously for his release. See Healey and Isserman, *California Red*, 77. The Scottsboro Boys were nine Black teenagers falsely accused of raping a white woman in Alabama in 1921. Harris, "Running with the Reds."

30. Andreu Iglesias, *Memoirs of Bernardo Vega*, 192–93.

31. "Massacre of Unarmed Arouses All Puerto Rico," *Daily Worker*, March 26, 1937.

32. "Puerto Rican Defense Group Calls Protest," *Daily Worker*, April 6, 1937.

33. Other Nationalist leaders in New York included Ramón Medina Ramírez, Julio Pinto Gandía, and Oscar Collazo, who was president of the Nationalist junta in Manhattan. Rosado, *Pedro Albizu Campos*, 283.

34. I have no doubt that the assault was upsetting to a large number of Puerto Ricans, an assertion that many currently living in the United States or in other places where mass violence is more and more common will readily understand. However, I have not been able to find testimonies that reveal how other Puerto Ricans felt.

35. Randall, *Pueblo*, 61–71. We know De la Cruz's story because Margaret Randall interviewed her when both were living in Cuba in the 1970s.

36. Dávila Marichal, "¡Atención, firmes, de frente, marchen!," 148.

37. "El alcalde de Lares no concede permiso para los actos nacionalistas a celebrarse mañana por la tarde allá," *Imparcial*, September 22, 1937.

38. Medina Ramírez, *Movimiento libertador*, 1:178.

39. Paralitici, *Sentencia impuesta*, 8.

40. Dávila Marichal, "¡Atención, firmes, de frente, marchen!," 147.

41. The Nationalist Party did not keep formal membership files, so I have been unable to determine how many people belonged to the party at any one time. FBI documents offer concrete numbers, although they are not likely to be exact. They do, however, provide a general sense of the downward trend in membership. According to FBI records, "3000 people belonged to the party in 1936," but only "approximately 500" did in 1950. These numbers undoubtably underestimate membership, do not include supporters, and thus fail to convey an accurate measure of support for the Nationalist Party. FBI, *Nationalist Party of Puerto Rico* (NPPR), 23:6, 42–44, 120.

42. For a discussion of their friendship, see Power, "Friends and Comrades."

43. Rodríguez-Fraticelli, "Pedro Albizu Campos," 29.

44. Sumner Welles to Franklin Roosevelt, May 22, 1943, Folder: Roosevelt, Franklin D., April–August 1943, Box 152, Sumner Welles Papers, Franklin D. Roosevelt Presidential Library and Museum. Welles adds, "I could, of course, only gain the impression that these three Nationalists [Albizu, Corretjer, and Silva, the treasurer] are of importance to him from the standpoint of the interests of the Communist Party." I thank Aaron Coy Moulton for generously sharing this document with me.

45. Rosado, *Pedro Albizu Campos*, 282.

46. Manorama Modak, "The Role of Foreign Missions in India," *Blitz* (Bombay), July 24, 1954. Manorama Modak was the son of Ramkrishna Modak, a pro-independence Indian who worked closely with the Nationalist Party. Lydia Collazo, interview with author, May 25, 2008, Levittown, P.R.

47. Ralph Templin, "Message to the Working Committee," folder 1, box 35, RRP.

48. "Our New York Ashram," folder "Templin, Ralph: Biographical items," RTC. Templin and Holmes Smith adapted the concept of an Ashram they had experienced during their time in India to their New York reality. They defined an Ashram as "a small community of kindred spirits living together in a deeply sharing and disciplined fellowship, and pursuing common spiritual and social ends." "Our New York Ashram," 1.

49. "The Harlem Ashram," 1, folder "Puerto Rico," RTC.

50. Dekar, *Creating the Beloved Community*.

51. "'Free Gandhi' Pickets Seized at British Embassy Here," *Times Herald* (Washington, D.C.), February 24, 1943.

52. Friedman, *Citizenship in Cold War America*, 124.

53. Reynolds, "People/Mi Gente," 46–47.

54. "Interview with Ruth Reynolds," *The Call*, folder 5, box 1, RPP.

55. "Interview with Ruth Reynolds."

56. "Interview with Ruth Reynolds." See also Rafael Cancel Miranda, "Julio Pinto Gandía," *Claridad*, August 21–28, 2008; and Materson, "Ruth Reynolds," 184.

57. The other nine advisers were John Haynes Holmes, E. Stanley Jones, Ramkrishna Modak, A. J. Muste, William Stuart Nelson, George L. Paine, A. Philip Randolph, Ralph Templin, and G. J. Watumull. Many of them were prominent figures in the pacifist movement who also took public positions in favor of Puerto Rican independence. Ruth Reynolds to Marge, February 25, 1945, folder 1, box 9, RRP.

58. See Stites Mor, *Human Rights and Transnational Solidarity*; and Hatzky and Stites Mor, "Latin American Transnational Solidarities."

59. "Minutes of Meeting on Puerto Rico," October 17, 1944, folder 2, box 18, RRP.

60. "Minutes of Meeting on Puerto Rico."

61. "Data on Non-Governmental Organizations," 1947, folder 4, box 18, RRP.

62. Ruth Reynolds to Dear Friend, November 29, 1944, file 5, box 18, RRP.

63. Thelma Mielke's Permanent Record and Transcript, Elmhurst College, July 23, 1937, and Student Yearbook, 1937, 62, 99, Rudolf G. Schade Archives and Special Collections, A. C. Buehler Library, Elmhurst College. I thank Elaine Fetyko Page, Elmhurst College archivist, for her help in locating these records.

64. Thelma Mielke, interview with author, September 22, 2008, New York. According to Mielke, the philosophy of theologian Reinhold Niebuhr, a 1910 graduate of Elmhurst, influenced her thinking and convinced her to become a socialist.

65. U.S. Senate, "Statement of Ruth M. Reynolds," 226.

66. Ruth Reynolds to Maxwell S. Stuart, December 8, 1944, file 1, box 8, RRP.

67. "Dear Friend," letter from Pearl S. Buck, March 22, 1945, folder 5, box 18, RRP.

68. For a longer list, see U.S. Senate, "Statement of Ruth M. Reynolds," 227. Medina Ramírez, *Movimiento libertador*, 1:216; Gosse, *Where the Boys Are*, 18; "For Immediate Release," July 21, 1945, folder 2, box 18, RRP; Hanson, *Mary McLeod Bethune*.

69. As César Ayala and Rafael Bernabe point out, the bill contained a catch in that it "provided for few transitional measures. For an economy totally oriented to [read dependent on] the U.S. market, independence under such conditions would bring considerable hardship." Ayala and Bernabe, *Puerto Rico in the American Century*, 111.

70. U.S. Senate, "Statement of Ruth M. Reynolds," 229.

71. Ayala and Bernabe, *Puerto Rico in the American Century*, 111–12; Gatell, "Independence Rejected," 34.

72. Rubenstein, *I Vote My Conscience*, 375.

73. Gatell, "Independence Rejected," 36–37.

74. Wertheim, "Instrumental Internationalism," 267.

75. However, the Philippines, India, Lebanon, and Syria, colonies that would soon become independent nations, were invited to the meeting and signed on to the U.N. Charter. Of the original 51 U.N. member states, only five—Poland, Byelorussia, Ukraine, the Soviet Union, and Yugoslavia—were socialist. Gautier Mayoral and del Pilar Arguelles, *Puerto Rico y la ONU*, 19.

76. As Stanley Meisler notes, the United Nations was FDR's brainchild, which is one key reason Eleanor Roosevelt was the lead U.S. representative at the San Francisco meeting where the international organization came into being. Meisler, *United Nations*, 3.

77. Blanshard, *Democracy and Empire*, 334–35.

78. Ana M. López and Gabriela Reardon, "Puerto Rico at the United Nations," NACLA, November 26, 2007, https://nacla.org/article/puerto-rico-united-nations.

79. Medina Ramírez, *Movimiento libertador*, 1:227.

80. Mielke interview.

81. Jay Holmes Smith to the Members of the Congress of the United States, July 24, 1946, 1, folder 6, box 18, RRP.

82. "Puerto Rico Asks UN for Freedom," *Chicago Defender*, August 17, 1946; "The American League for Puerto Rico's Independence vs. the United States of America," 2, folder 2, box 18, RRP. Chapter 11, art. 73, of the U.N. Charter states, "Members of the United Nations which have or assume responsibilities for the administration of territories whose peoples have not yet attained a full measure of self-government" have the responsibility "to develop self-government, to take due account of the political aspirations of the peoples, and to assist them in the progressive development of their free political institutions." "United Nations Charter, Chapter XI: Declaration Regarding Non-Self-Governing Territories," United Nations, www.un.org/en/about-us/un-charter/chapter-11.

83. "The American League for Puerto Rico's Independence vs. the United States of America," 5.

84. "The American League for Puerto Rico's Independence vs. the United States of America," 3–11. They are the "Senate of Argentina, 1936; Pan-American People's Congress, Buenos Aires, 1936; Pan-American Women's Peace Congress, Buenos Aires, 1936; World PEN Congress, Buenos Aires, 1936; Spanish-American Press Congress of Chile, 1937; First Pan-American Caribbean Congress, Havana, 1939; Pan-American Congress of Writers and Artists, . . . Mexico City, 1940; House of Deputies, Chile, 1940; Pan-American Labor Congress of the Confederation of Latin American Workers, Havana, 1941; Second Constitutional Convention of Cuba, 1942; Chamber of Deputies of Cuba, 1942; Confederation of Trade Unions of Latin America, Mexico City, 1943; Legislature of Guatemala, 1945." "The American League for Puerto Rico's Independence vs. the United States of America," 11.

85. Bethell and Roxborough, *Latin America*, 24.

86. Medina Ramírez, *Movimiento libertador*, 1:228–32.

87. Medina Ramírez, *Movimiento libertador*, 1:235–40. Ramón Medina Ramírez argues that "when the resolution came before the General Assembly, the colonial powers formed a compact opposition bloc, led by the United States." Medina Ramírez, *Movimiento libertador*, 1:239.

88. "Albizu Campos regresa a Puerto Rico," *El Mundo*, December 15, 1947, 1.

### Chapter Eight

1. Julio de Santiago, "A los Presidentes, Tesoreros de las Juntas Municipales Nacionalistas," April 28, 1948, file 28, box 15, Documentos Nacionalistas, AGPR.

2. Alejandrina Gotay to Julio de Santiago, May 14, 1948, file 28, box 15, Documentos Nacionalistas, AGPR.

3. Carr, *Puerto Rico*, 62. Barceló blamed Muñoz Marín for the Liberal Party's loss in the 1936 election. Zapata, *De independentista a autonomista*, 71.

4. Ayala and Bernabe, *Puerto Rico in the American Century*, 137.

5. Collado-Schwarz, *Truman y Puerto Rico*, 249.

6. Ayala and Bernabe, *Puerto Rico in the American Century*, 154, 161.

7. According to Eileen Suárez Findlay, an official picture of Muñoz Marín from 1944 conveys the idea that he is simultaneously a "leader, father, teacher, [and] preacher . . . [who] both embodies and leads the people." Suárez Findlay, *Left without a Father*, 46, 47.

8. Suárez Findlay, *Left without a Father*, 9.

9. "Estamos preparados para ganar la libertad: Luis Muñoz Marín," *El Universal*, December 16, 1947.

10. Sandra Pujals notes that the PPD derived the catchphrase from a Puerto Rican Communist Party slogan from the 1930s. Pujals, "'Soviet Caribbean,'" 263.

11. Dietz, *Economic History*, 205. Despite improvements, starvation stalked Puerto Ricans in the early 1940s. Attacks by German submarines on ships carrying goods to Puerto Rico led to a shortage and higher prices of food. Dietz, *Economic History*, 202–4.

12. Carr, *Puerto Rico*, 178. Several prominent Nationalist women—Margot Arce de Vázquez, Nilita Vientós, Mona Marti, Nieves Padilla, Iris Martínez, and Emelí Vélez de Vando—joined the PIP. Rivera de Alvarado, "Contribución de la mujer," 46.

13. Meyer, "Pedro Albizu Campos," 105.

14. Ayala and Bernabe, *Puerto Rico in the American Century*, 201.

15. Albizu issued a "General Amnesty Proclamation," which called on all those who had distanced themselves from the party to "rededicate themselves" and rejoin the struggle for independence in December 1947. Cited in Rosado, *Pedro Albizu Campos*, 311.

16. Paulino E. Castro to Señor Presidente de la Junta Municipal del Partido Nacionalista de Puerto Rico, ca. January–February 1948, file 5, box 14, Documentos Nacionalistas, AGPR. This is the oath that all PNPR members had been required to take since the 1930s.

17. I thank Neici Zeller for help with the translation. Letters from Rufino Rolón Marrero, February 11, 1948, Río Piedras; Noé Marty, March 5, 1948, San Germán; Julio de Santiago, June 6, 1948, Naguabo and Cayey; and Ana de Torres, Indian Head, Indiana, May 13, 1948, all in file 5, box 14, Documentos Nacionalistas, AGPR.

18. These events and proclamations had continued during the PNPR leaders' absence. For example, on March 26, 1946, the party commemorated the Ponce Massacre of 1937 with a proclamation that began with a quote from Dante, "To remember is to live," and continued, "Exactly nine years ago Yankee imperialism committed the most repugnant crime on the streets of Ponce that human eyes had ever seen." Partido Nacionalista de Puerto Rico, San Juan Bautista de Puerto Rico, May 18, 1946, file 2, box 15, Documentos Nacionalistas, AGPR. In April 1947, the Nationalist Party commemorated the birth of Ramón Emeterio Betances, who represented "an example of sacrifice and loyalty to the cause of freedom." The party called on "the Puerto Rican nation to fulfill its duty" and gather in Cabo Rojo, where Betances was born, and "plac[e] flowers on his remains." Julio de Santiago, "Conmemoración del día de Betances en la fecha e su natalicio," April 8, 1947, file 2, box 15, Documentos Nacionalistas, AGPR.

19. Partido Nacionalista de Puerto Rico, "Acta de protesta del nacionalismo puertorriqueño contra esa agresión imperialista yanqui," July 1948, file 2, box 15, Documentos Nacionalistas, AGPR.

20. Partido Nacionalista de Puerto Rico, "Solemne conmemoración del octogésimo aniversario del Grito de Lares," file 2, box 15, Documentos Nacionalistas, AGPR.

21. Stevens-Arroyo, "Catholic Worldview," 68. In 1949, some 19,000 U.S. military personnel representing the marines, navy, and army conducted military maneuvers in Vieques that included the simulated underwater explosion of atomic bombs. Hanson W. Baldwin, "Vieques 'Atom Test' Alters Navy Plans," *New York Times*, March 4, 1949. In addition to denouncing

the navy's usurpation of Viequenses' land, Albizu repeatedly warned that the presence of the U.S. military in Puerto Rico made the archipelago a target for an atomic attack. "Puerto Rico Base Atómica, Los Planes de Estados Unidos," radio show by PAC, July 2, 1950; *Puerto Rico Libre* 8, no. 147, June 30, 1950.

22. "El jefe nacionalista dijo que ha llegado la hora de la decisión," *El Mundo*, December 15, 1947, 1.

23. De Albizu Campos, *Albizu Campos y la independencia*, 119–21.

24. U.S. House of Representatives, "Selective Service Act of 1948."

25. "Memorándum en relación a los casos de violación del servicio military obligatorio," *Boletín Nacionalista*, June–March 1949, "A La Izquierda," reel 1, frame 208, Centro de Estudios Puertorriqueños, New York, emphasis in original.

26. "La criminal conspiración yanqui-fascista para encender la guerra en Asia: 'Korea para el imperialismo,'" *Puerto Rico Libre* 8, no. 147, June 30, 1950.

27. The six were Dario Berrios, Rafael Cancel Miranda, Luis Manuel O'Neill Rosario, Ramón Medina Maisonave, Miguel Angel Ruiz Alicia, and Reinaldo Trilla Martínez. "La criminal conspiración yanqui-fascista"; "Seis nacionalistas cumplirán Pena en Atlanta," *El Mundo*, July 16, 1949; Paralitici, *Sentencia impuesta*, 87–89.

28. Paralitici, *Sentencia impuesta*, 87–88.

29. The FBI kept close tabs on Puerto Rican Nationalists working in exile across Latin America. Because Puerto Rican Nationalists in Cuba worked closely with Cuban revolutionaries, the FBI was particularly interested in monitoring their activities. In the early 1950s, Puerto Rican exiles in Cuba "included Nationalists who had opposed the draft and refused to fight in Korea as well as participants in the 1950 revolt." FBI, "Subject: Pedro Albizu Campos," 11.

30. Cancel Miranda, *Remando bajo la lluvia*, 11.

31. Cancel Miranda, *Remando bajo la lluvia*, 20; Cancel Miranda, *Del cimarrón a los macheteros*, 11.

32. As noted in chapter 5, the FBI began surveillance of the Nationalists in January 1936, when Cecil Snyder, the U.S. federal judge in San Juan who presided in the trial of the Nationalist leaders, wrote to J. Edgar Hoover and asked him to keep an eye on the party. Aponte Vázquez, *Albizu*, 10–13.

33. Félix Benítez Rexach, an engineer, owned the luxury hotel, supported the Nationalist Party, and invited them to stay there. Rosado, *Pedro Albizu Campos*, 313.

34. De Albizu Campos, *Albizu Campos y la independencia*, 77.

35. Bosque-Pérez, "Political Persecution," 14. The story broke because of an investigation into the police's assassination of two young independentistas in 1978. See Bosque-Pérez and Colón Morera, *Carpetas*.

36. Several Nationalists showed me their carpetas, which is how I obtained this information.

37. The Smith Act "require[ed] that all aliens be registered and fingerprinted" and was a "peacetime sedition law" that allowed the government to charge someone for "simply talking about overthrowing the government 'by force and violence.'" Schrecker, *Many Are the Crimes*, 97–98.

38. Acosta-Lespier, "Smith Act Goes to San Juan." For a discussion of the geopolitical reasons why the law was passed in 1948 and the repressive repercussions of the law, see Acosta Lespier, *Mordaza*.

39. "Nacionalistas instan a ir al retraimiento," *El Mundo*, November 1, 1948.

40. U.S. Senate, "Approving Puerto Rican Constitution," 1.

41. Carr, *Puerto Rico*, 78.

42. Ayala and Bernabe, *Puerto Rico in the American Century*, 163. See chapter 8 for a helpful discussion of the process and politics of the formation of the ELA.

43. Harry S. Truman, "Special Message to the Congress Transmitting the Constitution of the Commonwealth of Puerto Rico," April 22, 1952, Public Papers of Harry S. Truman, Harry S. Truman Library, www.trumanlibrary.gov/library/public-papers/104/special-message -congress-transmitting-constitution-commonwealth-puerto.

44. Rosado, *Pedro Albizu Campos*, 322–23.

45. Dietz, *Economic History*, 183.

46. José E. López, conversation with author, March 25, 2006.

47. Although Jorge Duany uses the term in reference to a later period, it also applies to the 1950s. Duany, *Puerto Rican Nation on the Move*, 33. The Popular Democratic Party encouraged the out-migration of Puerto Ricans as an escape valve to alleviate the problem of "overpopulation" and as "an indispensable element of its development strategy." Suárez Findlay, *Left without a Father*, 91.

48. Sotomayor, *Sovereign Colony*, 21. For a fascinating discussion of how the United States used photographs, images, and the technology associated with their production to project itself as the force of modernity, progress, and civilization, see Llorens, *Imagining*.

49. "Statement Concerning the Selection of a Governor of Puerto Rico," Papers of Harry S. Truman, President's Secretary File, Harry S. Truman Library, as cited in Collado-Schwarz, *Truman y Puerto Rico*, 373.

50. "Puerto Rico: Interest and Attitude of Foreign Countries," Division of Research for American Republics, Office of Intelligence Research, "Bogota Conference," October 15, 1947, iii, entry 718, box 11, RG 43, Records of International Conferences, Commissions, and Expositions, NARA. I thank Ashley Black for sending me this report.

51. Leo R. Sack to Secretary of State, "Puerto Rican Independence Movement," San José, Costa Rica, May 29, 1936, box 864, Central Files Puerto Rico, RG 126, Records of the Office of Territories, NARA.

52. "Puerto Rico: Interest and Attitude of Foreign Countries," 54.

53. The municipalities consist of a mayor and local government office.

54. Ayala and Bernabe, *Puerto Rico in the American Century*, 168. The constitution Puerto Ricans voted on contained several human rights provisions, such as the right to an adequate standard of living and employment, which the U.S. Congress jettisoned. Ayala and Bernabe, *Puerto Rico in the American Century*, 168. For an excellent description of the back and forth between Muñoz Marín and Fernós Isern and the U.S. government on the points of contention between the two parties, see Collado-Schwarz, *Truman y Puerto Rico*, 413–20.

55. Collado-Schwarz, *Truman y Puerto Rico*, 420.

56. Truman, "Special Message."

57. Article 73(e) required nations that ruled non-self-governing territories to submit annual reports on their administration to the United Nations. Carr, *Puerto Rico*, 342.

58. Henry Cabot Lodge, "The United States Representative at the United Nations (Austin) to the Secretary-General of the United Nations (Lie)," New York, January 19, 1953, in *Foreign Relations of the United States, 1952–1954*, 1442.

59. On the PIP's challenge, see Carr, *Puerto Rico*, 344–45. On the Nationalists, see Medina Ramírez, *Movimiento libertador*, 2:493–99.

60. Ruth M. Reynolds, "Why Puerto Rico Cannot Be Removed from Classification as a Non-Self-Governing Territory by the United Nations," pp. 2, 20, 1253-4-1:07, folder "Puerto Rico (6)," RTC.

61. Carr, *Puerto Rico*, 347. For delegates' explanations of how they voted, see Medina Ramírez, *Movimiento libertador*, 2:512–13.

62. United Nations, *Official Records of the General Assembly*, 15th sess.

63. "Puerto Rico: Interest and Attitude of Foreign Countries," 20.

64. Iber, *Neither Peace nor Freedom*, 32–33.

65. Bethell and Roxborough, *Latin America*, 184. A U.S. Senate report described Toledano as the "top Communist labor organizer in the Western Hemisphere." U.S. Senate, "Report of the Subcommittee to Investigate Communist Aggression," 4.

66. "Excerpt from letter Headquarters Post of San Juan," State Department, September 29, 1938, 811C.01/80, box 5303, Decimal file 1930–39, RG 59 Department of State Central Files, NARA.

67. FBI Documents, reel 19, "Pedro Albizu Campos and the Nationalist Party," 1, 4.

68. FBI Documents, reel 20, "Pedro Albizu Campos and the Nationalist Party," 5. There is no record that the study took place.

69. Comité Cubano pro Libertad de Patriotas Puertorriqueños, *Bulletin* no. 5 (Havana, Cuba), September 1940, microfiche, New York Public Library.

70. Division of Research for American Republics, "Bogota Conference," 27.

71. FBI Documents, reel 20, "Pedro Albizu Campos and the Nationalist Party," 6.

72. Juarbe Juarbe, "Autobiografía," 2.

73. Juarbe Juarbe, "Autobiografía," 21.

74. Meneses de Albizu Campo, *Vida*, 27.

75. Juarbe Juarbe, *Puerto Rico*, 54–55; Ruth Reynolds Papers, Reynold's Untitled List of Latin American Contacts, Box 20, Folder 1, CEP, 1; Medina Ramírez, *El Movimiento Libertador*, 1:263.

76. Gilderhus, LaFevor, and LaRosa, *Third Century*, 116.

77. "Texts of Marshall Addresses for Hemispheric Cooperation at the Inter-American Conference," *New York Times*, April 2, 1948. Secretary of State George Marshall oversaw the European Recovery Plan, more commonly known as the Marshall Plan. The plan sought to rebuild Europe through the infusion of roughly $12.5 billion. U.S. goals were to ensure the restoration of capitalism and trade relations and, at the same time, to undercut the appeal of socialism and communism and the potential for internal revolt against pro-U.S. governments. For an excellent analysis of this policy, see Eisenberg, *Drawing the Line*, 318–63.

78. "Texts of Marshall Addresses."

79. Betancourt, "Discurso pronunciado," 253. The U.S. ambassador to Colombia noted that the delegates applauded Betancourt's comment about Puerto Rico. *Foreign Relations of the United States, 1948*, 33.

80. Reynolds's Untitled List, 1; Medina Ramírez, *Movimiento libertador*, 1:264; "Nacionalistas dan a conocer en Bogotá programa de 3 puntos," *El Mundo*, April 15, 1948, 5; *Foreign Relations of the United States, 1948*, 30.

81. *Foreign Relations of the United States, 1948*, 4. For background on this resolution and U.S. policy, see Trask, "Impact of the Cold War," 279–82.

82. *Foreign Relations of the United States, 1948*, 69.

83. The United States abstained. "For a Colonial Policy," *New York Times*, April 24, 1948.

84. *Foreign Relations of the United States, 1948*, 76.

85. *Foreign Relations of the United States, 1948*, 76; "Robert A. Lovett." No other American state held colonies in the Americas—only European powers did.

86. *Annals of the Organization of American States*, 135, emphasis added. I thank Ji-Yeon Yuh for obtaining this document for me.

87. Argentina, Colombia, Costa Rica, Cuba, Ecuador, El Salvador, Guatemala, Haiti, Honduras, Mexico, Panama, Paraguay, and Peru sent representatives to the meeting. Medina Ramírez, *Movimiento libertador*, 1:266.

88. Medina Ramírez, *Movimiento libertador*, 1:268–70.

89. "Organization of American States," 555.

90. *Foreign Relations of the United States, 1949*, 2:435.

91. I draw on Juan Antonio Corretjer's description of Albizu Campos as the leader of desperation to characterize the state of the Nationalist Party in this period. Corretjer, *Líder de la desesperación*.

### Chapter Nine

1. Canales, *Constitución*, 25–49. For a summary of Canales's life, see Jiménez de Wagenheim, *Nationalist Heroines*, 51–90.

2. Acosta Lespier, *Mordaza*, 62; Immerwahr, *How to Hide an Empire*, 253–54.

3. Canales, *La constitucion*, 53–54; Marín Torres, *Eran ellos*.

4. Rosado, *Pedro Albizu Campos*, 320. This declaration coincided with the House Un-American Activities Committee questioning and, in some cases, imprisoning Communists or suspected Communists in the United States. See Schrecker, *Many Are the Crimes*. The specific event that precipitated the revolt was the arrest on October 27, 1950, of Nationalist leaders in Santurce who were returning from a rally in cars carrying explosives and weapons. Seijo Bruno, *Insurrección nacionalista*, 73–75.

5. Collado-Schwarz, *Truman y Puerto Rico*, 403.

6. Zapata, *De independentista a autonomista*, 25.

7. Seijo Bruno, *Insurrección nacionalista*, 207–12. Jiménez de Wagenheim, *Nationalist Heroines*, 27. Nationalists took over the Selective Service Office in Jayuya since it "had all the records of the young men in Jayuya [the U.S. military] planned to draft and send to Korea." They burned the files. Heriberto Marín Torres, interview with author, May 20, 2008, San Juan.

8. Seijo Bruno, *Insurrección nacionalista*, 139.

9. Marín Torres interview.

10. Seijo Bruno, *Insurrección nacionalista*, 139.

11. Seijo Bruno, *Insurrección nacionalista*, 225.

12. As quoted in *El Imparcial*, November 2, 1950, in Medina Ramírez, *Movimiento libertador*, 2:333.

13. Seijo Bruno, *Insurrección Nacionalista*, 122.

14. Carlos Padilla, interview with author, May 29, 2015, San Juan.

15. Seijo Bruno, *Insurrección Nacionalista*, 169–172.

16. Collazo denied in court that he intended to kill the president. "Collazo niega intención de matar al president," *El Mundo*, March 2, 1951; Collazo, *Memorias*, 275–76.

17. Collazo, *Memorias*, 278.

18. Collazo, *Memorias*, 274–76.

19. Hunter and Bainbridge Jr., *American Gunfight*; Collazo, *Memorias*, 280–81.

20. Paralitici, *Sentencia impuesta*, 108.

21. "Revolt Flares in Puerto Rico; Soon Quelled with 23 Dead," *New York Times*, October 31, 1950. To reinforce his contention that communists were involved, Muñoz added, "The Nationalists, who often echo the Communist line, had staged the uprising to embarrass the Administration which is pledged to continue Puerto Rico's status as a territory of the United States. The Nationalists were said to have been planning a similar demonstration Nov. 4 when Puerto Ricans will register to vote on the island's new constitution." "Revolt Flares in Puerto Rico." The U.S. media erroneously reported that Juan Perón's government was connected to the Nationalist insurrection. "Peron Influence in Puerto Rican Uprising Is Seen by Inter-American Labor Leader," *New York Times*, November 4, 1950.

22. Muñoz Marín, "Declaraciones del gobierno," 572.

23. Paralitici, *Sentencia impuesta*, 108. That would be the equivalent of 87,500 people in the United States.

24. Meyer Berger, "Assassins' Kin and Friends Are Rounded Up in Bronx," *New York Times*, November 2, 1950, 1.

25. "Assassins' Kin and Friends"; Lydia Collazo, interview with author, May 25, 2008, Levittown, P.R.; Robert Meeropol, phone interview with author, July 30, 2009. Blanca Canales's cellmate in Alderson, West Virginia, was Tokyo Rose. José Enrique Ayoroa Santaliz, "Blanca Canales," *Claridad*, August 2–8, 1996, 20.

26. Carmen Zoraida was Collazo's daughter from a previous marriage, and Lydia and Iris were Rosa's from her previous marriage. Following Collazo's arrest, Lydia and Iris "adopted" him as their father and changed their last name to Collazo, a legal service CPUSA member Abraham Unger performed. They were grateful to Collazo for having raised them and "proud of his patriotism and his willingness to give his life for la Patria." Collazo Cortés, *Entre dos paréntesis*, 104–5.

27. Collazo Cortés, *Entre dos paréntesis*, 94.

28. Collazo Cortés, *Entre dos paréntesis*. For a gripping description of her arrest, questioning, and persecution, see pp. 87–101. Collazo interview.

29. Acosta Lespier, *Mordaza*, 117–21.

30. Paralitici, *Sentencia impuesta*, 110–14.

31. Marín Torres, *Eran ellos*, 22, 19. Marín Torres interview. Marín Torres attributes his early release to "international pressure from both the United Nations and Latin American governments, which pressured the U.S. president to release the Nationalist prisoners." Marín Torres interview. "Nacionalistas reciben las primeras visitas," *El Imparcial*, October 6, 1951. I thank José Manuel Dávila for sending me the article.

32. Reynolds explained her relationship to the Nationalist Party and her arrest in a letter to her sister, Helen. "I have been a friend of the Nationalist leadership since 1944. . . . I have never had an organic relationship with [the] group." She recounts that on November 2, 1950, "40 policemen and National Guard, armed with rifles, machine guns and revolvers, came to the house where I was living alone." She was arrested and convicted of violating Law 53, the Gag Law. Sentenced to six years, she was released on bond in June 1952. "Letter to Helen," June 21, 1951, file 3, box 9, Correspondence, RRP; Paralitici, *Sentencia impuesta*, 136.

33. Partido Nacionalista, *Tortura de los presos*, 70.

34. Partido Nacionalista, *Tortura de los presos*, 21–25, 46. Reynolds referred to the voices as "Loud Voice and Mr. Quiet." I surmise that the idea of a white woman being sexually and/or romantically attracted to men of color titillated the two white male speakers. At the same time, they probably hoped that their suggestive and unfounded comments would shame and undermine Reynolds.

35. Lynn, *There Is a Fountain*, 136.

36. Partido Nacionalista, *Tortura de los presos*, 80–81.

37. Partido Nacionalista, *Tortura de los presos*, 90.

38. The Soviet Union used a similar tactic when it diagnosed those who opposed the Socialist regime as crazy and sent them to psychiatric wards for treatment. See, e.g., the case of Vladimir Bukovksy: "Vladimir Bukovsky, Soviet-Era Dissident Who Exposed Communist Abuses, Dies," *Los Angeles Times*, October 28, 2019.

39. U.S. House of Representatives, Committee on Interior and Insular Affairs, "Nationalist Party," 11.

40. "Revolt Flares in Puerto Rico."

41. Friedman, *Citizenship in Cold War America*, 151.

42. For more on Duamy's report, see de Albizu Campos, *Albizu Campos*, 122–24. For an investigative study on Albizu's health, see Aponte, *¡Yo acuso!* For more on other Nationalist Party prisoners, see Partido Nacionalista, *Tortura de los presos*.

43. Friedman, *Citizenship in Cold War America*, 152.

44. As Leslie Bethell and Ian Roxborough point out, only Paraguay, El Salvador, Honduras, Nicaragua, and the Dominican Republic were not run by "popular and democratic" governments in the mid-1940s. However, by 1954, dictatorships or quasi-dictatorships ruled thirteen out of twenty-one nations in the region. Bethell and Roxborough, *Latin America*, 5, 18–19.

45. "Truman Doctrine, 1947."

46. Paralitici, *Sentencia impuesta*, 137–38; Padilla interview; Partido Nacionalista, *Tortura de los presos*, 81.

47. Meneses Albizu Campos and Lora Gamarra, *Vida de amor*, 28–29.

48. Collazo interview.

49. Medina Ramírez, *Movimiento libertador*, 2:383–85.

50. Medina Ramírez, *Movimiento libertador*, 2:383–85; "Desea enviar comisión aquí," *El Mundo*, November 1, 1950, 2.

51. "Desea enviar comisión aquí," 2; Medina Ramírez, *Movimiento libertador*, 2:383–85.

52. "Leuchsenring envía protesta al gobernador," *El Mundo*, November 2, 1950, 12. The governor's office replied, "Señor Roig is not familiar with Puerto Rico." "Leuchsenring envía protesta."

53. "Cuba Denies Drop in Amity for U.S.," *New York Times*, November 4, 1950; "Disuelvan manifestación pro nacionalista en Cuba," *El Imparcial*, November 31, 1950.

54. Meneses Albizu Campos and Lora Gamarra, *Vida de amor*, 29; Padilla interview.

55. Collazo, *Memorias*, 285.

56. Collazo, *Memorias*, 287. Ethel and Julius Rosenberg had been sentenced to death the day before. I thank Andrea Friedman for pointing this out to me.

57. Kanellos and Martell, *Recovering the U.S. Hispanic Literary Heritage*, 59; Jiménez de Wagenheim, *Nationalist Heroines*, 230; Collazo Cortés, *Entre dos paréntesis*, 111.

58. Jiménez de Wagenheim, *Nationalist Heroines*, 230. For a harrowing description of Rosa's time in prison, see Collazo Cortés, *Entre dos paréntesis*, 228–30.

59. Lydia Collazo communicated with backers across the hemisphere, in Europe, especially Italy, in Asia, and in countries "that were still fighting for their independence." Collazo Cortés, *Entre dos paréntesis*, 112, 115.

60. Ralph Templin stated the committee's position clearly: meetings were to be "strictly non-political." Supporting the demand to save Collazo's life, he said, "does not mean that you agree with the Puerto Rican nationalists either in purpose or method." Ralph Templin, "Plea for Oscar Collazo's Life," file 1, box 20, RRP.

61. Latin Americans' use of humanitarian discourse around Collazo in the 1950s recalls how they employed the language of the Good Neighbor Policy to criticize U.S. colonialism and imprisonment of Nationalist prisoners in the 1930s. See chapter 6.

62. Because Latin America was economically important to the United States, Washington paid attention to the region's political opinions. As Leslie Bethell and Ian Roxborough point out, in the postwar period, "Latin America remained the United States' most important export market and source of imports and, after Canada, the area in which most U.S. capital was invested." Bethell and Roxborough, *Latin America*, 24.

63. Collazo Cortés, *Entre dos paréntesis*, 116–19.

64. For a discussion of this issue, see Yasutake, "Preface."

65. Committee to Save the Life of Oscar Collazo, folder "Puerto Rico," RTC.

66. Peacemakers to President Harry S. Truman, July 16, 1952, folder "Puerto Rico," RTC.

67. The leaflet announcing the event appealed to the Puerto Rican and Hispanic communities of New York. It compared Collazo not only to such U.S. revolutionary heroes as Nathan Hale, Patrick Henry, and George Washington but also to Latin American ones such as Simón Bolívar, José de San Martín, José Martí, and Toussaint Louverture. "Hay que salvar a Oscar Collazo," file 1, box 20, RRP.

68. "Comités Collazo irán a Washington y a las N. Unidas," *La Prensa*, July 12, 1952.

69. Members of the committee compiled lists of individuals the Nationalists had worked with and added brief comments about them. For example, they wrote to Argentine Alfredo L. Palacios, "ex-pres of the univ. of La Plata . . . friend of PR; Dr. Henriquex [*sic*] Henriquez y Carjajal [*sic*], Santo Domingo, delegate of Nationalist party; or Dr. Joaquin Garcia Monge, *Repertorio Americano*" (Nationalist delegate to Costa Rica). Untitled, file 1, box 20, RRP.

70. "Carta de Luisa Quintero a Getúlio Vargas," July 9, 1952, classification c 1952.07.09/3, Fundação Getúlio Vargas. I thank Victoria Langland for sending me copies of these documents.

71. "Carta de Luisa Quintero." Vargas's response was in line with his government's general position on anticolonial struggles. Although Brazil "declar[ed] support for the right of self-determination" in general, "it supported the colonial powers, especially at the UN, on the grounds that it was necessary to achieve conciliatory solutions." Serra Coelho, "Brazil and India," 19. Indeed, in 1953 the Brazilian delegate to the United Nations agreed with the United States that Puerto Ricans had freely chosen their current status and, as a result, Washington no longer needed to transmit information on the archipelago to the international body. García Muñoz, "Puerto Rico in the United Nations," 66.

72. "Policy Statement Prepared in the Department of State," in *Foreign Relations of the United States, 1951*, 2:1429.

73. Nationalist Party of Puerto Rico, Foreign Relations Secretariat, "Our Gratitude," Havana, July 28, 1952, folder 4, box 29, RRP; Félix Ojeda Reyes, "La posibilidad de su muerte," *Claridad*, November 8, 2007.

74. "Grupo uruguayo pro libertad de Puerto Rico," *Marcha*, September 1, 1951.

75. Raúl F. Abadie-Aicardi to Rosa Collazo, Montevideo, July 9, 1952, folder 2, box 20, RRP.

76. "Una carta de R. F. Abadie Aicardi," *Marcha*, no. 553, November 17, 1950.

77. Ojeda Reyes, "Posibilidad de su muerte."

78. Anthony Leviero, "Assassin Spared by Truman in Gesture to Puerto Rico," *New York Times*, July 25, 1952. Truman likely concluded that sparing Collazo's life would add legitimacy to the Muñoz Marín government and Puerto Rico's new constitution, which was declared the next day. I thank Andrea Friedman for drawing this connection.

79. Secretary of State File: Memorandum of Conversations, July 1952, Dean G. Acheson Papers, Harry S. Truman Library. I thank Randy Sowell for locating this document for me.

80. "Commutation Approved," *New York Times*, July 26, 1952.

81. Reprinted in Medina Ramírez, *Movimiento libertador*, 2:470–76.

82. Nationalist prisoners held in isolation in La Princesa jail in San Juan received their first visits eleven months after their arrest. The visiting family members spoke little because they believed that their conversations were being taped and feared that the authorities could use their words against them and imprison them, too. "Nacionalistas reciben las primeras visitas," *El Imparcial*, October 6, 1951. For a description of how "the fear of long imprisonment in Puerto Rico is a real instrument of terror," see Ernest Bromley, Wallace Nelson, and Ralph Templin, "Visit to Puerto Rico," 11, folder "Puerto Rico (1)," RTC.

83. Because Congress was discussing a bill "governing the admission of Mexican farm laborers—referred to as 'wetbacks,'" several congressmen erroneously thought Lebrón was shouting, "Viva Mexico!" "5 Congressmen Shot Down," *Chicago Daily Tribune*, March 2, 1954. As *Time* wrote, Lebrón was "jabbering in Spanish." "The Capitol: Puerto Rico Is Not Free," *Time*, March 8, 1954.

84. Clayton Knowles, "Five Congressmen Shot in House by 3 Puerto Rican Nationalists; Bullets Spray from Gallery," *New York Times*, March 2, 1954.

85. The four, like Torresola and Collazo in 1950, had purchased one-way tickets to Washington, convinced they would not survive. Lolita Lebrón, interview with author, September 9, 2004, Chicago. "Five Congressmen Shot in House."

86. "Repudian en la cámara atentado al Congreso," El Mundo, March 2, 1954.

87. "Personas condenan," El Mundo, March 5, 1954; "Continúa rección en contra de atentado," El Mundo, March 9, 1954; "Senado condena atentado," El Mundo, March 3, 1954; "Da repudio en Caracas ataque a congresistas," El Mundo, March 3, 1954.

88. "Four Indicted," Chicago Daily Tribune, March 3, 1954.

89. "Congressmen Gun Victims All May Live," Chicago Daily Tribune, March 3, 1954.

90. "5 Congressmen Shot Down."

91. "Muñoz ofrece ayuda al Comité de Velde," March 4, 1954.

92. "Buscan nexo terroristas con rojos," El Mundo, March 4, 1954.

93. "Opina rojos han influído nacionalismo," El Mundo, March 5, 1954.

94. "Opina rojos han influído nacionalismo."

95. This is a paraphrase of the statement in the Insular Acts that Puerto Ricans are foreign in a domestic sense. See Burnett and Marshall, "Between Foreign and Domestic."

96. For different manifestations of anti-Semitism in the 1950s, see Antler, "Imagining Jewish Mothers."

97. According to one study from the 1950s, 95 percent of Americans thought that "it was impossible to be both a Communist and a loyal American." Friedman, Citizenship in Cold War America, 2.

98. For a nuanced discussion of who was included and who was excluded from being a full U.S. citizen, see Friedman, Citizenship in Cold War America, 9–12.

99. "Capturan Albizu y otros tres," El Mundo, March 6, 1954.

100. Paralitici, Sentencia impuesta, 451–50; Jiménez de Wagenheim, Nationalist Heroines, 199.

101. "13 Puerto Rican Terrorists Get Six Year Terms," Chicago Daily Tribune, October 27, 1954.

102. Jiménez de Wagenheim, Nationalist Heroines, 264.

103. Paralitici, Sentencia impuesta, 168.

104. See Power, "Friends and Comrades"; and "The Struggle for Puerto Rican Rights," N.Y. State Communist Party, January 1954, file 18, box 15, Clemente Soto Vélez Papers, Centro de Estudios Puertorriqueños, New York.

105. Indeed, both parties were already on the list of subversive organizations and targets of U.S. government repression. Acosta Lespier, "Smith Act Goes to San Juan," 61. The CPUSA was under siege from the FBI and the House Un-American Activities Committee and a hostile public convinced that Communists were traitors in service to the Soviet Union. For a description of common U.S. stereotypes of Communists, see Schrecker, Many Are the Crimes, 131–35. After being convicted of conspiracy to commit espionage, Communist Party members Ethel and Julius Rosenberg were executed in July 1953, which "bolstered the contention that Communists spied." Schrecker, Many Are the Crimes, 178.

106. "Niegan que inspiran atentado congresistas," El Mundo, March 4, 1954. The Communist leaders, like the Nationalists, were charged with being active in a subversive organization and thus violating Law 53.

107. "Puerto Rican Independence Still the Issue," Daily Worker, March 3, 1954.

108. "Puerto Rican Independence Still the Issue." The quotation may or may not have reflected what Lebrón thought at the time, but it clearly signaled a distance between the two parties. When I interviewed Lebrón in 2004, she offered a very different interpretation of her relationship with communists. She said, "They were friends. . . . I always got along very well with them. Once they invited me to speak at a program in New York City, but I don't remember when. I spoke and everyone liked what I said." Lebrón interview.

109. "Caracas and Puerto Rico," *Daily Worker*, March 9, 1954.

110. Two scholars who highlight them are Friedman in *Citizenship in Cold War America* and "Empire at Home"; and Materson, "Ruth Reynolds," 183–87.

111. "No Compromise," *MANAS Reprint*, August 11, 1948, 4.

112. "Ruth Reynolds Oral History," October 1, 1985, interviewed by Blanca Vázquez, tape no. 43, sides A and B, 12, RRP.

113. See "Lula Peterson letter" to Ruth Reynolds, January 11, 1950 [1951], folder 5, box 2, RRP; and Friedman, "Empire at Home."

114. "Actividades de Ruth Reynolds," file 14, box 48, RRP. Members of the Committee for Justice to Puerto Ricans included Sidney Aberman, Duncan Brackin, David Dellinger, Julius Eichel (Treasurer), Seymour Eichel, Royal W. France, Waldo Frank, Richard Gillies, Paul Jacobs, Rev. John Paul Jones, Roy Kepler, Sid Lens, Philip MacDougall, Normal Mailer, Chester Mannes, Isabel Monroe, Rev. A. J. Muste, Roger O'Neil, Rev. George Lyman Paine, Bayard Rustin, Rev. Robert Tapp, Arlo Tatum, Rev. Ralph Templin, and Harold Wurf. "Form Committee for Justice to Puerto Rico," *Peacemaker* 5, November 22, May 10, 1954, folder "Puerto Rico (6)," RTC; "Statement of Purpose," *Labor Action* 18, no. 22, May 31, 1954. Norman Mailer is known for his first novel, *The Naked and the Dead*, and for cofounding the *Village Voice*. Waldo Frank was a writer who wrote extensively about Latin America and Latino culture and a left-wing political activist who had been in the Communist Party in the 1920s and 1930s. See Gosse, *Where the Boys Are*, 140.

115. *Labor Action* 18, no. 22, May 31, 1954.

116. For a history of the use of the term "terrorist" against the Nationalists, see Friedman, *Citizenship in Cold War America*, 137–38. On the construction of a national, patriotic ethos that defended the function and practices of the state, Laura McEnaney notes that the term "national security" replaced "national defense" in the 1950s to "describe the close relationship between domestic politics, foreign policy, and military affairs. . . . [and] expressed hostility toward communism or nationalism." McEnaney, *Civil Defense*, 13. On the role the white, heterosexual family played in promoting and enforcing gender norms, patriotism, and national security, see May, *Homeward Bound*.

117. A. J. Muste to Ralph Templin, July 23, 1951, 2, folder "Puerto Rico (6)," RTC. For background on Peck, see Arsenault, *Freedom Riders*, 28–29.

118. Muste to Templin.

119. According to three members of Peacemakers who toured Puerto Rico, it was hard to convince U.S.-based pacifists to advocate for Reynolds because they depended "upon pacifists in Puerto Rico for information," who not only considered Reynolds a "non pacifist" but never "even attempted to visit Reynolds while she was in jail." Ernest Bromley, Wallace Nelson, and Ralph Templin, "Visit to Puerto Rico," October 6, 1951, 10, folder "Puerto Rico (1)," RTC. Ruth Reynolds was an active member of the Fellowship of Reconciliation and the War Resisters League and a founder of the Congress of Racial Equality. "From behind America's own curtain," folder 1, box 1, RRP.

120. "Comments on the Nationalist Party of Puerto Rico and the Revolt of October 1950," July 10, 1951, 1, folder "Puerto Rico (1)," RTC.

121. Carl Colodne (secretary of RRDC) to Ruth Reynolds, October 12, 20, 1951, folder 7, box 2, RRP.

122. "Comments on the Nationalist Party," 3. "For a discussion of his "dual tugs of caution and conscience," see Robinson, *Abraham Went Out*, 106–7. Muste thought that supporters should secure Reynold's release and raise the necessary funds to pay her bail and legal costs. "A. J. Muste Reports on Visit with Ruth Reynolds," *Peacemaker* 3, no. 4, July 21, 1951, 4, folder "Puerto Rico (6)," RTC.

123. "A. J. Muste Reports," 1.

124. "A. J. Muste Reports," 4.

125. A. J. Muste, "Memo on Puerto Rico," March 8, 1954, 3, 1, folder "Puerto Rico (2)," RTC.

126. "Free Puerto Rico," leaflet, undated, folder "Puerto Rico (2)," RTC.

127. "Peacemaker Delegation to Visit Puerto Rico," *Peacemaker* 3, no. 4, July 21, 1951, 1, folder "Puerto Rico (6)," RTC.

128. "Peacemaker Delegation to Visit Puerto Rico," 4. Andrea Friedman argues that these radical pacifists inspired "US activists [to] formulate a new model of anti-imperial struggle, one that insisted that a radical peace politics could stand in solidarity with those who use violence in national liberation movements." Friedman, "Empire at Home," 254.

129. Bromley, Nelson, and Templin, "Visit to Puerto Rico," 6. They wrote that "Ruth was haggard and emaciated and we hardly knew her when we saw her come into court, learning later that she was suffering from serious malnutrition and a kidney infection"; nonetheless, "her spirit was good throughout the trial." Bromley, Nelson, and Templin, "Visit to Puerto Rico," 6.

130. Bromley, Nelson, and Templin, "Visit to Puerto Rico," 12–13.

131. Seymour Eichel, interview with author, Bridgewater, N.J., June 26, 2008.

132. "This walk across Puerto Rico is sponsored by Peacemakers," folder "Puerto Rico (6), RTC; Ralph Templin, "Our Walk and Its Significance," *Peacemaker*, January 10, 1959, vol. 12, no. 1, folder "Puerto Rico (8)," RTC; Seymour Eichel and Al Uhrie, "A Week of Walking –Peacemakers Meet the People," January 31, 1959, 1, folder "Puerto Rico (8)," RTC.

133. "Cablegram to Ike," *Peacemaker*, January 31, 1959, vol. 12, no. 2, folder "Puerto Rico (8)," RTC.

134. Al Uhrie, "Why We Are Going to San Juan," 1, folder "Puerto Rico (8)," RTC.

135. Ruth Reynolds, "Why Albizu Campos, Other Puerto Ricans Are in Prison," A Call to Protest Political Imprisonment of Puerto Ricans, October 15, 1960, 3, folder "Puerto Rico (8)," RTC.

136. Ralph Templin, "Christmas Week in Puerto Rico," 1, folder "Puerto Rico (8)," RTC.

137. Collazo Cortés, *Entre dos paréntesis*, 146.

138. Earl Browder, secretary general of the CPUSA, predicted that "collaboration among the United States, Great Britain, and the Soviet Union would end colonial domination of the third world." Browderism, as his interpretation of communist strategy has come to be known, also believed that the mutually compatible interests of modernizing sectors of U.S. and Latin American capitalists would signal the end of imperialist exploitation. See Carr, *Izquierda Mexicana*, 24, 117. I thank Jacob Zumoff for sending me a copy of this book. For a discussion of Latin American communist parties' weaknesses, see Castañeda, *Utopia Unarmed*, 29–30.

139. The three do not fit the profile of Latin American political prisoners sent into exile by the military dictatorships that proliferated in the region in the 1960s and 1970s. Padilla and Juarbe chose exile in order to carry out the work of the Nationalist Party, while Meneses was stateless from 1948, when the U.S. government revoked her citizenship, to 1959, when the revolutionary Cuban government made her a citizen.

140. The Federación de Universitarios Pro Independencia (Federation of Pro Independence University Students) emerged in 1956, and the Movimiento Pro Independencia (MPI, Movement for Independence) formed in 1959. The MPI adopted Marxism-Leninism and evolved into the Puerto Rican Socialist Party in 1971. Paralitici, *Repression*, 113–17; Velázquez, Rivera, and Torres, *Revolution around the Corner*, 25–26.

141. Sznajder and Roneiger, *Politics of Exile*, 5.

142. Padilla interview.

143. Randall, *Haydée Santamaría*, 3–4.

144. Paterson, *Contesting Castro*, esp. 25. "Batista Lamenta Atentado Comunista," *El Mundo*, March 5, 1954.

145. "Cubans Seize 2 Puerto Rican Nationalists," *New York Times*, March 4, 1954. The Batista government had expelled Rafael Cancel Miranda, one of the four Nationalists who later attacked the U.S. Congress, in August 1952. "Rafael Cancel Miranda fué expulsado de Cuba," *El Mundo*, March 3, 1954.

146. Padilla interview.

147. Padilla interview.

148. Padilla interview. Carlos Padilla, phone interview with author, April 5, 2016, San Juan.

149. Gleijeses, "Agrarian Reform," 189; Schlesinger and Kinzer, *Bitter Fruit*. On "Guatemala's anti-imperialist attitude" during the Arbenz government, see García Ferreria, "'El caso de Guatemala,'" 27.

150. "Guatemala Snubs U.S. with Music; Ignores Anthem for a Dance Tune," *New York Times*, February 27, 1950. For a fuller discussion of the event and the suggestion that Juan Juarbe was responsible for the music selection, see Sotomayor, *Sovereign Colony*, 136–37.

151. The only other Latin American country to vote against the resolution was Mexico. On the U.N. debate on the status of Puerto Rico, different countries' positions on the issue, and the United States' role in influencing the vote, see García Muñiz, *Puerto Rico*, chap. 1. To explain the Latin American vote, García Muñiz points out, "Latin American countries like Colombia, Brazil, Panama, Paraguay and Nicaragua were under dictatorships pliable to the United States guidelines." India firmly opposed the U.S. resolution. García Muñiz, *Puerto Rico*, 51, 52.

152. For a personal account of her life with Guevara in Guatemala, see Gadea, *My Life with Che*. On Latin American exile communities in Guatemala and Mexico, see Black, "Politics of Asylum," 205–6.

153. Semán, *Ambassadors*, 210. Among those sheltering in the Argentine embassy were Guatemalan officials, Honduran and Dominican communists, revolutionary Cubans, and Nicaraguan peasant activists. For a complete list, see "Personas asiladas en la embajada de la República Argentina," *La Hora*, July 31, 1954. I thank Ernesto Semán for this reference.

154. Padilla interview; Padilla phone interview.

155. Corominas, *Puerto Rico Libre*.

156. Padilla interview. "Estatutos," Buenos Aires, August 4, 1956, folder 8, box 19, RRP; "Letter from Juan Juarbe Juarbe," October 25, 1956, folder 9, box 3, RRP. For a history of Argentine solidarity with Puerto Rico, see Ferreira de Cassone, *Claridad y el internacionalismo americano*, 256–61; and Palacios, *Nuestra América*.

157. Padilla phone interview.

158. Padilla interview.

159. Padilla Pérez, *Puerto Rico*, 7–8. I thank Andres Bisso for alerting me to this book.

160. "Ecuador y Puerto Rico," *El Imparcial*, October 4, 1957. I thank Ernesto Semán for sending me a copy of the article. For a fuller discussion of the congressional debate on the agreement, see Power, "Puerto Rican Nationalist Party."

161. María M. Santander and Rito D. Luna to Lydia Collazo and Ruth Reynolds, August 16, 1956, folder 3, box 19, RRP.

162. Letter to Jaime Benítez, August 3, 1956, Oscar Collazo Letters, no. 415, Colección Puertorriqueña, Universidad de Puerto Rico, Río Piedras.

163. "Letter to Jaime Benítez," "Hermanos argentines," folder 2, box 4, RRP; letter to Dag Hammarskjöld, September 15, 1958, Oscar Collazo Letters, no. 566, Colección Puertorriqueña, Universidad de Puerto Rico, Río Piedras; letter to Ruth Reynolds, February 12, 1959, folder 3, box 4, RRP; "Release of Albizu Asked from Argentina," *El Imparcial*, December 21, 1956, as cited in FBI, *Quarterly Summary Report*.

164. Juarbe Juarbe, "Autobiografía," 4. Mexican president Adolfo Ruiz Cortines offered asylum to exiles who did not challenge his government's politics. Rojas, *Historia mínima*, 59.

165. Meneses Albizu Campos and Lora Gamarra, *Vida de amor*, 31–32.

166. Meneses and Gadea became close friends; they were both Peruvian and had similar but not identical politics. According to Juarbe, Gadea supported "the democrats, José Figueres of Honduras, Romulo Betancourt of Venezuela, and Haya de la Torre, the Peruvian APRA leader," while Guevara, Juarbe, and Meneses did not. Juarbe Juarbe, "Autobiografía," 5. Gadea was a militant of APRA but broke with them in 1959 due to her support for armed struggle. Gadea, *My Life with Che*, 9, 138. I thank Ashley Black for referring me to Gadea's book. Meneses de Albizu Campos and Lora Gamarra, *Una Vida*, 31.

167. Gadea, *My Life with Che*, 174–75.

168. Juarbe, "Autobiografía," 6. Cuban Alberto Bayo had learned military skills fighting in defense of the Spanish Republic. Rojas, *Historia mínima*, 59.

169. Gadea, *My Life with Che*, 208.

170. The exile community consisted of Puerto Rican Nationalists, anti-Batista Cubans, Guevara, Gadea, Venezuelan, and Dominican revolutionaries. Juarbe Juarbe, "Autobiografía," 6.

171. Document 24/3.20/I.1/1–223, Expediente: Agregado Militar de la Embajada de Cuba en México, 15-5-1952–24-12-1956, Colección: Ejército, 1952–1958, Archivo del Instituto de Historia de Cuba. I thank Aaron Coy Moulton for sending me this document.

172. Juarbe Juarbe, *Derecho*.

173. Juarbe Juarbe, *Derecho*, vii.

174. In the article, "Puerto Rico Irredento," the editors state that because the journal is "the house of culture and the ideals of Indoamérica, unswerving in its ethical and humane position, always at the service of the dignity of people, it is honored to incorporate . . . the tireless apostle of Puerto Rico redemption [Juarbe]." *Humanismo*, January–February 1954, 82.

175. Juarbe Juarbe, "Puerto Rico lucha por su independencia," *Humanismo*, March–April–May 1954, 16–42.

176. Laura de Albizu Campos, "Carta a los hombres libres," *Humanismo*, September 1954, 20, 21, 29. For a discussion of Puerto Rican psychiatrists' "in the service of the state" diagnosis of Matos Paoli's insanity and the role art and faith played in his recovery and writing, see Rivera-Rivera, "Politics of Madness," esp. 2.

177. De Albizu Campos, "Carta a los hombres libres," 21, 29.

178. Lebrón interview.

## Conclusion

1. Rosado, *Pedro Albizu Campos*, 405, 406. Between 1956 and 1960, Albizu Campos's health declined sharply. He suffered a stroke that left him paralyzed on the right side and a cerebral thrombosis that rendered him unable to speak. Rosado, *Pedro Albizu Campos*, 393–402.

2. Ruth Reynolds, "The Funeral of Don Pedro Albizu Campos," 1, folder 1, box 31, RRP.

3. See "Sepelio de Don Pedro Albizu Campos," video posted by Joe Bruno, April 25, 2015, www.youtube.com/watch?v=UR-VE0ALU18.

4. For a description of the funeral, see Rosado, *Pedro Albizu Campos*, 406–11; and Reynolds, "Funeral of Don Pedro." For the Andreu quotations, see *El Imparcial*, April 24, 1965.

5. Rosado, *Pedro Albizu Campos*, 407, 409.

6. The United States canceled her U.S. citizenship, which she had acquired after marrying Albizu in 1922, in 1948. In 1956, when Albizu was very sick and in a coma, the U.S. government rejected her request to visit him. De Albizu Campos, *Albizu Campos y la independencia*, 137–141; "Pedro Albizu Campos, 73, Dies; Fiery Puerto Rican Nationalist," *New York Times*, April 22, 1965.

7. "Mensaje de duelo y funeral Don Pedro Albizu Campos," Archivos Medios Audiovisuales, Universidad de Puerto Rico, Río Piedras, video posted November 12, 2020, https://

www.youtube.com/watch?v=6fd54KmM1KM, Colección Juan Mari Bras del Archivo de Medios Audiovisuales, Escuela de Comunicación de la Universidad de Puerto Rico.

8. Reynolds, "Funeral of Don Pedro," 5. On Herrera Oropeza, see Ayala, "Experiencia del Comité Venezolano," 109; and Sant Roz, *Procónsul Rómulo Betancourt*, 492, 603. I thank Miguel Tinker-Salas for bringing this book to my attention.

9. "Mensaje de duelo y funeral Don Pedro Albizu Campos."

10. I have not found documentation to substantiate this, but it is likely that the U.S. government refused entry to representatives of the Cuban government who sought to speak at the funeral.

11. Waldo Frank, Oscar Gonzales-Suarez, Otto Nathan, Luisa Quintero, and Abraham Unger, "Dear Friends," August 23, 1962, Oscar Collazo Letters, no. 786, Colección Puertorriqueña, Universidad de Puerto Rico, Río Piedras. Carlos Santiago, "Dear Friend," July 1964, folder 6, box 28, RRP.

12. Paralitici, *Sentencia impuesta*, 183.

13. Letter to President Dwight D. Eisenhower, September 12, 1957, *Puerto Rico Libre* no. 7.

14. "Argentinos se dirigen al gobernador colonial," *Puerto Rico Libre*, Buenos Aires, September 3, 1957.

15. "Ecuatorianos lloran en visita a Albizu Campos," *El Imparcial*, December 22, 1957, cited in Padilla Pérez, *Puerto Rico*, 160–62.

16. Acosta-Lespier, *Mordaza*, 238. The Ley de Mordaza made it illegal to foment or advocate "the need, desirability, or convenience of overturning, destroying, or paralyzing the Insular Government." Acosta-Lespier, *Mordaza*, 13.

17. U.S. Committee to Free the Five Puerto Rican Nationalists, "The Case of the Five Puerto Rican Nationalists," New York, undated, 2. The names of the individuals who sponsored the call for the release of the Nationalists reads like a list of who's who of the U.S. left and progressive movement, ranging from Herbert Aptheker, CPUSA leader; to Ella Baker, Black civil rights leader; Noam Chomsky, prominent intellectual; Jane Fonda, actor and activist; Huey P. Newton, cofounder of the Black Panther Party; Irwin Silber, editor of the *Guardian*; Harold Washington, future mayor of Chicago; and Paul Sweezy of the *Monthly Review*.

18. National Committee to Free the Four Puerto Rican Prisoners of War, Document No. 1, Chicago, ca. 1978, 2. The committee changed its name from five to four after Andres Figueroa Cordero was released in 1977.

19. "Commutations Granted by President Jimmy Carter," U.S. Department of Justice, https://www.justice.gov/pardon/commutations-granted-president-jimmy-carter-1977-1981; "Puerto Rican Jailed in '54 Attack Freed by President, *Washington Post*, October 11, 1977; "Pardoned Activist Dies in Puerto Rico," *New York Times*, March 8, 1979.

20. Martin Tolchin, "President to Free 4 Puerto Ricans in Washington Shootings of 1950's," *New York Times*, September 7, 1979.

21. National Committee, "Charges and Documentation," 20.

22. National Committee, "Charges and Documentation"; Michael Deutsch, interview with author, August 16, 2010, Egg Harbor, Wis.

23. "Momentum Builds to Free Four Puerto Rican Nationalists," *Bay State Banner*, February 15, 1979.

24. "President to Free 4 Puerto Ricans."

25. "Puerto Rican Nationalist Prisoners of War Are Free," *Newsletter of the National Committee to Free Puerto Rican Prisoners of War* (Chicago) 1, no. 1 (n.d.); "4 Pardoned Terrorists to Meet Here," *Chicago Tribune*, September 8, 1979.

26. Tony Schwarz, "2 Freed Puerto Rican Nationalists Say They Can't Rule Out Violence," *New York Times*, September 12, 1979.

27. Collazo, "Memorias," cited in Jiménez de Wagenheim, *Nationalist Heroines*, 240.

28. Mara Siegal, interview with author, July 19, 2021, Phoenix, Ariz. Mara Siegal and Michael Deutsch worked at the People's Law Office in Chicago. Deutsch was the first U.S. attorney to visit Rafael Cancel Miranda in decades, and he and Siegal were both central to the campaign to free him and the other four Nationalists. They accompanied the Nationalists on their flight to Puerto Rico. Deutsch interview.

29. "Terrorists Given Welcome Home in Puerto Rico," *Washington Post*, September 13, 1979.

30. Jiménez de Wagenheim, *Nationalist Heroines*, 240.

31. "Terrorists Given Welcome Home."

32. On the armed clandestine organizations and/or the political prisoners, see Fernández, *Prisoners of Colonialism*; González-Cruz, *Nacionalismo revolucionario puertorriqueño*, and *Puerto Rican Revolutionary Nationalism*; González Cruz, Marquez Sola, and Terando, "U.S. Invasion of Puerto Rico; and Power, "From Freedom Fighters to Patriots."

33. Lolita Lebrón, interview with author, September 9, 2004, Chicago.

34. On the debt crisis, see Ed Morales, "The Roots of Puerto Rico's Debt—And Why Austerity Will Not Solve It," *Nation*, July 8, 2015. On the United States and the hurricanes in Puerto Rico, see Morales, "Puerto Rico." For more articles on the economic situation in Puerto Rico, see Puerto Rico Syllabus, https://puertoricosyllabus.com/.

35. Calle 13 was a Puerto Rican band consisting of three siblings. Popular across Latin America, winner of numerous Latin Grammy awards, the group rapped about independence, corruption, the political prisoners, and Latin American unity. See Hernández Prieto, "Calle 13."

36. Fernández, *Prisoners of Colonialism*; Power, "From Freedom Fighters to Patriots."

37. Flags were omnipresent in the protests of summer 2019 against then-governor Ricardo Barceló. See Patricia Mazzei and Frances Robles, "Puerto Ricans in Protest Say They've Had Enough," *New York Times*, July 18, 2019. On Puerto Ricans' use of the flag to assert their identity, see Carrión, "War of the Flags."

38. I thank Neici Zeller for bringing this to my attention.

# BIBLIOGRAPHY

## Archive Collections

A. C. Buehler Library, Elmhurst College
    Rudolf G. Schade Archives and Special Collections
Archivo del Instituto de Historia de Cuba, Havana
    Colección: Ejército, 1952–1958
Archivo General de la Nación, Mexico City
Archivo General de Puerto Rico, San Juan
Archivo Histórico Diplomático "Genaro Estrada" de la Secretaria de Relaciones Exteriores
    de México, Mexico City
Archivo Plutarco Elías Calles, Mexico City
Biblioteca Nacional del Perú, Lima
Centro de Estudios Puertorriqueños, New York
    Ruth M. Reynolds Papers
    Clemente Soto Vélez Papers
Franklin D. Roosevelt Presidential Library and Museum, Poughkeepsie, N.Y.
    Sumner Welles Papers
Fundação Getúlio Vargas, Rio de Janeiro
    Centro de Pesquisa e Documentação de História Contemporânea do Brasil
Harry S. Truman Presidential Library and Museum, Independence, Mo.
    Dean G. Acheson Papers
    Public Papers of Harry S. Truman
Instituto Riva-Agüero, Lima, Peru
International Institute of Social History, Amsterdam
    League against Imperialism Archives
National Archives and Record Administration, College Park, Md.
    RG 43, Records of International Conferences, Commissions, and Expositions
    RG 59, Department of State Central Files
    RG 126, Records of the Office of Territories
New York City Municipal Archives
    WPA Federal Writers' Project
New York Public Library
    Vito Marcantonio Papers
Schlesinger Library, Harvard Radcliffe Institute, Cambridge, Mass.
Special Collections and University Archives, Rutgers University Libraries
    Robert J. Alexander Papers
Special Collections Research Center, Syracuse University Libraries
    Earl Browder Papers
Tamiment Library and Robert F. Wagner Labor Archives, New York University
    Communist Party of the United States of America Oral History Collection
Joseph Regenstein Library, University of Chicago
United Methodist Church Archives—GCAH, Madison, N.J.
    Ralph T. Templin Collection
Universidad de Puerto Rico, Río Piedras
    Biblioteca José M. Lázaro

Centro de Estudios Caribeños
Colección Puertorriqueña
Oscar Callazo Letters

## Periodicals

Chicago Daily Tribune
Chicago Tribune
Bay State Banner (Dorchester, Mass.)
Blitz (Bombay)
CIO News (Chicago)
Claridad (Buenos Aires)
Claridad (San Juan, P.R.)
Daily Worker (New York)
FECH (Santiago)
Granma (Havana)
Harvard Crimson (Cambridge, Mass.)
Humanismo (Mexico City)
Imparcial, El (San Juan, P.R.)
Nación, La (San Juan, P.R.)
Palabra, La (San Juan, P.R.)

Listín Diario (Santo Domingo, D.R.)
Los Angeles Times
Marcha (Montevideo)
Mundo, El (San Juan, P.R.)
Nacionalista de Ponce, El (Ponce)
Nation, The
Nuevo Día, El (San Juan, P.R.)
New York Times
Prensa, La (New York)
Peacemaker (New York)
Revista Ilustrada de Nueva York, La
Time
Times Herald (Washington, D.C.)
Trinchera Aprista (Mexico City)
Vanguardia, La (San Juan, Costa Rica)

## Books, Articles, and Government Documents

Acosta, Ivonne. La mordaza: Puerto Rico, 1948–1957. Río Piedras: Editorial Edil, 1989.

Acosta-Belén, Edna. "Lola Rodríguez de Tió and the Puerto Rican Struggle for Freedom." In Latina Legacies: Identity, Biography, and Community, edited by Vicki L. Ruíz and Virginia Sánchez Korrol, 84–96. Oxford: Oxford University Press, 2005.

———. Puerto Ricans in the United States: A Brief Chronology. New York: Center for Puerto Rican Studies, 2015.

———. "Puerto Rican Women in Culture, History, and Society." In The Puerto Rican Woman: Perspectives on Culture, History, and Society, 1–29. New York: Praeger, 1986.

Acosta Cruz, María. Dream Nation: Puerto Rican Culture and the Fictions of Independence. New Brunswick, N.J.: Rutgers University Press, 2014.

Acosta Lespier, Ivonne. La mordaza. San Juan: Editorial Edil, 1987.

———. "The Smith Act Goes to San Juan: La Mordaza, 1948–1957." In Bosque-Pérez and Colón Morera, Puerto Rico under Colonial Rule, 59–66.

Albanese, Patrizia. Mothers of the Nation. Toronto: University of Toronto Press, 2006.

Albizu Campos, Pedro. "Concepto de la Raza." In Albizu-Campos Meneses and Rodríguez León, Albizu Campos Escritos, 26–27.

———. "Feminismo y la independencia de Puerto Rico." El Mundo, May 20, 1930.

———. "La mujer libertadora." El Mundo, May 24, 1930.

———. "Proclama ante la muerte de Sandino." In Albizu-Campos Meneses and Rodríguez León, Albizu Campos Escritos, 294–96.

———. "Sufragio." Revolución 1, no. 7, August 24, 1931.

———. "Discurso por el Dr. Pedro Albizu Campos." San Juan: Partido Nacionalista de Puerto Rico, 1971.

Albizu-Campos Meneses, Laura, and Fr. Mario Rodríguez León, eds. Albizu Campos Escritos. Hato Rey, P.R.: Publicaciones Puertorriqueñas, 2007.

"Algunos Miembros de la Comisión Organizadora de COSO." FECH, Quincenario de la Federación de Estudiantes de Chile 1, no. 2 (June 1937): 5.

Allende Gossens, Salvador. "Homenaje a la memoria de Ricardo Latcham, Ruben Azocar, Pedro Albizu Campos y Alfredo Palacios." Senate of Chile, Ordinary Session 39, April 28, 1965, 2159–62.

"Al señor Presidente de los Estados Unidos de Norte America." *FECH, Quincenario de la Federación de Estudiantes de Chile* 1, no. 4 (September 1937): 13.

Anderson, Carol. *White Rage: The Unspoken Truth of Our Racial Divide*. New York: Bloomsbury, 2016.

Anderson, Robert W. "Las elecciones de 1964 en Puerto Rico: Una evaluación." *Revista de Ciencias Sociales* 9, no. 3 (September 1965): 265–71.

Andreu Iglesias, César. *Independencia y socialismo*. San Juan: Librería Estrella Roja, 1951.

———, ed. *Memoirs of Bernardo Vega: A Contribution to the History of the Puerto Rican Community in New York*. New York: Monthly Review Press, 1984.

Andrew, N., and N. Cleven. "The Pan American Centennial Congress." *Hispanic American Historical Review* 6, no. 4 (November 1926): 175–93.

*Annals of the Organization of American States*. Vol. 1, no. 1. Washington, D.C.: Department of Public Information, Pan American Union, 1949.

*Annual Report of the War Department for the Fiscal Year Ended June 30, 1942*. Washington, D.C.: Government Printing Office, 1899.

Anti-imperialist League. *Protest against the Philippine Policy*. Boston: Anti-imperialist League, 1899.

Antler, Joyce. "Imagining Jewish Mothers." In *The Journey Home: Jewish Women and the American Century*, 233–58. New York: Free Press, 1997.

Aponte Vázquez, Pedro. *Albizu: Su persecución por el FBI*. San Juan: Publicaciones René, 2000.

———. *¡Yo acuso! Torturo y asesinato de don Pedro Albizu Campos*. San Juan: Publicaciones René, 1991.

Aretxaga, Begoña. *Shattering Silence: Women, Nationalism, and Political Subjectivity in Northern Ireland*. Princeton, N.J.: Princeton University Press, 1997.

Arroyo, Jossiana. "Living the Political: Julia de Burgos and Lolita Lebrón." *Centro Journal* 26, no. 2 (Fall 2014): 128–55.

———. *Writing Secrecy in Caribbean Freemasonry*. New York: Palgrave Macmillan, 2013.

Arsenault, Raymond. *Freedom Riders: 1961 and the Struggle for Racial Justice*. Oxford: Oxford University Press, 2006.

Ayala, César. *American Sugar Kingdom: The Plantation Economy of the Spanish Caribbean, 1898–1934*. Chapel Hill: University of North Carolina Press, 1999.

Ayala, César, and Laird Bergad. *Agrarian Puerto Rico: Reconsidering Rural Economy and Society, 1899–1940*. Cambridge: Cambridge University Press, 2020.

———. "Rural Puerto Rico in the Early Twentieth Century Reconsidered: Land and Society, 1899–1915." *Latin American Research Review* 37, no. 2 (2002): 65–97.

Ayala, César J., and Rafael Bernabe. *Puerto Rico in the American Century*. Chapel Hill: University of North Carolina Press, 2007.

Ayala, Mario. "La experiencia del Comité Venezolano de Solidaridad con el pueblo argentino (Caracas-Mérida, 1976–1983)." *Opción* 33, no. 83 (2017): 99–136.

Ayoroa Santaliz, José Enrique. *Contracanto al olvido patriotas*. Cayey, P.R.: Mariana Editores, 2009.

———. "Don Ramón Mayoral Barnés." *Claridad*, June 4–10, 1993.

———. "La Insurrección Nacionalista del año 1950." Unpublished ms., 2000.

———. "¿Quién es Juarbe Juarbe? ¿Por qué lo discriminan?" Unpublished ms., 1979.

Azize Vargas, Yamila. "The Emergence of Feminism in Puerto Rico, 1870–1930." In *Latino/a Thought: Culture, Politics, and Society*, edited by Francisco H. Vásquez and Rodolfo D. Torres, 175–84. Lanham, Md.: Rowman and Littlefield, 2009.

———. *La mujer en la lucha*. Río Piedras: Editorial Cultural, 1985.

Bacchetta, Paola, and Margaret Power. *Right-Wing Women around the World: From Conservatives to Extremists*. New York: Routledge, 2002.

Baker, Paula. "The Domestication of Politics: Women and American Political Society, 1780–1920." *American Historical Review* 89, no. 23 (June 1984): 620–47.

Baldoz, Rick, and César Ayala. "The Bordering of America: Colonialism and Citizenship in the Philippines and Puerto Rico." *Centro Journal* 25, no. 1 (Spring 2013): 76–105.

Barceló Miller, María de Fátima. *La lucha por el sufragio femenino en Puerto Rico, 1896–1935*. Río Piedras: Ediciones Huracán, 1997.

———. "Halfhearted Solidarity: Women Workers and the Women's Suffrage Movement in Puerto Rico during the 1920s." In *Puerto Rican Women's History: New Perspectives*, edited by Félix V. Matos Rodríguez and Linda C. Delgado, 126–42. New York: M. E. Sharpe, 1998.

Barney, William L. *The Passage of the Republic: An Interdisciplinary History of Nineteenth-Century America*. Lexington, Mass.: D. C. Heath, 1987.

Beisner, Robert L. *Twelve against Empire: The Anti-imperialists, 1898–1900*. New York: McGraw-Hill, 1968.

Bernand, Carmen. "Colón y la modernidad: De un Centenario a otro." In *Cristóbal Colón, 1506–2006: Historia y leyenda*, 335–44. Seville: Universidad Internacional de Andalucía, 2006.

Berbusse, Edward J. "The Unofficial Intervention of the United States in Mexico's Religious Crisis, 1926–1930." *Americas* 23, no. 1 (July 1966): 28–65.

Bergad, Laird A. "Agrarian History of Puerto Rico, 1870–1930." *Latin American Research Review* 13, no. 3 (1978): 63–94.

Betancourt, Rómulo. "En discurso pronunciado con ocasión de la IX Conferencia Interamericana, en Bogotá, Betancourt expone los que llamó un 'Enfoque Realista de los problemas Americanos' (6 de abril de 1948)." In *Rómulo Betancourt: Selección de escritos políticos, 1929–1981*, edited by Naudy Suárez Figueroa. Caracas, Venezuela: Fundación Rómulo Betancourt, 2006.

Bethell, Leslie, and Ian Roxborough, eds. *Latin America between the Second World War and the Cold War, 1944–1948*. Cambridge: Cambridge University Press, 1992.

———. "Latin America between the Second World War and the Cold War: Some Reflections on the 1945–8 Conjuncture." *Journal of Latin American Studies* 20, no. 1 (May 1988): 167–89.

Bhana, Surendra. *The United States and the Development of the Puerto Rican Status Question, 1936–1968*. Lawrence: University Press of Kansas, 1975.

Black, Ashley. "The Politics of Asylum: Stability, Sovereignty, and Mexican Foreign Policy in the Caribbean Basin, 1945–1959." PhD diss., Stony Brook University, 2018.

Blanshard, Paul. *Democracy and Empire in the Caribbean*. New York: Macmillan, 1947.

Bock, Gisela. "Racism and Sexism in Nazi Germany: Motherhood, Compulsory Sterilization, and the State." In *When Biology Became Destiny: Women in Weimar and Nazi Germany*, edited by Renate Bridenthal, Atina Grossman, and Marion Kaplan, 271–96. New York: Monthly Review Press, 1984.

Bolívar, Simón *El Libertador: Writings of Simón Bolívar*. Translated by Frederick H. Fornoff. Oxford: Oxford University Press, 2003.

"Bono a Favor de Puerto Rico." *FECH, Quincenario de la Federación de Estudiantes de Chile* 1, no. 4 (September 1937): 11.

Borges, Cristóbal A. "Unspoken Prejudice: Racial Politics, Gendered Norms, and the Transformation of Puerto Rican Identity in the Twentieth Century." PhD diss., University of Texas at El Paso, 2014.

Bosque-Pérez, Ramón. "Political Persecution against Puerto Rican Anti-Colonial Activists in the Twentieth Century." In Bosque-Pérez and Colón Morera, *Puerto Rico under Colonial Rule*, 13–47.

———. *The FBI and Puerto Rico: Notes on a Conflictive History*. Testimony before the Congressional Briefing Held by the Judiciary Committee Democratic Office, U.S. House of Representatives, March 28, 2006.

Bosque-Pérez, Ramón, and José Javier Colón Morera. *Las carpetas: Persecución política y derechos civiles in Puerto Rico*. Río Piedras: Centro para la Investigación y Promoción de los Derechos Civiles, 1997.

———. *Puerto Rico under Colonial Rule: Political Persecution and the Quest for Human Rights*. Albany: State University of New York Press, 2006.

Briggs, Laura. *Reproducing Empire: Race, Sex, Science, and U.S. Imperialism in Puerto Rico*. Berkeley: University of California Press, 2003.

Brown, Kathleen M. *Good Wives, Nasty Wenches, and Anxious Patriarchs: Gender, Race, and Power in Colonial Virginia*. Chapel Hill: University of North Carolina Press, 1996.

Burnett, Christina Duffy, and Burke Marshall. "Between the Foreign and the Domestic: The Doctrine of Territorial Incorporation, Invented and Reinvented." In Burnett and Marshall, *Foreign in a Domestic Sense*, 1–36.

Burnett, Christina Duffy, and Burke Marshall. *Foreign in a Domestic Sense: Puerto Rico, American Expansion, and the Constitution*. Durham, N.C.: Duke University Press, 2001.

Cabán, Pedro. *Constructing a Colonial People: Puerto Rico and the United States, 1898–1932*. Boulder, Colo.: Westview Press, 2009.

Calder, Bruce. *The Impact of Intervention: The Dominican Republic during the U.S. Occupation of 1916–1924*. Austin: University of Texas Press, 1984.

Campos, Ricardo, and Juan Flores. "Migración y cultura nacional puertorriqueñas: perspectivas proletarias." In *Antología del pensamiento crítico puertorriqueño contemporáneo*, edited by Anayra Santory Jorge and Mareia Quintero Rivera, 303–54. Buenos Aires: CLASCO, 1979. https://www.jstor.org/stable/j.ctvnpojr5.15#metadata_info_tab_contents.

Canales, Blanca. *La constitución es la revolución*. San Juan: Puerto Rico Comité de Estudios, Congreso Nacional Hostosiano, 1997.

Canales, Nemesio. "El voto femenino." In *Paliques* 72:175–77. San Juan: Ediciones Isla, 1967.

Cancel Miranda, Rafael. *Del cimarrón a los macheteros*. San Juan: Séptimo Ideario, 2008.

———. *Remando bajo la lluvia: sesenta y cinco anécdotas y tres poemas*. San Juan: Sexto Ideario, 2005.

Carr, Barry. *La izquierda mexicana a través del siglo XX*. Mexico City: Ediciones Era, 1996.

———. "Pioneering Transnational Solidarity in the Americas: The Movement in Support of Augusto C. Sandino, 1927–1934." *Journal of Iberian and Latin American Research* 20, no. 2 (2014): 141–52.

Carr, Raymond. *Puerto Rico: A Colonial Experiment*. New York: New York University Press, 1984.

Carrión, Juan Manuel. "Two Variants of Caribbean Nationalism: Marcus Garvey and Albizu Campos." *Centro Journal* 17, no. 1 (Spring 2005): 26–45.

———. "The War of the Flags: Conflicting National Loyalties in a Modern Colonial Situation." *Centro Journal* 18, no. 2 (Fall 2006): 101–23.

Carrión, Juan Manuel, Teresa C. Garcia Ruiz, and Carlos Rodríguez Fraticelli, eds. *La nación puertorriqueña: Ensayos en torno a Pedro Albizu Campos*. San Juan: Editorial de la Universidad de Puerto Rico, 1993.

Casanova de Villaverde, Emilia. *Apuntes biográficos de Emilia Casanova de Villaverde*. New York: n.p., 1874.

Casey, Matt. "Anti-Occupation Collaborations and Post-Colonial Intertwining in Haiti and the Dominican Republic." Paper presented at the 29th Annual Conference Haitian Studies Association, Tulane University, New Orleans, October 31, 2017.

Casteñeda, Jorge G. *Utopia Unarmed: The Latin American Left after the Cold War.* New York: Vintage, 1994.

Castillo Morales, José Ramón. "'Movimiento Libertador' en el primer congreso continental Bolivariano por nuestro América." Aquadilla, P.R.: n.p., 2005.

Castro, Paulino E. *Historia sinóptica del Partido Nacionalista de Puerto Rico.* San Juan: n.p., 1947.

Chase, Michelle. *Revolution within the Revolution: Women and Gender Politics in Cuba, 1952–1962.* Chapel Hill: University of North Carolina Press, 2013.

Chatterjee, Partha. *The Nation and Its Fragments: Colonial and Postcolonial Histories.* Princeton, N.J.: Princeton University Press, 1993.

Clark, Truman R. "Prohibition in Puerto Rico, 1917–1933." *Journal of Latin American Studies* 27, no. 1 (February 1995): 77–97.

Clark, Victor S. *Porto Rico and Its Problems.* Washington, D.C.: Brookings Institution, 1930.

Colby, Jason M. "Banana Growing and Negro Management: Race, Labor, and Jim Crow, 1884–1930." *Diplomatic History* 30, no. 4 (September 2006): 595–612.

Coll y Cuchí, José. *El nacionalismo en Puerto Rico.* San Juan: Gil de Lamadrid Hnos., 1923.

Collado-Schwarz, Angel. *Truman y Puerto Rico: El origen de un proyecto descolonizador fallido.* San Juan: Fundación Voz del Centro, 2019.

Collazo, Oscar. *Memorias de un patriota encarcelado.* San Juan: Fundación Manrique Cabrera, 2000.

Collazo Cortés, Lydia. *Entre dos paréntesis (Memorias de una nacionalista).* San Juan: Los Libros de la Iguana, 2018.

Colón, Alicia, Margarita Mergal, and Nilsa Torres. *Participación de la mujer en la historia de Puerto Rico.* Río Piedras: Centro de Investigaciones Sociales, 1986.

Comité Cubano Pro Libertad de Patriotas Puertorriqueños. *Por la independencia de Puerto Rico: Por la libertad de sus patriotas.* Vol. 1 of *Publicaciones del Comité Cubano pro Libertad de Patriotas Puertorriqueños.* Havana: n.p., 1939.

Committee in Solidarity with Puerto Rican Independence. *Towards People's War for Independence and Socialism in Puerto Rico: In Defense of Armed Struggle.* N.p., 1979.

Concepción de Gracia, Gilberto. *En nombre de la verdad.* San Juan: Fundación para la Libertad, 2007.

Conn, Stetson, Rose C. Engelman, and Byron Fairchild. *Guarding the United States and Its Outposts.* Washington, D.C.: Office of the Chief of Military History, 1964.

Connell, Robert W. *Masculinities.* Berkeley: University of California Press, 1987.

Corominas, Enrique V. *Puerto Rico libre.* Buenos Aires: El Editorial, 1950.

Corretjer, Juan Antonio, and Consuelo Tapia Lee. "Mariana Bracetti y Albizu Campos." In *Re: Mujer; A Reproduction of Writings by Juan Antonio Corretjer and Consuelo Tapia Lee,* 9–10. Ciales, P.R.: Casa Corretjer, 1997.

Corretjer, Juan Antonio. "Albizu Campos y las huelgas en los años 30." In *Albizu Campos,* 121–41. Chicago: El Coquí, 1970.

———. *El líder de la desesperación.* Guaynabo, P.R.: Federación Universitaria Pro Independencia, 1972.

Currier, Ashley. "The Aftermath of Decolonization: Gender and Sexual Dissidence in Postindependence Namibia." *Signs* 37, no. 2 (2012): 441–567.

Darío, Rubén. *Selected Writings.* Edited by Ilan Stevens. New York: Penguin Books, 2005.

Dávila Dávila, Ovidio. "Los bonos del Partido Nacionalista para la reconstitución de la República de Puerto Rico." *Revista de Instituto Cultura Puertorriqueña* 6, no. 11 (2005): 32–43.

Dávila Marichal, José Manuel. "¡Atención, firmes, de frente, marchen! Los Cadetes de la República, las Hijas de la Libertad y el Partido Nacionalista de Puerto Rico." M.A. thesis, Universidad de Puerto Rico, Río Piedras, 2012.

———. "Estudio del nacionalismo revolucionario puertorriqueño a través de una fotografía." *Revista Alborada, Universidad de Puerto Rico en Utuado,* June 2015–May 2016, 37–46.

———. "'La mujer no debe, no puede permanecer inhábil': Las Hijas de la Libertad— juventud, género, ideología y funcionamiento interno, 1932–1935." *Instituto de Cultura Puertorriqueño* 3, no. 7 (September 2017): 50–63.

De Albizu Campos, Laura. *Albizu Campos y la independencia de Puerto Rico.* Hato Rey, P.R.: Publicaciones Puertorriqueñas, 2007.

Degras, Jane. *The Communist International, 1919–1943, Documents.* Vol. 3, *The Seventh Comintern Congress.* London: Frank Cass, 1971.

De Jesús, Anthony. "I Have Endeavored to Seize the Beautiful Opportunity for Learning Here: Pedro Albizu Campos at Harvard a Century Ago." *Latino Studies* 9 (2011): 473–85.

Dekar, Paul R. *Creating the Beloved Community.* Telford, Pa.: Cascadia, 2005.

De la Fuente, Alejandro. *A Nation for All: Race, Inequality, and Politics in Twentieth-Century Cuba.* Chapel Hill: University of North Carolina Press, 2001.

Del Moral, Solsiree. *Negotiating Empire: The Cultural Politics of Schools in Puerto Rico, 1898–1952.* Madison: University of Wisconsin Press, 2013.

Deutsch, Sandra. *Las Derechas: The Extreme Right in Argentina, Brazil, and Chile, 1889–1939.* Stanford, Calif.: Stanford University Press, 1989.

Devés Valdés, Eduardo. *Del "Ariel" de Rodó a la CEPAL (1900–1950).* Santiago, Chile: Editorial Biblos, 2001.

Díaz Feliciano, Luis A. "El Partido Comunista Puertorriqueño y la táctica del Frente Popular, 1934–1945." MS thesis, Centro de Estudios Avanzados, San Juan, 2015.

Dietz, James. *Economic History of Puerto Rico: Institutional Change and Capitalist Development.* Princeton, N.J.: Princeton University Press, 1980.

Dimitrov, Georgi. "The Fascist Offensive and the Tasks of the Communist International in the Struggle of the Working Class against Fascism." *Georgi Dimitrov, Selected Works.* Vol. 2. Sofia, Bulgaria: Sofia Press, 1972.

———. *Report of the Seventh World Congress.* London: Modern Books, 1936.

Dirik, Dilar. "Overcoming the Nation-State: Women's Autonomy and Radical Democracy in Kurdistan." In Mulholland, Montagna, and Sanders-McDonagh, *Gendering Nationalism,* 145–63.

Domínguez, Jorge I. *Insurrection or Loyalty: The Breakdown of the Spanish American Empire.* Cambridge, Mass.: Harvard University Press, 1980.

Drake, Paul W. *Socialism and Populism in Chile, 1932–52.* Urbana: University of Illinois Press, 1978.

Duany, Jorge. "Nation on the Move: The Construction of Cultural Identities in Puerto Rico and the Diaspora." *American Ethnologist* 27, no. 1 (2000): 5–30.

———. *The Puerto Rican Nation on the Move: Identities on the Island and in the United States.* Chapel Hill: University of North Carolina Press, 2002.

Duncan, Natanya. "The 'Efficient Womanhood' of the Universal Negro Improvement Association: 1919–1930." Ph.D. diss., University of Florida, 2009.

Durham, Martin. *Women and Fascism.* London: Routledge, 1998.

Eddins, Crystal. "'Rejoice! Your Wombs Will Not Beget Slaves!': Marronnage as Reproductive Justice in Colonial Haiti." *Gender and History* 32, no. 3 (October 2020): 562–80.

Eisenberg, Carolyn. *Drawing the Line: the American Decision to Divide Germany.* Cambridge: Cambridge University Press, 1997.

Eley, Geoff. *Forging Democracy: The History of the Left in Europe, 1850–2000*. Oxford: Oxford University Press, 2002.

Emeterio Betances, Ramón. "A los puertorriqueños." In Ojeda Reyes and Estrade, *Obras completas*, 67–68.

———. "Los diez mandamientos de los hombres libres." In Ojeda Reyes and Estrade, *Obras completas*, 69–70.

———. "Patria, justicia, libertad." In Ojeda Reyes and Estrade, *Obras completas*, 59–66.

Enloe, Cynthia. *Bananas, Beaches, and Bases: Making Feminist Sense of International Politics*. Berkeley: University of California Press, 2000.

Estades-Font, María E. "The Critical Year of 1936 through the Reports of the Military Intelligence Division." In Bosque-Pérez and Colón Morera, *Puerto Rico under Colonial Rule*, 49–58.

Estrade, Paul. "Remarques sur le caractère tardif, et avancé, de la prise de conscience nationale dans des Antilles espagnoles." *Cahiers du Monde Hispanique et Luso-Brésilien* 38 (1982): 89–117.

Faber, Sebastian. "'La hora ha llegado': Hispanism, Pan-Americanism, and the Hope of Spanish/American Glory (1938–1948)." In *Ideologies of Hispanism*, edited by Mabel Moraña, 39–79. Nashville, Tenn.: Vanderbilt University Press, 2005.

Falcón, Luis M. "Migration and Development: The Case of Puerto Rico." In *Determinants of Emigration from Mexico, Central America, and the Caribbean*, edited by Sergio Díaz-Briquets and Sidney Weintraub, 145–88. Boulder, Colo.: Westview Press, 1991.

Fanon, Franz. *Black Skin, White Masks*. Translated by Richard Philcox. New York: Grove Press, 1967.

Federal Bureau of Investigation. FBI Documents during the Roosevelt Years, Reel 19. "Pedro Albizu Campos and the Nationalist Party."

———. FBI Documents during the Roosevelt Years, Reel 20. "Pedro Albizu Campos and the Nationalist Party." Hoover Supplemental Report to Hopkins. September 23, 1943.

———. FBI Report, Reel 19. "Nationalist Party Celebration of Grito de Lares." September 23, 1943.

———. *Nationalist Party of Puerto Rico (NPPR)*. Report SJ 100-3. Vol. 23. San Juan, July 31, 1952.

———. *Quarterly Summary Report*. 105-11898-NR. San Juan, January 31, 1957.

———. "Subject: Pedro Albizu Campos." File No. 105-105-11898. Section 15.

Feinberg, Leslie. *Transgender Warriors: Making History from Joan of Arc to Dennis Rodman*. Boston: Beacon Press, 1996.

Fernández, Ronald. *Prisoners of Colonialism: The Struggle for Justice in Puerto Rico*. Monroe, Me.: Common Courage Press, 1994.

Fernández-Olmos, Margarite, and Lisbeth Paravisini-Gebert. *Creole Religions of the Caribbean: An Introduction from Vodou and Santería to Obeah and Espiritismo*. New York: New York University Press, 2003.

Fernández Sanz, Yolanda. *Trina Padilla de Sanz: La hija del Caribe*. San Juan: Editorial Plaza Mayor, 1996.

Fernós López-Cepero, Antonio. *La correspondencia secreta entre Luis Muñoz Marín y Ruby Black, 1933–1946*. San Juan: Ediciones Puerto, 2010.

Ferrao, Luis Angel. *Pedro Albizu Campos y el nacionalismo puertorriqueño*. San Juan: Editorial Cultural, 1990.

Ferreira de Cassone, Florencia. *Claridad y el internacionalismo americano*. Buenos Aires: Editorial Claridad, 1998.

Flynn, Elizabeth Gurley. *My Life as a Political Prisoner*. New York: International Publishers, 1972.

Foner, Philip. *A History of Cuba and Its Relations with the United States.* New York: International Publishers, 1962.

*Foreign Relations of the United States Diplomatic Papers, 1936.* Vol. 5: *The American Republics.* Edited by Matilda F. Axton et al. Washington, D.C.: Government Printing Office, 1954.

*Foreign Relations of the United States, 1948.* Vol. 9: *The Western Hemisphere.* Washington, D.C.:, Government Printing Office 1972.

*Foreign Relations of the United States, 1950.* Vol. 2: *The United Nations; The Western Hemisphere.* Edited by S. Everett Gleason and Frederick Aandahl. Washington, D.C.: Government Printing Office, 1976.

*Foreign Relations of the United States, 1951.* Vol. 2: *The United Nations; The Western Hemisphere.* Edited by Ralph R. Goodwin, N. Stephen Kane, and Harriet D. Schwar. Washington, D.C.: Government Printing Office, 1979.

*Foreign Relations of the United States, 1952–1954.* Vol. 3: *United Nations Affairs.* Edited by Ralph R. Goodwin. Washington, D.C.: Government Printing Office, 1979.

Fortuño Janeiro, Luis. *Album histórico de Ponce.* Ponce, P.R.: n.p., 1963.

Franqui-Rivera, Harry. "Race and the Myth Surrounding the Military Service of Pedro Albizu Campos." inCOHERENT THOUGHTS (blog), April 21, 2021. https://incoherentthoughtsblog.com/2021/04/21/race-and-the-myth-surrounding-the-military-service-of-pedro-albizu-campos/.

———. *Soldiers of the Nation: Military Service and Modern Puerto Rico, 1868–1952.* Lincoln: University of Nebraska Press, 2018.

Friedman, Andrea. *Citizenship in Cold War America: The National Security State and the Possibilities of Dissent.* Amherst: University of Massachusetts Press, 2014.

———. "The Empire at Home: Radical Pacifism and Puerto Rico in the 1950s." In *A New Insurgency: The "Port Huron Statement" and Its Times,* ed. Howard Brick and Gregory Parker. Ann Arbor, Mich.: Maize Books, 2015. http://dx.doi.org/10.3998/maize.13545967.0001.001.

Friedman, Max Paul. "The Good Neighbor Policy." *Latin American History,* January 24, 2018. https://doi.org/10.1093/acrefore/9780199366439.013.222.

———. *Nazis and Good Neighbors: The United States Campaign against the Germans of Latin America in World War II.* New York: Cambridge University Press, 2003.

Fromm, Georg H. *Cesar Andreu Iglesias: Aproximación a su vida y obra.* Río Piedras: Ediciones Huracán, 1977.

Fusté, José. "Repeating Islands of Debt: Historicizing the Transcolonial Relationality of Puerto Rico's Economic Crisis." *Radical History Review* 128 (May 2017): 91–119.

Gadea, Hilda. *My Life with Che: The Making of a Revolutionary.* New York: St. Martin's Press, 2008.

Galicia Martínez, Alejandra G. "Sandino en Ariel: Representaciones del héroe en una revista antiimperialista." In *El imaginario antiimperialista en América Latina,* edited by Andrés Kozol, Florencia Grossi, and Delfina Moroni, 141–56. Buenos Aires: CLASCO, 2015.

Gannett, Henry. *Statistical Atlas of the United States.* Washington, D.C.: U.S. Census Office, 1903.

García Carrillo, Eugenio. *Cartas selectas de Joaquín García Monge.* San José, Costa Rica: Editorial Costa Rica, 1983.

García Ferreria, Roberto. "'El caso de Guatemala': Arévalo, Arbenz y la izquierda Uruguaya, 1950–1971." *Mesoamérica* 49 (January–December 2007): 25–58.

García Muñiz, Humberto. "Puerto Rico and the United States: The United Nations Role, 1953–1975." *Revista Jurídica de la Universidad de Puerto Rico* 53 (1984): 1–265.

———. "Puerto Rico in the United Nations, 1953: An Appraisal." *Caribbean Studies* 16, no. 2 (July 1976): 44–91.

———. "U.S. Military Installations in Puerto Rico: An Essay on Their Role and Purpose." *Caribbean Studies* 24, nos. 3, 4 (1991): 79–97.

———. "U.S. Military Installations in Puerto Rico: Controlling the Caribbean." In *Colonial Dilemma—Critical Perspectives on Puerto Rico*, edited by Edwin Meléndez and Edgardo Meléndez, 53–65. Boston: South End Press, 1993.

García Passalacqua, Juan Manuel. "Ariadne's Thread—Puerto Rican Nationality in the Caribbean." In *Ethnicity, Race and Nationality in the Caribbean*, edited by Juan Manual Carrión, 37–66. Río Piedras: Institute of Caribbean Studies, 1997.

García-Bryce, Iñigo. *Haya de la Torre and the Pursuit of Power in Twentieth-Century Peru and Latin America*. Chapel Hill: University of North Carolina Press, 2018.

Gates, John M. "Philippine Guerrillas, American Anti-imperialists, and the Election of 1900." *Pacific Historical Review* 46, no. 1 (February 1977): 51–64.

Gates, Merrill E., ed. "George Whitfield Davis." In *Men of Mark in America*, 277–79. Washington, D.C.: Men of Mark Publishing, 1905.

Gatell, Frank Otto. "Independence Rejected: Puerto Rico and the Tydings Bill of 1936." *Hispanic American Historic Review* 38, no. 1 (February 1958): 25–44.

Gautier Mayoral, Carmen, and María del Pilar Arguelles. *Puerto Rico y la ONU*. Río Piedras: Editorial Edil, 1978.

Geggus, David P., ed. *The Impact of the Haitian Revolution in the Atlantic World*. Charleston: University of South Carolina Press, 2001.

Gilderhus, Mark T. *The Second Century. U.S.–Latin American Relations since 1898*. Wilmington, Del.: Scholarly Resources, 2000.

Gilderhus, Mark T., David C. LaFevor, and Michael J. LaRosa. *The Third Century: U.S.–Latin American Relations since 1899*. Lanham, Md.: Rowman and Littlefield, 2007.

Gleijeses, Piero. "The Agrarian Reform of Jacobo Arbenz." *Journal of Latin American Studies* 21, no. 3 (October 1989): 453–80.

———. *Visions of Freedom: Havana, Washington, Pretoria, and the Struggle for Southern Africa, 1976–1991*. Chapel Hill: University of North Carolina Press, 2013.

Gluckstein, Donny. *A People's History of the Second World War: Resistance versus Empire*. London: Pluto Press, 2012.

Go, Julian. *American Empire and the Politics of Meaning*. Durham, N.C.: Duke University Press, 2008.

———. "Anti-imperialism in the U.S. Territories after 1898." In *Empire's Twin: U.S. Anti-imperialism from the Founding Era to the Age of Terrorism*, 79–96. Ithaca, N.Y.: Cornell University Press, 2015.

Gobat, Michael. "The Invention of Latin America: A Transnational History of Anti-imperialism, Democracy, and Race." *American Historical Review* 118, no. 5 (December 2013): 1345–75.

Godreau, Isar. *Scripts of Blackness: Race, Cultural Nationalism and U.S. Colonialism in Puerto Rico*. Urbana: University of Illinois Press, 2005.

Goebel, Michel. *Anti-imperial Metropolis: Interwar Paris and the Seeds of Third World Nationalism*. New York: Cambridge University Press, 2015.

González-Cruz, Michael. *Nacionalismo revolucionario puertorriqueño: La lucha armada, los intelectuales y los presos politicos y de guerra*. San Juan: Editorial Trastallares, 2021.

———. *Puerto Rican Revolutionary Nationalism (1956–2005)*. Binghamton: State University of New York, 2005.

González-Cruz, Michael, Alberto Marquez Sola, and Lorena Terando. "The U.S. Invasion of Puerto Rico: Occupation and Resistance to the Colonial State, 1898 to the Present." *Latin American Perspectives* 25, no. 5 (September 1998): 7–26.

Griffin, Roger. *The Nature of Fascism*. New York: Routledge, 1993.

Gosse, Van. "United States Textbooks and Puerto Rican History." *Modern American History* 2, no. 2 (2019): 179–82.

———. *Where the Boys Are: Cuba, Cold War America and the Making of a New Left*. London: Verso, 1993.

Grosfoguel, Ramon. "Puerto Ricans in the USA: A Comparative Approach." *Journal of Ethnic and Migration Studies* 25, no. 2 (April 1999): 233–49.

Gruening, Ernest. *Many Battles: The Autobiography of Ernest Gruening*. New York: Liveright, 1973.

Hamnett, Brian R. "Process and Pattern: A Re-Examination of the Ibero-American Independence Movements, 1808–1826." *Journal of Latin American Studies* 29, no. 2 (May 1997): 279–328.

Hanson, Joyce Ann. *Mary McLeod Bethune and Black Women's Political Activism*. Columbia: University of Missouri Press, 2018.

Harmer, Tanya. *Beatriz Allende: A Revolutionary Life in Cold War America*. Chapel Hill: University of North Carolina Press, 2020.

Harris, Lashawn. "Running with the Reds: African American Women and the Communist Party during the Great Depression." *Journal of African American History* 94, no. 1 (Winter 2009): 21–43.

Hart, Justin. *Empire of Ideas: The Origins of Public Diplomacy and the Transformation of U.S. Foreign Policy*. New York: Oxford University Press, 2013.

Hatzky, Christine. *Cubans in Angola: South-South Cooperation and Transfer of Knowledge, 1976–1991*. Madison: University of Wisconsin Press, 2014.

———. "Cuba's Concept of 'International Solidarity': Political Discourse South-South Cooperation with Angola, and the Molding of Transnational Identities." In Stites Mor, *Human Rights and Transnational Solidarity in Cold War Latin America*, 143–74.

———. *Juan Antonio Mella: Una biografía*. Santiago, Cuba: Instituto Cubano del Libro, Editorial Oriente, 2008.

Hatzky, Christine, and Jessica Stites Mor. "Latin American Transnational Solidarities: Contexts and Critical Research Paradigms." *Journal of Iberian and Latin American Research* 20, no. 2 (2014): 127–40.

Haya de la Torre, Victor Raúl. *Construyendo el aprismo: Artículos y cartas desde el exilio (1924–31)*. Buenos Aires: Colección Claridad, 1933.

Hays, Arthur Garfield. *Report of the Commission of Inquiry on Civil Rights in Puerto Rico*. Washington, D.C.: Commission of Inquiry on Civil Rights in Puerto Rico, 1937.

Healey, Dorothy Ray, and Maurice Isserman. *California Red: A Life in the American Communist Party*. Urbana: University of Illinois Press, 1993.

Hector, Michel. "Solidarité et luttes politiques en Haïti: L'action internationale de Joseph Jolibois Fils, 1927–1936." *Revue de la Société Haïtienne d'Histoire, de Géographie et de Géologie* 49, no. 176 (June 1993): 7–54.

Hernández Prieto, Carmen Esther. "Calle 13 y su discurso social." *Investigación y Desarrollo* 26, no. 2 (2018): 60–83.

Hill, Cyril D. "Citizenship of Married Women." *American Journal of International Law* 18, no. 4 (October 1924): 720–36.

Hoffnung-Garskof, Jesse. *Racial Migrations: New York City and the Revolutionary Politics of the Spanish Caribbean*. Princeton, N.J.: Princeton University Press, 2019.

———. "To Abolish the Law of Castes: Merit, Manhood and the Problem of Colour in the Puerto Rican Liberal Movement, 1873–92." *Social History* 36, no. 3 (October 2011): 312–42.

Hudson, Nicholas. "From 'Nation' to 'Race': The Origin of Racial Classification in Eighteenth-Century Thought." *Eighteenth-Century Studies* 29, no. 3 (1996): 247–64.

Hunter, Stephen, and John Bainbridge Jr. *American Gunfight: The Plot to Kill President Truman—and the Shoot-Out That Stopped It*. New York: Simon and Schuster, 2006.

Iber, Patrick. *Neither Peace nor Freedom: The Cultural Cold War in Latin America*. Cambridge, Mass.: Harvard University Press, 2015.

Immerwahr, Daniel. *How to Hide an Empire: A History of the Greater United States*. New York: Farrar, Straus, and Giroux, 2019.

James, Winston. *Holding Aloft the Banner of Ethiopia: Caribbean Radicalism in Early Twentieth-Century America*. London: Verso Press, 1998.

Jeifets, Lazar, and Víctor Jeifets. "Jaime Nevarez y la fundación del movimiento comunista y antiimperialista de Puerto Rico." *Pacarina del Sur* 5, no. 21 (October–December 2014). www.pacarinadelsur.comindex.php?option=com_content&view=article&id=1037&catid=5.

———. *América Latina en la Internacional Comunista, 1919–1943: Diccionario biográfico*. Santiago, Chile: n.p., 2015.

Jiménez Aponte, Christian J. "*La Urna como sepulcro*: La posición de Pedro Albizu Campos sobre el sistema electoral en Puerto Rico." Caguas, P.R.: n.p., March 2016.

Jiménez, Mónica. "Looking for a Way Forward in the Past: Lessons from the Puerto Rican Nationalist Party." In *Aftershocks of Disaster: Puerto Rico before and after the Storm*, edited by Yarimar Bonilla and Marisol LeBrón, 263–70. Chicago: Haymarket Books, 2019.

Jiménez de Wagenheim, Olga. *Nationalist Heroines: Puerto Rican Women History Forgot, 1930s–1950s*. Princeton, N.J.: Markus Wiener, 2016.

———. *Puerto Rico: An Interpretative History from Pre-Columbian Times to 1900*. Princeton, N.J.: Markus Weiner, 1998.

———. *Puerto Rico's Revolt for Independence: El Grito de Lares*. Boulder, Colo.: Westview, 1985.

Jiménez-Muñoz, Gladys M. "'Race' and Class among *Nacionalista* Women in Interwar Puerto Rico: The Activism of Dominga de la Cruz Becerril and Trina Padilla de Sanz." *Caribbean Review of Gender Studies* 12 (2018): 169–98.

———. "'So We Decided to Come and Ask You Ourselves': The 1928 U.S. Congressional Hearings on Women's Suffrage in Puerto Rico." In *Puerto Rican Jam: Essays on Culture and Politics*, 140–65. Minneapolis: University of Minnesota Press, 1997.

Johnson, Robert David. "Anti-imperialism and the Good Neighbour Policy: Ernest Gruening and Puerto Rican Affairs, 1934–1939." *Journal of Latin American Studies* 29, no. 1 (February 1997): 89–110.

Jones, Jean. *The League against Imperialism*. Socialist History Occasional Pamphlet Series, no. 4. Preston, U.K.: Lancashire Community Press, 1996.

Joseph, Miranda. *Against the Romance of Community*. Minneapolis: University of Minnesota Press, 2002.

"Juan Juarbe y Juarbe habla para la Fech." *FECH, Quincenario de la Federación de Estudiantes de Chile* 1, no. 3 (July 1937): 1–2.

Juarbe Juarbe, Juan. "Autobiografía." Unpublished ms. Havana, 1979.

———. *El derecho de Puerto Rico a su independencia*. Mexico City: Talleres de Impresiones Modernas, 1954.

———. *Puerto Rico: Problema internacional*. Havana: Editorial La Verdad, 1951.

———. "Puerto Rico lucha por su Independencia." *Humanismo: Revista Mensual de Cultura* 19/20 (March–April–May 1954): 16–43.

Kanellos, Nicolás, and Helvetia Martell. *Recovering the U.S. Hispanic Literary Heritage*. Houston, Tex.: Arte Público Press, 2000.

Kaplan, Caren, Norma Alarcon, and Minoo Moallem, eds. *Between Women and Nation: Nationalisms, Transnationalism Feminisms, and the State*. Durham, N.C.: Duke University Press, 2004.

Karush, Matthew, ed. *The New Cultural History of Peronism: Power and Identity in Mid-Century Argentina*. Durham, N.C.: Duke University Press, 2010.

Kersffeld, Daniel. *Contra el imperio: La historia de la Liga Anti-imperialista de las Américas*. Mexico City: Siglo Veintiuno Editores, 2013.

Kinsbruner, Jay. *Independence in Spanish America: Civil Wars, Revolutions, and Underdevelopment*. Albuquerque: University of New Mexico Press, 2000.

Kozol, Andrés. "Estaciones del antiimperialismo rioplatenses." In *El imaginario anti-imperialista en América Latina*, edited by Andrés Kozol, Florencia Grossi, and Delfina Moroni, 25–51. Buenos Aires: CLASCO, 2015.

Lang, George. "A Primer of Haitian Literature in Kreyol." *Research in African Literatures* 35, no. 2 (Summer 2004): 128–40.

Laó-Montes, Augustín. "Afro-Latin American Feminisms at the Cutting Edge of Emerging Political-Epistemic Movements." *Meridians* 14, no. 2 (2016): 1–24.

Latin American Task Force. *Vito Marcantonio: Fighter for Puerto Rico's Independence*. Philadelphia: American Friends Service Committee, n.d.

Legrás, Horacio. "La voluntad revolucionaria: Sobre las memorias de José Vasconcelos." *Revista de Crítica Literaria Latinoamericana* 33, no. 66 (2007): 53–76.

Levy, Teresita A. *Puerto Ricans in the Empire: Tobacco Growers and U.S. Colonialism*. New Brunswick, N.J.: Rutgers University Press, 2015.

Lewis, Gordon K. *Puerto Rico: Freedom and Power in the Caribbean*. New York: Harper Torchbooks, 1963.

Lloréns, Hilda. *Imagining the Great Puerto Rican Family: Framing Nation, Race, and Gender during the American Century*. Lanham, Md.: Lexington Books, 2014.

———. "'Racialization Works Differently Here in Puerto Rico, Do Not Bring Your U.S.-Centric Ideas about Race Here!,'" *Black Perspective*, March 3, 2020, https://www.aaihs.org/racialization-works-differently-here-in-puerto-rico-do-not-bring-your-u-s-centric-ideas-about-race-here/.

Lomas, Laura. "Migration and Decolonial Politics in Two Afro-Latino Poets: 'Pachín' Marín and 'Tato' Laviera." *Review: Literature and Arts of the Americas* 4, no 2 (2014): 155–63.

Love, Eric T. L. *Race over Empire: Racism and U.S. Imperialism, 1865–1900*. Chapel Hill: University of North Carolina Press, 2004.

Loveman, Mara. "The U.S. Census and the Contested Rules of Racial Classification in Early Twentieth-Century Puerto Rico." *Caribbean Studies* 35, no. 2 (July–December 2007): 79–114.

Loveman, Mara, and Jeronimo O. Muñiz. "How Puerto Rico Became White: Boundary Dynamics and Intercensus Racial Reclassification." *American Sociological Review* 72, no. 6 (December 2007): 915–39.

Lynn, Conrad. *There Is a Fountain: The Autobiography of a Civil Rights Lawyer*. Chicago: Lawrence Hill Books, 1993.

Mahan, Captain A. T. *The Influence of Sea Power upon History, 1660–1783*. 15th ed. Boston: Little, Brown, 1898.

Maldonado Denis, Manuel. "Las perspectivas del nacionalismo latinoamericano: El caso de Puerto Rico." *Revista Mexicana de Sociología* 38, no. 4 (October–December 1976): 799–810.

———. "Aproximación crítica al fenómeno nacionalista en Puerto Rico." In *Antología del pensamiento crítico puertorriqueño contemporáneo*, edited by Anayra Santory Jorge and Mareia Quintero Rivera, 277–302. Buenos Aires: CLASCO, 1977. https://www.jstor.org/stable/pdf/j.ctvnpojr5.14.pdf.

Mañach, Jorge. "Recuerdos de Albizu Campos." In *Hablan sobre Albizu Campos*, 6–13. San Juan: Editorial Jelofe, 1979.

Marino, Katherine. *Feminism for the Americas: The Making of an International Human Rights Movement.* Chapel Hill: University of North Carolina Press, 2019.

Marín Torres, Heriberto. *Eran Ellos.* 3rd ed. Río Piedras: n.p., 2000.

Martí, José. "Nuestra América." 1891. Translated by Esther Allen for Centro de Estudios Martianos. Accessed September 7, 2022. http://www.josemarti.cu/publicacion/nuestra-america-version-ingles/.

Márquez Macias, Rosario, ed. *Huelva y América: Cien años de Americanismo, revista "La Rábida."* Seville: Universidad Internacional de Andalucía, 2012.

Martínez-Fernández, Luis. "Political Change in the Spanish Caribbean during the United States Civil War and Its Aftermath, 1861–1871." *Caribbean Studies* 27, no. 1/2 (January–June 1994): 37–64.

Materson, Lisa G. "Ruth Reynolds, Solidarity Activism, and the Struggle against U.S. Colonialism in Puerto Rico." *Modern American History* 2, no. 2 (2019): 183–87.

McCaffrey, Katherine T. *Military Power and Popular Protest: The U.S. Navy in Vieques, Puerto Rico.* New Brunswick, N.J.: Rutgers University Press, 2002.

——. "Social Struggle against the U.S. Navy in Vieques, Puerto Rico: Two Movements in History." *Latin American Perspectives* 33, no. 1 (January 2006): 83–101.

McClintock, Anne. *Imperial Leather: Race, Gender, and Sexuality in the Colonial Context.* New York: Routledge, 2005.

McCullers, Molly. "'We Do It So That We Will Be Men': Masculinity Politics in Colonial Namibia, 1915–48." *Journal of African History* 52, no. 1 (2011): 43–62.

McEnaney, Laura. *Civil Defense Begins at Home: Militarization Meets Everyday Life in the Fifties.* Princeton, N.J.: Princeton University Press, 2000.

McGreery, David. "Wireless Empire: The United States and Radio Communications in Central America and the Caribbean, 1904–1926." *Southeast Latin Americanist* 33 (Summer 1993): 23–41.

McGuire, Danielle L. *At the Dark End of the Street: Black Women, Rape, and Resistance—A New History of the Civil Rights Movement from Rosa Parks to the Rise of the Black Power Movement.* New York: Penguin Random House, 2011.

McPherson, Alan. *The Invaded: How Latin Americans and Their Allies Fought and Ended U.S. Occupation.* New York: Oxford University Press, 2014.

——. "Joseph Jolibois Fils and the Flaws of Haitian Resistance to U.S. Occupation." *Journal of Haitian Studies* 16, no. 2 (2010): 120–47.

Meade, Teresa A. *A History of Latin America, 1800 to the Present.* Chichester, U.K.: Wiley-Blackwell, 2010.

Medina Ramírez, Ramón. *El movimiento libertador en la historia de Puerto Rico.* 3rd ed. Vol. 1. San Juan: Ediciones Puerto, 2016.

——. *El movimiento libertador en la historia de Puerto Rico.* Vol. 2. Santurce: Puerto Rico Printing, 1954.

Meisler, Stanley. *United Nations: The First Fifty Years.* New York: Atlantic Monthly Press, 1995.

Meléndez, Edgardo. *Patria: Puerto Rican Revolutionary Exiles in Late Nineteenth-Century New York.* New York: Centro Press, 2020.

Meléndez-Badillo, Jorell A. "Imagining Resistance: Organizing the Puerto Rican Southern Agricultural Strike of 1905." *Caribbean Studies* 43 (July–December 2015): 35–81.

——. "Mateo and Juana: Racial Silencing, Epistemic Violence, and Counterarchives in Puerto Rican Labor History." *International Labor and Working-Class History* 96 (Fall 2019): 103–21.

——. "A Party of Ex-convicts: Bolívar Ochart, Carceral Logics, and the Socialist Party in Early Twentieth-Century Puerto Rico." *Hispanic American Historical Review* 101, no. 1 (February 2021): 73–99.

———. *Voces libertarias: Los orígenes del anarquismo en Puerto Rico*. Santurce, P.R.: Ediciones C.C.C., 2013.

Melgar Bao, Ricardo. "The Anti-imperialist League of the Americas between the East and Latin America." *Latin American Perspectives* 35, no. 2 (March 2008): 9–24.

Mella, Julio Antonio. *Documentos y artículos*. Havana: Instituto de Historia del Movimiento Comunista y la Revolución Socialista de Cuba, 1975.

Meneses Albizu Campos, Cristina, and Silvia Lora Gamarra. *Una vida de amor y sacrificio*. San Juan: Publicaciones Puertorriqueños, 2009.

Metscher, Priscilla. *James Connolly and the Reconquest of Ireland*. Minneapolis, Minn.: MEP, 2002.

Meyer, Gerald. "Pedro Albizu Campos, Gilberto Concepción de Gracia, and Vito Marcantonio's Collaboration in the Cause of Puerto Rico's Independence." *Centro Journal* 23, no. 1 (Spring 2011): 87–123.

———. *Vito Marcantonio: Radical Politician, 1902–1954*. Albany: State University of New York Press, 1989.

Meyer, Jean A. *The Cristero Rebellion: The Mexican People between Church and State*. Cambridge: Cambridge University Press, 1976.

———. "Revolution and Reconstruction in the 1920s." In *Mexico since Independence*, edited by Leslie Bethell, 201–40. Cambridge: Cambridge University Press, 1991.

Meyer, Michael C., and William L. Sherman. *The Course of Mexican History*. 5th ed. New York: Oxford University Press, 1995.

Miller, Nicola. *In the Shadow of the State: Intellectuals and the Quest for National Identity in Twentieth-Century Spanish America*. London: Verso, 1999.

Mintz, Sidney W. "The Culture History of a Puerto Rican Sugar Cane Plantation, 1876–1949." *Hispanic American Historical Review* 33, no. 2 (May 1953): 224–51.

"Minutes of the Second Congress of the Communist International." Fourth Session, July 25, 1920. Marxists Internet Archive: History Archive, www.marxists.org/history /international/comintern/2nd-congress/ch04.htm.

Molina Jiménez, Iván. "Los comunistas y la publicidad en Costa Rica: El caso del periódico *Trabajo*." *Secuencia*, no. 77 (May–August 2010): 60–87.

Morales, Ed. "Puerto Rico: Belonging to, but Not Part of." *NACLA*, September 29, 2017. https://nacla.org/news/2017/09/29/puerto-rico-belonging-not-part.

———. "The Roots of Puerto Rico's Debt—and Why Austerity Will Not Solve It." *Nation*, July 8, 2015. https://www.thenation.com/article/archive/the-roots-of-puerto-ricos-debt -crisis-and-why-austerity-will-not-solve-it/.

Morales Carrión, Arturo. *Puerto Rico and the Non Hispanic Caribbean: A Study in the Decline of Spanish Exclusivism*. 3rd ed. Río Piedras: University of Puerto Rico Press, 1974.

Morrero, Carmen. *Luis Llorrens Torres (1876–1944): Vida y obra–bibliografía–antología*. New York: Hispanic Institute in the United States, 1953.

Morris, Nancy. *Puerto Rico: Culture, Politics, and Identity*. Westport, Conn.: Praeger, 1995.

Mosse, George L. *Nazi Culture*. New York: Schocken Books, 1981.

Mulholland, Jon, Nicola Montagna, and Erin Sanders-McDonagh, eds. *Gendering Nationalism: Intersections of Nation, Gender and Sexuality*. London: Palgrave Macmillan, 2018.

Muller, Dalia Antonia. *Cuban Emigrés, and Independence in the Nineteenth-Century Gulf World*. Chapel Hill: University of North Carolina Press, 2017.

Muñoz Marín, Luis. "Declaraciones del gobierno de Puerto Rico transmitidas por la radio con motive de los sucesos del 30 de octubre de 1950." In *Puerto Rico: Cien años de lucha política*, vol. 2, edited by Reece B. Bothwell González, 571–72. Río Piedras: Editorial Universitaria, 1979.

Nagel, Joane. "Masculinity and Nationalism: Gender and Sexuality in the Making of Nations." *Ethnic and Racial Studies* 21, no. 2 (1998): 242–69.

Nállim, Jorge. "Culture, Politics and the Cold War: The Sociedad de Escritores de Chile in 1950." *Journal of Latin American Studies* 51, no. 3 (February 2019): 549–71.

———. *Transformations and Crisis of Liberalism in Argentina, 1930–1955*. Pittsburgh: University of Pittsburgh Press, 2012.

National Committee for the Freedom of the Puerto Rican Nationalist Prisoners (Puerto Rico) and National Committee to Free the Four Puerto Rican Prisoners of War (United States). "Charges and Documentation of 25 Years of Human Rights Violations against the Imprisoned Puerto Rican Nationalists, Prisoners of War." In *25 Years of Struggle, 25 Years of Resistance*, 8–68. Chicago: n.p., 1979.

Navarro, Marysa. "Against *Marianismo*." In *Gender's Place: Feminist Anthropologies of Latin America*, edited by Rosario Montoya, Lessie Jo Frazier, and Janise Hurtig, 257–72. New York: Palgrave Macmillan, 2002.

Negrón de Montilla, Aida. *La americanización de Puerto Rico y la instrucción de educación popular, 1900–1930*. 2nd ed. Río Piedras: Editorial de la Universidad de Puerto Rico, 1990.

Nevin, Donal. *James Connolly, a Full Life: A Biography of Ireland's Renowned Trade Unionist and Leader of the 1916 Easter Uprising*. Dublin: Gill and MacMillan, 2005.

Nieves Falcón, Luis. *Un siglo de represión político en Puerto Rico (1898–1998)*. San Juan: Luis Nieves Falcón, 2009.

Nolla-Acosta, Juan José. *Puerto Rico Election Results, 1899–2012*. Self-published, 2013.

Nzongola-Ntalaja, [Georges]. "Amílcar Cabral and the Theory of the National Liberation Struggle." *Latin American Perspectives* 11, no. 2 (Spring 1984): 43–54.

Official Records of the General Assembly, Fifteenth Session, Supplement No. 2 (A/4494).

Ojeda Reyes, Félix. "Ramón Emeterio Betances, patriarca de la Antillanía." In Ojeda Reyes and Estade, *Pasión por la libertad*, 29–38.

———. *Peregrinos de la libertad: Documentos y fotos de exiliados puertorriqueños del siglo XIX localidazos en los archivos y bibliotecas de Cuba*. Río Piedras: Instituto de Estudios del Caribe, 1992.

Ojeda Reyes, Félix, and Paul Estrade, eds. *Obras completas*. Vol. 4. San Juan: Ediciones Puerto, 2013.

———. *Pasión por la libertad*. Río Piedras: Universidad de Puerto Rico, 2000.

Omi, Michael, and Howard Winant. *Racial Formation in the United States*. New York: Routledge, 1986.

"Organization of American States." *International Organization* 3, no. 3 (August 1949): 552–55.

Ortiz-Carrión, José Alejandro, and Teresita Torres-Rivera. *Voluntarios de la libertad: Puertorriqueños en defensa de la República Española, 1936–1939*. San Juan: Ediciones Callejón, 2015.

Padilla Pérez, Carlos. *Puerto Rico: Al rescate de su soberanía*. Buenos Aires: Publicaciones del Partido Nacionalista de Puerto Rico, 1958.

Pagán, Bolívar. *Historia de los partidos políticos puertorriqueños, 1895–1956*. Vol. 2. San Juan: Barcelona Pareja Montaña, 1959.

Palacios, Alfredo L. *Nuestra América y el imperialismo*. Buenos Aires: Editorial Palestra, 1961.

Palau de López, Awilda. *Veinticinco años de Claridad*. Río Piedras: Editorial de la Universidad de Puerto Rico, 1992.

Palieraki, Eugenia. "Chile, Algeria, and the Third World in the 1960s and 1970s." In *Latin America and the Global Cold War*, edited by Thomas C. Field Jr., Stella Krepp, and Vanni Pettiná, 274–300. Chapel Hill: University of North Carolina Press, 2020.

Palm, Risa, and Michael E. Hodgson. "Natural Hazards in Puerto Rico." *Geographical Review* 83, no. 3 (July 1993): 280–89.

Paralitici, Ché. *La represión contra el independentismo puertorriqueño: 1960–2010*. Río Piedras: Publicaciones Gaviota, 2011.

————. *Sentencia impuesta: 100 años de encarcelamientos por la independencia de Puerto Rico.* San Juan, P.R.: Ediciones Puerto, 2004.

Partido Nacionalista de Puerto Rico. *Tortura de los presos políticos en Puerto Rico.* Havana: Impresora Vega, 1952.

Pascoe, Peggy. *What Comes Naturally: Miscegenation Law and the Making of Race in America.* Oxford: Oxford University Press, 2009.

Pateman, Carole. *The Disorder of Women: Democracy, Feminism and Political Theory.* Stanford, Calif.: Stanford University Press, 1989.

Paterson, Thomas G. *Contesting Castro: The United States and the Triumph of the Cuban Revolution.* New York: Oxford University Press, 1995.

Paxton, Robert O. *The Anatomy of Fascism.* New York: Alfred A. Knopf, 2004.

Pérez Marchand, Rafael V. *Reminiscencia histórica de la Masacre de Ponce.* San Lorenzo, P.R.: Partido Nacionalista de Puerto Rico, 1972.

Pérez Velasco, Erik J. "La condición obrera en Puerto Rico (1898–1920)." *Plural* 3, nos. 1–2 (January–December 1984): 157–70.

Picó, Isabel. "The History of Women's Struggle for Equality in Puerto Rico." In *The Puerto Rican Woman: Perspectives on Culture, History, and Society,* edited by Edna Acosta-Belen, 46–58. New York: Praeger, 1986.

Pike, Frederick B. *Hispanismo, 1898–1936: Spanish Conservatives and Liberals and Their Relations with Spanish America.* Notre Dame, Ind.: University of Notre Dame Press, 1971.

Pineda Buitrago, Sebastián. "Entre el desprecio y la admiración: Visión de Estados Unidos en *Ulises criollo* de José Vasconcelos." *Latinoamérica: Revista de Estudios Latinoamericanos* 57 (2013): 125–51.

Piñero Cádiz, Genaro M. "La base aeronaval Roosevelt Roads: El Pearl Harbor del Caribe." In Rodríguez Beruff and Bolívar Fresneda, *Puerto Rico en la Segunda Guerra Mundial,* 233–59.

"Platform of the Anti-imperialist League." In *Speeches, Correspondence, and Political Papers of Carl Schurz,* edited by Frederick Bancroft, 6:77. New York: G. P. Putnam's Sons, 1913. http://sourcebooks.fordham.edu/mod/1899antiimp.asp.

Power, Margaret. "Friends and Comrades: Political and Personal Relationships between Members of the Communist Party USA and the Puerto Rican Nationalist Party, 1930s–1940s." In *Making the Revolution: Histories of the Latin American Left,* edited by Kevin Young, 105–28. Cambridge: Cambridge University Press, 2019.

————. "From Freedom Fighters to Patriots: The Successful Campaign to Release the FALN Political Prisoners, 1980–1999." *Centro Journal* 25, no. 1 (Spring 2013): 146–79.

————. "If People Had Not Been Willing to Give Their Lives for the *Patria* or There Had Not Been the Political Prisoners, Then We Would Be Nothing." *Radical History Review* 128 (May 2017): 36–43.

————. "The Puerto Rican Nationalist Party and Transnational Solidarity: Latin American Anti-colonialism vs. the United States during the Cold War in Latin America." In Stites Mor, *Human Rights and Transnational Solidarity in Cold War Latin America,* 21–47.

————. "Women, Gender, and the Puerto Rican Nationalist Party." In Mulholland, Montagna, and Sanders-McDonagh, *Gendering Nationalism,* 129–43.

Prados-Torreira, Teresa. *Rebel Women in Nineteenth-Century Cuba.* Gainesville: University Press of Florida, 2005.

Prasad, Vijay. *The Darker Nations: A People's History of the Third World.* New York: New Press, 2007.

Price, Richard, ed. *Maroon Societies: Rebel Slave Communities in the Americas.* Baltimore: John Hopkins University Press, 1996.

*Proceedings of the Twenty-Second Annual Meeting of the Mohonk Conference of Friends of the Indians and Other Dependent Peoples.* Reported by Wm. J. Rose. Lake Mohonk Conference, 1904.

Puerto Rico. Governor. *Twenty-Second Annual Report of the Governor of Porto Rico . . . for the Fiscal Year Ending June 30.* Washington, D.C.: Government Printing Office, 1923.

Puerto Rico. Official Records of the General Assembly. 15th sess. l. no. 2 (A/4494).

Pujals, Sandra. "De un pájaro las tres alas: El Buró del Caribe de la Comintern, Cuba y el radicalismo comunista en Puerto Rico, 1931–1936." *Op. Cit.* 21 (2012–13): 255–83.

———. "'La Brigada Móvil': Análisis preliminar de la base de datos del personal de la internacional comunista y sus agencias en América Latina y el Caribe." *Op. Cit.* 19 (2009–10): 1–32.

———. "¡Embarcados!: James Sager, la Sección Puertorriqueña de la Liga Anti-imperialista de las Américas y el Partido Nacionalista de Puerto Rico, 1925–1927." *Op. Cit.* 22 (2013–14): 1–32.

———. "A 'Soviet Caribbean': The Comintern, New York's Immigrant Community, and the Forging of Caribbean Visions, 1931–1936." *Russian History* 41 (2014): 263–64.

———. "La presencia de la Internacional Comunista en el Caribe, 1920–1940." *La Voz del Centro*, November 11, 2018. http://www.vozdelcentro.org/tag/dra-sandra-pujals/.

Putnam, Lara. *Radical Moves: Caribbean Migrants and the Politics of Race in the Jazz Age.* Chapel Hill: University of North Carolina Press, 2003.

Quijada, Mónica. "Latinos y anglosajones: El 98 en el fin de siglo suramericano." *Hispania* 57/2, no. 196 (1997): 589–609.

Quintero Rivera, Angel G. *Salsa, sabor y control! Sociología de la música tropical.* 2nd ed. Mexico City: Siglo Veintiuno Editores, 2005.

Rachum, Ilan. "Origins and Historical Significance of Día de la Raza." *Revista Europea de Estudios Latinoamericanos y del Caribe* 76 (April 2004): 61–81.

Randall, Margaret. *El pueblo no sólo es testigo: Historia de Dominga.* Río Piedras: Ediciones Huracán, 1979.

———. *Haydée Santamaría, Cuban Revolutionary: She Led by Transgression.* Durham, N.C.: Duke University Press, 2015.

———. *Sandino's Daughters Revisited: Feminism in Nicaragua.* New Brunswick, N.J.: Rutgers University Press, 1994.

Ransby, Barbara. *Ella Baker and the Black Freedom Movement: A Radical Democratic Movement.* Chapel Hill: University of North Carolina Press, 2003.

Renda, Mary A. *Taking Haiti: Military Occupation and the Culture of U.S. Imperialism, 1915–1940.* Chapel Hill: University of North Carolina Press, 2001.

Reyes-Santos, Irmary. "On Pan-Antillean Politics: Ramón Emeterio Betances and Gregorio Luperón Speak to the Present." *Callaloo* 36, no. 1 (Winter 2012): 142–57.

Reyes-Walker, Miguel Antonio. "El discurso albizuista en torno a las mujeres: El caso de Juanita Ojeda (1930–1950)." MS thesis, Centro de Estudios Avanzados de Puerto Rico y el Caribe, 2016.

Reynolds, Ruth M. "People/Mi Gente." *Centro de Estudios Puertorriqueños Bulletin* 2, no. 2 (Winter 1987–88): 44–48.

Ribes Tovar, Federico. *Albizu Campos El Revolucionario.* New York: Plus Ultra Educational, 1971.

Riddell, John, Vijay Prasad, and Nazeef Mollah. *Liberate the Colonies! Communism and Colonial Freedom, 1917–1924.* New Delhi: LeftWord Books, 2019.

Ripoll, Carlos. "La *Revista de Avance* (1927–1930): Vocero de vanguardismo y pórtico de Revolución." *Revista Iberoamericana* 30, no. 58 (July–December 1964): 261–82.

Rivera de Alvarado, Carmen. "La contribución de la mujer al desarrollo de la nacionalidad puertorriqueña." In *La mujer en la lucha hoy*, edited by Juan Angel Silén and Nancy A. Zayas, 37–47. Río Piedras: n.p., 1972.

Rivera-Rideau, Petra. *Remixing Reggaetón: The Cultural Politics of Race in Puerto Rico*. Durham, N.C.: Duke University Press, 2015.

Rivera-Rivera, Wanda. "The Politics of Madness in Francisco Matos Paoli's Prison Poem, *Canto de la locura*." *Revista Hispánica Moderna* 61, no. 2 (December 2008): 197–213.

Roa, Raúl. *El fuego de la semilla en el surco*. Havana: Editorial Letras Cubanas, 1982.

"Robert A. Lovett." Historical Office, Office of the Secretary of the Defense. https://history.defense.gov/DOD-History/Deputy-Secretaries-of-Defense/Article-View/Article/585251/robert-a-lovett/.

Robinson, Jo Ann Ooiman. *Abraham Went Out: A Biography of A. J. Muste*. Philadelphia: Temple University Press, 1981.

Rodríguez, Miguel. *Celebración de "La Raza": Una historia comparativa del 12 de octubre*. Mexico City: Universidad Iberoamericano, 2004.

Rodríguez Beruff, Jorge. "Prologue." In *"Volverán Banderas Victoriosas'": . . . Historia de Falange en Puerto Rico (1937–1941)*, ix–xiii. San Juan: Publicaciones Gaviota, 2019.

Rodríguez Beruff, Jorge, and José L. Bolívar Fresneda. *Puerto Rico en la Segunda Guerra Mundial: Baluarte del Caribe*. San Juan: Ediciones Callejón, 2015.

Rodríguez Cancel, Mario. "Conflictos ideológicos en el Partido Nacionalista de Puerto Rico a la luz de los documentos privados de Juan Gallardo Santiago." *Revista Universidad de América* 5, no. 2 (December 1993): 13–23.

Rodríguez de Tió, Lola. *Mi libro de Cuba*. Havana: Imprenta la Moderna, 1898.

Rodríguez-Fraticelli, Carlos. "Pedro Albizu Campos: Strategies of Struggle and Strategic Struggles." *Centro Journal* 4, no. 1 (1991–92): 25–33.

Rodríguez-Silva, Ileana M. *Silencing Race: Disentangling Blackness, Colonialism, and National Identities in Puerto Rico*. New York: Palgrave Macmillan, 2012.

Rojas, Rafael. *Historia mínima de la Revolución Cubana*. Madrid: Turner, 2015.

Romero-Cesaro, Ivette. "Whose Legacy? Voicing Women's Rights from the 1870s to the 1930s." *Callaloo* 17, no. 3 (Summer 1994): 770–89.

"Roosevelt en Puerto Rico." *FECH, Quincenario de la Federación de Estudiantes de Chile* 1, no. 4 (September 1937): 13.

Rosado, Marisa. *El nacionalismo y la violencia en la década de 1930*. San Juan: Ediciones Puerto, 2007.

———. *Pedro Albizu Campos: Las llamas de la aurora; Un acercamiento a su biografía*. 2nd ed. San Juan: n.p., 2003.

Rosario Natal, Carmelo, ed. *Albizu Campos: Preso en Atlanta; Historia del reo #5129A-a correspondencia*. San Juan: Producciones Históricas, 2001.

Rubenstein, Annette R., ed. *I Vote My Conscience: Debates, Speeches, and Writings of Vito Marcantonio*. New York: Queens College, CUNY, 2002.

Sánchez, Luis Alberto. *Testimonio personal: Memorias de un peruano del siglo XX*. Lima: Mosca Azul, 1980.

Sant Roz, José. *El Procónsul Rómulo Betancourt: Memorias de la degeneración de un país*. Caracas: Monte Ávila Editores Latinoamericana, 2009.

Santana, Arturo. "Puerto Rico in a Revolutionary World." In *Puerto Rico: A Political and Cultural History*, edited by Arturo Morales Carrión, 51–78. New York: W. W. Norton, 1983.

Santiago-Valles, Kelvin. "'Our Race Today [Is] the Only Hope for the World': An African Spaniard as Chieftain of the Struggle against 'Sugar Slavery' in Puerto Rico, 1926–1934." *Caribbean Studies* 35, no. 1 (January–June 2007): 107–40.

Scarano, Francisco A. "The Jíbaro Masquerade and the Subaltern Politics of Creole Identity Formation in Puerto Rico, 1745–1823." *American Historical Review* 101, no. 5 (December 1996): 1398–431.

Schaffer, Alan. *Vito Marcantonio: Radical in Congress*. Syracuse, N.Y.: Syracuse University Press, 1966.

Schlesinger, Stephen, and Stephen Kinzer. *Bitter Fruit: The Story of the American Coup in Guatemala*. Cambridge, Mass.: Harvard University Press, 1990.

Schoultz, Lars. *In Their Own Best Interest: A History of the U.S. Effort to Improve Latin Americans*. Cambridge, Mass.: Harvard University Press, 2018.

Schrecker, Ellen. *Many Are the Crimes: McCarthyism in America*. Princeton, N.J.: Princeton University Press, 1998.

Scott, James. *Weapons of the Weak: Everyday Forms of Peasant Resistance*. New Haven: Yale University Press, 1985.

Scott, Joan Wallach. *Gender and the Politics of History*. New York: Columbia University Press, 2018.

SECH [Sociedad de Escritores Chilenos]. "Primer Congreso de Escritores de Chile 3 de marzo y 1–4 de abril 1937." *Sociedad de Escritores Chilenos* 1, no. 5 (June 1937).

Seijo Bruno, Miñi. *La insurrección nacionalista en Puerto Rico, 1950*. Río Piedras: Editorial Edil, 1989.

Semán, Ernesto. *Ambassadors of the Working Class: Argentina's International Labor Activists and Cold War Democracy in the Americas*. Durham, N.C.: Duke University Press, 2017.

Sepúlveda, Isidoro. *El sueño de la Madre Patria: Hispanoamericanismo y nacionalismo*. Madrid: Fundación Carolina, Centro de Estudios Hispánicos e Iberoamericanos, 2005.

Serra Coelho, Miguel. "Brazil and India: A Brave New World, 1948–1961." In *Latin America and the Global Cold War*, edited by Thomas C. Field Jr., Stella Krepp, and Vanni Pettiná, 274–300. Chapel Hill: University of North Carolina Press, 2020.

Shaffer, Kirwin R. *Anarchists of the Caribbean: Countercultural Politics and Transnational Network in the Age of U.S. Expansion*. Cambridge: Cambridge University Press, 2020.

———. "Havana Hub: Cuban Anarchism, Radical Media and the Trans-Caribbean Anarchist Network, 1902–1915." *Caribbean Studies* 37, no. 2 (July–December 2009): 45–81.

Silén, Juan Angel. *Nosotros solos: Pedro Albizu Campos y el nacionalismo irlandés*. Río Piedras: Editorial Librería Norberto González, 1996.

Silvestrini, Blanca. *Los trabajadores puertorriqueños y el Partido Socialista (1932–1940)*. Río Piedras: Editorial Universitaria, 1979.

Silvestrini-Pacheco, Blanca. "Women as Workers: The Experience of the Puerto Rican Woman in the 1930's." In *Women Cross-Culturally: Change and Challenge*, edited by Ruby Rohrlich-Leavitt, 248–60. The Hague: Mouton, 1975.

Simón Arce, Rafael Ángel. *"Volverán banderas victoriosas . . .": Historia de Falange en Puerto Rico (1937–1941)*. San Juan: Publicaciones Gaviota, 2019.

Smith, Jean Edward. *Grant*. New York: Simon and Schuster, 2001.

Smith, Matthew J. *Red and Black in Haiti: Radicalism, Conflict, and Political Change, 1934–1957*. Chapel Hill: University of North Carolina Press, 2009.

Smith, Peter H. *Talons of the Eagle: Latin America, the United States, and the World*. New York: Oxford University Press, 2013.

Sotomayor, Antonio. *The Sovereign Colony: Olympic Sport, National Identity, and International Politics in Puerto Rico*. Lincoln: University of Nebraska Press, 2016.

Spear, Jennifer M. *Race, Sex, and Social Order in Early New Orleans*. Baltimore: Johns Hopkins University Press, 2009.

Spenser, Daniela. *In Combat: The Life of Lombardo Toledano*. Leiden: Brill, 2019.

"Statement of Purpose." *Labor Action* 18, no. 22 (May 31, 1954): 3.

Stein, Steve. *Populism in Peru: The Emergence of the Masses and the Politics of Social Control*. Madison: University of Wisconsin Press, 1980.

Stevens, Evelyn P. "Marianismo: The Other Face of Machismo." In *Female and Male in Latin America*, edited by Ann Pescatello, 89–101. Pittsburgh: University of Pittsburgh Press, 1973.

Stevens-Arroyo, Anthony M. "The Catholic Worldview in the Political Philosophy of Pedro Albizu Campos: The Death Knoll of Puerto Rican Insularity." *U.S. Catholic Historian* 20, no. 4 (Fall 2002): 53–73.

Stites Mor, Jessica, ed. *Human Rights and Transnational Solidarity in Cold War Latin America*. Madison: University of Wisconsin Press, 2013.

Stoler, Ann Laura. *Carnal Knowledge and Imperial Power: Race and the Intimate in Colonial Rule*. Berkeley: University of California Press, 2002.

Stoner, K. Lynn *From the House to the Streets: The Cuban Women's Movement for Legal Reform, 1898–1940*. Durham, N.C.: Duke University Press, 1991.

Suárez Findlay, Eileen J. *Imposing Decency: The Politics of Sexuality and Race in Puerto Rico, 1870–1920*. Durham, N.C.: Duke University Press, 1999.

———. *We Are Left without a Father Here: Masculinity, Domesticity, and Migration in Postwar Puerto Rico*. Durham, N.C.: Duke University Press, 2014.

Sullivan, Frances Peace. "'For the Liberty of the Nine Boys in Scottsboro, and against Yankee Imperialist Domination in Latin America': Cuba's Scottsboro Defense Campaign." *Canadian Journal of Latin American and Caribbean Studies* 38, no. 2 (2013): 282–92.

Swain, Carol M. *The New White Nationalism in America: Its Challenge to Integration*. Cambridge: Cambridge University Press, 2001.

Sweeney, George. "Irish Hunger Strikes and the Cult of Self-Sacrifice." *Journal of Contemporary History* 28, no. 3 (1993): 421–37.

Sznajder, Mario, and Luis Roneiger. *The Politics of Exile in Latin America*. Cambridge: Cambridge University Press, 2009.

Taller de Formación Política. *¡Huelga en la caña!* Río Piedras: Taller de Formación Política, 1982.

———. *No estamos pidiendo el cielo, huelga portuaria de 1937*. Río Piedras: Ediciones Huracán, 1988.

———. *Pedro Albizu Campos: ¿Conservador, fascista o revolucionario?* Río Piedras: Taller de Formación Política, 1991.

Taylor, Diana. *The Archive and the Repertoire: Performing Cultural Memory in the Americas*. Durham, N.C.: Duke University Press, 2003.

Thomas, Gwynn. *Contesting Legitimacy in Chile: Familial Ideals, Citizenship, and Political Struggles, 1970–1990*. University Park: Penn State University Press, 2011.

Tinajero, Araceli. *El Lector: A History of the Cigar Factory Reader*. Translated by Judith E. Grasberg. Austin: University of Texas Press, 2010.

Tirado Avilés, Amilcar. "La forja de un líder: Pedro Albizu Campos, 1924–1930." In Carrión, Garcia Ruiz, and Rodríguez Fraticelli, *La nación puertorriqueña*, 65–81.

Toledo, Josefina. "Ramón Emeterio Betances en la genesis de los clubs Borinquen y Mercedes Verona." In Ojeda Reyes and Estade, *Pasión por la libertad*, 15–30.

Torres, Benjamin J. "Albizu Campos y el Partido Nacionalista." In *Hablan sobre Albizu Campos*, 37–44.

———. *Hablan sobre Albizu Campos*. San Juan: Editorial Jelofe, 1979.

———. *Pedro Albizu Campos: Obras Escogidas, 1923–1936*. Vol. 1. San Juan: Editorial Jelofe, 1975.

Trask, Roger R. "The Impact of the Cold War on United States–Latin American Relations, 1945–49." *Diplomatic History* 1, no. 3 (Summer 1971): 271–84.

Trejo Castillo, Alfredo. *El Señor Don Samuel Zemurray y la soberanía de Honduras*. Tegucigalpa, Honduras: Tipografía la prensa libre, 1926.

"The Truman Doctrine, 1947." Office of the Historian, U.S. Department of State. https://history.state.gov/milestones/1945-1952/truman-doctrine.

Twinam, Ann. *Purchasing Whiteness: Pardos, Mulattos, and the Quest for Social Mobility in the Spanish Indies.* Stanford, Calif.: Stanford University Press, 2015.

Tyler May, Elaine. *Homeward Bound: American Families in the Cold War Era.* New York: Basic Books, 1999.

Ugarte, Manuel. *El destino de un continente.* Buenos Aires: Ediciones de la Patria Grande, 1962.

United Nations. *Official Records of the General Assembly.* 15th sess., suppl. 2, A/4494.

U.S. Bureau of Insular Affairs. *Report of the Chief of the Bureau of Insular Affairs, War Department.* Washington, D.C.: Government Printing Office, 1910.

U.S. Bureau of the Census. *Fifteenth Census of the United States 1930, Outlying Territories and Possessions, Census of Population and Housing.* www2.census.gov/library/publications/decennial/1930/abstract/00476589ch16.pdf.

———. *Fourteenth Census of the United States Taken in the Year 1920.* Vol. 3, *Population 1920,* "Outlying Possessions," 1203. www.census.gov/library/publications/1922/dec/vol-03-population.html.

U.S. House of Representatives. 80th Cong., 2nd sess. "Selective Service Act of 1948," June 19, 1948. www.loc.gov/rr/frd/Military_Law/pdf/act-1948.pdf.

———. Committee on Interior and Insular Affairs. "The Nationalist Party." Washington, D.C.: Government Printing Office, 1951.

U.S. Senate. Committee on Interior and Insular Affairs. 82nd Congress, 2nd sess. "Approving Puerto Rican Constitution." April 29, May 6, 1952.

U.S. Senate, Committee on Territories and Insular Affairs. "Statement of Ruth M. Reynolds, Secretary, the American League for Puerto Rico's Independence." April 24, 1945.

———. "Report of the Subcommittee to Investigate Communist Aggression in Latin America to the Select Committee on Communist Activities." 83rd Cong., 2nd sess., 1954.

———. Subcommittee of the Committee on Territories and Insular Affairs. "A Bill to Amend the Organic Act of Puerto Rico." 78th Cong., 1st sess., 1943.

———. "Terroristic Activity. The Cuban Connection in Puerto Rico. Castro's Hand in Puerto Rican and U.S. Terrorism." 94th Cong., 1st sess. Washington D.C.: Government Printing Office, July 30, 1975.

Valle-Ferrer, Norma. *Luisa Capetillo, Pioneer Puerto Rican Feminist.* Translated by Gloria Waldman-Schwartz. New York: Peter Lang, 2006.

Vasconcelos, José. *Indología:* "Text of the Speech of José Vasconcelias [sic] (Porto Rico) at the Congress-Meeting of February 10th, 1927." League against Imperialism Archives. International Institute of Social History.

Vaughan, Mary Kay. *The State, Education, and Social Class in Mexico, 1880–1920.* De Kalb: Northern Illinois University Press, 1982.

Vázquez, Blanca. "Ruth M. Reynolds." *Centro de Estudios Puertorriqueños Bulletin* 2, no. 2 (Winter 1987–88): 44–48.

Velázquez, José E., Carmen V. Rivera, and Andrés Torres, eds. *Revolution around the Corner: Voices from the Puerto Rican Socialist Party in the United States.* Philadelphia: Temple University Press, 2021.

Villaronga, Gabriel. *Toward a Discourse of Consent: Mass Mobilization and Colonial Politics in Puerto Rico, 1932–1948.* Westport, Conn.: Praeger, 2004.

Vivas Maldonado, José Luis. *Historia de Puerto Rico.* New York: Las Americas, 1962.

Walsh, Ellen. "'Advancing the Kingdom': Missionaries and Americanization in Puerto Rico, 1898–1930s." PhD diss., University of Pittsburgh, 2008.

———. "The Not-So-Docile Puerto Ricans: Students Resist Americanization, 1898–1930s." *Centro Journal* 26, no. 1 (Spring 2014): 148–71.

Weiner, Mark S. "Teutonic Constitutionalism: The Role of Ethno-Juridical Discourse in the Spanish-American War." In Burnett and Marshall, *Foreign in a Domestic Sense*, 48–81.

Weldon Johnson, James. "The Haitian Investigation." In *Eleventh Annual Report of the National Association for the Advancement of Colored People*, 9–12. New York: NAACP, 1921. www.archive.org/stream/naacpannualrepor1920nati#page/no/mode/2up.

Weaver, Kathleen. *Peruvian Rebel: The World of Magda Portal*. University Park: Pennsylvania State University Press, 2009.

Welter, Barbara. "The Cult of True Womanhood, 1820–1860." *American Quarterly* 18, no. 2 (1966): 151–74.

Wertheim, Stephen. "Instrumental Internationalism: The American Origins of the United Nations, 1940–3." *Journal of Contemporary History* 54, no. 2 (2019): 265–83.

West, Lois A., ed. *Feminist Nationalism*. London: Routledge, 1997.

Westad, Odd Arne. *The Global Cold War*. Cambridge: Cambridge University Press, 2007.

Whitman, James Q. *Hitler's American Model: The United States and the Making of American Race Law*. Princeton, N.J.: Princeton University Press, 2017.

Whitney, Robert. "War and Nation Building: Cuban and Dominican Experiences." In *The Caribbean: A History of the Region and Its Peoples*, edited by Stephan Palmié and Francisco A. Scarano, 361–72. Chicago: University of Chicago Press, 2011.

Yankelevich, Pablo. "En la retaguardia de la Revolución Mexicana: Propaganda y propagandistas mexicanos en América Latina, 1914–1920." *Mexican Studies/Estudios Mexicanos* 15, no. 1 (Winter 1999): 245–78.

Yasutake, Michael. "Preface." In *Can't Jail the Spirit: Political Prisoners in the U.S.*, 3rd ed., 5–6. Chicago: Editorial El Coquí, 1992.

Yuval-Davis, Nira, and Flora Anthias, eds. *Woman-Nation-State*. New York: St. Martin's Press, 1989.

Zapata, Carlos. *De independentista a autonomista: La transformación del pensamiento político de Luis Muñoz Marín*. San Juan: Fundación Luis Muñoz Marín, 2003.

Zeller, Neici. *Discursos y espacios femeninos en República Dominicana, 1880–1961*. Santo Domingo, D.R.: Editorial Letra Gráfica, 2012.

Zepeda Cortés, María Bárbara. *Cambios y adaptaciones del nacionalismo puertorriqueño: Del Grito de Lares al Estado Libre Asociado*. Morélia, Mex.: Universidad Michoacana de San Nicolás de Hidalgo, 2015.

# INDEX

Abreu de Aguilar, Isabel, 72
Acheson, Dean, 182
Acosta, Yvonne, 174
Acosta-Belén, Edna, 23–24
Acosta Velarde, Federico, 11, 74, 80, 101
Adams, Abigail, 72
Addams, Jane, 145
Albizu Campos, Pedro, 11–12, 60, 109, 121, 151; as dynamic speaker, 34, 46; efforts to discredit, 8, 9, 175–76, 211n33; in New York City, 136, 144–45, 146, 147–48, 150; prestige of, in Latin America, 6, 7, 15, 81, 120, 123, 127, 130, 199; surveillance of, 96, 114–15, 158–59
—background of, 65, 107–8, 232n100; ancestry of, 33, 35, 55, 65; Catholicism of, 19, 66, 93, 108; education of, 65, 107–8
—death of (1965), 7, 198–200
—imprisonment of, 12, 20, 191, 200; appeals for release of, 120, 121, 128, 129, 144, 178, 200; health problems worsened by, 136, 175, 176, 191, 200–201, 259nn1,6; limited visits allowed for, 124, 198, 228n15 259n6; release of (1943), 136, 143
—and Laura Meneses, 95, 96, 128, 176, 198–99; letters between, 10, 92, 93; marriage of, 82–83, 158–59
—as PNPR leader (1930–65), 44, 76; and armed actions, 1, 4–5; election of, 4, 55, 77, 101; encouragement of women's activism by, 1, 9–10, 11, 19, 54, 55, 68, 77, 108; and hostility to U.S. colonialism, 34, 35–36, 55, 209n15; and 1934 sugarcane workers' strike, 108–9, 236n77; and party's racial identity, 19; after return to Puerto Rico in 1947, 156, 157, 158, 173, 185; and World War II, 134
—and transnational solidarity, 12, 210, 229; and dream of Antillean Confederation, 229n47; 1927–30 travels by, 12, 19, 32, 45, 65, 77, 78–79, 81–96, 101, 116

—views of: on gender roles, 68–69; on race, 33, 55, 66–67; on women's suffrage, 71–72, 73
Alegria, José S., 83, 101
Allen, Devere, 148
Allende, Salvador, 5–6, 16
*Amauta*, 32, 90
American Anti-imperialist League, 37–38
American Committee for the Defense of Puerto Rican Political Prisoners, 141–43
American Committee on Dependent Territories, 168, 196
American Federation of Labor (AFL), 44, 110
Americanization, 19, 46–51, 52, 66, 160–61. *See also* English language
American League for Puerto Rico's Independence, 20, 135, 137, 146–49, 150, 151, 164, 187
Americans for Puerto Rico's Independence, 164. *See also* American League for Puerto Rico's Independence
anarchists, 3, 44
Anderson, Eleanor Copenhaver, 148
Anderson, Sherwood, 148
Andreu Iglesias, César, 110, 198, 236n92
Anthias, Flora, 69
Anthony, Marc, 50
Anti-imperialist League of the Americas, 93–94
Antillean Confederation, goal of, 3, 28–29, 88, 106, 229n47
APJP (Asociación Patriótica de Jóvenes Puertorriqueños, Patriotic Association of Young Puerto Ricans), 10, 106–7. *See also* Cadetes de la República
APRA (Alianza Popular Revolucionaria Americana, American Popular Revolutionary Alliance, Peru), 17, 95–96, 127–28, 166, 231n96, 259n166
Arbenz, Jacobo, 42, 154, 194, 195
Arévalo, Juan José, 154, 167, 181, 194

Chardón Plan, 113
Chatterjee, Partha, 8
Chile, 86, 129, 168; Puerto Rico solidarity
in, 5–6, 7, 15–16, 74, 121, 123, 124, 195,
200, 234n42, 240n32
Chisholm, Shirley, 202
*Claridad*, 130, 242n64
*Clarín*, 195
Clark, Victor S., 98
Club Borinquen, 222n44
Club Hostos, 140
coffee industry, 26, 42–43, 99, 218n56
Coffet, Lesley, 173
Collazo, Iris, 174, 179, 252n26
Collazo, Lydia, 174, 179, 252n26
Collazo, Oscar, 138, 179, 201, 244n33;
campaign to spare the life of, 170–71,
178–83, 254n78; family of, 138, 178, 179,
243n14, 252n26 (*see also* Collazo, Lydia;
Collazo, Rosa); in 1950 armed action,
173, 251n16; pardon of (1979), 202
Collazo, Rosa, 138, 178, 181, 182–83,
185–86, 252n26; imprisonment of, 174,
178, 185–86
Collazo, Zoraida, 174, 179, 252n26
Collins, Charles, 166
Coll y Cuchí, José, 34, 61, 74, 178, 222n48,
233n29; arrogant treatment of, by
Gov. Reily, 61–63, 222n51; attitude
of, toward United States, 34, 61–62,
65, 233n29; contrasts of, with Albizu
Campos 55, 65, 66–67; as a founder
of PNPR, 34, 62; ideas of, on race, 63,
64–65, 66–67, 76; and masculinity, 62,
63, 222n52
Colombia, 75, 115, 129, 169; Puerto Rico
solidarity in, 75, 121, 124, 125–26
Colón, Juana, 58
Columbus, Christopher, 66
Committee for Justice for Puerto Ricans,
187, 188, 256n114
Commonwealth. *See* Estado Libre Asociado
Communist International (Comintern), 3,
93–94, 125, 129; formation of, 241n58;
and Popular Front, 110, 129, 241n59;
and Puerto Rico, 89, 93–94, 110, 139,
236n89
Communist parties, 15–16, 129, 241n46;
in Costa Rica, 117, 129; in Cuba, 90,
230n58; in Mexico, 93–94, 165. *See also*

Communist International; Communist
Party USA; Partido Comunista
Puertorriqueño
Communist Party USA (CPUSA), 110,
238n134, 244n29, 255n105; and Puerto
Rican Communist Party, 110, 236n92
—and PNPR, 137–43, 186–87, 242n4,
243n21, 243n25; in New York City,
137–43, 144, 166–67, 236n87
Concepción de Gracia, Gilberto, 98,
139–40, 156
Congreso Mundial de la Prensa Latina
(World Congress of the Latino Media,
1928), 92, 95
Congress against Colonial Oppression and
Imperialism (Brussels, 1927), 32, 76
Connolly, James, 108
Conyers, John, 202
Corominas, Enrique V., 194–95
Corretjer, Juan Antonio, 20, 113, 126,
136, 143, 166; and Albizu Campos,
20, 65, 136, 229n47, 236n73; and Latin
American solidarity, 119, 120, 121,
127–28, 164–65, 237n113; as prisoner,
20, 119, 120, 121, 128, 242n1
Costa Rica, 124; newspapers in, 32, 90, 117,
128, 241n55; Puerto Rico solidarity in,
74, 90, 117, 124, 128, 129, 168–69
CTAL (Confederación de Trabajadores de
América Latina, Workers Confederation of Latin America), 165, 166
Cuba, 74, 86, 89–92, 94, 193; Albizu
Campos in, 19, 23, 78, 89–92, 95,
101; exiles in, 16–17, 158, 193–94,
248n29; Laura Meneses in, 123, 195,
198–99, 200, 257n139; longtime bonds
of, with Puerto Rico, 18, 19, 23–24,
28–30, 59–60, 200; post-1959, 14, 16;
Puerto Rico solidarity in, 121–22, 123,
128, 177–78, 182; revolution in, 193,
195–96, 222n53; under Spanish rule,
3, 22, 25, 26–27; and United States,
39–40, 42, 230n56; women activists
in, 91, 105
Cubillos, Vicente, 182–83
Cuchi Coll, Isabel, 178

*Daily Worker*, 186–87
Dario, Rubén, 31
Dávila, José Manuel, 13, 143, 144

Davis, George W., 39
de Diego, José, 34, 67, 84, 128, 216n1, 224n83
de Hostos, Eugenio María, 18, 22–23, 84, 90, 140, 203; and trans-Caribbean solidarity, 28, 79–80; and women's rights, 28, 213n9
de la Cruz, Dominga, 45, 70, 97, 105, 106, 143
Dellinger, Dave, 187
Dellums, Ronald, 202
Del Moral, Solsiree, 50
Depression of 1930s, 47, 98–100
de Santiago, Julio, 134, 153
Dessalines, Jean-Jacques, 78
de Valera, Éamon, 108
*Diario de Costa Rica*, 117
Díaz y Díaz, Bernardo, 201
Dietz, James, 43
divorce, 50
Dominican Republic, 42, 119, 168, 169; Albizu Campos's 1927 visit to, 83–86, 87, 88, 89, 101, 228n19; emigrants from, in United States, 137; nationalism in, 78–79, 85–86, 87, 228n29; Puerto Ricans living in, 74, 87, 96, 115, 228n21; Puerto Rican solidarity with, 80, 84–85; Puerto Rico solidarity in, 19, 74–75, 83–86, 87, 120, 137; under Spanish rule, 3, 18, 27–28; women's activism in, 91, 105, 234n47
draft, military, 36, 118, 132, 217n13; PNPR and, 132–34, 158, 180, 248n29, 251n7
Duamy, Orlando, 176
Duany, Jorge, 52–53, 160
Dulles, John Foster, 184

Ecuador, 168; Puerto Rico solidarity in, 15–17, 167, 195, 200
education. *See* schools
Eichel, Seymour, 191
Eisenhower, Dwight D., 16, 184, 191, 200
*El Mundo*, 10, 71, 85, 222n51
*El Nacionalista de Ponce*, 60, 74, 81, 95
*El Nacionalista de Puerto Rico*, 60
Enamorado Cuesta, José, 120, 166
Enfermeras de la República (Nurses of the Republic), 97, 100, 105–6, 143, 144, 198, 234n48; origins of, 105, 108; and PNPR's new militancy, 108, 112

English language, 48; in schools, under U.S. rule, 35, 46, 47, 48, 50, 51, 56, 63, 73, 219n84
Estado Libre Asociado (ELA, Free Associated State), 112, 186, 189, 197, 213n6; creation of, 21, 112, 152, 154, 160–63; impact of, 160–61; Muñoz Marín and, 17, 21, 112, 152, 160; PNPR and, 154, 160, 171–73; and United Nations, 163–65, 197
Estrade, Paul, 28

Faber, Sebastian, 31
Falcón, César, 76
FALN (Fuerzas Armadas de Liberación Nacional, Armed Forces of National Liberation), 5, 210n21, 238n124
Fanon, Franz, 53
fascism, 9–11, 32, 107, 111, 132–34, 210n27; Communist parties' hostility to, 129, 139, 241n59; false linking of PNPR to, 9–11, 107, 110, 176
Federación Universitaria Pro Independencia (Federation of Pro Independence University Students), 191, 257n140
Federal Bureau of Investigation (FBI), 13, 243n21, 255n105
—targeting of PNPR by, 13, 113–15, 136, 171, 184, 192, 234n42; in Cuba, 193, 248n29; estimates of PNPR membership by, 244n41; in New York City, 174, 187; and Puerto Rican police, 13, 113, 158–59
Feliú, Angel, 138
Fellowship of Reconciliation (FOR), 145, 146, 147, 188, 189
Fernós-Isern, Antonio, 163, 184
Ferrao, Luis Angel, 9–10, 114
Figueroa Cordero, Andres, 1, 2, 5, 183, 201, 260n18
Figueroa Hernández, Sotero, 30, 215n48
Flores, Irvin, 1, 5, 183, 201
FLT (Federación Libre de Trabajadores, Free Federation of Labor), 44–45, 56–58, 109–10, 223n66, 236n77; women workers in, 44–45, 58, 70–71
Foraker Act (1900), 36, 39, 42, 43, 49
France, 28, 209n12. *See also* Paris
Franco, Francisco, 9, 11, 107
Frank, Waldo, 187
Franqui-Rivera, Harry, 25

Free Associated State. *See* Estado Libre
    Asociado
Friedman, Andrea, 145, 176
Fusté, José, 38

Gadea, Hilda, 194, 195, 196, 259n166
"Gag Law." *See* Law 53
Gandhi, Mahatma, 11, 145
Gandía, Julio Pinto, 97–98, 136, 146
Garay, Narciso, 128–29
García, Robert, 202
García Monge, Joaquín, 128
Garvey, Marcus, 4
Gay Galbo, Enrique, 90
Germany, 20, 129; U.S. rivalry with, 20, 42,
    118–19, 131, 132; and World War II, 42,
    118, 131, 132, 145, 247n11
Go, Julian, 51
Gómez, Juan Vicente, 96
Gompers, Samuel, 56
Gonzalo Marín, Francisco (Pachín Marín),
    30, 215n48
Good Neighbor Policy, 20, 118–20; Puerto
    Rico as prominent exception to, 20,
    117–18, 119–20, 121–30, 134–35, 253n61
Gorky, Maxim, 76
Gotay, Alejandrina, 153, 154
Grant, Ulysses, 29
Great Britain, 42, 145, 151, 167
Grito de Lares uprising (1848), 18, 22, 25,
    27, 68, 110, 214n29; commemorations
    of, 72, 103–4, 110, 140, 143–44, 157,
    165–66, 203
Grove, Marmaduke, 129
Gruening, Ernest, 112, 113, 114, 237n102,
    239n4
Guatemala, 167, 193–94, 196; Puerto Rico
    solidarity in, 154, 167, 168–69, 171, 181,
    182, 193–94; U.S. coup in (1954), 42, 194
Guayama, 109
Guevara, Ernesto "Che," 194, 195–96
Gusti, Carmen María, 67
Guzmán, Julio Alfredo de, 75

Haiti, 78, 87–89, 169, 229n47; Albizu
    Campos in, 19, 78, 87–89, 101; Puerto
    Rican solidarity with, 87–88, 89, 95;
    Puerto Rico solidarity in, 14, 157; slave
    rebellion in, 26, 28; U.S. domination of,
    87, 89, 229n39

Hammarskjöld, Dag, 195
Harding, Warren G., 62, 63
Harlem Ashram, 136–37, 145–47, 190;
    formation of, 136, 145, 245n48; and
    Puerto Rico solidarity, 8, 20, 135, 136,
    146–47, 180; Ruth Reynolds and, 8, 17,
    147, 180
Hart, Justin, 118–19
Haya de la Torre, Victor Raúl, 17, 95, 127
Henríquez García, Enriquillo, 78, 227n1
Henríquez y Carvajal, Federico, 85, 86, 87
*Heraldo de la Mujer*, 68
Hernández, Rafael, 50–51
Hernández-Cata, Alfonso, 121–22
Herrera Oropeza, José, 199, 200
Hijas de la Libertad (Daughters of
    Freedom), 105, 140, 243–44n26. *See also*
    Enfermeras de la República
Hispanismo, 19, 30–31, 33, 213n71
Hoffnung-Garskof, Jesse, 52
Honduras, 74, 75, 169, 253n44
Hoover, J. Edgar, 113
House Un-American Activities Committee
    (HUAC), 184, 251n4, 255n105
Hull, Cordell, 117
hurricanes: Irma (2017), 203, 218n49; María
    (2017), 83, 203, 218n49; San Ciprián
    (1932), 99; San Felipe (1928), 83, 99

Iber, Patrick, 165
Ichaso, Francisco, 90
Ickes, Harold, 112
Iglesias Pantín, Santiago, 56–57
India, 10–11, 145, 246n75; anticolonial
    positions of, in U.N., 151, 164, 258n151
Indigenous peoples, 33, 51, 94–95; and
    Albizu Campos's views on race, 66, 67,
    94–95; of Puerto Rico (Taino), 22, 26,
    67, 226n127
Infante, Pedro, 50
Insular Cases, 38, 217n29
Insular Police. *See* Puerto Rican police
Inter-American Peace Conference (Buenos
    Aires, 1936), 118–20, 121
InterAmerican Student Congress (Brazil,
    1952), 182
International Congress of American
    Democracies, 129
International Labor Defense (ILD), 139,
    141, 243n21

Padilla, Carlos, 12, 173, 193–94, 197; imprisonment of, 173, 175, 193; travel by, as PNPR representative, 12, 15, 177

Padilla de Sanz, Trina, 68, 72, 225n121

Palacios, Alfredo, 130, 195

Panama, 75, 117, 128–29, 169, 258n151. *See also* Panama Canal

Panama Canal, 3, 35, 41–42, 81, 131

Pan American Centennial Congress (Panama, 1926), 75

Paraguay, 14, 86, 169, 253n44, 258n151

Paralitici, Ché, 132, 200

Paris, 80, 215n38

Parra Velasco, Antonio, 167

Partido Comunista Puertorriqueño (PCP, Puerto Rican Communist Party), 13, 110–11, 236n92, 238n122; and CGT, 110, 111; founding of, 110, 236n89; and PNPR, 13, 110–11, 186–87, 151, 198, 232n5; repressive measures against, 13, 151, 174, 186; and World War II, 132–34

Partido Nacionalista Puertorriqueño (PNPR, Puerto Rican Nationalist Party)
—before 1930: Albizu Campos's travels on behalf of (*see under* Albizu Campos, Pedro); early leadership of, 34, 53, 59–62 (*see also* Coll y Cuchí, José); founding of, 4, 6, 30, 59–62, 76; and gender, 67–68, 76; racial identity of, 64–65, 76, 226n127; response of colonial government to, 46, 58, 61–63, 222n51; stance of, toward U.S. government, 4, 34, 61–62, 76
—in 1930s: Albizu Campos's election as president of (1930), 4, 55, 77, 101; changing racial identification in, 19, 65–67, 77; greater militancy of, 4, 19, 108, 112; growing presence of, in New York City, 135, 136–43; harder line of, toward U.S. colonialism, 34, 77; increased role of women in, 19, 68–70, 77; Latin American solidarity with, 20, 117–18, 119–20, 121–30, 253n61; repressive measures against, 98, 112, 114, 115–16, 120, 143–44, 240n40 (*see also* Ponce Massacre)
—in 1940s: appeals of, to United Nations, 149–51; move of leaders of, to New York City, 135, 143–44; and peacetime military draft, 158; repression against,

5, 21, 170–71, 174–76, 184–86 (*see also* Law 53); and World War II, 118–19, 130–34, 161, 247n11
—in early 1950s: armed actions by, 4, 21 (*see also* Truman, Harry S.: attempted assassination of; uprising of October 1950; U.S. Congress: 1954 attack on); criminal trials of members of, 1, 158, 174, 178, 185–86, 193; response of, to creation of Estado Libre Asociado (1950), 154, 160, 171–73 (*see also* uprising of October 1950); successful campaign of, for commutation of Oscar Collazo's death sentence, 170–71, 178–83, 254n78; weakened presence of, in Puerto Rico amid repression, 143, 183–84
—in late 1950s and after, 191–92; and clemency campaigns, 191–92, 200–203; and declining years of Albizu, 191–92, 198–200, 259n1, 259n6; and gradual release of prisoners, 201–3
—international solidarity for, 5, 14–16, 21, 32–33; in Latin America, 4, 5, 14–16, 21, 33, 74–75, 81–96, 165–69, 177–83, 200; in North America, 20, 135, 138–49, 150–51, 164, 178–83. *See also under* Nationalist prisoners
—members of, in prison. *See* Nationalist prisoners
—version of nationalism championed by, 8–9, 21; and anti-imperialism, 19, 24, 32, 53, 79–80; and gender, 12, 67–70; and identification as part of Latin America, 6, 73–75, 78–79, 70, 199; nineteenth-century roots of, 22–25, 28–29, 213n12; and race, 64–67; and transnational solidarity, 4, 14–15, 19, 29, 73–74, 78–80, 105, 199, 210n24

Partido Popular Demócrata (PPD, Popular Democratic Party), 20–21, 111, 154–56, 160, 174, 189; close work of, with U.S. government, 21, 154, 169, 184; development strategy of, 155–56, 249n47; electoral success of, 152, 154–55, 156, 163; Muñoz Marín and, 36, 153–55, 237n107

Partido Unión (Union Party), 57, 58–59, 63, 71; and birth of PNPR, 55, 58–59, 60, 61, 74, 76; and goal of independence, 54, 58–59, 67, 69, 76

Party for Independence (1912–14), 226n124
Patria, 59–60
Peacemakers, 180, 188; A. J. Muste and, 180, 188; origins of, 187; and Puerto Rico solidarity, 180, 187, 188, 189–92; Ralph Templin and 189–90, 191
Peck, Jim, 188
Peco, José, 120
Pérez, Carmen, 173, 175, 185
Pérez Pagán, Pedro, 134
Perón, Juan, 194, 195
Peru, 17, 32, 68, 90, 129, 169, 229n35; Albizu Campos in, 12, 19, 95, 123, 166; Laura Meneses in, 19, 82–83, 92, 95, 123, 166. See also APRA
Pierre-Paul, Antoine, 78, 87, 88, 101
Piñero, Jesús T., 36, 163
Pinto Gandía, Julio, 97–98, 136, 146
Platt Amendment, 89, 117, 230n56
PNPR. See Partido Nacionalista Puertorriqueño
Ponce, 60, 61, 81, 109, 172. See also El Nacionalista de Ponce; Ponce Massacre
Ponce Enríquez, Camilo, 15
Ponce Massacre (1937), 20, 45, 97–98, 141–43, 212n49; deaths in, 98; responses to, 98, 100, 106, 111, 121, 141, 143, 144, 247n18
Popular Front, 124, 129, 241n61; Comintern and, 110, 129, 241n59
Prío Socarrás, Carlos, 16–17
prisoners. See Nationalist prisoners
PROMESA (Puerto Rican Oversight, Management, and Economic Stability Act, 2016), 203
Pro-Oscar Collazo Defense Committee, 178–80, 182, 253n60
Puerto Rican Falange, 11
Puerto Rican Independence Party (PIP), 5, 156, 161, 164, 174, 183, 247n12; in elections, 156, 160
Puerto Rican police: and FBI, 13, 113, 158–59; tactics used by, 13, 20, 97–98, 113–14, 144, 158–59, 173, 174, 185, 191 (see also Ponce Massacre). See also Riggs, Francis E.
Puerto Rican Reconstruction Administration, 113
Puerto Rican Republican Party, 44, 56, 57, 109, 223n66; as representative of sugar producers, 59

Puerto Rican Socialist Party (Partido Socialista), 44, 56, 57, 109, 110; women in, 44, 48, 58, 70–71
Putnam, Lara, 3

Quintero, Luisa, 178, 179, 180, 181

Ramirez, Francisco, 104
Randolph, A. Philip, 8, 148
Reily, E. Mont, 46, 58, 61–63, 222n51, 223n63
Renda, Mary, 87
Repertorio Americano, 32, 90, 117, 128, 241n55
Republican Council of Cuba and Puerto Rico, 29
retraimiento, 4, 159, 225n117
Revista Puerto Rico, 138
Reynolds, Ruth, 8–9, 12, 145–49, 164, 192, 195, 256n119; and American League for Puerto Rico's Independence, 147, 148–49, 175, 187; arrests and imprisonment of, 9, 146, 175, 190–91, 252n32, 256n119; background of, 145–46; and Harlem Ashram, 8, 17, 145, 146; and PNPR, 8, 146, 187, 189, 252n32
Riggs, Francis E., 100, 114, 148
Rio Pact of 1947, 176
Rivera Walker, Alvaro, 173
Rodó, José Enrique, 31, 32, 213n71
Rodríguez, Artemio, 100
Rodríguez de Tió, Lola, 18, 22–24, 213n4; as inspiration long after her death, 24, 79–80, 203; "La Borinqueña," 22–23, 97, 104, 194, 202, 213n7; and trans-Caribbean solidarity, 23, 28, 29, 79–80; and women's rights, 22, 23, 28
Rodríguez-Silva, Ileana, 64
Roig de Leuchsenring, Emilio, 90, 123, 128, 177, 178, 230n61
Rolland, Romain, 76, 101
Rondón, Isolina, 70
Roosevelt, Eleanor, 112
Roosevelt, Franklin D., 119–20, 122, 238–39n4; appeals addressed to, 120, 121, 129, 130, 143, 144, 238n130; on Puerto Rico's status, 130–31, 242n68. See also Good Neighbor Policy
Roosevelt, Theodore, 31, 41
Roosevelt Roads naval base, 42, 132
Rosado, Hiram, 114

Rosado, Isabel, 106, 185
Rosado, Marisa, 11, 34, 59
Rosenberg, Ethel, 174
Roy, M. N., 125
Ruiz Belvis, Segundo, 28, 84, 214n33
Russell, John H., 87
Ruth Reynolds Defense Committee
    (RRDC), 187, 188

Sabás Alomá, Mariblanca, 91
Sack, Leo R., 117, 130, 162
Sager, James, 94
Sánchez, Alberto, 110, 111
Sánchez, Luis Alberto, 17
Sánchez Vilella, Roberto, 54
Sandino, Augusto César, 10, 81, 148,
    227n9
Sandino Battalion, 10
Santander, María, 195
Santiago-Valles, Kelvin, 88
Santos Rivera, Juan, 111
Scarano, Francisco, 25, 26
schools, 46–48, 50; gender gap in, 47;
    language used in, 46, 47, 48, 50, 56,
    63
Schurz, Carl, 37
Seijo Bruno, Miñi, 13
Semán, Ernesto, 194
Sepulveda, Isidro, 30
Seventh International Conference of
    American States (Montevideo, 1933),
    119
Sharpe, A. C., 39
Simón Arce, Rafael Ángel, 11
Sinclair, Upton, 76
slavery, 28, 29, 56, 97
Smith, Jay Holmes, 145, 147, 150, 187, 188
Smith, Peter, 81
Smith Act (Alien Registration Act, 1940),
    159, 248n37
Snyder, Cecil, 113, 115
Somoza, Anastasio, 119
Sotomayor, Antonio, 161
Soto Vélez, Clemente, 120, 143
Spain, 42, 217n13; fascism in, 9, 11, 107;
    and Hispanismo, 30–31
    —as colonial power, 14, 25–29; and
    construction of race, 35; in Cuba, 23,
    25, 26–27; defeat of, 29, 31, 34, 56–57;

in Dominican Republic, 18, 28, 29;
    in Puerto Rico, 23, 25–27, 28, 51–52,
    150, 214n17, 214n29; 217n13, 220n102,
    226n127; revolts against, 3, 18, 22–23,
    27–28, 29, 103, 214n29
Spanish-American War, 34, 36, 38
Spanish language, 48–49, 53, 66, 88,
    219n84; attempted replacement of, by
    English in schools, 35, 46, 47, 48, 50, 51,
    56, 63, 73, 219n84
Stoler, Ann Laura, 63
strikes, 51, 109–10; by dockworkers, 109–10,
    140, 243n25; by sugarcane workers, 44,
    100, 109; women in, 58, 109
Stimson, Henry, 241n47
student organizations, 120, 121, 122,
    181–82; in Puerto Rico, 114, 178, 191
Suárez Findlay, Eileen, 49, 52,155
sugar industry, 42, 43, 44, 99, 113, 233n16;
    in Dominican Republic, 96, 228n21; and
    party politics, 56, 59; strikes in, 44, 100,
    109; workers in, 35, 43, 49–50, 218n56

Tagore, Rabindranath, 82
Taino people, 22, 215n47, 226n127
Taller de Formación Política (TFP, Political
    Training Workshop), 10
Taylor, Maxwell, 191
Teatro Puerto Rico, 179
Templin, Ralph, 17, 145, 180–81, 187,
    189–90, 191
Tenth Inter-American Conference
    (Caracas, 1954)
Three Kings Day, 50
Tió Segarra, Bonocio, 22
tobacco industry, 42, 43, 218n56; workers
    in, 44, 45, 57, 59, 99, 218n56, 219n72
Toledano Lombardo, Vicente, 165–66
Torregrosa, Fernando, 72
Torres, Alejandrina, 48–49, 50, 219n87
Torresola, Angelina, 105–6
Torresola, Carmen Dolores, 174, 178
Torresola, Doris, 173, 175, 185
Torresola, Elio, 172, 173
Torresola, Griselio, 173
Trejo Castillo, Alfredo, 75
Trujillo, Rafael, 119
Truman, Harry S., 36, 160; appointment
    of Puerto Rican as governor by, 36,

163; attempted assassination of, 5, 169, 170, 171, 173, 178, 186, 189, 196; and commutation of Oscar Collazo's death sentence, 179–82, 194, 254n78

Truman Doctrine, 177

Trump, Donald, 1, 203

Tugwell, Rexford 161

26th of July Movement, 171, 193, 195, 196

Tydings, Millard, 148, 149, 154

Ugarte, Manuel, 32, 76, 101, 119–20, 125

Uhrie, Al, 191

Unger, Abraham, 179–80, 181

United Nations, 149–51, 163–65, 200, 246n75; charter of, 150, 246n82; founding of, 149, 162, 246n76; PNPR's appeals to, 9, 147, 149, 150–51, 172, 175, 181, 195; U.S. influence in, 149–50, 151, 154, 165, 169, 258n151; votes in, regarding Puerto Rico's status, 154, 164, 194, 197, 258n151

United Negro Improvement Association (UNIA), 4, 209n15, 234n48

University of Puerto Rico, 54, 75, 94–95

uprising of October 1950, 4–5, 13, 21, 165, 169, 214n29, 251n4; in Jayuya, 70, 115, 170, 172–73, 234n49, 251n7; repression following, 8–9, 13, 21, 54, 106, 159, 170, 173–76, 252n32; timing of, 152, 169, 171, 214n29, 251n4; women in, 54, 70, 105. See also Truman, Harry S.: attempted assassination of

Uruguay, 86, 129, 169, 181; Puerto Rico solidarity in, 181, 182, 195

U.S. citizenship, 36, 39, 74, 132, 217n13; revocation of Laura Meneses's, 257n139, 259n6

U.S. Congress, 62, 184; lack of Puerto Rico representation in, 36, 134; legislating by, for Puerto Rico, 36, 39, 131, 160, 163, 203, 249n54 (see also Jones Act); 1954 attack on, 1–2, 5, 18, 106, 170, 183–86, 189, 196, 201

U.S. Department of the Interior, 112, 182. See also Ickes, Harold

U.S. military bases, 40–42, 132, 134, 157–58, 161, 247n21; protests over, 157, 203, 247n21

U.S. Supreme Court, 38–39, 137, 217n29

U.S. War Department, 112, 133, 237n111. See also U.S. military bases

Utuado, 172

Valero de Bernabé, Antonio, 25

Vargas, Getúlio, 181

Varona, Enrique José, 90, 230n61

Vasconcelos, José, 32, 75–76, 81, 125, 231n77; and Albizu Campos, 76, 81, 93; and Mexican politics, 93, 231n77; and PNPR, 32, 65, 75–76, 81, 101

Vázquez, Filiberto, 140

Vázquez, Horacio, 84–85

Vega, Bernardo, 140

Velázquez, Luis F., 136, 143

Vélez Alvarado, Antonio, 30, 59–60, 101

Venezuela, 19, 22, 96, 115, 129, 166; Puerto Rico solidarity in, 166, 167, 168, 198, 199, 200

Vieques island, 68–69, 190; protests over, 157, 203, 247n21; U.S. military use of, 132, 157–58, 203, 247n21

Viscal, Olga, 196–97

voting rights, 56, 216, 225n109; for governorship, 36, 51, 155, 163; and literacy, 56, 71; Puerto Ricans' lack of, in federal elections, 36, 39, 134. See also women's suffrage

Walker, William, 29, 215n46

Walsh, Richard, 147

War Resisters League, 147, 188, 189

Weiner, Mark, 37

Welles, Sumner, 144

Wertheim, Stephen,

White, Francis, 96

Winship, Blanton, 11, 97–98, 114, 115, 141, 143, 212n49

women's activism, 44–46, 58, 70–71, 91, 234n47; in Cuba, 91, 105; in Dominican Republic, 91, 105, 234n47; in nineteenth century, 225n114 (see also Rodríguez de Tió, Lola); in Socialist Party, 58; in unions, 44–45, 58, 70–71

—in PNPR, 12, 13–14, 45–46 67–70, 105–8, 121, 143; Albizu Campos's encouragement of, 19, 55, 67, 69, 77, 92; in New York City, 138 (see also Mielke, Thelma; Reynolds, Ruth).

women's activism, in PNPR (*cont'd.*)
  *See also* Canales, Blanca; Enfermeras de
  la República; Lebrón, Lolita; Meneses,
  Laura
Women's Organization for Independence,
  121
women's suffrage, 56, 58, 70–73, 91,
  221n28, 225n109; PNPR and, 71–73;
  struggle for, 35, 44, 68, 70–73
women workers, 43, 44, 219n72; in unions,
  44–45, 58, 70–71. *See also* needleworkers
World War I, 3–4, 42, 134, 161

World War II, 118–19, 130–34, 161, 247n11;
  military draft in, 132–34; PNPR and,
  10–11, 118, 132–34; U.S. bases in, 42,
  132, 161

Yankelevich, Pablo, 81
Yrigoyen, Hipólito, 66, 86
Yuval-Davis, Nira, 69

Zamora, Antonio, 130
Zapata, Carlos, 171

www.ingramcontent.com/pod-product-compliance
Lightning Source LLC
Chambersburg PA
CBHW020501270326
41926CB00008B/690